Aiming at Heaven, Getting the Earth

Aiming at Heaven, Getting the Earth

The English Catholic Novel Today

Marian E. Crowe

LEXINGTON BOOKS

A division of
ROWMAN & LITTLEFIELD PUBLISHERS, INC.
Lanham • Boulder • New York • Toronto • Plymouth, UK

LEXINGTON BOOKS

A division of Rowman & Littlefield Publishers, Inc.
A wholly owned subsidiary of The Rowman & Littlefield Publishing Group, Inc.
4501 Forbes Boulevard, Suite 200
Lanham, MD 20706

Estover Road
Plymouth PL6 7PY
United Kingdom

British Library Cataloguing in Publication Information Available

Library of Congress Cataloging-in-Publication Data

Crowe, Marian E., 1941-
  Aiming at heaven, getting the earth : the English Catholic novel today /
Marian E. Crowe.
    p. cm.
  This study analyzes the fiction of four contemporary Catholic novelists:
Alice Thomas Ellis, David Lodge, Sara Maitland, and Piers Paul Read.
  Includes bibliographical references and index.
  ISBN-13: 978-0-7391-1640-1 (cloth : alk. paper)
  ISBN-10: 0-7391-1640-1 (cloth : alk. paper)
  ISBN-13: 978-0-7391-1641-8 (pbk. : alk. paper)
  ISBN-10: 0-7391-1641-X (pbk. : alk. paper)
  1. English fiction—Catholic authors—History and criticism. 2. English fiction—
20th century—History and criticism. 3. Catholic fiction—History and criticism.
4. Christianity in literature. 5. Catholics in literature. I. Title.
  PR120.C3C76 2007
  823'.9140938282--dc22   2006100598

Printed in the United States of America

∞™ The paper used in this publication meets the minimum requirements of
American National Standard for Information Sciences—Permanence of Paper
for Printed Library Materials, ANSI/NISO Z39.48-1992.

This book is dedicated to the men in my life:
Michael, Mark, Jeff, Andy, Kevin, and Benjamin.

Contents

Part III: Sara Maitland

Part IV: Piers Paul Read

Acknowledgments

Grateful acknowledgment is made to the following for permission to reprint excerpts from copyrighted works: To David Lodge: *Souls and Bodies*, [*How Far Can You Go?*], *Paradise News*, and *Therapy*. To Sara Maitland: *Daughter of Jerusalem*, *Virgin Territory*, *Brittle Joys*, and *A Big-Enough God*. To Piers Paul Read: *Monk Dawson*, *Polonaise*, and *On the Third Day*. To Peters Fraser & Dunlop Group: *Birds of the Air*, *The 27th Kingdom*, *Unexplained Laughter*, and *Serpent on the Rock*, by Alice Thomas Ellis. To Loyola Press: *The Vital Tradition: The Catholic Novel in a Period of Convergence* by Gene Kellogg (Loyola University Press, 1970). Farrar, Straus & Giroux, and The Flannery O'Connor Charitable Trust, via Harold Matson Co., Inc.: "The Fiction Writer & His Country," "The Nature and Aim of Fiction," "Novelist and Believer," and "Catholic Novelists and Their Readers" from *Mystery and Manners* by Flannery O'Connor, copyright © 1969 by the Estate of Mary Flannery O'Connor. New Directions Publishing Corp.: "On Belief in the Physical Resurrection of Jesus" by Denise Levertov, from *Sands of the Well*, copyright © 1996 by Denise Levertov. Some material on Piers Paul Read originally appeared in "A Modern *Psychomachia*: The Catholic Fiction of Piers Paul Read," *Christianity and Literature* 47, no. 3 (spring 1998). "Intimations of Immortality: Catholicism in David Lodge's *Paradise News*," was published in a slightly different form in *Renascence: Essays on Values in Literature* 52, no. 2 (winter 2000). "In the Bleak Midwinter: *The Birds of the Air*" was published in a slightly different form in *Logos: A Journal of Catholic Thought and Culture*, 8, no. 2 (spring 2005). All Bible passages are from the New American Bible © 1970.

I would like to extend heartfelt thanks to the following: To David Lodge, Sara Maitland, Piers Paul Read, and the late Alice Thomas Ellis, all of whom generously took time out of their busy schedules to talk with me about their work; To Don Sniegowski and Rev. Nicholas Ayo, C.S.C., colleagues at the University of Notre Dame, who encouraged and supported me in this project; To the Erasmus Institute at the University of Notre Dame, which granted me the opportunity to spend two weeks at a summer institute on religion and literature with Sara Maitland at Saint Edward's University in Austin, Texas, in the summer of 1999; To the reference librarians at the University of Notre Dame for their invaluable help in locating materials; To all the good sisters who taught me, but especially Sister Wilfred, Sister Mary Paul, Sister Laurentia, and Sister Mary Patricia, who awakened and nurtured my love of literature, especially literature with religious themes; To my good friends, Sidney Blanchet-Ruth and Ann Carey, who read portions of the manuscript and made helpful suggestions; To my husband Michael, who encouraged and supported me in this project.

Preface

A Catholic putting Catholicism into a novel, or a song, or a sonnet, or anything else, is not being a propagandist; he is simply being a Catholic. Everybody understands this about every other enthusiasm in the world.

—G. K. Chesterton, "On the Novel with a Purpose"

Catholic writers see a drama of good and evil that others do not see.

—Piers Paul Read, Interview

The Catholic novel is dying. In fact, it may already be dead. So say several scholars and critics. In 1982 one critic referred to his book on the Catholic novel as an "elegy for an apparently dying form," and two years later another wrote, "the religious spiritual novel is in some sense only a memory."[1] Some assert that the Catholic novel is dying because of changes in Catholicism since Vatican II. Others offer a more draconian analysis: that Christianity itself is dying. They argue that the dissent and chaos that have come in the wake of the Second Vatican Council are simply the death throes of a religion that is not sustainable in an age that is increasingly secular, liberal, scientific, and pluralistic.

Although many secular people think that the imminent demise of Christianity is so obvious as to require no evidence, the proposition is certainly debatable. Christianity in Africa and other areas of the developing world shows remarkable vitality and growth, and even in the United States, sociologist Andrew Greeley claims:

> As difficult as it is for members of the academic and media elites to comprehend the fact, religion is important to most Americans. There is no sign that this importance has declined in the last half century (as measured by survey data from the 1940s). Skepticism, agnosticism, atheism are not increasing in America, as disturbing as this truth might be to the denizens of midtown Manhattan.[2]

Colleen Carroll's recent book *The New Faithful* describes reports that "a small but committed core of young Christians is intentionally embracing organized religion and traditional morality. Their numbers—and their disproportionately powerful influence on their peers, parents, and popular culture—are growing."[3] Although Carroll's study focuses on the United States, there are indications of the same phenomenon in Europe among the young people who have responded enthusiastically to Pope John Paul II. Although rates of church attendance in Europe are very low, there are hints that the spark of a genuine and fervent Christian faith is still alive.[4]

Even if Christianity is not in its death throes, should the Catholic novel survive? Some think that the great Catholic novels of the past reflect the fortress mentality of the pre-Vatican II Catholic ghetto and have no place in a pluralistic and ecumenical age. Others argue that not only Catholics, but non-Catholic readers and critics as well, appreciate these distinguished novels as a unique and valuable part of our literary heritage.

In the pages that follow, I argue that the Catholic novel in England is not dead.[5] It certainly does, however, reflect developments in society and in the Church since Vatican II and consequently looks very different from the classic Catholic novels of François Mauriac, Georges Bernanos, Graham Greene, and Evelyn Waugh. I begin with a discussion of the theory of the Catholic novel, exploring the philosophical and literary problems inherent in combining literature and religion, especially in novels. The next chapter traces the birth of the Catholic novel in France and its development in England up to the Second Vatican Council. Readers with little interest in these theoretical and historical matters might wish to begin with chapter 3, "The English Catholic Novel Today," which introduces the four novelists who are the primary subjects of this book: Alice Thomas Ellis, David Lodge, Sara Maitland, and Piers Paul Read. There follows a series of chapters that discuss three novels by each writer. The concluding chapter considers the distinctive contributions of these novelists and offers some speculations about the future of the Catholic novel.

My purposes in this book are these:

- To foster an appreciation of the special achievement of the Catholic novel as more than a novel that uses Catholic material, but as one that provides a distinctive way of looking at the world (what Andrew Greeley calls "the Catholic imagination") and that manages to incorporate serious religious themes without becoming didactic or polemical.
- To give Catholic readers an appreciation of their heritage of the Catholic novel, together with an awareness of the extraordinary achievement of Catholic novelists who attempt to be faithful to both their faith and their art.
- To explain why Catholics both like and need good Catholic novels that reflect their own religious experience and that nourish and enrich their faith.
- To show how contemporary Catholic novels both reflect developments in Catholicism since the Second Vatican Council and provide various perspectives through which to interpret and understand these developments.
- To propose that Catholic novelists have made a distinctive and valuable contribution to English literature and that the disappearance of such literature in the future would be a significant loss.
- To suggest some probable directions in future English Catholic novels based on the achievements of Ellis, Lodge, Maitland, and Read, and on some predictions about Catholicism in the years ahead.

My method in this book is to some extent dictated by the fact that it is aimed primarily at an American audience, which is not as familiar with the works of Ellis, Lodge, Maitland, and Read as are English readers. I have chosen therefore to include substantial amounts of plot summary and generous quotations in order to provide a framework for discussing the novels' themes and to convey the flavor of the writing. I have tried to do this in a way that will not detract from the pleasure of reading the novels, since my fondest hope is that, having enjoyed the tidbits, my readers will want the whole feast.

The title, *Aiming at Heaven, Getting the Earth: The English Catholic Novel Today*, refers to a passage in C. S. Lewis's *Mere Christianity*:

Hope is one of the Theological virtues. This means that a continual looking forward to the eternal world is not (as some people think) a form of escapism or wishful thinking. . . . It does not mean that we are to leave the present world as it is. If you read history you will find that the Christians who did most for the present world were just those who thought most of the next. . . . It is since Christians have largely ceased to think of the other world that they have become so ineffective in this. Aim at Heaven and you will get earth "thrown in"; aim at earth and you will get neither.[6]

Although Lewis's remarks here are directed more toward religious, social, and political achievements than to literary ones, I argue that an analogous point could be made for writers whose imagination is informed and enriched by Christian—and in this case, Catholic—faith. I make no claim that in their writing Ellis, Lodge, Maitland, and Read are consciously "aiming at heaven." Indeed they would be appalled at such a suggestion, for it implies that their work is merely thinly disguised proselytizing, the charge that continually plagues the writer who wishes to integrate faith into his or her art. I would argue, however, that Lewis's theory of the Christian's plenitude applies here. Because these writers look at the earth through the eyes of faith, they *see* more.[7] Because their vision makes room for heaven (or at least the hope of it), acknowledges the sacred, and sees human acts as freighted with moral consequence, they not only get the earth "thrown in"; they get an earth that is extraordinarily rich, vivid, engaging, and compelling. In their portrayal of this world, these writers also point toward something that is in short supply these days: hope.

NOTES

1. Albert Sonnenfeld, foreward to *Crossroads: Essays on the Catholic Novelists* (York, S.C.: French Literature Publications Co., 1982), viii; Richard Gilman, "Salvation, Damnation, and the Religious Novel," *New York Times Book Review*, December 2, 1984, 7, quoted in Theodore P. Fraser, prologue to *The Modern Catholic Novel in Europe* (New York: Twayne, 1994), xi.

2. Andrew Greeley, *The Catholic Revolution: New Wine, Old Wineskins, and the Second Vatican Council* (Berkeley: University of California Press, 2004), 104.

3. Colleen Carroll, *The New Faithful: Why Young Adults are Embracing Christian Orthodoxy* (Chicago: Loyola Press, 2002), 4.

4. With respect to England, according to Monsignor Keith Baltrop, director of the Catholic Agency to Support Evangelisation:

> There are many initiatives at grassroots level: people reaching out to drug addicts and the marginalized, parishes training people to knock on doors in the parish and offer the Good News, youth initiatives such as Youth 2000 and the Life Teen group I met in Liverpool recently. The new movements are a great source of hope, but there are good things going on in parishes also. Another great sign of hope is the thirst the laity have for solid theological and pastoral formation.

Greg Watts, "Innovation Key to Renewal of Catholic Evangelization," *Our Sunday Visitor*, 12 December 2004, 4.

5. My focus on England should not be taken to mean that that there is no significant Catholic fiction being written in the United States. There is indeed high

quality American Catholic fiction, and others have amply explored that subject. Rather, I focus on England because English literature is the primary subject of my interest and scholarship and because American readers are less familiar with English novelists than with American ones.

6. C. S. Lewis, *Mere Christianity*, rev. ed. (New York: Macmillan, 1960) 118.

7. Flannery O'Connor surely believed this, for she wrote that "the chief difference between the novelist who is an orthodox Christian and the novelist who is merely a naturalist is that the Christian novelist lives in a larger universe." "Catholic Novelists and Their Readers," in *Mystery and Manners*, ed. Sally and Robert Fitzgerald (New York: Farrar, Straus & Giroux, 1969), 175.

1

✛

The Theory of the Catholic Novel

The task of philosophy or theology is to make certain statements or to propose certain hypotheses about the general nature of the human person as lucidly and truthfully as possible, whereas that of imaginative literature is to provide a picture of it in specific circumstances.

—J. C. Whitehouse, *Vertical Man*

The Catholic novel can be seen as arrogant, often filled more with hate than with love. And if its arguments are spurious and even sometimes wicked, it has the "grandeur of a great struggle and the endurance of great Renaissance sculpture."

—Albert Sonnenfeld, *Crossroads: Essays on the Catholic Novelists*

I do not conceive it my vocation to preach the Christian faith in a novel, but as it happens, my worldview is informed by a certain belief about man's nature and destiny which cannot fail to be central to any novel I write.

—Walker Percy, Catholic novelist

"Literature is drenched in religious concerns—modern and contemporary literature at least as much as any other," says literary critic John Neary.[1] Although to the ancients it was obvious that religion was central to poetry and drama, it was Christianity that saw problems with the combination. In the early third century the great Christian scholar Tertullian, asked "What has Athens to do with Jerusalem?" Athens, of course, represents art and culture, while Jerusalem symbolizes Christianity. Tertullian thought the two spheres were entirely separate and should stay

1

that way. Throughout the following centuries and continuing to the present day, the question has provoked countless debates. Christians have often been suspicious of the seductive power of art in all its forms. Even before the Puritans of the seventeenth century, the Iconoclasts of the eighth and ninth centuries railed against the use of images, which not only could distract the Christian but could even contaminate the spiritual nature of one's relationship with God.[2]

As literacy spread and more Christians had access to art made from words, the debate focused on literature. The fact, however, that a book, the Bible, is the foundation of the Christian faith, has paradoxically given support both to the supporters and the adversaries of literature. Those who see the Bible as all-sufficient see no need for profane literature, which can in no way even compare to the eminence of Scripture. Others see Scripture as endorsing humans' desire to write and read stories and poetry. The fact that God has chosen literary forms as the means to reveal His truth is seen as encouragement for humans to use the same means. As Leland Ryken puts it, "If the message of the Bible were all that mattered, there would have been no good reason for biblical poets to put their utterances into intricately patterned verse form, or for biblical storytellers to compose masterfully compact and carefully designed stories."[3] Also, the repeated emphases in the book of Genesis on the goodness of creation have suggested to some writers and artists that their own acts of creation, in imitating God the Creator, are expressions of filial piety.

Yet God's pronouncement of creation as "very good" precedes the Fall that has tarnished the work of the Creator. Philosopher Jacques Maritain reminds us that although "grace heals the wounds of nature," Christian art, although not impossible, "is difficult, doubly difficult—difficulty squared, because it is difficult to be an artist and very difficult to be a Christian, and because the whole difficulty is not merely the sum but the product of these two difficulties multiplied by one another, for it is a question of reconciling two absolutes."[4]

The other major fear about Christian art is not that it will lead us to sin, but rather the opposite—that it will try to keep us from sin, in other words, that it will be didactic. Even people who don't mind being preached to in church, object to it strongly when they sit down to read a novel. People are sometimes edified, inspired, or morally challenged by what they read, but if a writer's intent to edify or preach is too obvious, the reader is likely to rebel. Dante stated forthrightly in a letter his purpose in writing the Divine Comedy: "to remove those living in this life from the state of misery and to lead them to a state of bliss."[5] Yet his magnificent poetry, unforgettable characters, and stunning imagery have made Dante's readers willing to overlook his moralistic purpose. Novelist Joyce Cary has argued that every piece of writing is to some extent didactic: "We are told that novelists must not preach. This is nonsense. All serious artists preach—they are perfectly convinced of the truth as they see it, and they write to communicate that truth. . . . For a reader must never be left in doubt about the meaning of a story."[6] Walker Percy, however, says, "Nothing is worse than a novel which seeks to edify the reader."[7] The operative word here is surely *seeks*. Any didactic purpose must be subtle, oblique, understated. Above all, it must not overpower the primary purpose of giving artistic delight. Brian Godawa, writing about film, makes an important point that is as pertinent to literature as to film.

> The rejection of "messages" in movies as "preachy" or "propagandistic" is a recent phenomenon of the Cartesian dualistic worldview that results in the splitting of reality into secular/sacred distinctions. This view is the denial of man's holistic existence, a gnostic divorce of mind from body, meaning from behavior, as if a story about human beings relating to one another could exist in a vacuum without reference to values or meaningfulness.[8]

"Values or meaningfulness," however, are one thing. Advocating belief in Christianity or promoting the validity of one denomination is something else. No reader will object to a piece of literature concerning itself with values or with illuminating some aspect of the human condition, but most will balk at the idea that an author is allowing his advocacy of religion to eclipse his art of storytelling. In fact, this aversion to any hint of the didactic in literature is by far the most common objection to writing that attempts to introduce religious themes. Contemporary people rarely eschew literature for fear that it will lead them into sin, although this fear is not entirely a thing of the past. So endemic, however, is the tension at the heart of the project of creating Christian literature that one critic says that "Christianity stands in radical opposition to the creative imagination and . . . a Christian writer of any power will necessarily tend toward a heresy."[9]

Yet despite these difficulties, there are still writers who want to combine religion and literature and readers who like the combination. In spite of Tertullian's warning, there is a long and venerable tradition of Christian writers who saw the blending of their faith and their art as a kind of sacred marriage and produced such masterpieces as *The Divine Comedy*, *Paradise Lost*, *Pilgrim's Progress* and the poems of John Donne, George Herbert, and Gerard Manley Hopkins. In the sixteenth century Sir Philip Sidney wrote a classic defense of literature, *An Apology for Poetry*, where he argued that poetry could actually be a positive aid in the moral life. He maintained that if it is true "that no learning is so good as that which teacheth and moveth to virtue, and that none can both teach and move

thereto so much as poetry, then is the conclusion manifest that ink and paper cannot be to a more profitable purpose employed."[10] Even some
clergy recognized that good literature could be a help to theology. Martin
Luther wrote:

> I am persuaded that without knowledge of literature pure theology cannot at
> all endure, just as heretofore, when letters have declined and lain prostrate,
> theology, too, has wretchedly fallen and lain prostrate. . . . Certainly it is my
> desire that there shall be as many poets and rhetoricians as possible, because
> I see that by these studies as by no other means, people are wonderfully fit-
> ted for the grasping of sacred truth and for handling it skillfully and happily.[11]

Another churchman, John Henry Newman, in *The Idea of a University* advocated that a Catholic university ought to promote the creation of
Catholic literature written not just by writers who happen to be Catholics,
but also by those who would treat their subjects "as a Catholic would naturally treat them, and as he only can treat them."[12] A more contemporary
churchman who shared that view was Pope John Paul II, who in 1999 in
an Easter letter to artists said that the Church needs art:

> In order to communicate the message entrusted to her by Christ, the Church
> needs art. Art must make perceptible, and as far as possible attractive, the
> world of the spirit, of the invisible, of God. It must therefore translate into
> meaningful terms that which is in itself ineffable. . . . The Church has need
> especially of those who can do this on the literary and figurative level, using
> the endless possibilities of images with symbolic force.[13]

J. C. Whitehouse put it well when he wrote that novelists are valuable because theological and philosophical ideas that "may seem restrictive and
straitened assume a new richness when filtered through an individual literary sensibility."[14]

Aidan Nichols, speaking primarily of visual art, could also be speaking
of the art of fiction when he writes that in a moment of communion with
an art object, a person

> finds himself reorganizing his own world of meaning, what counts for him
> as "the real," in its light. In the course of that, just as the artwork can shape
> an existence, moving us to the suppression of self so that fidelity to ultimate
> values may replace the distortions of the relentless ego, so the revelatory
> event proves able to place us in touch with an absolutely satisfying and com-
> plete hold on the reality that blesses us with its own truth, even if it calls on
> us for a painful reshaping of our lives.[15]

Literature is revelatory because it clarifies the human situation. Even if a
literary work has no obvious Christian themes or material, it can elucidate

and give concreteness to the belief that we live in a fallen world and render the need for salvation more compelling. Novelist and critic David Lodge uses the term defamiliarization to describe fiction's ability to "overcome the deadening effects of habit by representing familiar things in unfamiliar ways."[16] Christian fiction brings to life doctrines rendered insipid and prosaic due to long familiarity and frequent repetition in creeds and liturgy. Graham Greene's *The Power and the Glory* conveys dramatically the Roman Catholic theology of the Eucharist and the priesthood; and no theological treatise, no matter how learned and profound, can disclose the action of God's grace in the world as powerfully as Georges Bernanos's *The Diary of a Country Priest*.

The seventeenth century Puritans in their fear of literature were right about one thing: literature can and does affect us—and not always for the better. T. S. Eliot cautions that much modern literature "repudiates, or is wholly ignorant of, our most fundamental and important beliefs: and . . . in consequence its tendency is to encourage its readers to get what they can out of life while it lasts, to miss no "experience" that presents itself, and to sacrifice themselves, if they make any sacrifice at all, only for the sake of tangible benefits to others in this world either now or in the future."[17]

Literature can induce cynicism and licentiousness, as well as benevolence and gratitude. Yet Sir Philip Sidney's assertion that poetry "teacheth and moveth to virtue" surely applies to much fiction as well as to poetry.[18] For the religious person, fiction can be a means of increasing self-knowledge and thereby enhancing growth in the spiritual life. Moreover, fiction can also affect behavior. Here again, Eliot makes the case:

> The common ground between religion and fiction is behaviour. Our religion imposes our ethics, our judgement and criticism of ourselves, and our behaviour toward our fellow men. The fiction that we read affects our behaviour towards our fellow men, affects our patterns of ourselves. When we read of human beings behaving in certain ways, with the approval of the author, who gives his benediction to this behaviour by his attitude toward the result of the behaviour arranged by himself, we can be influenced toward behaving in the same way.[19]

Readers know that good novels can help us to be better people, and religious people know that some novels can enhance and fortify our faith. Yet for a novel to *seem* to have that as its primary purpose is tantamount to literary suicide.

Today a Christian novel is problematic for two reasons. The first is our secular culture. The second is the novel form itself. Although many people still consider themselves religious, a greater percentage of people are nonbelievers than ever before. People may be attracted to church for

fellowship, community, and instruction in broad ethical principles yet
have little belief in central Christian dogmas like the Incarnation or
Atonement. Much of the Christian ethical code is universal. Judaism, Islam, Hinduism, and Buddhism all teach that we should help the less fortunate, be honest, and resist becoming too attached to material things.
Rather it is the central and distinctive beliefs of Christianity that are
problematic: the Trinity, the Incarnation, and humanity's need for salvation through Jesus Christ. As Flannery O'Connor says, "Redemption is
meaningless unless there is cause for it in the actual life we live, and for
the last few centuries there has been operating in our culture the secular
belief that there is no such cause."[20]

Writing in his diary in 1945, Catholic novelist Julian Green pondered
the contrast between the medieval world, where almost everyone believed and doubt was rare, to our present world. He wondered how for
us who live in a world "where doubt is, to a certain extent, the general
opinion, how can we not feel isolated and like lost children in modern civilization, we and our singular ideas about the incarnation and the tran-
substantiation (singular in the eyes of the world, but as natural to us as
the sun in the sky)?"[21] Since 1945 challenges to the faith from evolutionary biology, cosmology, modern Biblical criticism, and the shameful aspects of Christian history, all disseminated through the media, have accelerated the attack on traditional Christianity, making faith more difficult
than it was in a more credulous and less sophisticated age.

Flannery O'Connor describes the situation this way:

> We live in an unbelieving age but one which is markedly and lopsidedly spir-
> itual. There is one type of modern man who recognizes spirit in himself but
> who fails to recognize a being outside himself whom he can adore as Creator
> and Lord; consequently he has become his own ultimate concern. . . .
>
> There is another type of modern man who recognizes a divine being not
> himself, but who does not believe that this being can be known anagogically
> or defined dogmatically or received sacramentally. Spirit and matter are sep-
> arated for him. . . .
>
> And there is another type of modern man who can neither believe nor con-
> tain himself in unbelief and who searches desperately, feeling about in all ex-
> perience for the lost God.
>
> At its best our age is an age of searchers and discoverers, and at its worst,
> an age that has domesticated despair and learned to live with it happily.[22]

This situation creates a disjunction between the worldview of the writer
with serious Christian beliefs and that of a large segment of the reading
public. O'Connor says that "the Catholic writer often finds himself writing in and for a world that is unprepared and unwilling to see the meaning of life as he sees it."[23] Since O'Connor wrote these words over forty

years ago, the arts, the media, popular culture, and the intellegentia have become even more unabashedly secular, making the combination of religion and literature more difficult than it was for writers who could assume that most of their readers were also believers.[24]

Not only secular readers but even church-going Christians are apt to be offended or discomfited if a novel seems too intent on moralizing or evangelizing or if there is a hint of a self-righteous or overly certain tone. If, as Walker Percy says, "Nothing is worse than a novel which seeks to edify the reader," how is a novelist who is also a serious Christian to incorporate religious themes into a novel that will not seem smug, moralistic, or admonitory? The Christian writer may choose to do so by avoiding explicitly religious content. In *Narrative Elements and Religious Meaning* theologian Wesley Kort explores the reasons why narratives, even when not explicitly religious, often seem to convey religious meaning. Kort contends that narrative naturally comports with religious experience because the elements of narrative—atmosphere, character, plot and tone—correspond to aspects of religious faith.[25]

Atmosphere, to a large degree determined by setting, suggests what the character is up against, that which is beyond his understanding and control. Often the atmosphere is threatening, oppressive or antagonistic, and sometimes it reveals a radical discontinuity between the human and his situation; but it always speaks of the presence of limits. In this way atmosphere suggests otherness—or in religious terms—transcendence.

Character, on the other hand, expresses human possibilities. Whereas atmosphere connotes limits, character implies the potential to know and manage the world. A character in a novel is a kind of paradigmatic figure, in some cases comparable to exemplary or authoritative religious figures—mediators, prophets, or saints. In its most extreme form, this leads to the "Christ figure," a character whose person and experience have certain parallels to Jesus, which the author highlights with imagery and details.[26]

Plots show processes, and they reflect humans' resistance to chaos and their need to impose order and meaning on sequential linear time. Frank Kermode in *The Sense of an Ending* argues that the desire for an ending is a basic human need.[27] Just as religious rituals reenact great religious events of the past, plots propose human actions as meaningful and coherent and somehow lifted out of linear time and given a kind of paradigmatic status.

Tone, generally understood as an author's attitude toward his material, is conveyed by the author's selection of material and his language choices. Tone is that which constitutes the subjective presence in the narrative because it is the way in which the writer is most personally present to the reader. It projects the author's worldview, and by representing a world he has believed in enough to create, it suggests belief in and affirmation of a world other than the one empirically given to our senses.

Thus the four primary elements of narrative—atmosphere, character, plot, and tone—correspond to basic elements of religious experience—transcendence, paradigmatic religious figures, religious rituals, and belief. In sum, Kort's argument is that modern fiction, even when not explicitly religious, can convey religious meaning because the elements of narrative correspond to elements of religious experience.

Kort's intriguing analysis explains why some readers find compelling religious themes in narratives that have no obvious or explicit religious content—a fact that irritates some secular critics, who accuse religious readers of reading into the book what they want to find. Nevertheless, using such approaches may enable a novelist to write about Christianity without *seeming* to write about it by using suggestion, imagery, and symbolism, but avoiding explicitly Christian content. This strategy may enable the novelist to avoid writing what Charles Moeller calls the "literature of salvation." Moeller claims that contemporary readers "are suspicious of salvation for they see in it a kind of stopgap. Their impression is that believers have ready-made answers, as if one could press a button on an automatic machine for the answer to the problem of death or the problem of love. They think that faith suppresses the flavor of life, its risks and its authenticity."[28] One critic complains that the emphasis on the Fall, sin, and grace leads to the human environment being "rendered as suffocating dullness and pettiness" and human achievements "shown to be inadequate, egoistic, evil, just in being themselves, in being human."[29]

Moeller contrasts the literature of happiness and the literature of salvation: "With its intention of making man more human, the literature of happiness supposes that he is already human. It wants to embellish and improve his life. The literature of salvation is its antithesis: the house is burning or threatens to burn."[30] Moeller believes that the problem is largely due to vocabulary. The very word salvation immediately raises the question, "Saved from what?" The concept of original sin and a fall from a state of original bliss just does not mesh with what science tells us about the beginning of the human species on this planet. Even many Christians who give intellectual assent to the need for salvation seldom feel it in a compelling way. Thus the Christian novelist who wishes to present Christianity in a forceful and dramatic way faces a daunting challenge.

Allied with the fact that salvation and redemption are not meaningful categories to contemporary people is the fact that they have lost a language for talking about evil, and in having lost that language, they have also largely lost belief in the reality of evil. In *The Death of Satan* Anthony Delbanco writes: "A gulf has opened up in our culture between the visibility of evil and the intellectual resources available for coping with it. . . .

The repertoire of evil has never been richer. Yet never have our resources been so weak. We have no language for connecting our inner lives with the horrors that pass before our eyes in the outer world."[31] Delbanco, a secular liberal, feels that on balance it is a good thing that the religious worldview has passed away and that people no longer really believe in the devil as an objectively real entity. He does question, though, whether contemporary people can do without a metaphor to which they can direct their feelings about evil. But it is language and metaphor he craves, not belief in a real supernatural world. He is forthright about the impossibility of such belief in our world:

> Whether we welcome or mourn this loss, it is the central and irreversible fact of modern history that we no longer inhabit a world of transcendence. The idea that man is a receptor of truth from God has been relinquished, and replaced with the idea that reality is an unstable zone between phenomena (unknowable in themselves) and innumerable fields of mental activity (which we call persons) by which they are apprehended.[32]

Despite Delbanco's certainty about the impossibility of religious faith (suggesting that he is addressing only a secular audience), he is correct about the different tenor of Christian faith today with its greatly diminished emphasis on sin, damnation, and Satan, and its tendency to focus on humanistic values it shares with the culture at large. He further claims that it is not just that beliefs have changed, but that the very capacity to believe is eroding.

> We have reached a point where it is not only specific objects of belief that have been discredited but the very capacity to believe. This is new. In the past, when old ways of seeing the world gave way, it was possible to discern at least the outlines of a new way that would take their place; and the succession, it was generally believed, would result in a better vision of truth. . . . But the process we are living through today is sufficiently different in degree that it has become different in kind. It is divestiture without reinvestment.[33]

This development, even if not as dire as Delbanco suggests, is useful for understanding the challenge for the contemporary Christian novelist. If many people today have lost the very "capacity to believe," what does this mean for the novelist who wishes to include Christian beliefs as a substantive part of his fiction? He must either narrow his audience to the tiny minority (evidently too few even to be counted in Delbanco's analysis) who really do think that religious beliefs correspond to an existing reality, or write about these beliefs as a kind of myth or metaphor enabling one to portray certain aspects of human experience. Yet for the novelist who considers his religious beliefs a truthful account of the most important realities, the second approach may amount to a compromise of his personal and artistic integrity.

Although the novelist's faith may create a problem in terms of his audience, it may, in fact, actually aid his art. Flannery O'Connor certainly believed this. Rather than seeing faith as something that closes off parts of life to the writer, O'Connor insists that "the chief difference between the novelist who is an orthodox Christian and the novelist who is merely a naturalist is that the Christian novelist lives in a larger universe. He believes that the natural world contains the supernatural."[34] Dogma, which is commonly thought of as a limit on what one can think, closing off the questioning, exploring mind, in O'Connor's view, empowers the novelist, for it is "an instrument for penetrating reality."

> Those who have no absolute values cannot let the relative remain merely relative; they are always raising it to the level of the absolute. The Catholic fiction writer is entirely free to observe. He feels no call to take on the duties of God or to create a new universe. He feels perfectly free to look at the one we already have and to show exactly what he sees. . . . Open and free observation is founded on our ultimate faith that the universe is meaningful, as the Church teaches.[35]

Yet this "open and free observation" does not mean that the novelist will produce flat, naturalistic fiction. On the contrary, says O'Connor, Christian dogma "affects his writing primarily by guaranteeing his respect for mystery."[36] Reality and mystery may seem to be—if not exactly opposites—at least poles apart; for reality suggests that which is clear, understandable, and obvious, whereas mystery is that which is unknowable, enigmatic, and elusive. For O'Connor, however, the two are brought together in good fiction, for the mind of the reader has "its sense of mystery deepened by contact with reality, and its sense of reality deepened by contact with mystery."[37] Although O'Connor is convinced that the Christian novelist "lives in a larger universe" than the secular writer, she is fully aware of the fact that "what is to us an extension of sight is to the rest of the world a peculiar and arrogant blindness, and . . . no one today is prepared to recognize the truth of what we show unless our purely individual vision is in full operation."[38] Hence O'Connor's insistence that the Christian novelist scrupulously cultivate an unprejudiced and penetrating vision. He must see more—not less—than the secular writer.

Yet this enlarged vision can be problematic for writing fiction. O'Connor succinctly states the challenge for the Christian novelist: "Just how can the novelist be true to time and eternity both, to what he sees and what he believes, to the relative and the absolute? And how can he do all this and be true at the same time to the art of the novel, which demands the illusion of life?"[39]

This question leads to the second element that complicates the project of the Christian novel: the literary genre itself. The novel—of all forms of literature—is most closely wedded to realism. The novel came of age in the eighteenth century when the rising middle class favored a literature that would reflect the empirical world they knew rather than the world of chivalry or myth.[40] As David Lodge says, "If realism of presentation was not actually invented by the eighteenth-century novelists and their nineteenth-century successors, it was certainly developed and exploited by them on a scale unprecedented in earlier literature"[41] Religious faith seems more naturally adapted to poetry, as attested to in the rich tradition of devotional poetry and exemplified in the poems of Milton, Donne, Herbert and others. Although novelists—particularly in the twentieth century—have experimented with nonrealistic techniques, including fable, fantasy, and magical realism, the novel's foundational ties to realism continue to exert a bias toward the empirical.[42] Some experimental forms of narrative, such as the stream of consciousness technique, can be seen as the result of a desire to be *more* realistic, to include a part of reality not previously described accurately or fully.

How then is the Christian novelist to incorporate the supernatural and the spiritual in a work of fiction? Some do it by what they leave out. A sudden plot reversal or change in character is not adequately accounted for; the intimation being that the transcendent has broken into the natural order. Some use broken off, unfinished sentences, as in François Mauriac's *The Viper's Tangle* (*Le Noeud de vipères*), where the main character, who had been an agnostic, dies, leaving as the last entry in his journal, "a Love whose name at last I know, whose ador . . ."[43]

Some novelists even go so far as to include miracles in their stories, although they often allow for an alternate naturalistic explanation. Some try to suggest the supernatural through the use of shock and surprise. Flannery O'Connor explained the grotesque elements in her fiction by saying that "to the hard of hearing you shout, and for the almost-blind you draw large and startling figures."[44] These attempts to jolt the reader into an awareness of the supernatural are meant to function like parables by subverting the reader's expectations of the ordinary and predictable. According to theologian Sallie McFague, in parables "people are not asked to be 'religious' or taken out of this world; rather the transcendent comes *to* ordinary reality and disrupts it."[45]

Yet sometimes these techniques do not have the desired effect, especially if the reader is not a believer. For such a reader, any attempt to include the supernatural in a work of fiction is likely to be annoying, if not downright jarring. Albert Sonnenfeld, who has given a full and sensitive account of the ways Catholic novelists try to deal with the supernatural, is himself not a believer, and he expresses the frustration of secular readers when religious writers try to include the supernatural in their fiction. Referring to the claim of French Catholic novelist Georges Bernanos that by demonstrating to the reader that human weakness is not an adequate explanation for evil, he compels the reader "to throw himself on his knees, if not with love then at least through fear, and to call God," Sonnenfeld argues that the secular reader does not, in fact, fall to his knees. Instead he finds explanations in sexual pathology, vestigial Romantic satanism, or *Schadenfreude* and is unwilling to enact the willing suspension of disbelief that would be necessary in order to engage the novel on its own terms.[46] Sonnenfeld also notes that answered prayers abound in Catholic novels, and he finds it "distinctly irritating" when "at a crucial moment of tension, a character utters a prayer."[47]

Some religious novelists try to make their depiction of something supernatural—a miracle, conversion, or the effect of grace—more palatable to the nonbeliever by using a skeptical narrator. Here again, however, the strategy does not always succeed. Piers Paul reports that his use of a skeptical narrator in *Monk Dawson* brought him "the dubious satisfaction of being congratulated by a Russian critic during the Soviet era for demonstrating so clearly that Christian belief was a form of insanity."[48] Evelyn Waugh used this technique, making the skeptical Charles Ryder the narrator in *Brideshead Revisited*. "I had no religion. . . . The view implicit in my education was that religion was a hobby which some people professed and others did not; at the best it was slightly ornamental, at the worse it was the province of 'complexes' and 'inhibitions'—catchwords of the decade—and of the intolerance, hypocrisy, and sheer stupidity attributed to it for centuries."[49] Yet the apparent deathbed conversion of Lord Marchmain and Julia's decision to obey Church teaching that she cannot marry Charles because they are both divorced elicits this comment from one critic: "If *Brideshead Revisited* proves nothing else, it demonstrates that sentimentality and the religious dimension cannot mix in a modern novel without destroying its impact and its art. Filtered through sentimentality, what is intended as power becomes melodrama and what is introduced to touch the emotions descends to bathos."[50] Another critic has this to say about Julia's decision to give up Charles:

> Non-Catholic readers can surely be forgiven their revulsion at the seeming smugness of this dismissal of love. The set speech comes so easily from the rhetoric of the rectory. God has made the laws, down to their last canon, and we who have been initiated into His great legal fraternity, we understand. Pity we cannot make others understand.

Was Waugh trying to make others understand when he constructed his canonist's copybook adultery? Had he given up irony for apologetics?[51]

A similar tone is evident in Sonnenfeld's criticism of Mauriac's "lapses of novelistic taste," maintaining that "the preachy post-Nobel Prize Mauriac of 1954 needed to affirm, to prove, not merely to adumbrate the supernatural."[52]

It is perhaps in the hope of avoiding such criticism that some Christian novelists are drawn to the view that the best way to reveal the supernatural is to simply let the ordinary be itself without trying to shock the reader or subvert expectations. German Catholic novelist Heinrich Böll's had a strong conviction "that the most simple and natural modes allowing human beings to communicate . . . [such as] sharing food, drinking bouts, and card games . . . are sacred and possess authentic sacramental dimensions."[53] Peter Hebblethwaite, author of a book on Bernanos, stated in an article entitled "How Catholic Is the Catholic Novel?" that the word *supernatural* is largely misunderstood and that "it does not refer to the miraculous nor to a shadowy parallel world into which one might escape." His preference is for the supernatural to be conveyed in fiction as "a dimension of everyday existence, as everyday existence seen in depth," making the supernatural seem "credible and natural."[54] Although such views may be theologically respectable, conveying the supernatural by simply presenting "everyday existence seen in depth" would be a daunting challenge for any novelist. One wonders how many readers would get the point?

No Christian writer wants to limit his audience to his fellow Christians. He surely wants to reach the widest possible audience, not simply for commercial success, but because he wants to create a literary work that has universal meaning rather than one that is sectarian or parochial. Yet the more committed a novelist is to his faith, the more likely it is that he would be pleased by the possibility that through his book a secular reader might become more open to the transcendent or feel the first faint stirrings of a response to the Spirit. Still, it is obvious that a reader who shares the writer's religious views will experience the novel differently than one who does not. Kurt Reinhardt goes so far as to claim "authors who advance a religious or theological thesis, whether expressed in a theoretical treatise or in a work of literature, can be appreciated only by readers who live and think sympathetically and empathetically within a similar frame of reference."[55]

Recently several Christian novelists have been turning to the comic mode. For a long time Christianity labored under the misperception that religion is opposed to happiness and joy and is intent upon limiting human beings' pleasure in this world. A traditionally tragic—or at least serious—tone was often considered more appropriate for a novel with a religious theme. Such a view, although not extinct, is much attenuated in our day. Some writers may simply find the comic to be the natural bent of their narrative voice, but others may find it a more judicious approach, which is less likely to bring the charge of moralizing.

In *The Comedy of Redemption* Ralph Wood argues that the "message of redemption in Christ finds a larger reflection and analogue in comic than in tragic art."[56] Wood points out, however, that Christians have had good reasons for their traditional suspicion of the comic. Comedy has roots in pagan festivals and often included violence and eroticism. Comic characters do not seem to undergo the moral struggles that tragic ones do. Comedy can easily spill over into an absurdist view, becoming more black comedy than high-spirited farce. It can also become quite vicious satire that is more mean-spirited than corrective. Comedy shines a light on all that is foolish and contemptible in human beings. Yet, Wood insists, "God has reclaimed us as his own. We have been repossessed as the property of the God who wants us gladly to give back our lives to him in faith and to the world in service. . . . Faith, in this reading, is the supremely comic act."[57]

Another critic who sees the comic as entirely compatible with a Christian imaginative vision is Jesuit priest William Lynch. His book *Christ and Apollo* valorizes the finite and the definite, symbolized by Christ, as against the abstract and infinite, symbolized by Apollo. He uses the interesting analogy of looking through a telescope to compare the tragic and the comic.

> The essential difference between the tragic and the comic is that between the two finites into which each enters. In tragedy the finite is looked at through the narrow and normal end of the telescope; therefore the limited in the human situation is regarded as an enormous abyss of non-being, which indeed it is. . . .
>
> . . . Comedy turns the telescope around so that the eye looks through the greater end, and everything has become, not sea incarnadine, but a disconcertingly small puddle.
>
> . . . By being turned around, the telescope reveals the actual contours, the interstices, the smells, of the beastly man.[58]

Thus the comic helps us more honestly engage with the definite and the concrete, which Lynch sees as so valuable. As for the comic being somehow easier or more comfortable than the tragic, Lynch argues that, "the way of comedy taxes the imagination and the whole soul more than does tragedy, and requires even more courage as a way into God. It is a more terrible way, requiring a greater ascesis, requiring more faith in the finite, the pure finite, as an entrance thereinto." Lynch even speaks of "the courage of the comic."[59]

> Indeed, its whole function is to be a perpetual and funny, if disconcerting, reminder that it is the limited concrete which is the path to insight and salvation. Its whole art is to be an art of anamnesis, or memory, of the bloody human (in the sense in which the English use that adjective) as a path to God, or to any form of the great.
> . . . Comedy is perpetually reminding the uprooted great man that in some important sense he was once, and still is, a bit of a monkey. . . .
> The one offense, therefore, which comedy cannot endure is that a man should forget he is man, or should substitute a phony faith for faith in the power of the vulgar and limited finite.[60]

However novelists may choose to make their work more palatable for nonreligious readers, a Christian novel must somehow project a Christian worldview. Many novels use overtly Christian material without ever becoming what could accurately be called a Christian novel. Some writers who have rejected the religion of their youth use it to provide colorful and provocative background. This is not really what is meant by a Christian novel. On the other hand, a work of fiction can powerfully present a Christian point of view using little, if any, Christian terminology. For Flannery O'Connor, it is a matter of how one sees the world. "I see from the standpoint of Christian orthodoxy. This means that for me the meaning of life is centered in our Redemption by Christ and what I see in the world I see in its relation to that. I don't think that this is a position that can be taken halfway or one that is particularly easy in these times to make transparent in fiction."[61] As one English professor put it, what makes a Christian novel distinctive is "the angle of vision, the nuances that a different pair of eyes can yield, a way of understanding, not subject matter."[62]

In addition to a Christian worldview, another requirement for a genuinely Christian novel is that it must be suffused with charity. In an essay on the American Catholic novelist Jon Hassler, Anthony Low says that the difference between Hassler and Sherwood Anderson, who both depict small town life, is that "Hassler loves even his most deplorable creatures."[63] This does not mean that the Christian novelist should gloss over evil or sentimentalize human failings. On the contrary, the religious writer should be even more scrupulously realistic than the secular writer, yet without becoming cynical, bitter, or caustic. J. Hillis Miller says "the proper model for the relation of the critic to the work he studies is not that of scientist to physical objects but that of one man to another in charity."[64] Could not the same be said of the relation of the Christian writer to his characters? Jacques Maritain goes so far as to insist that a work of art will be Christian "in proportion as the love is alive. Let there be no mistake: it is the actuality of love, contemplation in charity, which is here required."[65]

There is one other quality that is perhaps not essential for a Christian novel, but is, I suggest, characteristic of the best of the genre: room for doubt. Making room for doubt does not at all cancel out the Christian worldview. Doubt can be enfolded in faith and often is.[66] In his article on Jon Hassler, Low says, "Like most of us, and like many of his characters, Hassler has plenty of room for doubts."[67] Presbyterian minister and novelist Frederick Buechner says that "if you don't have any doubts, you are either kidding yourself or asleep. Doubts are the ants in the pants of faith. They keep it awake and moving."[68] A novel should reflect awareness that, at least for most people, religious faith is not experienced as certain knowledge. Saint Paul says, "Now we see indistinctly, as in a mirror; then we shall see face to face. My knowledge is imperfect now; then I shall know even as I am known (1 Corinthians 13:12). For the fiction writer, *indistinctly* and *imperfect* are the key words.

There are myriad ways in which a novelist can communicate the tentative nature of faith. Sometimes it is just a matter of tone; sometimes it is through a sympathetic nonbelieving character or through a believer's own struggle with faith. Graham Greene's Monsignor Quixote has a nightmare in which Christ comes down from the cross, proving his divinity. "There was no ambiguity, no room for doubt and no room for faith at all." Monsignor Quixote feels that this is "a kind of Saharan desert without doubt or faith, where everyone is certain that the same belief is true. He had found himself whispering, 'God save me from such a belief.'"[69] Without allowing doubt a legitimate place in the narrative universe, a Christian novel risks becoming brittle and inhuman.

The writer who wishes to incorporate Christian faith into a novel certainly faces a daunting array of challenges and pitfalls. What about the Catholic novelist, who wishes to write about Catholicism in all its richness and particularity? The Catholic novelist faces all of the challenges of any Christian writer but also confronts an array of other difficulties that can complicate his task. For a writer whose Catholicism is superficial or only residual, the problem is minimal; but the more genuine and ardent his attachment to Catholicism, the more acutely he is likely to feel these particular challenges.

First of all, in Catholicism the institutional church looms so large. It is not just that Roman Catholicism is the largest Christian denomination, but its tightly knit hierarchical structure, its emphasis on authority, and its systematic oversight of orthodoxy all combine to present a formidable aspect to other Christians (even to some Catholics), and a downright sinister one to nonbelievers. George Orwell thought the very idea of a Catholic novelist a contradiction in terms.

"The atmosphere of orthodoxy is always damaging to prose; and above all it is completely ruinous to the novel, the most anarchical of all forms of literature. How many Roman Catholics have been good novelists? Even the handful one could name have usually been bad Catholics. The novel is practically a Protestant form of art; it is a product of the free mind, of the autonomous individual."[70]

Like Orwell, many secular readers approach a novel by a Catholic with a negative bias based on their feelings about the Catholic Church. David Lodge, a Catholic novelist himself, expresses the dilemma this way:

> In seeking to convey to his non-Catholic audience a technical and emotional understanding of Catholic experience, the Catholic novelist risks arousing in this audience whatever extraliterary objections and suspicions it entertains about the Catholic Church as an active, proselytizing institution; while on his own part he has to grapple with the problem of retaining his artistic integrity while belonging to a Church which has never accepted the individual's right to pursue intellectual and artistic truth in absolute freedom.[71]

There is also the danger of the "Catholic neurosis" defined by Thomas Woodman as a condition "compounded out of authoritarianism, superstition and the peculiarities of Catholic moral teaching."[72] This "neurosis," although not the same as the intellectual constriction that Orwell laments, could conceivably restrict the free flow of creative energy, which may be siphoned off by the tension of believing what seems incredible and subverting the naturally human. It may seem as if some Catholic novelists embody an improvisation of John 8:32 attributed to Flannery O'Connor: "You shall know the truth, and the truth shall make you odd."[73] Furthermore, the Catholic belief in the teaching authority of the Church, reinforced before Vatican II by religious instruction largely through memorized answers to questions, can lead to what Woodman calls the "routinism of certainty."[74] What the Catholic may experience as the liberation of a reliable source of truth, may be perceived by the reader as stultifying.

In addition, Catholic writers—much more than Protestant ones—are apt to be drawn to the Middle Ages, when the Catholic Church was at its height of power and influence and all of Europe was united in one faith. With the exception of the Norwegian Sigrid Undset, few Catholic novelists actually write about the Middle Ages, but their idealization of the period is evident in some writers, such as G. K. Chesterton. Others, while not so enamored of the Middle Ages, may look back nostalgically to another earlier time when religious faith was stronger and moral principles more faithfully followed. Even if an attachment to an earlier period is not evident, some readers sense that the Catholic writer is judging the modern world in a medieval tribunal and failing to see it clearly. These tendencies

often earn Catholic writers the epithet of *romantic* or *reactionary*. Sonnenfeld asserts that their distaste for their own period leads "Catholic roman-
tics to idealize the asceticism and self-mortification of the medieval
monks" and believes that it was "possibly perverse and reactionary nos-
talgia which made the Catholic Novel possible."[75]

Catholic novelists have at their disposal Catholicism's rich symbol system and poetic liturgy. Yet even this advantage can backfire. For many
secular readers, this symbolic and sacramental system may lead the
writer to see coherence where there is complexity, to impose an artificial
pattern on what should be allowed to be chaotic.

> The Catholic novelist still believes in the rules of the game, in a coherent sys-
> tem of meaningful symbols. He is constantly tempted by them to make the
> supernatural manifest: the novel would then become a vehicle for theologi-
> cal exegesis, not for literary criticism, since these symbols would not be or-
> ganic to the particular novel under study. . . . It would be all too easy to cre-
> ate a network of recondite religious symbols which draw on the Church's
> symbolic view of the universe, whereas it is extremely difficult to use conse-
> crated symbolism in such a way that it seems to grow out of the very sub-
> stance of the novel.[76]

With all of these potential hazards for the Catholic novelist, it is understandable that Graham Greene, Georges Bernanos, and François Mauriac,
insisted that they were not "Catholic novelists" but "merely novelists who
happened also to be Catholic."[77] Yet one would hope that a Catholic novelist's religion would be more than a burden, more than a series of hur-
dles to be cleared or literary rapids to be cautiously navigated. Catholic
novelists Flannery O'Connor and Evelyn Waugh were straightforward
and unabashed about writing *as* Catholics and believed it improved their
art. After writing *Brideshead Revisited*, his first novel with an explicitly
Catholic theme, Waugh announced in *Life* magazine, "So in my future
books there will be two things to make them unpopular: a preoccupation
with style and the attempt to represent man more fully, which, to me,
means only one thing, man in relation to God."[78]

Catholicism does, in fact, provide many resources and advantages for
the novelist. The most obvious one, of course, is Catholic material, which
can enliven a plot and add a wealth of texture and color—mean nuns, the
mystique of priesthood, confessions, sexual angst, marriage and divorce
problems and so forth. Yet many novels contain this material, but would
not qualify as a Catholic novel as I define it. On the other hand, Flannery
O'Connor, one of the greatest American Catholic writers of fiction, uses
very little Catholic material. J. R. R. Tolkien provides an intriguing example of a Catholic novelist who uses no Catholic material, yet he himself insisted that his *Lord of the Rings* trilogy is "a fundamentally religious and

Catholic work."[79] Tolkien did not like allegory and therefore did not want to write a story with obvious Christian parallels as did his friend C. S. Lewis in *The Chronicles of Narnia*. Instead he wished to create a world that reflects the fundamental metaphysical realities of Christianity: the corruption through sin of a creation originally intended to be good, destruction wrought through pride and the will to power, and redemption through sacrificial suffering. Ian Ker suggests that obvious elements and themes which one would expect to find in the work of Catholic writers—"aestheticism, a love of ritual, ceremony, tradition, the appeal of authority, a romantic triumphalism, the lure of the exotic and foreign, a preoccupation with sin and guilt"—are, in fact, used much more by lesser Catholic writers than by really accomplished ones.[80]

David Lodge points out that even in the fiction of Graham Greene, who didn't want to be known as a Catholic novelist, Catholicism provides

> a system of concepts, a source of situations, and a reservoir of symbols with which he can order and dramatize certain intuitions about the nature of human experience—intuitions which were gained prior to and independently of his formal adoption of the Catholic faith. Regarded in this light, Greene's Catholicism may be seen not as a crippling burden on his artistic freedom, but as a positive artistic asset.[81]

One factor that distinguishes some Catholic novels is the Catholic imagination. Many scholars and critics have been influenced by the work of theologian David Tracy, who in *The Analogical Imagination and the Culture of Pluralism* argues that the analogical imagination, which emphasizes similarities, closeness and connection, is more characteristically Catholic, and the dialectical imagination, which emphasizes differences, distance and separation, is more characteristically Protestant. Although Tracy's study is primarily directed at theologians, sociologists, and Catholic priests, Andrew Greeley (a priest and sociologist) uses Tracy's concepts to examine the Catholic imagination as embodied in visual art, architecture and literature, as well as popular culture. According to Greeley,

> Tracy noted that the classic works of Catholic theologians and artists tend to emphasize the presence of God in the world, while the classic works of Protestant theologians tend to emphasize the absence of God from the world. The Catholic writers stress the nearness of God to His creation, the Protestant writers the distance between God and His creation; the Protestants emphasize the risk of superstition and idolatry, the Catholics the dangers of a creation in which God is only marginally present. Or, to put the matter in different terms, Catholics tend to accentuate the immanence of God, Protestants the transcendence of God. Tracy is consistently careful to insist that neither propensity is superior to the other, that both need each other. . . . Nonetheless, they are different one from another.[82]

Another important point in Tracy's analysis is that neither the analogical nor the dialectical is pure—at least not if it is healthy. Each must contain—at least by implication—traces of the other: "Where analogical theologies lose that sense for the negative, that dialectical sense within analogy itself, they produce not a believable harmony among various likenesses in all reality but the theological equivalent of 'cheap grace': boredom, sterility and an atheological vision of a deadening univocity."[83] On the other hand, "without the similarities produced through differences and negations, without the continuities, the order and even the possible, actual or proleptic harmony produced by an internal theological demand for some new mode of analogical language, negative dialectics, left to itself, eventually explodes its energies into rage or dissipates them in despair."[84] Although the analogical and dialectical imaginations need each other, Tracy believes that the analogical is particularly needed in the extremely pluralistic times in which we live. He insists that it is not just explicitly analogical writing, but rather the analogical imagination that can help all thinkers—not just theologians—avoid "the brittleness of self-righteous ideologies" or "the privatized sloth of an all too easy pluralism," for "we understand one another, if at all, only through analogy."[85]

John Neary in his *Like and Unlike God* considers Thomism to be the "most obvious blossoming of the analogical imagination in Christian history."[86] Thomas Aquinas's positive view of the natural world as basically good, although fallen, is a contrast to that of the dialectical imagination, which stresses the depravity of the fallen world. For Aquinas, grace builds on nature, and the supernatural on the natural; thus the natural order is a good way—indeed, the best way—for the Christian to apprehend supernatural realities. Although few Catholic novelists may have formally studied Aquinas, Thomism has been so influential in Catholic thought, working its way into countless sermons, devotional works and catechetical materials, as to become the Catholic way of looking at the world. Furthermore, it is only natural that a religion that has at the center of its liturgical life seven sacraments that use material things to make the sacred present would encourage and sustain an analogical vision. In the Church's understanding of sacrament, the physical matter and form are empowered, and not just a sign of a spiritual reality. They confer grace *ex opere operato* ("by the very fact of the action's being performed"). According to the *Catechism of the Catholic Church*, "From the moment that a sacrament is celebrated in accordance with the intention of the Church, the power of Christ and his Spirit acts in and through it, independently of the personal holiness of the minister."[87]

Obviously, a religion that holds that God's divine power can be communicated through such mundane material as water, bread, wine, and oil must convey a sense of matter as being a kind of divine language. Furthermore, a religious tradition that has traditionally decorated its churches with statues, pictures, and stained glass, and whose treasured belief in the Communion of Saints means that those who are in heaven can hear our prayers and help us in our own struggle toward heaven suggests that the wall separating the human and the divine is porous.[88] It also suggests that God is not displeased by our use of material things to celebrate what we believe. The Catholic understanding of sacrament, however, is not simply a celebration or memorial of a religious belief. Rather, sacraments effect what they celebrate; they "confer the grace that they signify."[89]

This belief that God loves the material world enough to make it the vehicle of sharing his life with humanity is a natural consequence of the central Christian dogma of the Incarnation.[90] This positive view of the world is called incarnational or sacramental. According to the *HarperCollins Encyclopedia of Catholicism*, the principle of sacramentality means "the notion that all reality, both animate and inanimate, is potentially or in fact the bearer of God's presence and the instrument of God's saving activity on humanity's behalf."[91] It is in this spirit that Catholic Jesuit poet Gerard Manley Hopkins exclaims, "The world is charged with the grandeur of God./It will flame out, like shining from shook foil" ("God's Grandeur") and "Christ plays in ten thousand places,/Lovely in limbs, and lovely in eyes not his" ("As Kingfishers Catch Fire").[92]

Although the terms *sacramental* and *analogical* are often used interchangeably, they are not really equivalent. John Neary claims that critic Nathan Scott—although his theological stance is "sternly dialectical," rejecting images or models of God and stressing God's unlikeness to the world or human experience—has a sacramental imagination.[93] For Scott, the sacramental principle means "that certain objects or actions or words or places belonging to the ordinary spheres of life may convey to us a unique illumination of the whole mystery of our existence, because in these actions and realities . . . something 'numinous' is resident, something holy and gracious."[94] The task of such an imagination is primarily to be open to all that is, not to see correspondences. Neary describes such a vision as "lyrical, epiphanic experiences of an oozing sacramental sacredness" and contrasts it to the more explicitly analogical vision of William Lynch, whose portrayal of God Neary describes as "a dramatic experience of the unfolding of autonomous—specific, historically embedded—personhood."[95] Thus the sacramental vision tends toward more diffuseness, whereas the truly analogical vision inclines toward more definite, concrete, and dramatic parallels. Yet both visions—the sacramental and the analogical—seem to flow from Catholicism's incarnational theology and sacramental practice.

Andrew Greeley claims that of all the major religions, "Catholicism is the most at ease with creation."[96] This assertion might seem preposterous

when one thinks of the hundreds of canonized saints who fled the pleasures of the world and tortured their bodies, and of the way the Church
has exalted virginity and celibacy. As far as sex is concerned, Greeley suggests that there are actually two traditions in the Church: the high tradition and the popular tradition.

> The high tradition is the Catholicism you learned in schools; the popular tra-
> dition is the Catholicism you learned in great part before you went to school.
> The former is contained in the teaching of theologians and the magisterium.
> It is cognitive, propositional, didactic. It is prosaic Catholicism. The latter is
> contained in the teaching of parents, family, neighbors, and friends. It is
> imaginative, experiential, narrative. It is poetic Catholicism.[97]

Although he admits that an ascetic antagonism to the flesh and sexuality
runs through Catholicism (exacerbated by Jansenism)[98] and is transmitted
through the "high tradition," Greeley insists that a love for the material
world, sensory beauty and the pleasures of the flesh has stubbornly per-
severed in the popular tradition.

Greeley also asserts that stories are central to Catholicism, arguing
"when a church ceases to be the center of events which bind together sacred time and sacred space through sacred narrative, it may be a very
beautiful, dignified, reverent place, but it isn't Catholic anymore. When a
church stops being a treasure house of stories, it stops being Catholic."[99]

Catholic novelist Ron Hansen has this to say about the way his Catholic
childhood nurtured his vocation as a writer:

> Looking back on my childhood now, I find that church-going and religion
> were in good part the origin of my vocation as a writer, for along with
> Catholicism's feast for the senses, its ethical concerns, its insistence on seeing
> God in all things, and the high status it gave to scripture, drama, and art,
> there was a connotation in Catholicism's liturgies that storytelling mattered.
> Each Mass was a narrative steeped in meaning and metaphor, helping the
> faithful to not only remember the past but to make it present here and now,
> and to bind ourselves into a sharing group so that, ideally, we could continue
> the public ministry of Jesus in our world.[100]

The gospels and the other narratives of Scripture are fundamental in all
Christian traditions, but Catholicism, with its rich lore of saints' lives
and legends, has perhaps foregrounded the narrative aspect of Christianity more than other denominations. Michel Foucault even argues in
the History of Sexuality that the practice of confession played a part in the
development of erotic narrative.[101] Andrew Greeley also sees Catholicism as less afraid of the imaginative dimension of religion than are Judaism, Islam, or Protestantism and thinks that Catholics are more likely

than others "to see the transcendent lurking in the objects, events, and people of creation."[102]

Greeley's claims for Catholicism may be debatable, but it must be remembered that he is positing these characteristics of the tradition as a whole, not of each individual Catholic. Greeley readily acknowledges there are Catholics whose religion is completely spiritual and who see nothing of the Divine in the material world:

> Many Catholics act as if creation is Godforsaken, while many who are not Catholic act as if the whole of creation is sacramental and revelatory of God. I merely suggest that there is a propensity among Catholics to take the objects and events and persons of ordinary life as hints of what God is like, in which God somehow lurks, even if (as is perhaps often the case) they are not completely self-conscious about these perceptions of enchantment.[103]

If Tracy and Greeley are right about the propensity of Catholicism to nurture an analogical imagination, a sacramental view of the world, and a propensity to tell stories of faith, we may expect to see Catholic novelists producing fiction that conveys a sense that, as Greeley says, "Catholics live in an enchanted world, a world. . . . haunted by a sense that the objects, events, and persons of daily life are revelations of grace."[104]

At this point it is necessary to provide a definition for the Catholic novel as I propose to use it in this book. The term is ambiguous, for by some accounts, a Catholic novel is any novel written by a Catholic or a former Catholic, yet many Catholic writers produce novels that contain no Catholic material or any recognizable Catholic theme. Some novels, though including clearly recognizable Catholic material, use it primarily as sociological or colorful background, without any sense of serious commitment to or engagement with the ideals and beliefs of the Catholic Church. Novels that use Catholicism simply as vivid sociological background do not really qualify as Catholic novels in my sense. Nor do novels that are thinly disguised apologetics. What I mean by a Catholic novel, is, first of all, a work of substantial literary merit. Catholic novelist Valerie Sayers provides the following catechism for Catholic writers:

> Question 1: What is the duty of the Catholic novelist?
>
> Answer: The duty of the Catholic novelist is to write a good story.
>
> Question 2: What is the duty of the Catholic novelist who chooses to write about the church?
>
> Answer: The duty of the Catholic novelist who chooses to write about the church is to write a good story.[105]

Catholic novels of mediocre or even inferior literary quality have been enjoyed by countless Catholic readers, but my particular interest here is to
explore the possibility of Catholic fiction that has comparable literary
merit to the best secular fiction, and to consider the possibilities for such
fiction in our own era.

Albert Sonnenfeld defines a Catholic novel as "a novel written by a
Catholic, using Catholicism as his informing mythopoeic structure or gen-
erative symbolic system, and where the principal and decisive issue is the
salvation or damnation of the hero or heroine."[106] This definition fits the
novels Sonnenfeld analyzes in his book (especially those of Graham
Greene and Georges Bernanos), but in my opinion this definition is too restrictive in making salvation or damnation the decisive issue. Thomas
Woodman, whose *Faithful Fictions* surveys the entire range of the British
Catholic novel, broadens the definition of a Catholic novel to "one that
deals with specifically Catholic themes or subject matter or indeed with
any themes or subject matter from a distinctively Catholic perspective
and with a sufficient degree of inwardness."[107] This last phrase "with a
sufficient degree of inwardness," though a bit imprecise, points to an essential element in a Catholic novel: that it is not content to describe surface reality but is interested in a deeper spiritual dimension.

Gene Kellogg in *The Vital Tradition: The Catholic Novel in a Period of Convergence* defines a Catholic novel as one "whose mainspring of dramatic
action depends upon Roman Catholic theology, or upon the history of
thought within one of the world's large Roman Catholic communities, or
upon 'development' of Roman Catholic 'ideas' in Newman's sense."[108] I
share Kellogg's belief that Catholic theology and thought must have a
substantial presence within the narrative, but would not insist that those
ideas be the "mainspring of dramatic action." It is true that the novels he
discusses—mainly from the 1930s and 1940s, generally considered to be
the "golden age" or flowering of the Catholic novel—*do* have such an essential connection to Catholic doctrine as to merit the metaphoric use of
mainspring to describe it. Furthermore, it may be that the most dramatic,
compelling, and memorable Catholic novels will always have that strong
link to the heart of Catholicism.

For me then a Catholic novel is a work of substantial literary merit, in
which Catholic theology and thought have a significant presence within
the narrative, with genuine attention to the inner spiritual life, often
drawing on Catholicism's rich liturgical and sacramental symbolism and
enriched by the analogical Catholic imagination.

I must add one further qualification. Some novels are deeply engaged
with Catholic material, but almost exclusively in a negative or hostile
sense.[109] Such novels are plentiful, for no one is as angry at Catholicism as
a former Catholic. Such novels are sometimes considered Catholic novels,

and indeed, many loyal Catholics find it bracing and expansive to enter a fictional space that confronts them with the shadow side of the Church. I think Catholics need such novels and I would be loath to deny them the designation of Catholic novel.

Yet the Catholic novels that most engage my interest and are the subject of my study in this book are those that include some kind of sense that Catholicism, no matter how flawed the institutional Church and no matter how weak and sinful individual Catholics, is a locus of truth. I must emphasize, however, that these Catholic novels do not necessarily exclude criticism of the Church. On the contrary, it would be difficult to find a Catholic novel that does *not* include it—including those of the so-called golden age of the Catholic novel. It may criticize the Church for being too materialistic, too complacent, too indifferent to the suffering of the poor and oppressed, too bourgeois, too rigid in its sexual teaching, too compliant with the spirit of the age, inattentive and insensitive to the needs and special gifts of women, and in our own day, for having either insufficiently or overly complied with the spirit of Vatican II. Yet these critiques are more like lovers' quarrels or marital arguments. They are deeply felt and painful, yet still encased in love for the beloved, in this case, for the Church as the earthen vessel that contains the good news.

Let us now turn to a review of the Catholic novel as it developed in France and England up to the mid-twentieth century.

NOTES

1. John Neary, *Like and Unlike God: Religious Imaginations in Modern and Contemporary Fiction* (Atlanta: Scholars Press, 1999), 3.

2. During this period the Byzantine emperors sponsored the destruction of religious images.

3. Leland Ryken, "Thinking Christianly About Literature," in *The Christian Imagination*, rev. ed., ed. Leland Ryken (Colorado Springs: WaterBrook Press, 2002), 26.

4. Jacques Maritain, "Christian Art" in *Art and Scholasticism: With Other Essays*, trans. J. F. Scanlon (New York: Charles Scribner's Sons, 1924), 53.

5. James Collins, *Pilgrim in Love: An Introduction to Dante and His Spirituality*. (Chicago: Loyola University Press, 1984), 47.

6. The excerpt from Cary's *Art and Reality* is quoted in Ryken, *The Christian Imagination*, 131.

7. Walker Percy, "On Being a Catholic Novelist," excerpted from *Conversations with Walker Percy*, ed. Lewis A. Lawson and Victor A. Kramer (Jackson: University Press of Mississippi, 1985) in Ryken, *The Christian Imagination*), 194.

8. Godawa, Brian. "Redemption in the Movies" in Ryken, *The Christian Imagination*, 439.

9. Rayner Heppenstall, *Léon Bloy* (Cambridge: Bowes & Bowes, 1953), 19.

10. Sir Philip Sidney, *An Apology for Poetry*, ed. Forrest G. Robinson (Indianapolis: Bobbs-Merrill, 1970), 56.

11. Martin Luther's letter to Eoban Hess (1533), quoted in Ryken, *The Christian Imagination*, 8.

12. John Henry Newman, *The Idea of a University*, ed. Martin J. Svaglic (New York: Holt, Rinehart & Winston, 1960), 222.

13. Wojtyla, Karol (Pope John Paul II). "Letter to Artists." 1999. <http://www.ewtn.com/library/papaldoc/jp2artis.htm> (10 April 2006).

14. J. C. Whitehouse, *Vertical Man: The Human Being in the Catholic Novels of Graham Greene, Sigrid Undset, and Georges Bernanos* (London: Saint Austin Press, 1999), 206.

15. Aidan Nichols, *The Art of God Incarnate* (New York: Paulist, 1980) 113.

16. David Lodge, *The Art of Fiction* (New York: Penguin, 1992) 53.

17. T. S. Eliot, "Religion and Literature," in *Selected Essays*, new ed. (New York: Harcourt, Brace & Co., 1950), 354.

18. Sidney, *Apology for Poetry*, 56.

19. Eliot, "Religion and Literature," 347.

20. O'Connor, "The Fiction Writer and His Country," in *Mystery and Manners*, 33.

21. Julian Green, *Diary 1928–1957*, sel. by Kurt Wolff, trans. Anne Green (New York: Harcourt, Brace & World, 1964), 159.

22. O'Connor, "Novelist and Believer," in *Mystery and Manners*, 159.

23. O'Connor, "Catholic Novelists and their Readers," 185.

24. In the analysis that follows I am limiting my discussion to North America and western Europe, the milieu which has produced the novelists and the readership with which I am concerned.

25. Wesley Kort, *Narrative Elements and Religious Meanings* (Philadelphia: Fortress Press, 1975).

26. For example, the whiskey priest in Graham Greene's *The Power and the Glory* (New York: Penguin, 1977) thinks of his betrayer as Judas (91), hears a cock crow when he is in prison (100), goes to his martyrdom riding a mule (178), and is urged to save himself by a "good thief" named Calver (187). Graham Greene, *The Power and the Glory* 1940 (London: Penguin, 1968).

27. Frank Kermode, *The Sense of an Ending* (New York: Oxford University Press, 1967).

28. Moeller, *Man and Salvation*, 44.

29. Martin Green, *Essays on Literature and Religion: Yeats's Blessings on von Hügel* (London, Longman, 1967), 116, 74, quoted in Woodman, *Faithful Fictions*, 140.

30. Moeller, *Man and Salvation*, 4.

31. Andrew Delbanco, *The Death of Satan: How Americans Have Lost the Sense of Evil* (New York: Farrar, Straus & Giroux, 1995), 3.

32. Delbanco, *Death of Satan*, 220.

33. Delbanco, *Death of Satan*, 210.

34. O'Connor, "Catholic Novelists and Their Readers," 175.

35. O'Connor, "Catholic Novelists and Their Readers," 178.

36. O'Connor, "Fiction Writer," in *Mystery and Manners*, 31.

37. O'Connor, "The Nature and Aim of Fiction," in *Mystery and Manners*, 79.

38. O'Connor, "Catholic Novelists and Their Readers," 180. O'Connor goes on to add, "When the Catholic novelist closes his own eyes and tries to see with the eyes of the Church, the result is another addition to that large body of pious trash for which we have so long been famous."

39. O'Connor, "Catholic Novelists and their Readers," 177.

40. See Ian Watt's *The Rise of the Novel* (Los Angeles: University of California Press, 1957).

41. David Lodge, "The Novelist at the Crossroads," in *The Novelist at the Crossroads and Other Essays on Fiction and Criticism* (Ithaca: Cornell University Press, 1971), 4.

42. According to the *Harper Handbook to Literature*, magical realism refers to "the practice of Latin American writers who mix everyday realities with imaginative extravaganzas drawn from the rich interplay of European and native cultures. [It enlarges] a reader's ordinary sense of the real to include magic, myth, hallucinations, and miracles." *The Harper Handbook to Literature*, 2nd ed., ed. Northrop Frye et al. (New York: Longman, 1997), 280.

43. François Mauriac, *The Viper's Tangle*, trans. Gerard Hopkins (New York: Carroll & Graf, 1987), 199. My practice in citing novels not written in English will be to give the English title followed by the title in the original language. The documentation will be for the English translation since that will probably be more useful to my readers.

44. O'Connor, "Fiction Writer," 34. O'Connor also says that writing informed by this kind of prophetic vision results in "realism which does not hesitate to destroy appearances in order to show a hidden truth." "Catholic Novelists and Their Readers," 179.

45. Sallie McFague, *Speaking in Parables: A Study in Metaphor and Theology* (Philadelphia: Fortress Press, 1975), 3.

46. Sonnenfeld, *Crossroads*, 25–26. Bernanos's statement is from an interview with Frédéric Lefèvre and is quoted on p. 25.

47. Sonnenfeld, *Crossroads*, 36.

48. Piers Paul Read, "The Catholic Novelist in a Secular Society" in *Hell and Other Destinations: A Novelist's Reflections on This World and the Next* (San Francisco: Ignatius Press, 2006), 209–10.

49. Evelyn Waugh, *Brideshead Revisited: The Sacred and Profane Memories of Captain Charles Ryder* (Boston: Little, Brown and Company, 1945), 85–86. Although the conclusion of the novel reveals that Charles does, in fact, eventually convert to Catholicism, throughout the novel the reader has no reason to think of Charles as anything other than completely secular.

50. Gene Kellogg, *The Vital Tradition: The Catholic Novel in a Period of Convergence* (Chicago: Loyola University Press, 1970), 110.

51. Barry Ulanov, "The Ordeal of Evelyn Waugh," in *The Vision Obscured: Perceptions of Some Twentieth-Century Catholic Novelists*, ed. Melvin J. Friedman (New York: Fordham University Press, 1970), 89.

52. Sonnenfeld, *Crossroads*, 39.

53. Fraser, *The Modern Catholic Novel*, 153. Böll was highly critical of the German Catholic Church not only for its appeasement of the Nazi regime, but also for being overly concerned with its own financial well-being and its insufficient efforts

to help refugees after the war. He withdrew from the formal practice of Catholicism in the late 1960s, but he never denied that he was "spiritually Catholic" and desired a Church burial at his death (157–58).

54. Peter Hebblethwaite, "How Catholic Is the Catholic Novel?" *Times Literary Supplement*, 27 July 1967, 679.

55. Kurt F. Reinhardt, *The Theological Novel of Modern Europe: An Analysis of Masterpieces by Eight Authors* (New York: Frederick Ungar, 1969), 3. Paul Lacey makes a point about religious poetry that applies equally well to the Christian novel:

> Religious poetry and political poetry have this in common: where the writer speaks out of personal experience and deep feelings, those who share neither may see only abstractions or tendentious opinions. The writer tries to speak of the flesh-and-blood experience behind beliefs and convictions; readers who have not shared the experience may see only doctrine—unfamiliar to some, too familiar to others, a source of resentment to still others.

Paul A. Lacey, "'To Meditate a Saving Strategy': Denise Levertov's Religious Poetry," *Renascence* 50, Nos. 1–2 (fall 1997/winter 1998): 18.

56. Ralph C. Wood, *The Comedy of Redemption: Christian Faith and Comic Vision in Four American Novelists* (Notre Dame, Ind.: University of Notre Dame Press, 1988), 23.

57. Wood, *Comedy of Redemption*, 32.

58. William F. Lynch, S.J. *Christ and Apollo: The Dimensions of the Literary Imagination*. Notre Dame (Indiana: University of Notre Dame Press, 1960), 93–95.

59. Lynch, *Christ and Apollo*, 94.

60. Lynch, *Christ and Apollo*, 96–97.

61. O'Connor, "Fiction Writer," 32.

62. Chad Walsh, "A Hope for Literature," in *The Climate of Faith in Modern Literature*, ed. Nathan A. Scott, Jr. (New York: Seabury Press, 1964), 232.

63. Anthony Low, "Jon Hassler: Catholic Realist," *Renascence* 47, no. 1 (fall 1994): 60.

64. J. Hillis Miller, "Literature and Religion" in *Religion and Modern Literature: Essays in Theory and Criticism*, ed. G. B. Tennyson and Edward E. Ericson, Jr. (Grand Rapids: Eerdmans, 1975), 45.

65. Maritain, "Christian Art," 55.

66. According to the *Catechism*, "Even though enlightened by him in whom it believes, faith is often lived in darkness and can be put to the test. The world we live in often seems very far from the one promised us by faith. Our experiences of evil and suffering, injustice, and death, seem to contradict the Good News; they can shake our faith and become a temptation against it." *Catechism of the Catholic Church* (New York: Doubleday, Image Books, 1995), 164. Quotations from the *Catechism* are referred to by item number.

67. Low, "Jon Hassler: Catholic Realist," 68.

68. Frederick Buechner, *Wishful Thinking: A Seeker's ABC*, rev. ed. (San Francisco: HarperSanFrancisco, 1973, 1993), 23.

69. Graham Greene, *Monsignor Quixote*, (London: Vintage, 2000), 77.

70. George Orwell, "Inside the Whale," in *A Collection of Essays* (New York: Doubleday, 1954), 246.

71. Lodge, "Graham Greene," in *Novelist at the Crossroads*, 88–89.

72. Thomas Woodman, *Faithful Fictions: The Catholic Novel in British Literature* (Milton Keynes, England: Open University Press, 1991), 27.

73. This remark of Flannery O'Connor was quoted in a lecture by Ralph Wood at the University of Notre Dame on November 10, 2003. I have been unable to locate the source of the quotation.

74. Woodman, *Faithful Fictions*, 27.

75. Sonnenfeld, *Crossroads*, 18, viii.

76. Sonnenfeld, *Crossroads*, 39.

77. Sonnenfeld, foreward to *Crossroads*, vii.

78. Evelyn Waugh, "Fan-Fare," in *The Essays, Articles and Reviews of Evelyn Waugh*, ed. Donat Gallagher (Boston: Little, Brown and Company, 1983), 302. The article was originally published in the April 8, 1946 issue of *Life*.

79. Quoted in Jason Boffetti, "Tolkien's Catholic Imagination," *Crisis*, November 2001, 34. There are, however, some hints and allusions to Tolkien's Christian framework. Aspects of Christ are present in Frodo, Gandalf, and Aragorn. The Virgin Mary is reflected in Galadriel and Elbereth. (Tolkien wrote in a letter, "I think it is true that I owe much of this character to Christian and Catholic teaching and imagination about Mary." [Stratford Caldecott, "The Lord & Lady of the Rings: The Hidden Presence of Tolkien's Catholicism in *The Lord of the Rings*," *Touchstone*, January 2002, 55]). The Hobbits are sustained on their journey by the Eucharist-like lembas. Most telling, perhaps, is the fact that the Ring of Power, representing the evil of the corrupted will, is destroyed on March 25, the feast of the Annunciation, when Mary's acceptance of God's will began the reversal of sin's power through the Incarnation.

80. Ian Ker, *The Catholic Revival in English Literature, 1845–1961* (Notre Dame, Ind.: University of Notre Dame Press, 2003), 203.

81. Lodge, "Graham Greene," 89.

82. Andrew Greeley, *The Catholic Imagination* (Berkeley: University of California Press, 2000), 5.

83. David Tracy, *The Analogical Imagination: Christian Theology and the Culture of Pluralism* (New York: Crossroad, 1981), 413.

84. Tracy, *Analogical Imagination*, 421.

85. Tracy, *Analogical Imagination*, 454.

86. Neary, *Like and Unlike God*, 23.

87. *Catechism*, 1128.

88. Unfortunately, some of the Catholic churches that were built after Vatican II were plain to the point of being austere and almost completely devoid of religious art. To some extent, this trend was a reaction against the mediocre and tawdry decoration of many pre-Vatican II Catholic churches. The cure, however, was in most cases worse than the disease. An analysis of this unfortunate development is given in Michael Rose's *Ugly as Sin: How They Changed Our Churches from Sacred Places to Meeting Spaces and How We Can Change Them Back Again* (Manchester, N.H.: Sophia Institute Press, 2001).

89. *Catechism*, 1127.

90. G. K. Chesterton makes the point that, although early Christianity was strongly influenced by Platonic ideas that devalued matter, the centrality of the idea of the Incarnation in European civilization, made it "inevitable that there would be a return to materialism, in the sense of the serious value of matter and the making of the body." G. K. Chesterton, *St. Thomas Aquinas* in *The Collected Works of G. K. Chesterton*, vol. 2 (San Francisco: Ignatius Press, 1990), 493.

91. "Sacramentality" in *The HarperCollins Encyclopedia of Catholicism*, ed. Richard P. McBrien (San Francisco: HarperSanFrancisco, 1995), 1148.

92. Gerard Manley Hopkins, *Poems and Prose of Gerard Manley Hopkins*, ed. W. H. Gardner (Harmondsworth, Eng.: Penguin, 1953), 27, 51.

93. Neary, *Like and Unlike God*, 109.

94. Nathan Scott, *The Wild Prayer of Longing: Poetry and the Sacred* (New Haven: Yale University Press, 1971), 49, quoted in Neary, *Like and Unlike God*, 114.

95. Neary, *Like and Unlike God*, 124. The titles of two of Lynch's books, *Christ and Apollo* and *Christ and Prometheus*, emphasize that for Lynch the primary revelation of God is Christ, and this fact anchors the Christian's imagination in "Christ's specific, dramatic historicity over against forms of solipsistic thinking that, rather than engaging the real, fly off into ungrounded ('romantic') fantasy or pure, unimaginative cognition or willful absolutism." Neary, *Like and Unlike God*, 124.

96. Greeley, *Catholic Imagination*, 10.

97. Greeley, *Catholic Imagination*, 76.

98. Jansenism was a reform movement in seventeenth century France that taught a very pessimistic view of human nature and stressed predestination and humanity's inability to perform good works without God's grace. See "Jansenism" in *HarperCollins Encyclopedia of Catholicism*, 687–88.

99. Greeley, *Catholic Imagination*, 36.

100. Ron Hansen, preface to *A Stay Against Confusion: Essays on Faith and Fiction* (New York: HarperCollins, 2001), vii.

101. Michel Foucauld, *An Introduction*, vol. 1 of *The History of Sexuality*, trans. Robert Hirley (London: Allen Lane, 1979), 19–23, referenced in Woodman, *Faithful Fictions*, 147.

102. Greeley, *Catholic Imagination*, 77.

103. Greeley, *Catholic Imagination*, 18.

104. Greeley, *Catholic Imagination*, 1.

105. Valerie Sayers, "Being a Writer, Being Catholic," *Commonweal*, 4 May 2001, 14.

106. Sonnenfeld, foreward to *Crossroads*, vii.

107. Woodman, introduction to *Faithful Fictions*, xi.

108. Kellogg, *Vital Tradition*, 1.

109. Examples of such novels would be *Sucking Sherbet Lemons* (1988) by Michael Carson and *Knowledge of Angels* (1994) by Jill Paton Walsh. James Joyce is often identified as a great Catholic writer. His writing is saturating with Catholicism, and many Catholics take special delight in Joyce's rich use of Catholic imagery and symbolism. One could argue that Joyce's novels present Catholicism as true in some deep mythic sense, in the way that his *Ulysses* discloses the "truth" of Homer's *Odyssey*. Yet Stephen's *"Non serviam"* ("I will not serve") in *Portrait of the Artist as a Young Man* overlays all Joyce's fiction and strongly contravenes any affirmation of Catholism. The Catholicism is there primarily to be rejected.

2

✝

The History of the
Catholic Novel in England

Catholic fiction can evoke questions in the heart and mind of a reader, questions that have been by and large banished from the mainstream culture.

—Michael O'Brien, Catholic novelist

A recent, very incomplete bibliography of "The Catholic Novel" lists over seventeen hundred examples as well as a variety of criticism.

—Thomas Woodman, *Faithful Fictions:*
The Catholic Novel in British Literature

Catholic writers see a drama of good and evil that others do not see.

—Piers Paul Read, Catholic novelist

Fyodor Dostoyevsky, although not a Roman Catholic, is sometimes called the father of the Catholic novel because he is the first European novelist for whom the drama of salvation is at the center of his fiction.[1] Furthermore, for Dostoyevsky, salvation is not the kind of self-realization advocated by Enlightenment thinkers, but a total submission to Jesus Christ and outpouring of the self in service to others. Furthermore, this Christianity is stubbornly resistant to all rationalistic and empirical accounts of human welfare, as dramatized in the famous "Grand Inquisitor" episode of *The Brothers Karamazov*. Dostoyevsky, however, was Russian Orthodox and not friendly to Roman Catholicism. The Catholic novel actually had its beginnings in France, and since the major British Catholic novels were strongly influenced by the writers of the

31

French Catholic Renaissance, it is useful to look first at this flowering of Catholic literary art across the channel.

The nineteenth century was a chaotic time in France. After the violent and bloody upheavals of the French Revolution at the end of the eighteenth century and the brief burst of Napoleonic glory followed by the humiliating defeat at Waterloo, France was left with two strong competing strains: the democratic impetus for *liberté, égalité, fraternité,* and an equally ardent yearning for order and stability. The turmoil of the Revolution and its aftermath left the Catholic Church much weakened in France. The Revolution had unleashed violent anticlerical feeling, which had long been latent; but the revolutionaries' violence against the Church—putting large numbers of priests and nuns to death, and turning the Cathedral of Notre Dame into a temple of the goddess of Reason—led others to look to the Church as a force for social order and political stability. With the restoration of the Bourbon monarchy, many people from the middle and upper classes, who had previously been seduced by Deism and other Enlightenment ideas, returned to the Church, but not necessarily from religious fervor as much as from a desire for the social order seen as necessary for their own continuing prosperity.

Before the century was over, France would see many more changes in government—a second Empire, two more republics, and a war with Prussia resulting in another humiliating defeat and loss of territory. Through all of this, advances in science nourished an optimistic belief in the upward, progressive trajectory of civilization and a conviction that truth was to be found in science and materialism, not in faith and religion. In France, most of the great intellectual and cultural figures— Ernest Renan, Émile Durkheim, Hippolyte Taine, Guy de Maupassant, Émile Zola—exemplified this attitude, known as Positivism. A French philosopher, Auguste Comte, regarded as the founder of Positivism, stated, "any proposition which does not admit of being ultimately reduced to a simple enunciation of fact, special or general, can have no real or intelligible sense," expresses the movement's disdain for metaphysical abstractions and dogma.[2]

Meanwhile as the century progressed, the hostility and mutual suspicion between the republican and Catholic factions was exacerbated by the papacy's condemnation of modern ideas in the *Syllabus of Errors* in 1864 and the definition of papal infallibility at the First Vatican Council (1869–1870). The Church for its part was dismayed by the excesses of the Paris commune and the way that modern thinkers were challenging Biblical and ecclesiastical authority. Eventually, however, even some secular people began to feel that the currents of materialism, naturalism, scientism, and determinism were choking off vitality and beauty. Those of a literary bent disliked what these developments had done to the novel.

Novelists had portrayed human life as determined by brute, mechanistic forces. In this fiction human behavior was shaped—not by ideals, valor, intelligence, cowardice or villainy—but by impersonal laws of biology and sociology. Naturally, this literature made readers feel helpless. No matter what the new science said, they wanted to feel once more the freedom and the grandeur of the human person.

Gene Kellogg, who traces the development of the Catholic novel from its roots in France to the mid-twentieth century, points out the irony in the fact that under the Third Republic the intellectual and cultural currents actually made people feel less free and less in control of their own lives:

> Emotionally the Republic bore an odd crop: not a bright daylight flowering of confidence in progress but night-blooming superstition, metaphysical despair, and a longing to demonstrate liberty by every conceivable excess. The result was the "decadence" of the period eventually to be known as the "fin de siècle," a period which by curiously convoluted processes ended by giving way to a revival of Catholicism in France.[3]

One of the young men drawn to the decadent movement in the arts in an attempt to assuage their emotional hunger, was Jules Barbey d'Aurevilly, the first self-proclaimed Catholic novelist. Like many young Frenchmen of the time, Barbey d'Aurevilly had thrown off his childhood faith, but he reconverted at the age of thirty-seven and went on to write highly dramatic novels, in which sin (especially sexual sin) and the issues of salvation and damnation play a major part. In their morbid and exotic elements, such as sorcery and Satanism, they show the influence of the decadent movement. For a new edition of his novel, *An Old Mistress* (*Une vielle maitresse*) (1851), he wrote a preface that articulates a manifesto for Catholic novelists. Barbey addresses his critics who charged that he could not be a good Catholic and write about human corruption, lechery, and degradation. Insisting that Catholicism has nothing prudish or puritanical about it, he argues that a Catholic could write about anything as long as he did not do so in a way that encouraged sin or made it appear that "good is bad and bad is good."[4] In fact, Barbey seems to be anticipating Flannery O'Connor's argument that the Catholic writer's faith frees him to see more and to see the world as it is. "That which is morally and intellectually magnificent in Catholicism is that it is large, comprehensive, immense; that it embraces human nature in its totality."[5] He insists that "Catholicism does not cripple art for fear of scandal" and that the Catholic writer's responsibility is "to lay hold of human reality, crime or virtue, and to make it live by the full power of inspiration and expression, to show the reality, to make it live."[6] The "morality of the artist is in the power and truth of his portrayal."[7] These words, although written in the middle of the nineteenth century, are ones that most Catholic writers would heartily endorse today.

Another important early French novelist, also attracted to the fin de siè-cle decadence in reaction against the stultifying limitations of materialism and determinism was Joris-Karl Huysmans. His novels provide fictional accounts of his experience of despair and physical collapse in his attempt to satisfy his desire for every kind of sensory experience. Ultimately, he, like Barbey d'Aurevilly, was drawn back to the faith of his childhood, but in his case, the primary attraction was aesthetic. Enthralled by the beauty of the liturgy and plain chant, he came to see the Catholic faith itself as an exemplar of spiritual as well as aesthetic beauty, described in this passage from his novel *En Route* (1895):

> As for plain chant, the agreement of its melody with architecture is also cer-tain; it also bends from time to time like the sombre Romanesque arcades, and rises, shadowy and pensive, like complete vaulting. . . .
> Sometimes, on the other hand, the Gregorian chant seems to borrow from Gothic its flowery tendrils, its scattered pinnacles, its gauzy rolls, its tremu-lous lace, its trimmings light and thin as the voices of children.[8]

After his conversion, Huysmans's novels show his continuing fascination with the spiritual beauty of Catholicism. He also uses what is sometimes called the theme of mystical compensation or sacrificial substitution (also called reversibility or interresponsibility). This idea, based on the Catholic doctrine of the communion of saints, is that all Christians, living and dead, are spiritually connected and can offer their own suffering or good works for the redemption of another, a prime example being intercessory prayer. This theme, which would become very popular with Catholic novelists, is expressed by a Trappist monk in *En route*:

> "The world does not even conceive that the austerity of the abbeys can profit it. The doctrine of mystical compensation escapes it entirely. It cannot repre-sent to itself that the substitution of the innocent for the guilty is necessary when to suffer merited punishment is concerned. Nor does it explain to itself any more that in wishing to suffer for others, monks turn aside the wrath of heaven, and establish a solidarity in the good which is a counter-weight against the federation of evil. God knows, moreover, with what cataclysms the unconscious world would be menaced, if in consequence of a sudden dis-appearance of all the cloisters, the equilibrium which saves it were broken."[9]

That the novels of both Barbey d'Aurevilly and Huysmans were quite pop-ular in their day with secular as well as Catholic readers may seem pecu-liar, given the breach between the secular and religious segments of French society. Kellogg provides the following explanation of this phenomenon:

> During the era of the "decadents," the average French Catholic's sense of separation between Catholicism and the secular environment was acute. At

the same time convergence was beginning. A curiosity about Catholicism, so long despised by the secular world, was growing within that world. Ironically, the victory of secularism had carried in its results—determinism, license, aspirituality—the seeds of a Catholic renaissance. This renaissance would affect not only the secular world from which such converts as Huysmans came, but have an even more powerful effect on the isolated Catholic community, whose isolation would finally dissolve in a fever of creative expression, addressed both to the secular environment and to Catholics themselves, as the two communities approached on what amounted to a collision course of mutual recognition. The Catholic generation of 1876 was growing up, and without its own schools the Catholic community could no longer maintain its young in insulated apartness. Young Catholics were thrown into the secular environment, and the secular environment had to receive them.[10]

By the turn of the century, Catholicism in France had suffered from the anti-Catholic and anti-clerical policies of the Third Republic. Education had been secularized and the Jesuits and most other teaching orders expelled in the 1880s. By 1904 no members of religious orders were allowed to teach. Religion was banished from the public square as crosses were removed from courtrooms, public prayers prohibited, and diplomatic relations with Rome broken off. Divorce was introduced and Sunday working permitted. Separation of church and state became the law of the land. Catholicism was tolerated but not supported. On the contrary, it was seen by significant segments of the population as inimical to people's well being. Those who retained ties with Catholicism were mostly from the upper classes who had a sentimental attachment to the Church, which they associated with the glory days of the powerful monarchy. Some of the bourgeois clung to the Church as a force for social order, which was good for commerce. The poor and the peasants, who had been largely de-Christianized and given only rudimentary and inadequate religious instruction, relied on the Church primarily for baptisms, marriages or funerals. Even for those who regularly practiced their religion, nineteenth-century Catholicism seemed largely sluggish and inert.

Yet even in this dismal situation, there were serious and sensitive Catholics, and their fervor was increased by their sense of being an embattled community under siege. An impressive number of intellectuals and cultural figures followed the same pattern as Barbey d'Aurevilly. Having abandoned their childhood faith and become atheists in their youth, they reconverted to Catholicism in their adulthood. Among them were Paul Claudel, who wrote poetry and plays stressing sacrifice, chivalry, and nobility; Léon Bloy, whose novels expressing the doctrine of the communion of saints called attention to the poor as an integral part of that communion and depicted poverty as both a social evil and source of sanctification; and Charles Péguy, an early socialist, who, like Bloy, stressed the importance of the poor and seemed to embody the best ideals of both the republican and religious traditions of France.[11] Bloy's novels made a strong critique of the hypocrisy and materialism of many nominal Catholics, a theme that would be repeated in future Catholic novels. Jacques Maritain, who was raised as a liberal Protestant, converted to Catholicism under the influence of Bloy and interpreted the philosophy and theology of St. Thomas Aquinas for the modern world. These converts were leading figures in the revitalized Catholicism of the early twentieth century, which is referred to as the Catholic Revival or the French Catholic Renaissance. Although Bloy was the only novelist among them (Huysmans had died in 1907), the ideas of all these thinkers contributed to the creative ferment in which the Catholic novel matured.

The greatest novelists of the French Catholic Renaissance were François Mauriac and Georges Bernanos, most of whose novels appeared in the 1920s and 1930s. Unlike Barbey d'Aurevilly, Huysmans and Bloy, Mauriac and Bernanos did not lose their faith and reconvert, but were lifelong Catholics. One of the major differences between them and Barbey d'Aurevilly and Huysmans, who focused their critique on the secular world, is that, like Bloy, they were more intent on scrutinizing the flaws in the Catholic community. Mauriac's faith had a strong strain of Jansenism in it, and his novels evince a fascination with evil and sin.[12] He wrote, "I make the Catholic universe of evil palpable, tangible, pungent. The theologians offer us an abstract idea of the sinner; I present him in flesh and blood."[13] Many of the sins that Mauriac disclosed were certainly in the secular world as well, but the ones that fell most fully under the novelist's scrutiny were those of Catholics whose faith was dry, lifeless, uncharitable, or hypocritical. Mauriac's earlier books concentrated on sexual sin to such an extent that he was accused by some critics of taking a kind of perverse pleasure in describing acts and situations that he ostensibly condemned as immoral and drawing his readers into voyeurism.[14]

Mauriac's fiction reflects the influence of Blaise Pascal, with whom Mauriac shared a view of the degradation and misery of humanity in its natural state and the necessity of God's grace to rise above its slavery to passion and greed. The atmosphere of Mauriac's novels is grim, repressive, almost hopeless—except for intimations of grace underlying a desolate universe. *The Viper's Tangle (Le noeud de vipères)* (1932) is considered by many to be Mauriac's most outstanding depiction of the action of grace upon a human soul. The protagonist, a miserly agnostic, is converted shortly before his death, partly, it is suggested, through the intercession of his daughter, who, before she died in childhood, expressed the wish to die for her father. This is an example of the theme of sacrificial substitution: one person offering his life or suffering for the spiritual well being of another. Although the novel depicts the protagonist's agnosticism as choking off the wellsprings of spiritual vitality and human joy, its greatest scorn is directed at the superficial, mechanistic Catholicism of the rest of his family.

Mauriac's novels, like those of Huysmans, were popular with secular as well as religious readers, which is curious, given their overt spiritual themes and heavy emphasis on sin and salvation. Again, one explanation is the state of French society at the time. The common struggle of all the French in the first world war had brought the secular and Catholic factions closer together, and the antagonism between the two groups had been somewhat attenuated. The old bitterness between the religious and the secular was being tempered by mutual respect. According to Kellogg, this new convergence included "at least as much mutual curiosity as abrasiveness."[15] The lessening of tension and growth of mutual respect between the two factions was reflected in Mauriac's election to the French Academy in 1932. This newfound esteem from the secular world was given international prominence when he was awarded the Nobel Prize for literature in 1952.

Like Mauriac, Georges Bernanos was a lifelong Catholic and more critical of the Catholic community than of the secular world. Also like Mauriac, he denied the goodness of natural man without grace to lift him out of the mire of sin. Yet in his fictional world, one has the sense of grace being more available, for the boundary between the secular and the sacred seems more permeable. In fact, they seem to interpenetrate each other.[16] As the dying priest in Bernanos's *Diary of a Country Priest* (*Journal d'un curé de campagne*) (1936) says, "'Grace is everywhere.'"[17] Yet Bernanos does not in any way minimize the power of evil. His sense of the universe as engaged in a great struggle between God and Satan is most dramatically depicted in his first novel *Under the Sun of Satan* (*Sous le soleil de Satan*) (1926), where Satan actually appears as a bourgeois horse trader and bestows on a young priest the gift/curse of being able to clearly see Satan's power throughout the world, especially in the spiritual lives of his penitents.[18] Bernanos also has a way of making the reader aware of the world of time and the world of eternity running along parallel to each other. While both Mauriac and Bernanos have a psychological focus, depicting change in a human soul, Bernanos's novels have a more cosmic scope, where the forces of Satan and the kingdom of heaven are engaged. Yet Bernanos's fiction often seems more psychologically convincing than Mauriac's because his fictional world seems less determined. Although, like Mauriac, he shines a harsh light on the world of sin, there is a greater sense of human solidarity and freedom. Therefore, many readers find him less pessimistic and more affirmative than Mauriac.

Bernanos, who as a young man had wanted to become a priest, came to see his vocation as a writer as a kind of priesthood,[19] and two of his most famous protagonists are priests: Abbé Donissan in *Under the Sun of Satan* and the young curé in *The Diary of a Country Priest*. They are both unrefined, minimally educated, and lacking in theological sophistication or preaching ability. Yet, although they may be ignorant of the complexities of academic theology, they have an intense love of God and an uncanny ability to see directly into the heart of their parishioners and to call them out of their selfishness, resentment, or bitterness.

Bernanos was a political and social conservative, yet in his fiction his sympathies were primarily with the poor and deprived. He saw poverty not simply as an economic issue, however, but as a manifestation of a morally degenerate society. He admired chivalry, but in a moral rather than a military sense. His humble priest protagonists take on a chivalric heroism. Though sometimes accused of being a reactionary, Bernanos looked to the past—not to revel in the power and splendor of the medieval Church—but to contrast what he believed was a time of more genuine and fervent faith to the eviscerated Catholicism of his day, which had largely neglected the poor and adopted the values of the materialistic bourgeoisie.

Like Mauriac, Bernanos enjoyed wide popularity with the French reading public. This phenomenon can be explained, not only by the gradual rapprochement between the religious and secular segments of French society, but by two other factors. In the early twentieth century, the reigning vogues of surrealism, cubism, fauvism and various sorts of experimental writing contributed in all the arts to the sense of a fragmented, meaningless world. Mauriac and Bernanos eschewed these techniques, writing in a basically realistic mode, yet they were able to transcend the sense of dullness and limitation conveyed by the materialist determinism of earlier nineteenth century realists and naturalists like Zola and Balzac. The world portrayed realistically by Mauriac and Bernanos is palpitating with the very breath of God. Their novels depict a universe where, as the poet Gerard Manley Hopkins wrote in "God's Grandeur," "the Holy Ghost over the bent/World broods with warm breast and with ah! bright wings."[20] Probably what most appealed to readers was the sense that in these books, the individual human being matters enormously, has dignity even in the most squalid circumstances, and is loved by a power beyond understanding.[21]

Whatever the reasons for their popularity, Mauriac and Bernanos had clearly demonstrated that the spiritual world could have a dynamic presence even in that most secular of literary forms, the novel, and had also introduced into it a new kind of interiority that was completely different from the stream of consciousness technique used by James Joyce, Virginia Woolf and others. They had developed and expanded on several themes already introduced by earlier Catholic novelists—the pursuit of the sinner by God, the criticism of materialism and hypocrisy, the futility of life without God, regenerative suffering, and the motifs of sacrificial substitution and intercessory prayer—to which they added a critique of the Catholic community, especially its superficial pieties, its materialism, its arrogance, and its neglect of the poor. Yet even in this critique, they disclosed sources of spiritual vitality within the Church—the sanctity of some of its most humble priests, and of the poor, the unchurched, and even the sinners. For the sinner in their works is not simply someone to be corrected and saved. Rather, Mauriac and Bernanos both show how the sinner is at the very heart of Christianity, an idea perhaps best expressed by Péguy:

> The sinner is at the very heart of Christianity. . . . The sinner and the saint, one can say, are two equally integral parts . . . of the mechanism of Christianity. Both are equally indispensable and mutually complementary entities. . . . [W]hoever is not a Christian or competent in the matter of Christianity is someone who does not commit sin. . . . Whoever is literally a sinner . . . is because of this already a Christian. . . . The sinner, together with the saint, enters into the system of Christianity. . . . The sinner holds out his hand to the saint because the saint gives his hand to the sinner. And, both drawing the other, ascend to Jesus in their unbreakable grasp.[22]

This concept would be dramatized in English Catholic novels, where sinners like Sebastian in *Brideshead Revisited* or Sarah in *The End of the Affair* not only are enmeshed in a web of grace that draws them in, but also help the larger community of the "saints."[23] This and many other themes explored by these French novelists would animate the imaginations of some very talented Catholic writers on the other side of the English Channel, and it is to England that we now turn.

———

English Catholic writers had some similarities to their French co-religionists. Like them, they were repelled by the social dislocations and ugliness spawned by industrialism and appalled by the greed and materialism unleashed by unfettered capitalism. In fact, this sense of dismay may have been even greater in England, the birthplace of the Industrial Revolution. These writers also resented the way in which advances in science and technology tended to undermine spiritual values and diminish the importance of the person. This distaste for the modern world led them, like Huysmans, Claudel and others, to look to the Middle Ages—its gothic architecture and religious art, the Latin liturgy, and God-centered world view—for moral clarity and spiritual beauty. In the nineteenth century the Oxford Movement and Pre-Raphaelitism in the arts—both of which were not Catholic movements[24]—reinforced this attraction to medievalism.

The primary difference between French and English Catholics was that in France the dominant form of Christianity was Catholicism, whereas in England it was Anglicanism. French Catholics defined their religious stance over against atheistic secularism, whereas the earlier English Catholics saw themselves primarily in opposition to Protestantism.[25] At least until well into the twentieth century, secularism had not made the kinds of inroads in England that it had made in France, and most of the English were Christian. The French saw their Catholic community as about half of the nation, and French culture reflected its ancient Catholic roots. English Catholics, on the other hand, saw themselves as a tiny, embattled minority, whose religion was considered unpatriotic at best, and positively perverse at worst.

Consequently, most of the early Catholic novels in England reflect this struggle of English Catholics to defend their allegiance to this "foreign power," and they insist on the validity of Catholicism's claim to be the only true and authentic form of Christianity. John Henry Newman's novel *Loss and Gain* (1848) recounts in an amusing yet sensitive way the tribulations of a young Anglican who converts to Catholicism. His other novel *Callista* (1856), the story of a third century convert and martyr, reflects Newman's interest in establishing Catholicism's essential link with early Christianity. Several Catholic women writers in the latter part of the nineteenth century gained a wide readership among Catholics. Lady Georgiana Fullerton, Cecilia Caddell, and Josephine Mary Ward wrote some fiction about the suffering of Catholics during the Reformation, but most of their work deals with what Margaret Maison calls the "heroine-lover-faith triangle."[26] These novels feature adultery, mistaken identity, conversions, convents, renegade priests and, of course, Jesuits. In most of them earthly love must be renounced for the sake of a higher good, often with the heroine entering the convent or the hero becoming a priest. *The School for Saints* (1897) and *Robert Orange* (1900) by Pearl Craigie (who published under the name of John Oliver Hobbes), an American expatriate, divorcée, and Catholic convert, were the first of these novels by Catholic women to attract much notice from the non-Catholic literary establishment.

The early twentieth century saw the production of some rather bizarre Catholic novels by converts. Frederick Rolfe was a convert who entered the seminary but was dismissed, presumably for homosexuality. Thereafter he led a bohemian and dissipated life yet seemed to retain a sincere belief in Catholicism. His novel *Hadrian VII* (1904), concerns a fictitious English pope, who, convinced that the wealth of the Vatican is a scandalous contradiction of gospel values, sells its art treasures and gives the money to the poor. He also insists on opening up Vatican windows that had been closed and walking through the streets of Rome. He makes

peace with political leaders and makes ecumenical and conciliatory over-
tures to non-Catholics and non-Christians.[27] Another noteworthy convert
and writer of this period was Robert Hugh Benson, the son of the Anglican archbishop of Canterbury. He wrote an historical novel, *Come Rack!
Come Rope!* (1912), based on the Jesuit martyr Edmund Campion during
the Elizabethan persecution. In addition to some contemporary novels focusing on conversion, Benson also wrote two futuristic novels that show
the marked influence of H. G. Wells. In *Lord of the World* (1907), set about
a hundred years in the future, the forces of secularism have won out, the
Church is reduced to a tiny remnant, and the pope and the few remaining
cardinals are hiding out in the Palestinian desert as the apocalypse approaches. Although Benson's predictions of such things as commercial air
travel and other technological advances are noteworthy, his portrayal of a
secular utopia is even more striking:

> War, apparently, was now extinct, and it was not Christianity that had done
> it; union was now seen to be better than disunion, and the lesson had been
> learnt apart from the Church. In fact, natural virtues had suddenly waxed
> luxuriant, and supernatural virtues were despised. Friendliness took the
> place of charity, contentment the place of hope, and knowledge the place of
> faith.[28]

Benson may be trying to clarify that the Church is not simply a mechanism for achieving social progress, a view that was common in the nineteenth century. He may also be trying to show the limits of secular progressive movements, for this "utopia" also contains unsavory elements,
such as legal euthanasia and assisted suicide. In *The Dawn of All* (1911)
Benson presents an opposing scenario in which Catholicism has tri-
umphed. The human attempts to perfect human life through science, political systems, social engineering, and the arts have all been found wanting, and in the end everyone "found themselves looking once more into
the serene, smiling face of Catholicism."[29]

Although the premises of the two novels seem diametrically opposed,
they both identify the Church with the institution, especially the papacy,
for even in *Lord of the World*, the tiny remnant Church is primarily the
Pope and a few cardinals. These novels reflect the growing tendency of
English Catholics at this time to identify with ultramontanism (literally,
"beyond the mountains," i.e., Rome), an intellectual and cultural movement in the late nineteenth and early twentieth centuries that looked to
the papacy as a symbol of all that was great and glorious in Catholicism
and as a bulwark against much that was threatening in modern liberalism, socialism, and scientific materialism.[30] Cardinal Manning had cham-
pioned this view and exulted in the definition of papal infallibility in

1870. Although there had been an impressive number of converts as a result of the Oxford Movement, and distinguished intellectuals continued to join the Church in the early twentieth century, Catholics were still very much a minority in England; and the majority of them, being poor or working class, felt especially marginalized. The papacy was a symbol that they belonged to a Church with enormous influence and prestige and was therefore a very important part of their Catholic identity. Even Rolfe's *Hadrian VII,* although critical of the material trappings of the papacy, still identifies it as the moral and spiritual center of Catholicism.

Hilaire Belloc and G. K. Chesterton, although primarily known today for their non-fiction—especially their vigorous defense of Catholicism[31]— did write some fiction which had bearing on the development of the English Catholic novel. Chesterton used allegory and fantasy to express religious themes, a technique that would be utilized by later novelists. Although weak in terms of character development, his novels like *Napoleon of Nottinghill* (1904), *The Man Who Was Thursday* (1908), *The Ball and the Cross* (1909), and *The Return of Don Quixote* (1927) effectively convey Chesterton's sense of Christianity as a robust, life-affirming religion, and a vision of humanity as flawed and unable to improve without supernatural help.

Belloc's essays and nonfiction reinforced English Catholics' sense of apartness, for he elaborated Catholicism's claim to be the only authentic Christianity and thus superior to the Church of England. In historical works like *How the Reformation Happened* (1928), *Characters of the Reformation* (1936), and *Europe and the Faith* (1920), in which he claims "The Faith is Europe. And Europe is the Faith,"[32] he provided an alternative view of history from the standard English one, in which Catholics were unpatriotic traitors manipulated by devious Jesuits. In Belloc's version Catholics nobly clung to the truth, while unscrupulous villains, hungry for the wealth of the monasteries and of affluent Catholic families, corrupted the English Church and severed its vital link with Rome. In *Survivals and New Arrivals* (1929), Belloc describes the difficult hostile atmosphere in which English Catholic writers have worked. He contrasts the situation in England with that in countries with a large Catholic population, where Catholic literature, ideas, and history are known. "But in the English-speaking world it is otherwise. *There* Catholicism re-entered late as an alien phenomenon after the character of society had become 'set' in an anti-Catholic mould. There all national literature, traditions, law and especially history were (and are) fundamentally anti-Catholic."[33]

Belloc's pugnacious brand of Catholicism, now often referred to as *triumphalist,* has fallen out of favor in this ecumenical age. Yet Belloc certainly was not blind to the failings of the Catholic Church, for he is reputed to have said, "for unbelievers a proof of its divinity might be found in the fact that no merely human institution conducted with such knavish imbecility would have lasted a fortnight."[34] Belloc's most popular book, *The Path to Rome* (1902), a delightful descriptive account of a pilgrimage he made on foot, conveys his love for the Church and the sense in which it is embedded in European culture, without the off-putting polemics of many of his other books.

Belloc's nonfiction, then, was a major contribution to Catholics' growing sense of pride in their religion. His fiction, though little read today, may also have influenced the shape of the Catholic novel in England. There is a possibillity that Belloc, who spent a good part of his youth in France (his father was French), may have read Huysmans and some of the other French novelists, for in his novel *Emmanuel Burden* (1904), a satire on the moral debasement of a mercantile English family, he writes with the kind of interiority and emphasis on the salvation of one's soul typical of the French Catholic writers.[35]

Evelyn Waugh and Graham Greene, both of whom started publishing fiction in the late 1920s, were the most important English Catholic novelists of what is referred to as the golden age of the Catholic novel. Waugh came from an upper middle class family and attended Oxford, where he was known for snobbery and decadence, lived what he himself described as an "idle, dissolute and extravagant" life, and was eventually sent down for bad behavior.[36] He was a great admirer of craftsmanship of all kinds and attended art school for a while. After some frustrating and unsuccessful attempts at school teaching, he married in 1928, but the marriage lasted only a few months. That same year he published his first novel, *Decline and Fall*, a satire on the decadence of the twenties. As divorce proceedings were going forward, Waugh began religious instructions with Father Martin D'Arcy, a London Jesuit well-known for his skill in apologetics. In 1930 Waugh was received into the Catholic Church. Waugh's conversion was almost entirely a matter of intellectual conviction. Father D'Arcy said, "'I have never myself met a convert who so strongly based his assents on truth. . . . He had convinced himself very unsentimentally—with only an intellectual passion—of the truth of the Catholic faith.'"[37] After his previous marriage was annulled, Waugh married Laura Herbert from an upper class Catholic family and proceeded to settle into family life, eventually having a family of six children and a house in the country.

Decline and Fall was followed by several more novels in the same satiric vein: *Vile Bodies* (1930), *A Handful of Dust* (1934), and *Scoop* (1938). Waugh's satires are so delightfully pungent and caustic that he has been called by some "the greatest satirist since Swift" in spite of the fact that for contemporary tastes his satire can seem "so mordant and politically incorrect that one is almost surprised to see it displayed openly on booksellers' shelves."[38] Although he would continue to write satire after his conversion, his writing definitely took a different turn when he published *Brideshead Revisited* in 1945, as indicated by his announcement in *Life* magazine that he intended in the future to write about man in relation to God.[39] Waugh's prediction that this would make his books unpopular was prescient. Although his books continued to be popular, many critics cite *Brideshead Revisited* as the beginning of Waugh's decline as a writer.

Brideshead Revisited is completely different from Waugh's earlier novels. It is not satiric and is only occasionally funny. It is an account in lush, romantic prose of a young man's involvement with an old aristocratic Catholic family. The tone is elegiac and wistful, rather than satiric or cynical. In the end the dying father, who has been estranged from his wife and living with a mistress, apparently is reconciled with the faith when he makes the sign of the cross on his deathbed. This apparent conversion is not convincing to some readers, and, as has been noted earlier, many are repelled by the way Julia submits to Church law and refuses to marry Charles, thus sacrificing human love for what these readers see as inhuman legalism. Some Catholics are put off by the way that the "good Catholics" in the novel—Lady Marchmain, Cordelia, and Bridey—are much less appealing than the more dissolute members of the family. As one American reader wrote to Waugh, "Your *Brideshead Revisited* is a strange way to show that Catholicism is an answer to anything. Seems more like the kiss of Death."[40]

Waugh continued to write some satire, the best-known being *The Loved One* (1948), a lampoon of the American funeral industry, based on his visit to Forest Lawn in Los Angeles. In his trilogy, *Sword of Honor*, based on his military experience in World War II—*Men At Arms* (1952), *Officers and Gentlemen* (1955), and *Unconditional Surrender* (1961)—Waugh shows the absurdity of modern war; yet the satire, which lacks the trenchant humor of his early novels, is more subdued. These novels also are reminiscent of *Brideshead Revisited* in that the protagonist is a scion of an aristocratic Catholic family whose link to the faith is reinvigorated by his wartime experience. His father, Guy Crouchback, is an exemplar of an ideal Catholic gentleman.[41]

Waugh is probably the best example of the problem of the Catholic novelist and his audience. Catholic readers and non-Catholic readers have vastly different responses to him. Waugh relates that after the publication of *Brideshead Revisited*, Edmund Wilson, who had been positive about his earlier work, "was outraged . . . at finding God introduced into my story."[42] The standard view among many readers and critics is that his early satires are good, but that "the satirist was spoiled by his religion."[43] Gene Kellogg, who believes that Waugh's future reputation will rest on his satires, exemplifies this point of view. "The comparison between early and late Waugh invariably reminds one of a rapier which by the continual addition of weight has turned into a sledgehammer."[44] As for *Brideshead Revisited*, Kellogg believes that it illustrates "too simplistic a morality to make compelling fiction. The most Waugh can achieve is melodrama and sentimentality."[45] Barry Ulanov claims that although the novels before *Brideshead Revisited* are comic masterpieces, the ones that follow it (with the exception of *The Loved One*) "are blighted by the disease of Brideshead, an egregious inclination to take religion seriously, accompanied by a marked distaste for the world that does not share that inclination—the modern world."[46] Donat O'Donnell is put off by Waugh's version of Catholicism:

> The Gothic dream, nostalgia for childhood, snobbery, neo-Jacobitism—this whole complex of longings, fear and prejudices, "wistful, half-romantic, half-aesthetic," to use a phrase of Mr. Waugh's—must be taken into account in approaching the question of Mr. Waugh's Catholicism. . . . But the Catholicism of Mr. Waugh, and of certain other writers, is hardly separable from a personal romanticism and a class loyalty. . . . In Mr. Waugh's theology, the love of money is not only not the root of all evil, it is a preliminary form of the love of God.[47]

Yet even O'Donnell concedes that "the intense romantic and exclusive piety of [Waugh's] maturer years gives him strength and eloquence" and that in *Brideshead Revisited* "the texture of Mr. Waugh's writing is both finer and stronger than is usual in Proust."[48]

Other readers sympathetic to Catholicism see more to admire in Waugh's later works than his craftsmanship. F. J. Buckley finds the Catholic novels "ripping good reads" and considers *Sword of Honor* "the best fiction to come out of World War II."[49] He argues that belief in the Fall is critical for understanding Waugh:

> More than any other English writer, Waugh saw past our self-delusions to the inner core of selfishness, spite, and indifference. There is no one more amusing, but there is always a tension in his satires. We sit in the dark at the back of the theater as folly and sin are revealed, secretly fearing that we too will be called forward and our vices exposed. The greater the tension, the greater the laughter when we dodge the bullet. That is why Waugh's satires are so much more hilarious than the gentle comedy of Wodehouse. "For Mr. Wodehouse," Waugh noted, "there has been no Fall of Man; no 'aboriginal calamity.' His characters have never tasted the forbidden fruit. They are still in Eden."[50]

In "The Triple Conversions of *Brideshead Revisited*," Laura Mooneyham makes the point that the conversions that strike secular readers as contrived and unmotivated were deliberately written to show the inexplicability of grace, and that the novel is not really about conversion so much as the re-conversion of the lapsed—not only Lord Marchmain, Sebastian and Julia, but the narrator Charles as well. Although Charles appears to be converted at the time of Lord Marchmain's death, the older Charles, who narrates the story, although known as a Catholic, appears "sunk in moral sloth and bitterness, the sin of *accidie*."[51] His faith seems to be regenerated when he is billeted at Brideshead during World War II, relives his involvement with the Marchmains, and realizes that for him now the most important part of the magnificent estate is the sanctuary lamp in the chapel. This theme may have been inspired by Waugh's own experience. Margaret Oertling argues that "Waugh realized during World War II that he had make [sic] mistakes in his conversion, followed the right course but gone about it in the wrong way, for wrong reasons. But like the wise men, Waugh "'got there in the end.'"[52] The reference is to something Waugh said in a letter to his wife during the war. "The wise men committed every sort of *betise* . . . but they got there in the end and their gifts *were* accepted."[53] This theme would have special meaning to Catholics and other committed Christians who understand conversion, not as some *deus ex machina* trick, but as an arduous journey that requires continual refueling.

I believe this lengthy excursus through critics' pronouncements on Waugh's work has been worthwhile because they illustrate so powerfully the particular problems of the Catholic novelist who wishes to put the Catholic faith at the center of a novel. Perhaps because of his robust enthusiasm for his new faith and his pugnacious disposition, Waugh made no apology for the less salient aspects of Catholicism. He may, in fact, have taken a particular delight in dramatizing the way that the Church kept Charles and Julia apart, as if to say, "Look, the Church is of a completely different order of being than the world, which sees natural human happiness as the highest good. There is something higher." By making that choice, Waugh produced novels that arouse repugnance in secular readers (as well as in some Catholics), but also provide for many Catholic readers a fiction that explores with great depth and subtlety the religious world in which they live. Although Waugh's approach alienates some, it is possible that his boldness in unabashedly insisting on Catholicism as a supernatural entity gives his fiction a depth and intensity that resonates with many readers, even many secular ones.

Like Waugh, Graham Greene was a convert. Shortly after taking a degree at Oxford, he was received into the Church, largely due to the influence of his Catholic fiancée. Greene had suffered depression during his youth, attempted suicide, and undergone some psychoanalysis. Catholicism seemed to offer him hope and a sense of direction. He did newspaper journalism for a while, and his early novels are in the vein of "thrillers," dealing with crime, espionage, and political intrigue. Greene termed these novels and others he would write in this vein as "entertainments." The publication of *Brighton Rock* in 1938 inaugurated what would come to be known as Greene's Catholic novels. In addition to *Brighton Rock*, they include *The Power and the Glory* (1940), *The Heart of the Matter* (1948), *The End of the Affair* (1951), *A Burnt-Out Case* (1961) and (although not always listed among his Catholic novels) *Monsignor Quixote* (1982).

Whereas Waugh looked to the Church as a principle of order in the chaotic decadence of modern life, Greene was more focused on the personal drama of good and evil, sin and grace. Also, although Greene had no illusions about the depravity to be found in the secular world and depicted it in stark detail, he was also attentive to a critique of the Catholic community. Perhaps for this reason, he did not arouse as much ire among critics as did Waugh. Like Mauriac, whom he very much admired, Greene is particularly hard on self-righteously pious Catholics who keep the letter of the law but have little charity.

Although many Catholic writers, such as Bernanos and Waugh, are classified as reactionary, Greene's sympathies are clearly more leftist. He even joined the Communist party briefly in his youth. As he got older, he became disillusioned with progressive humanism, and in *The Lawless Roads* (1939), he inveighed against "Progress, Human Dignity, great empty Victorian concepts that life denies at every turn."[54] Yet, unlike many other disillusioned liberals, Greene never moved to the political right. Perhaps because he was never able to find a social and political philosophy in which he could comfortably settle, there is a strong sense of agitation and anxiety in his fiction.[55]

Greene, like Mauriac and Bernanos, favored realistic fiction, and he was a master of it. His ability to describe a setting with startling immediacy is most evident in his rendering of "Greeneland," those shabby, squalid locales, reeking of decay, that are Greene's typical settings, whether the novel is set in Africa, Mexico, or Brighton. The opening of *The Power and the Glory* is a good example of how Greene thrusts the reader into this harsh and comfortless place:

> Mr Tench went out to look for his ether cylinder, into the blazing Mexican sun and the bleaching dust. A few vultures looked down from the roof with shabby indifference: he wasn't carrion yet. A faint feeling of rebellion stirred in Mr Tench's heart, and he wrenched up a piece of the road with splintering finger-nails and tossed it feebly toward them. One rose and flapped across the town: over the tiny plaza, over the bust of an ex-president, ex-general, ex-human being, over the two stalls which sold mineral water, towards the river and the sea. It wouldn't find anything there: the sharks looked after the carrion on that side. Mr Tench went on across the plaza.[56]

Greene disliked experimental modernist techniques and fiction which concentrated so exclusively on the interior life that the outer world was barely present. He praised Mauriac "for whom the visible world has not ceased to exist, whose characters have the solidity of men with souls to save or lose."[57] For Greene spiritual concerns did not render the physical world *less* real, but *more* real. He also liked to be an intrusive author and defended this technique against those who considered it a passé encumbrance of Victorian novels.

Greene's themes in both his entertainments and his Catholic novels are primarily pursuit, suspicion, betrayal, guilt, and failure. Death (often violent or suicidal) not only occurs in every Greene novel except one, *Loser Takes All* (1955), but it continually hovers over the action.[58] Trust, responsibility, and solidarity are exhibited mostly through their opposites, although integrity is explicitly present, for example, in the courage of the whiskey priest in *The Power and the Glory*, who goes to minister to the dying Mestizo even though he knows it will mean his death at the hands of the state, Rose's willingness to sacrifice herself for Pinky in *Brighton Rock*, and Sarah's fidelity to her vow in *End of the Affair*. There are moments of genuine communion, intimacy, and affection, all the more poignant because of their rarity.

Greene did not want to be known as a "Catholic writer." In his autobiography, *Ways of Escape*, he laments that he "was discovered to be— detestable term!—a Catholic writer . . . . Many times since *Brighton Rock* I have been forced to declare myself not a Catholic writer but a writer who happens to be a Catholic."[59] Yet it is difficult to see the Catholicism in Greene's novels as nothing more than the raw material of his art.[60] The theological issues are too intense, too personal, too much the informing vision of his narrative world. The Catholicism in Greeneland is hardly the steady, daily routine of religious practices undergirded by a steady belief in God and fidelity to Church teaching. In the limit situations that characterize his fiction (the aforementioned guilt, betrayal, suffering, and of course, death), Greene stresses how faith is a kind of gamble, a Pascalian wager. It is akin to what Karl Jaspers describes as the philosophical faith of a believer who says, "I do not know; I do not even know whether I believe; however, such faith, expressed in such propositions, strikes me as meaningful; I will venture to believe in this way, and I hope I shall have the strength to live by my faith."[61]

Like other Catholic novelists, Greene is trying to describe the action of grace. Kurt Reinhardt asks, "Is grace conceived by Greene as saving, renovating, and sanctifying grace in the orthodox Catholic sense? The answer will have to be that obviously it is not. Greene's conception of grace . . . has validity only with respect to a forgiving grace which is gratuitously offered by an infinitely merciful God."[62] Those who agree may attribute this fact to what they see as Greene's pessimism. He portrays grace, not so much as a nurturing supportive presence of God in one's life, as a momentary sense of His forgiveness or some other temporary flash of insight. In a symposium published in *Partisan Review* entitled "The Intellectual's Return to Religion," Jean Guitton and others argue that Greene—as well as Mauriac, Bernanos, and Waugh—are "portraying characters who do not participate in grace so much as they are knocked over the head by it."[63] Yet there is always that dim awareness of another supernatural world hovering just out of reach over the disappointment, corruption, and suffering that constitute human existence, and it is that awareness that contributes such dramatic tension to Greene's novels. It is precisely the pain and suffering in life, which for so many people negates the existence of a good God, that for Greene points to His existence, for the conditions of life create a yearning for a place of order and peace that must exist. Although the nonbeliever may see this as simply wishful thinking, for some readers the novels' portrayal of a kind of faith that is as much hope as it is belief seems to resonate with their own religious experience.

After *The End of the Affair*, Greene did not write with such frequency or intensity about Catholicism, and in the two subsequent books that do make substantial use of Catholic material—*A Burnt-Out Case* and *Monsignor Quixote*—his mode is more nuanced and skeptical with regard to faith. Theodore Fraser divides Greene's long career into two phases corresponding with his relationship with the Catholic Church:

> The first begins with his conversion and continues up through a period of commitment and intellectual adherence to Catholicism that seems to have come to a close at about the time his novel *The Quiet American* was published in 1955. The second—extending from the mid-1950s up to his death (and during which time he described himself as having become a lapsed Catholic)—reveals a dramatic shift in tone and emphasis. No longer would he rely on the certainty of Catholic truths and teachings to give meaning to the fallen world, but he would now portray the universe as increasingly unilluminated by any divine presence or pattern and defined more realistically by such factors as the absurd.[64]

David Lodge also sees a shift in Greene's perspective around the time of *The Burnt-Out Case*, but attributes it, at least in part, to the influence of the thought of Teilhard de Chardin, which Greene acknowledged. Teilhard's spiritualized evolution seemed to give Greene new hope in the possibilities of human progress, as evidenced perhaps in the sympathetic portrait of the atheistic/agnostic Querry, a Catholic architect who has become famous for his church designs, but has lost his faith and come to Africa to work in a leper colony. The atheist lieutenant in *The Power and the Glory* had also been sympathetically portrayed, yet there was never any doubt that his program was doomed to failure, whereas the whiskey priest, for all his flaws, had the right answers. In *A Burnt-Out Case*, however, the answers are more elusive. Hope does seem available in the direction of human service, generosity, and affection, as Querry learns with his affection for Deo Gratias, his African servant.

The late *Monsignor Quixote* (1982) also shows Greene once more seriously engaged with the idea of Christian faith. What is so striking about this novel is that the drama of redemption has moved out of Greeneland. It is set in present-day Spain, a land relatively stable and at peace; and the atmosphere is pastoral as Monsignor Quixote and his friend Sancho, an atheist and the Communist mayor of El Toboso, drive through Spain on holiday. A loose parody of *Don Quixote*, the novel has as its central theme the question of fact and fiction, (and faith and doubt) with the central joke of the book being that Monsignor Quixote claims to be the descendant of a fictional character, Don Quixote. A Trappist monk at the monastery where Quixote and Pancho are staying tells a visitor, who says he prefers fact to fiction, "Fact or fiction—in the end you can't distinguish between them—you just have to choose."[65] Monsignor Quixote and Sancho compare their respective faiths—Quixote's in Christianity and Sancho's in Communism—and find much commonality, especially the coexistence of faith and doubt. Quixote confesses: "I am riddled by doubts, I am sure of nothing, not even of the existence of God, but doubt is not treachery as you Communists seem to think. Doubt is human. Oh, I want to believe that it is all true—and that want is the only certain thing I feel. I want others to believe too—perhaps some of their belief might rub off on me."[66] Despite the danger of attributing a character's opinions to an author, it is tempting to think that Monsignor Quixote here speaks for Greene, especially in light of what he wrote to his friend Father Leopoldo Duran in 1984: "I am to a certain extent an agnostic Catholic. I am quite unable to believe in Hell which contradicts my faith that if there is a God he must be a loving God or else why bother to invent the Devil?. . . . One must distinguish between faith and belief. I have a continuing faith that I am wrong not to believe and that my lack of belief stems from my own faults and failure in love."[67]

Unlike in Greene's other Catholic novels, in *Monsignor Quixote* damnation is not really a question, for Monsignor Quixote—like Greene himself—cannot really believe that anyone is in hell. In this novel, Greene emphasizes love and gentleness, and he mutes the stark contrast between doubt and faith and between the secular and the sacred that informed his earlier novels. The Eucharist is important in this novel, as it was in *The Power and the Glory*; but whereas the whiskey priest was desperate to obtain genuine wine to say Mass, Monsignor Quixote, sedated from an injury in a car crash, gets up in the middle of the night and in some kind of trance says a truncated version of the old Latin Mass (to which he is much attached). He says the words of consecration, *Hoc est enim corpus meum*, even though there is *no* host or wine. He gives "communion" to Sancho by laying his fingers "like a Host, on his tongue" and telling him "*Companero*, . . . you must kneel."[68] A few moments later, without regaining consciousness, Quixote dies.

Sancho, one of the monks, Father Leopoldo, and a visiting professor discuss Monsignor Quixote's "Mass" and Sancho's "communion." The professor, a lapsed Catholic, insists there was no consecration and no real Mass because there was no host and no wine. Father Leopoldo agrees that there was no bread or wine but insists that "'Monsignor Quixote quite obviously believed in the presence of the bread and wine. . . . Do you think it's more difficult to turn empty air into wine than wine into blood? Can our limited senses decide a thing like that? We are faced by an infinite mystery.'"[69] The novel ends with Sancho speculating on what has happened, especially the love that he and Monsignor Quixote had come to have for each other. "Why is it that the hate of a man—even of a man like Franco—dies with his death, and yet love, the love which he had begun to feel for Father Quixote, seemed now to live and grow in spite of the final separation and the final silence—for how long, he wondered with a kind of fear, was it possible for that love of his to continue? And to what end?"[70]

It is tempting to see this ending as endorsing a kind of Christian gnosticism, the view that the physical components (the Thomistic "matter") of the sacrament are unimportant and that it is only the love that flows from it that is meaningful—a far cry from the whiskey priest who was convinced that he could not make God present without genuine wine. John Desmond sees in this novel another example of Greene's affinity for Teilhard de Chardin's theories. "For in this novel, Greene, like Teilhard, affirms the spirituality of matter and the energy of love within matter driving creation toward convergence."[71] This interpretation, however, veers easily into a kind of gnostic vision that opposes Monsignor Quixote's way of practicing the faith. His attachment to the old Latin liturgy and to his "books of chivalry," (St. Augustine's *Confessions* and the works of St. Francis de Sales), and his horror at the vulgar desecration of a statue of Mary suggest that the physical "stuff" of his faith is an important component, and not just a springboard to a higher spirituality.

At any rate, the novel affirms that doubt—far from being the enemy of religious faith—can, in fact, be essential in nurturing a mature faith, as opposed to a rigid ideology. Almost twenty years before the publication of *Monsignor Quixote*, Greene had written: "Perhaps the most important historical point in the future will be when the Christian says 'I do not always believe' and the Marxist agrees with him. A good future based on the failure always to believe. Comprehension and charity also follow. Violence

comes when we are afraid to admit that we do not always believe. By violence we try to kill the doubt in ourselves."[72]

The evolution of Greene's fiction goes beyond his changing understanding of faith and his degree of adherence to Catholic dogma. More
than ten years before the publication of *Monsignor Quixote*, David Lodge
detected in Greene's work a "progress from fiction based on a 'tragic' conflict between human and divine values, to fiction conceived in terms of
comedy and irony in which the possibility of religious faith has all but retreated out of sight in the anarchic confusion of human behaviour."[73]
Whether or not "the possibility of religious faith has all but retreated out
of sight" in Greene's late work is debatable, but it is undeniable that there
has been a convergence of the type spoken of by Desmond. Yet this new
view—albeit more optimistic and predictive of harmony—may not be
good news for fiction; for Lodge goes on to admit that "the permeation of
[Greene's] later work with negative and sceptical attitudes, characteristically filtered through the consciousness of a laconic, disillusioned narrator, has resulted in some loss of intensity."[74]

Looking at Greene's career in some detail is instructive, not only because
he is considered by some people to be the finest British Catholic writer of
the twentieth century, but also because it exemplifies a major shift in
Catholic life and thought that would impact all subsequent Catholic fiction. Significant changes in Catholics' attitudes toward religious belief and
practice have occurred since the Second Vatican Council. Theodore Fraser
sees these transformations as falling into three broad categories.

First there is "the perspective from below," meaning that the Church
came to have greater respect for secular life, to see much good—even
sacramental meaning—in it. Secondly, there was a turn away from a dualistic dichotomy between soul and body toward a more holistic view of
human nature and a more positive attitude toward the body.[75] Third, the
Church modified its self-concept and the way it presented itself to the
world. There was less emphasis on the Church as an institution and more
on the Church as a pilgrim people, less emphasis on the infallibility and
authority of the Church and more on its flawed humanity, even its sin.[76]
Of course, one can see some of these concepts in the work of Mauriac,
Bernanos, Waugh, and Greene. But novelists have always seen aspects of
the Church that diverged from that conveyed in the catechisms and books
of theology. What was different after Vatican II was that these views had
been "canonized" by the official Church.

Muriel Spark, whose career spanned this period of transition, is one of
the most important English Catholic novelists after Waugh and Greene.
She began writing novels in the pre-Vatican II period, but most of her
very prolific output was produced after the Council. Born in Edinburgh
in 1918 of a Jewish father and Presbyterian mother, she married young

and moved with her husband to Rhodesia. After her marriage ended, she returned to London with her son in 1944 and earned a precarious living first as a freelance writer and then as editor for *Poetry Review*. Although brought up as a Presbyterian, she had little commitment to Christianity until her conversion to Anglicanism in 1953 and to Catholicism the following year, largely as a result of reading Newman. In 1957 she published her first novel, *The Comforters*. Graham Greene took great interest in her work and gave her financial support and encouragement. She is probably best known for *The Prime of Miss Jean Brodie* (1961) about a charismatic teacher who tries to exert a godlike control of her students' lives. She died in 2006.

Spark believed that her conversion enabled her to write: "Nobody can deny that I speak with my very own voice as a writer now, whereas before my conversion I couldn't do it because I was never sure what I was. . . . I didn't get my style until I became a Catholic because you just haven't got to care, and you need security for that."[77] One critic refers to Spark's Catholicism as her "'rock,' a position from which the believer can survey the human condition."[78] She herself said that Catholicism helped her become a satirist. "The Catholic belief is a norm from which one can depart. It's not a fluctuating thing."[79] Spark's narrative voice is sure and confident, able to survey the foolishness in a fallen world without ever quite falling into cynicism. The irony, though sharp, is open to the possibility that God may bring good out of sin and evil.

The Comforters, written shortly after her conversion, is about a woman—like Spark, a Catholic convert and a novelist—who begins hearing an imaginary novelist typing a novel about her, in the style of an intrusive author with access to Caroline's thoughts and feelings. David Lodge explains how this bizarre plot expresses Spark's efforts to come to terms with her new faith:

> In writing her first novel about the experience of conversion to Catholicism (an experience which we know, from external sources, was one of considerable psychological strain for the author herself), Muriel Spark wittily combined the two issues: the heroine's subconscious resentment of the sacrifice of individual freedom entailed in conversion is projected in the fantasy of an omniscient and intrusive narrator who seems to be directing her life.[80]

At the end of the novel Caroline has come to terms with the demands of her new faith and feels secure in it.

Although Catholicism may have given her a moral anchor, Spark has no illusions about the Church. Caroline, the heroine of *The Comforters*, finds that "the True Church was awful, though unfortunately, one couldn't deny, true."[81] One of the characters in that novel, Georgiana

Hogg, is a thoroughly obnoxious, self-righteous Catholic.[82] Furthermore, there is no sense that Catholicism gives Spark's Catholics facile answers or makes their lives easy. For most of them, their faith just gives them a lens for seeing more truly (the same advantage Flannery O'Connor claimed for the Catholic novelist). Yet this perspective does not give the reader—whether a believer or not—a sense of enlightenment. Jennifer Randisi puts it this way: "It is precisely because they challenge our ability to arrive at moral truth by using human reason that Spark's novels are disturbing. Rather than knowing more after reading her novels, one feels one knows less."[83]

Spark's compact novels are written in pithy, elegant prose and are replete with eccentric characters. One critic notes that her novels "are so involved with the eccentric event and the odd personality that they have virtually no content."[84] There is little sense of character development. For an author interested in religious themes, it is striking that there is so little revelation of the characters' interior life. The effect is somewhat like the brilliantly painted flat surface of an icon. Nor is there much sense of community. Even when the characters are in the midst of other people, they seem isolated. The Catholic characters, usually converts, are quite isolated in their faith. In Spark's later novels, there is less use of Catholic material, although she does turn her satiric eye on some of the trendy reforms carried out in the name of Vatican II in *The Abbess of Crewe* (1974). Also unusual for a woman author, there is very little attention to love—although there are some lovers. Her Catholic heroines have a positive attitude toward sex and are remarkably unburdened by sexual guilt or scruples, reflecting Spark's rejection of a dualistic philosophy that sees the physical as inimical to faith.

Many critics have commented on the detachment in her fiction. Woodman suggests that her "deliberate understatement and detached wit comes from an attitude of religious irony at a fallen world, but they are also a personal and social response."[85] In Spark's own words, "I think it's bad manners to inflict a lot of emotional involvement on the reader—much nicer to make them laugh and keep it short."[86] This tone helps to account for the fact that, although Spark's work is filled with mayhem and evil, she adopts one of the traditional Christian strategies for dealing with the devil: to treat it as a figure of fun and thus rob it of some of its power. Sparks's tone of extreme detachment may serve the function of dissipating evil to some extent. Ruth Whittaker sees in her work "a sense of suppression, an air of controlled panic restrained through the use of rigorous, economic prose. It is as if the precision of the language might have an exorcising function, like stepping carefully over the cracks in the pavement."[87]

In Spark's fiction there is no mistaking that the relationship of the human and the divine is paramount, and the contrast between the human perspective and a God's eye view is part of the irony. The reader has the feeling of being in a two level universe—like a two-storey building—the supernatural level mysterious yet orderly; the natural level, bizarre, chaotic, quirky, with periodic incursions from the supernatural, including the occasional miracle. Spark takes up several of the motifs and themes of earlier Catholic novelists: the critique of unattractive, pious Catholics, the unexplained miracles and conversions, and suspended closure (to allow for providence). Like all Catholic writers, she is accused of trying to convert the reader. "Mrs. Spark returns again and again to thematic deceptions and conversions as she tries to deceive and convert us."[88] Non-Catholic or non-Christian readers seem inevitably to see attempts to convert them, whereas fellow believers are more likely to see a vision of the universe as it appears to a Catholic who is keenly aware of the quirky ways of providence and the murky regions of the human soul.

Muriel Spark's first novel, *The Comforters*, was published in 1957 and her last, *The Finishing School*, in 2004. Thus her career spanned almost half a century, beginning in the pre-Vatican II period and continuing through the period of upheaval, experimentation, dissent and transformation that has characterized the post-Vatican II era. I have alluded briefly to the way changes in society and in Catholicism are reflected in the later fiction of Greene and Spark, but we must now look in a more systematic and sustained way at the factors that have affected the English Catholic novels written during this period.

Pluralism has become a fact of life in England, as it has in most Western countries. This diversity has disproportionately affected Catholics who no longer live in tightly knit Catholic enclaves that remained fairly homogeneous until the Second World War. Before mid century the "other" for English Catholics was primarily Protestantism or secularism; but since that time there has been massive immigration, especially from countries that were part of the former British empire. Consequently, English Catholics now live, work, study, and even socialize with Hindus, Buddhists, and Muslims, as well as other Christians. There are now many "others," and Catholics often feel peculiar—not just for adhering to the Church of Rome—but for believing in Christianity at all.[89] Secondly, the secular media have in recent years become much more aggressively hostile to Christianity in general and Catholicism in particular.

The sexual revolution and feminism are really at the heart of the contemporary secular world's quarrel with the Catholic Church. The sexual revolution called the Church's traditional sexual morality into question. The first teaching to be challenged was the ban on artificial contraception. The development of the birth control pill had led to expectations that it would be acceptable, but Pope Paul VI's 1968 encyclical *Humanae Vitae* reaffirmed the Church's ban on all methods except natural family planning (refraining from sexual intercourse during a woman's fertile periods). The anger and dissent that erupted eventually led to serious questioning of Church teaching on all aspects of sexual morality: premarital sex, abortion, homosexuality, and divorce and remarriage. As divorce became easier and more socially acceptable, Catholics began to divorce in about the same proportion as the rest of society.[90]

Regardless of whether or not they agree with official Church teaching on sexual matters, Catholics are in a peculiar position. If they oppose church teaching, other people wonder why they stay in the Catholic Church when there are plenty of other Christian denominations whose teachings are more compatible with their opinions. On the other hand, if they support the Church's teachings, Catholics are likely to be branded as extremist, intolerant, homophobic, or reactionary. It may have been difficult to be a Catholic in England when Catholics were despised as traitorous subjects of a foreign power or as being in collusion with scheming Jesuits. But at least those Catholics had the comfort of being united in the faith with their coreligionists. Today that sense of unity is hard to come by in the increasingly polarized Catholic Church.

Yet in spite of internal tension and even dissent over these matters, the Catholic Church has continued to take a firm stand against premarital sex, artificial contraception, abortion, and homosexual acts. Although all of these practices were once condemned by all Christian sects and even by civil society, the Catholic Church is now almost the only mainline denomination that clearly denounces all these behaviors as sinful.[91] Although many evangelical or fundamentalist sects also hold to these traditional views, somehow they just do not make as convenient targets for the media as a celibate pope and bishops in their ecclesiastical regalia. Furthermore, the Church's refusal to sanction homosexual love or approve of condom use as a way to fight AIDS and of in vitro fertilization to achieve pregnancy are seen as cruel and heartless.

The feminist movement has also been on a collision course with the Church. Although feminism at first concentrated on the right of married women to work outside the home, receive equal pay for equal work, and have equal access to all professions, it soon demanded unrestricted rights to abortion. However, many Catholic women who rejected abortion as an option embraced feminism and saw the fundamental issue as a demand that women's abilities and contributions be recognized and that their special propensities for nurturing and emotional intimacy, as well as their strength and endurance—qualities much more identified as masculine traits—be valued and honored.

Feminism most powerfully impacted Catholicism in its appeal to religious orders of women, who responded enthusiastically to calls for women's empowerment. Many sisters resented the undervaluing of

women's work, especially within the Church. The issue of women's ordination became pivotal. Although many priests and Catholic laypeople
supported women's ordination, sisters and former sisters were the most
outspoken and visible advocates for this cause. As the Episcopal Church
in the United States began to ordain women, followed by the Church of
England in 1992, this issue generated increasing anger and disappointment. Large numbers of sisters left their convents to seek more fulfilling
lives in the world. Many of them married men who were leaving the
priesthood, as the sexual revolution weakened the commitment to
celibacy, and anger and dissent over *Humanae Vitae* fueled disillusionment
within the Church.

The loss of so many sisters changed the character of Catholic schools,
which were increasingly staffed by lay teachers. The more substantive
change in Catholic education, however, was due to the philosophical shift
that transformed Catholic education, homiletics, and evangelization. The
emphasis was on the love of God, rather than the fear of God. Affective
education was preferred to dogmatic or intellectual. Rote memorization
was discarded and replaced with storytelling, faith sharing, art projects,
and service work. Consequently, a generation of young Catholics reached
adulthood having almost no substantive knowledge of Church doctrine,
moral teaching, Church history, or apologetics. Preaching also became
less doctrinal, although it became more scriptural. It was Christian or humanistic, rather than Catholic, and many Catholics thought of themselves
primarily as Christian rather than Roman Catholic. They were losing that
Catholic "oddness."

In comparison with all these social upheavals, philosophical shifts, and
contested issues of gender and sexuality, the liturgical changes initiated
by Vatican II might seem to be a superficial and cosmetic matter. Yet the
changes in liturgy and church architecture and design were unsettling to
many Catholics. The Mass was now said in English, congregational
singing became common, and lay Communion ministers and lectors were
introduced. Catholics who were discomfited by these changes were as-
sured that nothing really important had changed. Yet not everyone was
convinced. The emphasis was less on the Mass as a sacrifice and solemn
worship, and more on a community celebration. Not only was the form of
the Mass changed, but its preeminence was stressed to the point that other
popular devotions, such as Benediction, Stations of the Cross, novenas,
and processions became very rare or nonexistent. Ironically, the practice
of going to confession, perhaps due to the decreased emphasis on sin, experienced a great decline just as the rite was revised to allow for a face to
face, less formulaic and more "humanized" version. The actual church
buildings also changed. New churches were built in an austere style, often in the round and with no kneelers, and old ones were "restored" to

make them less ornate. The use of religious art was minimized. These changes were not simply cosmetic, nor even aesthetic. Liturgists insisted they restored the rites to their original purity and cast off later accretions; but some of the laity were not enthusiastic, resenting the loss of what they had experienced as an uplifting and solemn form of worship for one, which was mundane and embarrassingly banal. Both the style of the new Mass and the changed character of religious education tended to minimize the supernatural aspects of religion and to emphasize the human. Humanist ethics took precedence over the Ten Commandments and the catechism. Rules were out. Feelings were in. Miracles and martyrdom gave way to soup kitchens and peace marches.

All of these developments in Catholic life are reflected in the novels of this period. This fiction depicts married people struggling with *Humanae Vitae*, liturgical mayhem, nuns and priests questioning their vocations, women striving for empowerment and celebrating their femaleness, a nonjudgmental attitude toward homosexuality, less of a focus on sex as sin, and more emphasis on its power to heal, renew, and open one to new dimensions of self-knowledge, communication and love.

Yet the changes in the Catholic novel go far beyond a mimetic reflection of these social and religious upheavals and transformations. The novels find within the turmoil the Catholic essence, (or as some would say, the Catholic "oddness") struggling to assert itself and maintain its integrity amid the flux. Furthermore, they continue to take up the familiar themes and motifs of the earlier Catholic novels, but since they are dramatized in a changing Church and world, they must necessarily be expressed in new forms. They also take up new themes not prominent in earlier fiction. The next chapter will look in some detail at Catholic novels of this period.

NOTES

1. It was André Gide who pointed out in his book on Dostoyevsky that he was the first European novelist to make a character's relationship with God the heart of a novel. Before Dostoyevsky, according to Gide, "the novel with but rare exception concerns itself with relations between man and man, passion and intellect, with family, social, and class relations, but never, practically never between the individual and his self and with God." André Gide, *Dostoyevsky* (New York: New Directions, 1923, 1961), 15, quoted in Fraser, *Modern Catholic Novel*, 5.

2. Samuel Enoch Stumpf, *Socrates to Sartre: A History of Philosophy*, 3rd ed. (New York: McGraw-Hill, 1982), 329. Stumpf defines positivism as follows:

Positivism is best defined as a general attitude of mind, a spirit of inquiry, an approach to the facts of human existence. Its central feature is first of all negative in that it rejects the assumption that nature has some ultimate purpose or end. Secondly, positivism gives up any attempt to discover either the "essence" or the internal or secret causes of things. On the positive side, its spirit is expressed in the attempt to study facts by observing the constant relations between things and formulating the laws of science simply as the laws of constant relations between various phenomena. 328–29.

3. Kellogg, *Vital Tradition*, 14

4. Jules Amédée Barbey d'Aurevilly, preface to *Une Vieille Maitresse*, nouvelle ed., tome premier, *Oeuvres de J. Barbey d'Aurevilly* (Paris: Librairie Alphonse Lemerre, n.d.), 8. Translations are by the author.

5. Barbey d'Aurevilly, preface, 7.

6. Barbey d'Aurevilly, preface, 10.

7. Barbey d'Aurevilly, preface, 11.

8. Joris-Karl Huysmans, *En route*, 3rd. ed., trans. C. Kegan Paul (London: Kegan Paul, Trench, Trubner & Co., 1908), 6. Most English translations retain the French title.

9. Huysmans, *En Route*, 301.

10. Kellogg, *Vital Tradition*, 16–17.

11. Although he did not formally return to the Church, Péguy called himself a Catholic convert and was Catholic in his views.

12. See chapter 1, "The Theory of the Catholic Novel," endnote 98.

13. François Mauriac, "On Writing Today," in *Second Thoughts: Reflections on Literature and Life* (New York: World, 1961), 16. Quoted in Fraser, *Modern Catholic Novel*, 37.

14. Mauriac was so chastened by criticism from Catholics in this regard that he decided that for a while he would write no novels with explicitly Catholic content and thereby not be identified as a Catholic novelist. *The Desert of Love* (*Le Désert de l'amour*), published in 1925, the first novel he wrote after his crisis of conscience, though less explicitly Catholic, does, in fact, have more theological depth. An English translation is *The Desert of Love*, trans. Gerard Hopkins (London: Eyre & Spottiswoode, 1949). Later Mauriac returned to greater use of explicitly Catholic material.

15. Kellogg, *Vital Tradition*, 44.

16. Kellogg says that in Bernanos's fiction "the physical world is not separated from the metaphysical but enfolded within it." *Vital Tradition*, 53.

17. Georges Bernanos, *The Diary of a Country Priest*, trans. Pamela Morris (Garden City, N.Y.: Image), 232. A literal translation of the French (*"Tout est grâce"*) is "Everything is grace."

18. Georges Bernanos, *Under the Sun of Satan*, trans. Harry L. Binsse (New York: Pantheon, 1949).

19. In the interview quoted in the previous chapter, Bernanos admits, "The lived experience of divine love does not fall within the novel's province," but he hopes to "force the reader to descend to the depths of his own conscience" and persuade him "that human weakness is not the final explanation, that this weakness is sustained and exploited by a ferocious and somber being." With reference to the evil he witnessed in the trenches of World War I and in post-war Paris, he said, "I did want to die without bearing witness." Sonnenfeld, *Crossroads*, 25, 44.

20. Gerard Manley Hopkins, *Poems and Prose of Gerard Manley Hopkins*, ed. W. H. Gardner (Harmondsworth, Eng.: Penguin, 1953), 27.

21. Mauriac and Bernanos must have been familiar with some of the ideas of Jacques Maritain, who was such an important figure in the French Catholic Renaissance. According to Kellogg, "Maritain drew his distinction between the 'individual,' who is a citizen and member of society, and the 'person,' who is rooted in eternity." Kellogg, *Vital Tradition*, 36.

22. Charles Péguy, "Un Nouveau théologien: M. Fernand Laudet," *Oeuvres de prose, 1909–1914* (Paris: Gallimard/Bibliothèque de la Pléiade, 1961), 1074–76, quoted in Fraser, *Modern Catholic Novel*, 21.

23. This dynamic is perhaps best seen in the whiskey priest of *The Power and the Glory*, whose martyrdom clearly builds up the faith of the persecuted Christians. Even the atheistic lieutenant has developed a respect for the priest, which may very possibly prepare an opening for grace. Also, sinners like Sarah and Sebastian whose acts flagrantly violate Christian morality, nevertheless possess a certain freshness, honesty and humility, which is a reproach to self-righteous and uncharitable Catholics, and which, after their conversions, may infuse the Catholic community with new life.

24. The Oxford Movement actually began in the Church of England among churchmen who were trying to bring about doctrinal and spiritual renewal in the Anglican Communion by study of the early Church Fathers and the seventeenth-century Anglican divines. Although anti-papal, they stressed the Catholic character of the Anglican Church, such as its sacraments and bishops, who they claimed were in the apostolic succession. They also favored more ornate and formal liturgy. The movement actually led to a number of conversions to Roman Catholicism, the most outstanding example being John Henry Newman. The Pre-Raphaelite Movement began with a group of painters who tried to recapture the simplicity, truthfulness, and spiritual vividness they saw in Italian painting before Raphael. Their ideals were taken up by poets as well, who, like the painters, were fond of using medieval themes.

25. Some Anglicans insist that the Church of England *is* Catholic, one of the three main branches of Catholic orthodoxy—the other two being Roman Catholicism and Eastern Orthodoxy. Yet the more common understanding is that it represents a Protestant denomination, as is reflected in the long struggle to ensure the Protestant succession to the throne; therefore, I use the term *Protestant* to refer to the Church of England, as well as the other Christian sects in England.

26. Margaret M. Maison, *The Victorian Vision: Studies in the Religious Novel* (New York: Sheed & Ward, 1961), 159.

27. Modern readers of *Hadrian VII* have been quick to see in Hadrian a prefiguring of Pope John XXIII, who in convening the Second Vatican Council, spoke of opening up the Church's windows to the world. Gene Kellogg, however, cautions, "It is an exaggeration to see Hadrian as an early type of John XXIII, for Rolfe gives no portrayal of a tide of change surrounding Hadrian and following him. Hadrian does not stir Catholic thinkers of all nations and the Catholic people of all communities as John did" (*Vital Tradition*, 94).

28. Robert Hugh Benson, *Lord of the World* (London: Sir Isaac Pitman & Sons, 1907), 157.

29. Robert Hugh Benson, *The Dawn of All* (London: Hutchinson, 1911), 41.

30. For a fuller account of ultramontanism see "Ultramontanism" in *Harper-Collins Encyclopedia of Catholicism*, 1278.

31. Chesterton's most famous apologetical work, *Orthodoxy*, was actually published in 1908, well before his conversion to Catholicism in 1922. It argued on behalf of orthodox Christianity (what C. S. Lewis would later call "mere Christianity"). Chesterton's insistence on a historical and literal understanding of the gospel and the creeds is today more compatible with Catholicism than with some of the more liberal Protestant denominations. After his conversion Chesterton wrote his other famous apologetical work, *The Everlasting Man* (1925), as well as some works specifically defending Roman Catholicism.

32. Hilaire Belloc, *Europe and the Faith* (New York: Paulist Press, 1920), 261. For Belloc "the Faith" means not just Christianity, but specifically Roman Catholicism.

33. Hilaire Belloc, *Survivals and New Arrivals* (New York: Macmillan, 1929), 31.

34. Robert Speaight, *The Life of Hilaire Belloc* (London: Hollis & Carter, 1957), 378.

35. Kellogg, *Vital Tradition*, 97.

36. David Daiches, ed., *The Avenel Companion to English & American Literature*, vol. 1 (New York: Avenel Books, 1981), 546.

37. F. J. Buckley, "The Satirist of the Fall," *Crisis*, January 2003, 28.

38. Buckley, "Satirist," 27.

39. See chapter 1, "The Theory of the Catholic Novel," endnote 78.

40. Evelyn Waugh, "Fan-Fare," 304.

41. In the character of Guy Crouchback, Waugh succeeded in doing what he had failed to do in *Brideshead Revisited*—create a sincerely devout Catholic, who is neither tiresomely pious, moralistic or naïve, but rather a thoroughly likeable character.

42. Waugh, "Fan Fare," 302.

43. Buckley, "Satirist," 29.

44. Kellogg, *Vital Tradition*, 105.

45. Kellogg, *Vital Tradition*, 109. The attitude of many critics to *Brideshead Revisited* is aptly expressed by the title of Kingsley Amis's attack on the novel, "How I Lived in a Very Big House and Found God," *Times Literary Supplement*, 20 November 1952, 1352. The essay is actually a review of the British televised serial based on the novel.

46. Ulanov, "Ordeal of Evelyn Waugh," 79.

47. Donat O'Donnell [Conor Cruise O'Brien], *Maria Cross: Imaginative Patterns in a Group of Modern Catholic Writers* (New York: Oxford University Press, 1952), 125–26.

48. O'Donnell, *Maria Cross*, 127. O'Donnell adds this *caveat*: "This is not to imply that *Brideshead Revisited,* as a totality, comes within measurable distance of Proust's achievement in *Remembrance of Things Past.*"

49. F. J. Buckley, "Satirist," 29.

50. F. J. Buckley, "Satirist," 31.

51. Laura Mooneyham, "The Triple Conversions of *Brideshead Revisited*," *Renascence* 45, no. 4 (Summer 1993): 227.

52. Margaret Oertling, "A Response to Critics of *Brideshead Revisited*," The Espositor (Trinity Univ.) 2 (1990): 65–75. Quoted in Mooneyham, "Triple Conversions," 232.

53. Evelyn Waugh, *The Letters of Evelyn Waugh*, ed. Mark Amory (London: Weidenfield and Nicholson, 1980), 197.

54. Graham Greene, *The Lawless Roads*, quoted in Lodge, "Graham Greene," 97.

55. David Lodge suggests that "Greene's whole fictional world seems ripe for dissolution rather than revolution" (*Novelist at the Crossroads*, 97).

56. Greene, *Power and the Glory*, 7.

57. Graham Greene, "François Mauriac," in *The Lost Childhood and Other Essays* (New York: Viking Press, 1951), 70.

58. Lodge, "Graham Greene," 91.

59. Graham Greene, *Ways of Escape* (New York: Simon and Schuster, 1980), 77.

60. Greene insisted that he is simply "a writer who in four or five books took characters with Catholic ideas for his material." From *In Search of a Character*, quoted in J. C. Whitehouse, *Vertical Man: The Human Being in the Catholic Novels of Graham Greene, Sigrid Undset, and Georges Bernanos* (London: Saint Austin Press, 1999), 41.

61. Karl Jaspers, *Way to Wisdom*, trans. Ralph Manheim (New Haven: Yale Univ. Press, 1954), 95.

62. Reinhardt, *Theological Novel*, 199.

63. Reinhardt, *Theological Novel*, 200.

64. Fraser, *Modern Catholic Novel*, 95.

65. Greene, *Monsignor Quixote*, 238.

66. Greene, *Monsignor Quixote*, 205.

67. Leopoldo Duran, *Graham Greene*, trans. Euan Cameron (San Francisco: HarperCollins, 1994) 289.

68. Greene, *Monsignor Quixote*, 250.

69. Greene, *Monsignor Quixote*, 253–54.

70. Greene, *Monsignor Quixote*, 256.

71. John Desmond, "The Heart of the Matter: The Mystery of the Real in *Monsignor Quixote*," *Religion and Literature* 22, no. 1 (Spring 1990): 68.

72. Maria Couto, *Graham Greene: On the Frontier* (New York: St. Martin's Press, 1988), 214. An article published on the occasion of Greene's death in 1991, stated, "When asked toward the end of his life 'Are you still hounded by God?' he replied: 'I hope so. I'm not very conscious of His presence, but I hope He is dogging my footsteps.'" Jack Kroll, "Map of Greeneland," *Newsweek*, 15 April 1991, 75.

73. Lodge, "Graham Greene," 117.

74. Lodge, "Graham Greene," 117–18.

75. This admission of the existence of this spirit/flesh dualism in Catholicism seems to contradict Greeley's and Tracy's assertion that dualism is more typical of the dialectical (and more typically Protestant) imagination. Yet Greeley and Tracy admit that both the dialectical and analogical impulses are present in both traditions, and Vatican II marked a deliberate movement in Catholicism to more fully embrace the analogical (both/and) spirit.

76. Fraser, *Modern Catholic Novel*, 149–50.

77. Muriel Spark, "My Conversion," *Twentieth Century*, 170 (autumn 1961): 61–62.

78. Irving Malin, "The Deceptions of Muriel Spark," in Friedman, *Vision Obscured*, 102.

79. Spark, "My Conversion," 60.

80. Lodge, "The Uses and Abuses of Omniscience: Method and Meaning in Muriel Spark's *The Prime of Miss Jean Brodie*," in *Novelist at the Crossroads*, 121. For more on Spark's difficulties in converting to Catholicism, Lodge refers the reader to Derek Stanford's *Muriel Spark* (London, 1963), p. 62.

81. Muriel Spark, *The Comforters* (London: Macmillan, 1957), 89.

82. In her essay "My Conversion," Spark admits, "I didn't like some of the Roman Catholics I met awfully much, and they put me off for a long time." 59.

83. Jennifer Lynn Randisi, *On Her Way Rejoicing: The Fiction of Muriel Spark.* (Washington, D.C.: Catholic Univ. of America Press, 1991), 23.

84. Frederick R. Karl, *A Reader's Guide to the Contemporary English Novel*, rev. ed. (New York: Octagon Books, 1986), 280. The fact that Karl goes on to say that Spark's novels are "light to the point of froth" (280) suggests that he fails to see the extraordinary effects she gets with this odd material. This comment, however, is based only on four early novels. In a section written for the revised edition of this book when five more of her novels had been published, he admits that Spark "has always been earnest beneath her sense of play" (349).

85. Woodman, *Faithful Fictions*, 74–75.

86. Muriel Spark, interview by Ian Gillham, *Writers of Today*, no. 4, BBC World Service script. Quoted in Ruth Whittaker, *The Faith and Fiction of Muriel Spark* (New York: St. Martin's Press, 1982), 15.

87. Whittaker, *Faith and Fiction*, 12.

88. Malin, "Deceptions," 107.

89. This sense of peculiarity is probably more pronounced for English Catholics than for those in the United States, where church going is still quite popular. According to a recent article in *Newsweek*, only 7 percent of British people attend church regularly. Liat Radcliffe, "Log On for Salvation," *Newsweek*, May 31, 2004, 10.

90. In 1979 Sociologists Michael Hornsby-Smith and R. M. Lee reported that "overall, Catholics are not any less prone to divorce than members of the population at large." Michael Hornsby-Smith and R. M. Lee, *Roman Catholic Opinion: A Study of Roman Catholics in England and Wales in the 1970s* (Guildford: University of Surrey, 1979), 117, cited in Michael P. Hornsby-Smith, *Roman Catholic Beliefs in England: Customary Catholicism and Transformations of Religious Authority* (Cambridge: Cambridge Univ. Press, 1991), 183. Hornsby-Smith reaffirmed this finding in 1999. "There seems little doubt that Catholic marriages are just as likely to break down as anyone else's." Michael P. Hornsby-Smith, "A Transformed Church," in *Catholics in England 1950–2000: Historical and Sociological Perspectives*, ed. Michael P. Hornsby-Smith (London: Cassell, 1999), 11.

91. Although official Church teaching is consistent, many individual Catholics (including some theologians) no longer concur in the Church's view of all these behaviors as sinful. Furthermore, the hierarchy has not been as outspoken as some Catholics would like in denouncing these practices. Nevertheless, the clear and consistent teaching on these matters has been enough to anger the secular media and launch frequent attacks upon the Church.

3

✝

The English Catholic
Novel Today

The reform was experienced by many as the joyful clearing away of outmoded lumber, by others as the vandalising of a beautiful and precious inheritance.

—Eamon Duffy, *Saints and Sinners: A History of the Popes*

The air that Catholic writers and their readers have breathed over the last few decades is very different from that breathed by their counterparts of forty or fifty years ago.

—J. C. Whitehouse, *Vertical Man*

The post-Vatican II period may go down in history as the most turbulent and challenging era in the Catholic Church since the Reformation. In contrast, the period preceding it, although a time of wars and economic depression, was—in terms of Church life—placid and unified, with a largely docile laity and large numbers of obedient priests and religious. Although the intellectual and theological currents that would come to fruition in Vatican II were present in Catholic intellectual life during the 1930s, 1940s and 1950s, most average Catholics were not aware of them. Nor had they any inkling of the massive social changes that the 1960s and 1970s would bring. It is not surprising, therefore, that the Catholic novels of the post-Vatican II period are markedly different from those written before Vatican II.

One of the most obvious differences is the treatment of sexuality. In earlier Catholic novels, sex was depicted primarily as sin—as temptation either given in to or heroically resisted. Adultery, fornication, and references to homosexual behavior, as in *Brideshead Revisited*, were part of the

65

fabric of those novels, but were rarely at the center of dramatic interest. Even in Graham Greene's novels *The Heart of the Matter* and *The End of the Affair*, where adultery is a pivotal part of the plot, the emphasis is more on faith, the struggle to believe, and the failure to understand the scope of God's mercy and love. Furthermore, before the 1960s sexual sins were denounced, not only by the Church, but by the larger society as well. Thus, in *The Heart of the Matter* and *The End of the Affair*, there is never any question of adultery not being seriously sinful or any sense that the Church was being unduly harsh in its condemnation of this conduct. Yet Greene evinced great sympathy for his adulterers and managed to show how God's love and desire for the sinner could penetrate even a tangled web of immorality. In *The End of the Affair* an adulterous affair is actually a catalyst for a character's conversion. In her journal Sarah addresses God: "I might have taken a lifetime spending a little love at a time, doling it out here and there, on this man and that. But even the first time, in the hotel near Paddington, we spent all we had. You were there, teaching us to squander, like You taught the rich man, so that one day we might have nothing left except this love of you."[1] In 1951 it seemed a bold and daring stratagem for Greene to connect so intimately adultery and God, and in fact, many Catholics were disturbed by it.

In recent Catholic novels there is less of the emphasis on sin characteristic of earlier Catholic fiction.[2] The writers seem more inclined to follow the lead of Greene in *The End of the Affair*. Nonmarital sexual love as often as not provides an entrée for the love of God, and both writers and readers seem quite comfortable with such a conjunction. This development is not surprising, given the more positive approach to sexuality in contemporary Catholic theology and the greatly diminished emphasis on sexual sin in both cathechetics and homiletics. This muting of the sense of sin, however, together with less attention to the supernatural and miraculous, and liturgy with a diminished sense of mystery, creates a real problem for the novelist. It is difficult to write fiction that is incisive, dramatic, and compelling against a backdrop of religion that is so comfortable, humane, and prosaic.

The note of protest and critique of the secular world, which was a strong feature of earlier Catholic novels is not absent, but is more muted and oblique. The once strong dividing line between the godless secular world and the redeemed world of the Church is more nebulous.[3] Although some of the fiction may still endorse Catholicism as a locus of meaning or the fullest expression of the gospel, there is not as strong a sense of the Church as an island of sanity and order in the midst of the chaos of modernity that was characteristic of earlier writers, especially Belloc and Chesterton. On the contrary, there is plenty of craziness in the Catholic Church as well, and many of the novels convey a sense of disappointment that the Church fails—either for accommodating or failing to accommodate itself to the modern world—and in either case doing it with deplorably bad taste.

Contemporary Catholic novelists do not critique their own Catholic community in the same way as earlier writers did. Whereas the earlier novels often criticized the failings of individual Catholics who were sunk in spiritual lethargy, mired in materialism, or indifferent to the poor, recent ones seem more sympathetic to Catholics' plight in the post-Vatican II Church. *Both* Church and world are chaotic, and one must navigate as best one can. The novels are more critical of the institutional Church itself, either in its failure to be pastorally sensitive to the needs of laypeople— especially in the areas of gender, sexuality, and marriage—or in some of the new liturgical and pastoral practices which are shown to be more detrimental than helpful and in the jettisoning of old rites and practices that were comforting and beneficial.

These critiques are often made through satire, which exemplifies another significant trend in recent Catholic fiction: a more extensive and creative use of the comic mode. The recent turn to the comic owes much to the witty novels of Muriel Spark, which appeared with great frequency during the post-Vatican II period. Also, a kind of cross-fertilization may have taken place with English writers being stimulated and inspired by the work of comic American Catholic writers Flannery O'Connor and Walker Percy.

Gene Kellogg claims, "Catholic novels of the highest quality virtually ceased to appear after the mid-1960s."[4] He argues that the spark that had ignited the imaginations of the greatest Catholic novelists was a certain "abrasiveness" and that from the beginning the typical stance of the Catholic novelist was in opposition either to the secular community or to certain elements in the Catholic community or to both. Kellogg also maintains that the fiction that focused on criticizing the Catholic community is superior to the earlier fiction (Huysmans, Belloc, Chesterton, Waugh) that criticized the secular world because Catholic beliefs were "nearer the quick of [the Catholic writer's] own heart and intellect."[5] It was this nearness, he believes, that produced the most compelling and influential Catholic novels.

The condition that most nourished Catholic creativity from the mid-1920s to the mid-1950s, according to Kellogg, was the convergence of the Catholic community and the surrounding secular community.

If the Catholics cleared away many of the corruptions of their faith that had repelled secularists, so also did secularists abandon many of their own superstitions. Catholics were no longer forced into opposition by the secular belief in scientific determinism which repelled Claudel and Maritain. There was also erosion in the secular belief that the profit system was a source of automatic "progress," and that the poor and ignorant could be ignored because ultimately the benefits trickling down to their level would eliminate the conditions from which they suffered. A recognition that material advances can go with spiritual and moral impoverishment also grew strongly among most thinking secularists from 1920 to the present. . . . If Catholics approached the modern world, it was because the modern world finally arrived at recognitions that made possible an approach by a people oriented to values of the spirit.[6]

This convergence produced what Kellogg calls assimilative writing: writing that reflects a secular order and a religious order that are both self-critical, have permeable boundaries, and are receptive to insights and achievements of the other. The religious person and the secular person both alter their thinking and learn new respect for those of different beliefs. Yet each still keeps its own distinct identity. The boundaries may be permeable, but they are still very much boundaries.

One might argue that this convergence really came to fruition with the Second Vatican Council and that therefore the greatest Catholic novels should have appeared during and following the years of the Council, that is, after the mid-1960s. The Council may be seen as an expression of the fruit of the convergence that had been going on for several decades.[7] This period of convergence, however, was followed by a period of confluence when the two communities began to merge into each other. This is what Kellogg believes happened during and after the Second Vatican Council:

> So much assimilation had taken place that there was a crisis of identity. Catholics, no longer so critical of secularism, became by an unfortunate corollary often also no longer critical of the inroads of secularism into Catholicism's own essence. It became difficult for many Catholics to discern what Catholics advocated that was not also advocated by most men of good will. . . . The primary and defiant Catholic emphasis upon the spirit, which for so many generations had generated the creative spark between the Catholic communities and the secular environment, virtually ceased.

The Catholic novels produced during this period, according to Kellogg, had less vigor than the earlier ones, and "their assertions were frail echoes of what they once had been."[8]

Referring to the insistence of Graham Greene and others that they were not "Catholic novelists" but novelists who happened to be Catholic, Albert Sonnenfeld asserts: "They were wrong, I believe, but ironically they were also, in this and in so many matters, prophetic. . . . Their disclaimers notwithstanding, they had an inner dread of becoming novelists who happened also to be Catholic. That prophecy is now well on the way to fulfillment."[9] Sonnenfeld suggests that the Catholic novel has become the psychological novel or the novel of political and social justice. He cites a remark of Thomas Hardy used by Graham Greene as the epigraph of his 1973 novel *The Honorary Consul* that seems to articulate the mode of thought behind many recent Catholic novels: "All things merge into one another—good into evil, generosity into justice, religion into politics."[10] Such themes, while they may make interesting novels, seem trivial compared to those in which a person's salvation or damnation was at stake. J. C. Whitehouse in *Vertical Man: The Human Being in the Catholic Novels of Graham Greene, Sigrid Undset*[11] *and Georges Bernanos* comes to a similar conclusion: "Works informed by that older Catholic view of man as a creature of enormous individual worth, living in a special and dynamic relationship with his Creator, taught by the Church Christ founded and moving gradually towards salvation or damnation no longer seem quite relevant to the newer, post-Council and conciliatory Catholic world of community and communications."[12]

David Lodge was asked in a radio interview in 1968 what he thought about the Catholic novel. His response, while compatible with the views expressed above, focuses less on the changing worldview of Catholics and more on the way the Church is perceived:

> I don't think that one can talk of the Catholic novel in quite such sharply-defined terms anymore, partly because Catholicism itself has become a much more confused—and confusing—faith, more difficult to define, mainly in the last ten or fifteen years as a result of Pope John and the Vatican Council. The Church no longer presents that sort of monolithic, unified, uniform view of life which it once did.[13]

These opinions suggest that the highest achievements in the genre of the Catholic novel were possible only because a window of opportunity appeared as Catholicism was venturing out from its defensive posture and entering into conversation with the secular world yet still maintained a clear and robust sense of its own identity. If this thesis is correct, we are not likely to see again Catholic novels of the quality of the best of Mauriac, Bernanos, Greene, and Waugh or other European Catholic novelists of the years preceding Vatican II.[14]

The Catholic writers who produced the flowering of the Catholic novel faced the perennial challenges of all Christian novelists: how to show the workings of grace and allow for the miraculous and supernatural without violating psychological credibility or the canons of realism, how to make salvation or damnation seem important to a secular reader, and how to convey a worldview based on a deeply held personal faith without appearing to engage in underhanded apologetics and evangelization. We have seen that not all critics agree that they met all these challenges successfully, yet some novelists found ways to navigate these difficulties and produce fiction of exceptionally high quality and wide appeal for secular as well as Christian readers. To what extent these extraordinary achievements in Catholic fiction were the result of the uncommon situation of the Church—an unprecedented openness to secularity while still retaining a clear and strong sense of its own identity—and to what extent they were the result of the appearance of several extraordinarily gifted Catholic writers must remain a matter for speculation.[15]

If many Catholics today have lost a strong sense of their Church as a unique source of religious truth, the guardian of orthodoxy, and the custodian of essential sacramental life, it stands to reason that some Catholic novelists will also lack the clearly defined faith that made earlier novelists willing to take the risk of using that faith (which they knew many of their readers would reject) as the framework for their novels. American Catholic novelist Valerie Sayers says, "if we aspire to Catholic writing, then we had better let the Gospels propel us."[16] Yet if it is the gospels propelling the writer, without the ballast of the distinctive Roman Catholic tradition, will the novels still have the same arresting quality that caught the attention of the reading public in the 1930s, 1940s, and 1950s? It is worth noting, as Kellogg points out with reference to the great novels of earlier Catholic writers, "how deeply Roman Catholic the novels are. Historic Roman Catholic theological and philosophical ideas furnished the mainsprings of dramatic action."[17] Many good Christian novels are written by Protestants of various denominations, yet one never hears of the Presbyterian novel or the Lutheran novel. Whether it is due to the Catholic imagination, as defined by Greeley and others, the rich texture of the Catholic liturgical and sacramental tradition, or the accumulated detritus of a tumultuous, two thousand year history, the Catholic novel is distinctive.

In an era when attending to sectarian differences can seem retrograde and divisive, it may seem more attractive for a Catholic novelist to focus on seminal Christian motifs, such as the lessons of the parables or the beatitudes. The American Catholic Ron Hansen, for example, has effectively transposed the story of the Prodigal Son to our own day in *Atticus.* Another option is to use Catholic material to add texture, interest, and sociological detail, much as the late nineteenth-century writer Kate Chopin used Creole culture in her stories. Yet neither of these two options is likely to capture the fullness of a Catholic novel that is both explicitly Catholic and informed by Catholic theology.

In 1967 Peter Hebblethwaite published an article entitled "How Catholic Is the Catholic Novel?" He pointed out that the French Catholic novelists at the turn of the century were not afraid to stress "all those aspects of Catholic faith which are most paradoxical and craggy." He concluded, however, that now if a Catholic writer wishes to speak to others besides Catholics, "his Catholicism will have to be a centre of coherence rather than a demagogic party line." He also expected that Catholic novelists would be influenced by the "new theology," one stressing God's immanence more than His transcendence, and would therefore see grace less as "a kind of moral *Deus ex machina,*" than as a "quality of human existence." Hebblethwaite predicted, "the novelist who happens to be a Catholic will prefer to discern the patterns that emerge, fumblingly, in the chiaroscuro of faith, through characters in situation. I would expect him therefore to be increasingly less 'different,' less sheerly provoking, in a word, more deeply Catholic."[18]

To some extent Hebblethwaite's prediction seems to have been borne out. Nevertheless, four Catholic novelists writing in England at the beginning of the twenty-first century are not afraid to be different: Alice Thomas Ellis, David Lodge, Sara Maitland, and Piers Paul Read. They do not hesitate to include the "craggy" and "paradoxical" parts of Catholicism. Yet—perhaps because they have been influenced by immanentist theology or possess Greeley's Catholic imagination—they have produced highly accomplished fiction in which religious meaning emerges from and is inextricably entwined with human experience. Some of their novels make extensive use of explicitly Catholic material. Others are deeply informed by a Catholic vision without much use of explicitly Catholic material. Maitland, Lodge, and Read are still writing; Ellis died in 2005. Clearly they have not been doing the same kinds of things that Mauriac, Bernanos, Waugh, and Greene did, yet their fiction exemplifies exciting possibilities for the Catholic novel. Why only these four? I make no claim that they are the only significant English Catholic novelists writing at this time, nor even that they are a representative cross section. Yet they have, more than most contemporary English novelists, allowed their faith to inform their writing and have exemplified very different and interesting ways of integrating Catholicism into their work in ways that are substantial, imaginative, and serious.

In giving his rationale for using Graham Greene, Sigrid Undset, and Georges Bernanos as the subjects for his book, J. C. Whitehouse makes the point that Undset and Bernanos "attracted great attention as writers of non-fictional works, particularly as moralists, political and philosophical essayists and as figures active in the ideological struggles of their time."[19] A similar claim could be made for Ellis, Maitland, and Read. Ellis's nonfiction *Serpent on the Rock* (1994) and Maitland's non-fictional books *A Map of the New Country: Women and Christianity* (1983) and *A Big Enough God: A Feminist's Search for a Joyful Theology* (1995) are important contributions are important contributions to the ongoing task of making faith both relevant to the contemporary situation and faithful to the orthodox tradition. Ellis,

Maitland, and Read have contributed articles to Catholic periodicals and newspapers on subjects pertaining to the contemporary Church and faith, not just on literary subjects. Some of Ellis's have now been collected in *God Has Not Changed* (2004) and Read's in *Hell and Other Destinations: A Novelist's Reflections on This World and the Next* (2006).

David Lodge, while not outspoken on religious matters, nevertheless is known among his Catholic readers as one who clearly articulates the experience of those who are conflicted about some of the Church's teachings, yet are unwilling to abandon what they also see as a source of meaning and a connection to the transcendent. Lodge's novels reveal an impressive grasp of developments in contemporary Catholicism. In *How Far Can You Go?* Lodge actually steps outside the narrative to offer his own analysis of the encyclical *Humanae Vitae*, which reasserted the traditional condemnation of artificial contraception. Bernard Bergonzi claims this interpolated essay "is far more cogent than the theological discussions I have come across."[20] Whitehouse argues that Greene, Undset, and Bernanos were "Catholic writers in the strict sense, that is, authors whose faith had personal meaning and value, informed their minds, imagination and work, and made its presence felt."[21] I believe that the same is true of Ellis, Lodge, Maitland, and Read. My final reasons for choosing these four novelists are personal. I have had the opportunity to meet all four of them and discuss their work, and—the best reason—I love their novels.

ALICE THOMAS ELLIS

The human race has always had a tendency to hate God. It crucified Him, after all. Now it is trying to convince itself that He does not exist or that, if He does, He is indulgent to and indeed identifies with its every whim, even the most sinful. We have no trust and will not face the dark for the fear that it is endless.

—Alice Thomas Ellis, *Serpent on the Rock*

All of her sentences seem lit from their own spark of intelligence; at their best, they are epigrammatically clever and composed summaries of vast tracts of social and emotional experience.

—James Mustich, afterward to *Unexplained Laughter*

Alice Thomas Ellis is the pseudonym for Anna Haycraft. She was born in Liverpool in 1932, but during World War II she and her mother lived for a time in Wales to be away from the danger of bombing. After secondary school she studied at the College of Art. As a young adult, partly because of her Catholic relatives on her father's side (his sister had married a

Catholic) and her inevitable contact with the Church because of Liverpool's large Catholic population, she became a Catholic.

> Then after due time and instruction I became a Catholic because I no longer found it possible to disbelieve in God. . . . I felt entirely at home with the conviction, aims and rituals of the Church and secure in the certainty that it was immune from frivolous change and the pressures of fashion; primarily concerned with the numinous rather than with the social and political concerns of its members.[22]

Shortly after her conversion, Ellis entered a religious order but had to leave because of a serious back problem.[23] She later married publisher Colin Haycraft, and joined him at the Duckworth Publishing Company, where she became the fiction editor. She had seven children, of whom two are deceased. She died on March 8, 2005.

Perhaps the word one encounters most often in reviews of Ellis's novels is *wit*. Peter Ackroyd reviewing her first novel, *The Sin Eater*, said that the distinguishing quality of the book is "its wit: the relentlessness of domestic life, the knives only just sheathed in time, the tart little phrases bouncing around like Molotov cocktails."[24] The reviewer of another novel noted that the seriousness of her themes should not obscure her reputation as "one of the wittiest writers currently at work."[25] Ellis's novels are replete with eccentric characters with odd names, bizarre situations, and scintillating dialogue. Also frequently mentioned by reviewers is her elegant style. What Julia O'Faolain wrote with respect to *Unexplained Laughter* is true of all her novels: "In the end the novel cannot be summarized and this is proof of its excellence. The author's quicksilver perceptions can be conveyed adequately in no words but her own."[26] In analyzing Ellis's fiction one is forced to include ample quoted passages because paraphrase simply cannot convey an adequate sense of the novel.[27]

Yet her work is not merely brilliant surface. As John Nicholson noted in his review of *The Other Side of the Fire*, the underlying themes of Ellis's fiction are serious indeed. Her subjects include sexual betrayal, deceit, treachery of all kinds, and bereavement. Yet it is not simply the subject matter that makes Ellis's short novels so compelling, but her unusual perspective on these familiar subjects. For example, Nicholson refers to "Ellis's chillingly effective dissections of the damage people do to each other when they stretch out the hand of *friendship*, or, worse still, *love*" (emphasis added).[28]

It is difficult to read much of Alice Thomas Ellis without thinking of Muriel Spark and the early Evelyn Waugh. Like them, she writes witty, satiric novels in a tight elegant prose. Some critics detect in her work a snobbish humor reminiscent of Waugh. Yet whereas Waugh's readers tended to identify the snobbishness with the author, Ellis clearly stands over and against her characters' snobbishness. Although she will turn her devastating wit on those characters she dislikes, it is difficult to see any partiality to the upper classes. Like Muriel Spark, she builds her novels around highly intelligent women with penetrating insight. One of the best analyses of how Ellis manages to address weighty metaphysical and theological themes in novels with such a light bright surface is provided by James Mustich in an afterward he wrote for *Unexplained Laughter*:

> While the author's deft, brilliant portrayal of social milieux is amusing, even arresting, it is the otherworldly shadow her inventions ingeniously cast that distinguishes her novels; through its dim illumination questions kept at a distance by the frantic business of modern life (and the ironic stance of most contemporary literature) are allowed to creep near. Matters of metaphysical moment that are often on the fringes of our awareness—but that seldom raise their heads in the commotion of everyday event [*sic*] because we are embarrassed by their ominous logic, and by the language, lore and even the liturgy of their superstitious legacies—are slipped into the conversation of Ellis's fictional gatherings with an only slightly disconcerting frankness, appearing (and disappearing) as quickly as a tray of exotic but alluring canapés. With the sleight of hand of a clever and accomplished hostess, the author invites deep themes into the room and lets them make themselves familiar. And despite our best efforts to ignore their insistent gaze, we recognize her portentous guests and avoid them at our spiritual peril.[29]

Ellis rarely uses Catholic material in the explicit way that Lodge and Read do. Yet in her non-fiction, she has been very forthright about expressing both her affection for the preVatican II Church and her dismay at developments following the Council. Speaking of the Catholicism she encountered during her young life in Liverpool, she writes:

> It is presently *de rigeur* to claim that Catholicism thirty-odd years ago was repressive, hidebound and frightening, but I found in it great richness and an abundance of people who made me laugh: a release from fear and the vague oppression of a childhood shadowed alike by the joyless strictures of Protestantism and the horrors of fairy-tale and terrifying legend.[30]

In contrast, here is her reaction when, in the name of Vatican II, her parish priest discarded clerical garb and insisted on being addressed by his first name:

> He professed himself delighted with the prospect of universal singing and dancing in the aisles and round the altar and gave an overwhelming impression of goofiness. I was startled, for he was an elderly person, and elderly persons are not usually changeable. It filled me with a strange feeling, a sense

of the possibility of impermanence, of ultimate worthlessness and the prospect of the triumph of chaos and old night.[31]

She describes contemporary Catholic life as "new or re-ordered churches of Lutheran barrenness, all Catholic culture, all tradition lost."[32]

The reader familiar with Ellis's religious opinions from other sources will see her Catholic sensibility weaving through her novels, even when there is little explicit use of Catholic material. There is usually one Catholic or ex-Catholic in her cast of characters. In *The Sin Eater* Rose reflects the views of her author when she says of the local parish priest:

> "To do him justice, . . . he does still dress in the proper fashion. He hasn't taken to going round in jeans and a T-shirt and a little cross on a chain round his neck imploring people to call him Roger, and he hasn't left the church to marry and devote his life to rewriting theology to conform with his own lusts and itches, and drivel on about the self-transcending nature of sex, like all those treacherous lecherous jesuits [*sic*] mad with the radiant freedom of contemporary thought. But it isn't enough. Now the Church has lost its head, priests feel free to say what they think themselves, and they don't have any thoughts at all except for some rubbish about the brotherhood of man. They seem to regard Our Lord as a sort of beaten egg to bind us all together. . . ."
> "It is as though . . . one's revered, dignified and darling old mother had slapped on a mini-skirt and fishnet tights and started ogling strangers. A kind of menopausal madness, a sudden yearning to be attractive to all. It is tragic and hilarious and awfully embarrassing."[33]

Such passages earn Ellis disparaging comments from reviewers, such as Peter Ackroyd, who deplores the "unnecessary good will . . . heaped upon the ancient rites of the Catholic Church."[34]

In his study of the British Catholic novel, Thomas Woodman includes Ellis in a section called "Catholic chic," by which he means the portrayal of Catholicism as having a certain glamour or cultural stature. Catholicism can seem attractive—not in spite of—but precisely because of its complex theology and stringent moral demands. It is difficult to see how Ellis's fiction quite fits this category since her use of Catholicism is so oblique. The central concerns of the novels are not specifically Catholic as much as moral, and in some cases, Christian. As she put it to me, "Once you take away the religious element—absolutes of good and evil—you can't write fiction. (Well, you can, but it's boring.)"[35]

Ellis's fiction is anything but boring. Harriet Waugh nicely sums up the basic premise of an Ellis novel: "In her short, edged comedies of human failure in the face of some ultimate good, Alice Thomas Ellis manoeuvres to pit the world against the spirit and then stands back to see which will win."[36]

DAVID LODGE

I would regard myself as a liberal, and in some ways a rather secular kind of liberal in spite of the fact that I'm a Catholic—I'm not the kind who wishes to persuade other people to accept his Catholic beliefs. Catholicism happens to be the ideological milieu I grew up in, that I know and write out of.

—David Lodge, Interview by John Haffenden

Lodge joins an honorable and great tradition by restoring the primacy of the soul in fiction.

—John Podhoretz, review of *How Far Can You Go?*

David Lodge is both a distinguished literary critic and the author of twelve novels and a novella. He was a Professor of modern English literature for many years at the University of Birmingham but is now retired from teaching. Born in 1935, Lodge was the only child of a Catholic mother and a nondenominational Christian father who was one quarter Jewish.[37] He is married and has three children.

In 1993 Lodge, who is a cradle Catholic, wrote an introduction for the republication of his first novel, *The Picturegoers* (1960), in which he described his theological perspective as "demythologized, provisional, and in many ways agnostic."[38] A fuller account of Lodge's religious position is provided in an essay by Bernard Bergonzi, "A Conversation with David Lodge," which was published in 1999:[39]

Lodge said that he disliked having to define his theological position but that he was prepared to try. Graham Greene, in his later years, after he had moved away from the tormented orthodoxy of his Catholic novels, defined himself as a "Catholic agnostic"; Lodge prefers to reverse the terms and call himself an "Agnostic Catholic." He remains in the Church as a practising Catholic, though he is agnostic about the ultimate reality behind the symbolic languages of liturgy and scripture. He has abandoned much of the traditional Catholic worldview which he grew up with and expressed in *The Picturegoers*, now regarding it as over literal and anthropomorphic; at the same time, he insists that religious language is not empty of meaning. It is a perennial symbolic and speculative mode in which we articulate the contradictions and anxieties which are ineradicably part of the human condition. By traditional standards—perhaps those he would have upheld himself as a young man—Lodge acknowledges that he is probably a heretic; but he thinks that many theologians, including Catholic ones, would now hold similar attitudes.[40]

Although Lodge is probably best known for his academic novels, *Changing Places, Small World,* and *Nice Work,* in which Catholicism plays no part, many of his other novels make substantial use of Catholic material. *The Picturegoers*, published when he was only twenty-five, concerns a lapsed Catholic who comes to lodge with a large Catholic family and ends up returning to the faith, whereas the adult daughter, who has left the convent, loses hers. Although the plot sounds as if it could be from a novel of Greene or Waugh, what makes it distinctive is that that the Catholic characters are so ordinary. "There are no dissolute aristocrats . . . or men undergoing spiritual intensities in exotic parts of the world. . . . The frame of reference is sociological rather than literary-theological."[41]

In his third and fourth novels Lodge uses Catholic material primarily for comedy. *The British Museum Is Falling Down* (1965) zeroes in on birth control, detailing the stratagems to which Catholic couples had to go in order to try to avoid pregnancy.[42] In *Out of the Shelter* (1970), Catholicism, as part of the protagonist's sheltered upbringing, is again used primarily for sociological background and comedic possibilities.

Lodge depicts the contemporary world as confusing, unpredictable, and comical. Although one can see a gentle critique of modern society (the insanity in modern university life in *Changing Places* and *Small World* and the depersonalized world of industry and business in *Nice Work)*, yet one does not find in his fiction the severe or moralizing critique of the secular world that characterized the work of so many earlier Catholic novelists. Similarly, Lodge uses comedy and satire to critique the Church, particularly what he sees as a rigid, puritanical sexual morality taught in the decades preceding Vatican II. Lodge's ebullient comic spirit catches all the ridiculous aspects of Catholic life, together with a righteous anger at what he sees as unreasonable sexual demands. There is also a sensitivity to vast discrepancies between the descriptions of the human situation in the carefully formulated pronouncements of Catholic theology and catechisms and the unpredictable, sometimes comic, sometimes absurd circumstances in which human beings often find themselves.

Lodge explains what attracted him as a young man to the fiction of the important Catholic novelists of that day. He found himself struggling with tensions between his respect for Catholic theology and his rejection of the narrow "Catholic ghetto" culture:

Literature, specifically the "Catholic novel" of Greene, Mauriac and others, helped me to resolve these tensions and paradoxes, by presenting authentic religious belief as something equally opposed to the materialism of the secular world and to the superficial pieties of parochial Catholicism. The idea of the sinner as a representative Christian was appealing to the adolescent mind, suggesting (in a wholly theoretical way, for I was as timid as I was innocent) that being a Catholic need not entail a life of dull, petty-bourgeois respectability. The extreme situations and exotic settings on which these writers thrived were, however, very remote from my experience; and when I

came to try and write fiction for myself I domesticated their themes to the
humdrum suburban parochial milieu that I knew best.[43]

As a university student, Lodge found that, although Joyce had to leave
the Church to escape a cultural stranglehold, Lodge himself found that to
be a Catholic in the entirely different context of a university in the secular
England of the fifties "was to strike a rather interesting, almost exotic pose
before one's peers."[44]

In fact, however, when Lodge's Catholic novels appeared, they were
anything but exotic. Nor were they marked by the stark tension of the
drama of salvation or damnation, the dramatic conflict between sin and
grace, the overriding sense of a supernatural realm hovering just out of
sight, or a relentless God in pursuit of a soul. Lodge is not much interested
in conversion, the subject of so many earlier Catholic novels, but in the
long, slow, ongoing process of living with a faith, particularly one handed
on in childhood. In an amusing paragraph from *The Picturegoers* Lodge
clarifies two different experiences of Catholicism:

> The common mistake of outsiders, that Catholicism was a beautiful,
> solemn, dignified, aesthetic religion. But when you got inside you found it
> was ugly, crude, bourgeois. Typical Catholicism wasn't to be found in St.
> Peter's, or Chartres, but in some mean, low-roofed parish church, where
> hideous plaster saints simpered along the wall, and the bored congrega-
> tion, pressed perspiration tight into the pews, rested their fat arses on the
> seats, rattled their beads, fumbled for their smallest change, and scolded
> their children. Yet in their presence God was made and eaten all day long,
> and for that reason these people could never be quite like other people, and
> that was Catholicism.[45]

This paragraph, while delightfully humorous, is also arresting in calling
our attention to a serious paradox within Catholic life. Sometimes the
grand tradition of Aquinas, Dante, Palestrina, St. Theresa of Avila, and
John Henry Newman seems so far away from people's direct contact with
Catholicism, which is their local parish, with—more often than not—
dreadful music, anemic preaching, a bored congregation, and uninspired
liturgy in a drab church. Most Catholics *do* believe that there *is* a connection between Catholicism's grand tradition and their local parish, yet
sometimes find that belief hard to maintain. This paragraph from *The Picturegoers* exemplifies what Lodge does so well in all his Catholic novels:
extract and highlight the comic element in what is a profound disjunction
in Catholic life and yet still manage to keep the seriousness substantive
and undiminished. Thomas Woodman points out that "Lodge shows well
here one way that sophisticated Catholics try to get the best of both
worlds. They retain themselves a strong sense of the Catholic high-art tra-

dition and of their own superiority to the popular forms, but in accepting the latter they at the same time defend themselves against the charge that aestheticism has anything to do with their allegiance."[46]

Lodge has contributed something new to the English Catholic novel in his extraordinarily detailed depiction of the day-to-day life of average Catholics. With the exception of Belloc, who was a cradle Catholic, most of the earlier Catholic novelists had been highly intellectual converts. Their experience was not typical of average Catholics. Lodge, however, portrays the Catholic milieu in a way that Bernard Bergonzi found "disturbingly accurate," exemplified in this passage from *The Picturegoers*.[47]

> The kitchen into which he was ushered confirmed his suspicions about Mrs Mallory's religious background: the evidence of the plastic holy water stoup askew on the wall, the withered holy Palm, stuck behind a picture of the Sacred Heart which resembled an illustration in a medical text-book, and the statue of St Patrick enthroned upon the dresser, was conclusive.[48]

Most Catholic readers feel a certain delight in seeing their familiar world rendered so accurately. Yet Bergonzi's adverb *disturbingly* catches the disorienting experience of seeing details one associates with faith and the supernatural embedded in such a prosaic setting. Although Catholic readers may live comfortably with such a juxtaposition in their daily lives, seeing it described in a novel makes them see it with startling freshness, what Lodge calls *defamiliarization*. Bernanos and Mauriac had provided glimpses into ordinary Catholic homes in France, but usually with a negative tone, pointing up the parochialism or hypocrisy of those who lived there. Lodge's tone is different, combining a certain affection for these Catholics with a refusal to either idealize or denounce them. He sympathizes with their struggles to survive in a world which frequently is bewildering and frustrating, and to find meaning in a religion that often seems out of sync with their own experience.

Sex is important in Lodge's fiction, not so much as the archetypal sin to be conquered, but as a delightful and comic part of life, although one that requires some restraint and discipline. His novels suggest that the Church's overly strict and heavy-handed approach to sexual morality has caused needless anguish to some Catholics and alienated others. Yet in Lodge's fiction sex never becomes purely a form of recreation or a source of comedy. Beneath the comic situations, Lodge usually manages to point to serious underlying questions of commitment and responsibility. Theodore Fraser even claims that sex in Lodge's novels has "tragic undertones and consequences"[49] Sex is also an important way in which some of his characters experience a connection with the transcendent. Even for those on the margin of religious faith, a generous response to the gift of sexual love is usually indicative of an openness to or potential for a relationship with God.

Lodge has a clear grasp of many of the issues that have been so important in Catholicism in the second half of the twentieth century. To my knowledge no other Catholic writer has described so cogently the moral dilemma of Catholics who simply could not find the arguments of *Humanae Vitae* persuasive, as well as the way in which this controversy called into question the whole network of Catholic moral teaching. He also portrays how Catholics, deprived of their old certainty of an authoritative moral guide, try to live in a sexually permissive society by relying on the best that secularity has to offer: a good heart and a desire not to hurt others. Lodge also sees the disruptive nature of the pace, extent and quality of liturgical and other changes in Catholicism, as well as the profound ramifications of a loss of belief in hell and a greatly attenuated belief in immortality.

Whereas Evelyn Waugh depicted aristocratic Catholics and Greene portrayed anguished sinners in exotic settings, Lodge's Catholic characters are resolutely middle class, and their locales—London and Birmingham—are about as far away from Greeneland as you can get. Even when his characters take excursions to Copenhagen, Spain, or Hawaii, they bring middle class English life along with them. Their very ordinariness is what makes his novels so appealing to ordinary readers—even secular ones. Yet many Catholics see more in them. In the words of sociologist priest Andrew Greeley, "David Lodge's novels are hard to summarize because his ironic wit defies summary. His protagonists are often swept up by some kind of salvation—an imperfect and problematic salvation perhaps, but one in which there are not only grounds for hope but also powerful hints of grace."[50]

SARA MAITLAND

In all of Maitland's novels the reader becomes aware of the sacred potential within and outside of each of her characters' consciousness.

—Sally Cunneen, "Big Enough for God: The Fiction of Sara Maitland"

The production of art is quite simply a particular participation in the divine; it is a specific and vital form of theology—defined simply as the capacity to tell stories about the divine, and of course the capacity to hear them—and as Christians we fail to value it at our peril.

—Sara Maitland, *A Big-Enough God*

Sara Maitland was born in 1950 and was brought up in the Scottish Presbyterian faith. She had abandoned any form of Christian belief, however, by the time she went to Oxford, where she became a committed socialist and feminist. She was also inspired, however, by the radical commitment to social justice of some of the Christians there, especially some Dominican priests, and she recommitted to Christianity, not as a Presbyterian, but as an Anglican.[51] At the age of twenty-two she married an American, who later became an Anglican priest, with whom she had a daughter and a son. They were subsequently divorced. Maitland did postgraduate study in theology with Rowan Williams, the present archbishop of Canterbury.[52] In 1993 she converted to Roman Catholicism.

> In 1993 I became a Roman Catholic; there has been no doctrinal nor liturgical change for me, merely a repositioning of my relationship to authority; a reaffirmation, despite its many sillinesses (and I must say wrongnesses) that a church can, and must, be universal, can be large scale through time and space—can indeed be big enough.[53]

Big enough for what? One does not need to read much of Maitland's work to encounter the expansiveness of her theology. Not only does she love the Bible, liturgy, and legends and stories of the saints, but she also retains her passionate commitment to social justice and to feminism. She is intent on disclosing the ways in which women's religious experience has been devalued and misunderstood because of patriarchal attitudes in Christianity. She is also captivated by the discoveries of modern science. "It is perfectly possible to believe in the Big Bang, in evolution, and in genetics and still believe nonschizophrenically that God made the world, that we are beloved, that we have free will and that virtue matters."[54] Like Annie Dillard, she finds science to be—not an enemy of religion—but an amazing and continual source of spiritual renewal.[55]

> I am certain that accepting all of this randomness and unknowability gives us more, if we dare to receive it, than it takes away. I believe what we have gained is complexity, freedom and loveliness. We have gained a universe so extraordinary that it should stun us into awe, and a God so magnificently clever and creative that we can have confidence in such a creator's ability to sort out tiny little problems like the resurrection of the body without too much trouble. We are shown a universe that can keep us on our toes, agog with excitement.[56]

Maitland insists that her theology is orthodox, and one suspects that her conception of orthodoxy reflects Chesterton's understanding of it as an unwillingness to exclude any element of the faith, especially the paradoxical ones, the ones that lead us into mystery. Her remark quoted above about the resurrection of the body is an indication of the way she clings tenaciously to elements of the Creed that most contemporary Christians have either discarded or choose to ignore. She also believes very seriously in angels and in the Devil. "I really do believe in angels and I am glad that I do." "I believe in the Devil—not the horns and tail bit necessarily, . . . but I do believe."[57]

Maitland asserts that "we urgently need to reclaim the art of telling stories, and hearing stories, about the divine if we are to have a joyful faith."[58] Her fiction incorporates myth, fable, fantasy, and science, and her five novels have been much praised. Her first, *Daughter of Jerusalem*, won the Somerset Maugham best first novel award. Yet Maitland feels that the novel, of all literary forms, is the least congenial for expressing religious experience, primarily because it is *the* genre of the post-Enlightenment. The novel form reflects its birth in a period that was enamored of empirical science, rational analysis, and the rights of the individual, and is therefore not hospitable to the supernatural, the spiritual, the divine. Maitland says that this Enlightenment inheritance takes four forms.

First, modern psychology sees the self as an autonomous entity bounded by the body.[59] Modern novels are expected to reflect this psychology. Second, the novel seeks closure. The novel form militates against the kind of opening out that is inherent in religious experience. "If the fundamental purpose of religious experience is to move the individual not just away from their individualism but away from closure, then it is obviously difficult to represent this in a genre which requires such a closure."[60] Third, the influence of postmodernism, which calls into question the possibility of any objective truth and any correspondence of the written word to an outside reality, has rendered the novel an even more problematic form for depicting religious experience.[61] Fourth, our declining ability to use myth means that we have less access to allegory, metaphor, symbol, and story. Since we can only speak of God by way of analogy, we have "a massive problem as to how on earth one could insert experiences of the divine Other . . . into contemporary novels."[62]

The part of religious experience that most engages Maitland's imagination is transformation, what religion traditionally calls conversion, but not necessarily in the sense of accepting a certain denomination or even assent to Christianity. Maitland is engaged with transformation in the larger sense of a fundamental change, which brings one closer to God. In her own words: "There is a fundamental Christian journey which has always been the same and always will be: the journey out of Egypt and into the painful freedom of wilderness; out of Babylon and exile back to our true home; out of sin, through death, towards the difficult experience of free life."[63] Maitland's attempt to make the novel form accommodate religious experience—in particular, transformation—gives her fiction the following qualities:

First, surprise and reversal of expectations are frequent. One of her favorite techniques is to use familiar stories from the Bible or folklore but give them a surprising twist. In her version of Cinderella the stepmother is the heroine. She incorporates diverse voices—not in the commonly understood sense of multiculturalism or socioeconomic diversity—but by including voices from a completely different realm of reality or juxtaposing stories from different historical periods with no explicit connection. In *Daughter of Jerusalem*, stories of Old Testament women are interpolated in the story of a contemporary English woman. In *Virgin Territory*, a nun hears the disembodied voices of the God of the Old Testament, the Fathers of the Church, and other patriarchal figures from Church history. In *Brittle Joys*, one of the main characters is an angel. These voices act as a kind of chorus, opening a wider angle of vision on the main action.[64] These surprises, reversals, and abrupt conjunctions of different time periods and modes (familiar Biblical story or fairy tale/realistic narrative in the contemporary world) strike some readers as "a stagey device," "too self-conscious in execution," or embarrassing "bursts of purple."[65] Others, however, find these experiments bracing and delightful adventures in an expansive, imaginative realm informed by a powerful religious imagination. Maitland has tried hard to resist the closure inherent in the novel form, and her endings may displease readers who long for a sense of resolution and completeness. Her novels, like the theology she favors, open out.

Maitland's protagonists are contemporary women, some Christian, some secular. Two aspects of her treatment of sexuality are noteworthy. One is the way in which she validates the importance and beauty of women's bodily experience—all aspects of it, not simply the erotic. The second is her frank acceptance of homosexuality. The three novels I examine each have at least one homosexual character. One does not get the impression that she is trying to make some kind of statement about homosexual people or their treatment by society. Her homosexual characters are likeable and have some endearing traits, but they also have faults like all the other characters. They are not anguished victims of homophobia.[66]

In choosing to include Sara Maitland among my four contemporary Catholic novelists, I am taking a certain liberty. As she herself pointed out to me, all her novels before *Brittle Joys* were written before she was a Roman Catholic. Yet, as she says in *A Big-Enough God*, her theology as an Anglican was very orthodox, very catholic,[67] and it is difficult not to see that catholicism in her earlier novels, especially the biblically rich *Daughter of Jerusalem* and *Virgin Territory* with its sensitive exploration of the meaning of consecrated virginity. Maitland's deep interest in Catholic nuns and sisters is evident from her discussion of them in her 1983 book *A Map of the New Country: Women and Christianity*. Therefore, by virtue of her 1993 conversion I am co-opting Sara Maitland as a Catholic novelist.

PIERS PAUL READ

The principal moral benefit of religion is that it permits a confrontation with the age in which one lives in a perspective that transcends the age and thus puts it in proportion.

—Peter Berger, *A Rumor of Angels*

Though our population practises no kind of religion, it is left with a curiosity about those who try.

—Piers Paul Read, *Monk Dawson*.

Piers Paul Read was born in 1941. His father, Herbert Read, the well known art critic and author of *The Green Child*, was an agnostic. His mother was a Catholic convert, and Piers was raised and educated as a Catholic. He went to Cambridge to study moral sciences (philosophy, logic, ethics, and psychology) but exasperated by the extreme skepticism of the students and professors, he decided to study history instead.[68] He is married and has four children.

Although best known for his nonfiction book *Alive* (1974), the story of the survivors of a 1972 airplane crash in the Andes, Read has produced fourteen novels since 1966. One reviewer calls Read's work "fascinatingly unlike much other novel writing of quality in England at present," and Malcolm Bradbury has referred to him as "one of Britain's most intelligent and disturbing writers."[69] One reason that Bradbury and others may find Read's work disturbing is that he is actually writing contemporary *psychomachia*, a literary form popular in the early Middle Ages, which focused on the battle between good and evil in the human soul. An atmosphere of urgency, drama—even apocalyptic doom—hangs over his novels, and his fictional landscape is shot through with an almost Manichaean dualism. He has said that he cannot imagine writing fiction if one is not Catholic or Christian because, in his opinion, the only thing that makes really good fiction is the conflict between good and evil. One of his favorite novelists is Dostoyevsky.[70]

Eschewing experimental techniques, Read writes in a straightforward realistic mode.[71] He uses a wide variety of settings—Warsaw and Paris (*Polonaise*), France, (*The Villa Golitsyn* and *The Free Frenchman*), Boston and Berkeley (*The Professor's Daughter*), Jerusalem (*On the Third Day*), Russia

(*Alice in Exile* and *A Patriot in Berlin*). These places do not have the seediness and squalor of Greeneland, nor are they as exotic as Graham Greene's Mexico, Liberia, Vietnam, or Haiti. Nevertheless, Read has a remarkable ability to evoke a rich and palpable sense of place in locales that have a certain glamour and allure. His plots include the material of popular fiction—espionage, sexual promiscuity, marital infidelity, social climbing, prostitution, incest, drug dealing, suicide, abortion, murder, and even infanticide and Satanic rituals—but with a refusal to place them in an amoral universe. Read's imagination is largely shaped by his conservative Roman Catholicism, which he portrays as a steady and authoritative moral voice that is unwelcome—not only in secular society—but even to many within his Catholic community.

There is a notable scarcity of wit, humor, and irony, distinguishing Read's work from that of Waugh and Spark, as well as from that of his contemporaries, David Lodge and Alice Thomas Ellis. Read's seriousness, coupled with his clear moral framework, strikes some readers as heavy-handed and blatantly apologetic. One reviewer complained that *A Married Man* is "theology that masquerades as fiction" and its protagonist "not really a free character in a free fictional universe but a football destined to be booted about by an author bent on scoring theological goals."[72] In his recent book *Hell and Other Destinations*, Read laments being identified as a "stern moralist," adding, "This is not how I see myself, nor how I want to be seen. . . . My novels, though they frequently had a moral denouement, were hardly works of Catholic propaganda."[73]

In some of his novels, however, the Catholic Church is definitely a mediating presence. So obvious is this premise that one critic says that "to Read, there is only one sure way of fulfilling oneself or saving one's soul, and that is through religion, through Roman Catholicism."[74] In some novels like *Monk Dawson* and *On the Third Day*, the Catholic Church is practically a major character. Yet Read's is not an uncritical view of the contemporary Church's performance as mediator, as is evident in a letter from one of his Catholic characters, responding to her confessor's explanation of why the Church has dropped the term *mortal sin*:

> I see what you mean about sins still being serious even if they aren't automatically mortal, but it doesn't make things easier. In the old days you at least knew that death *en flagrant délit* meant Hell-fire forever. You had to hope you'd survive long enough to repent in a moment of post-coital *tristesse*. Now you feel that a good Guardian Angel could get you off with five hundred days in Purgatory. . . . You see once the Church says that a sin isn't necessarily fatal to one's relationship with God then I'm afraid the floodgates are opened. . . . If adultery won't necessarily land me in Hell then it makes it awfully tempting to indulge now and pay later.[75]

Read is concerned with the way the Church, especially in its institutional form—its creaking and cumbersome apparatus, its laws, doctrines, canon law, prohibitions, and pronouncements (so attenuated in the contemporary Church)—mediates between God and the human person. The novel quoted above is typical of much of Read's work, which sees a diminution of the contemporary Church's ability or resolve to mediate effectively. In his own words, the Church has "lost the plot."[76]

Yet if Read makes a critique of the Church, he makes an even stronger one of the secular world. In this respect, Read differs from those who regard the secular world as the home of humane and democratic values that the Church would do well to emulate. Although most writers are horrified by the blatant violence and cruelty in the world, Read is distrustful of the world even in its more benign aspects. In fact, he seems intent on pointing out that the more harmless it may appear, the more dangerous the world is by the very fact that the naïve Christian is off his guard. Every kind of sin is depicted in Read's novels, but what is distinctive is the serious portrayal of the destructiveness of sexual sin. In this respect Read is more similar to earlier Catholic writers than to his own contemporaries. Without the restraining discipline of moral principles, his fiction suggests, sex is, at best, disordered, and at worst, predatory and destructive. In some of his later novels, however, Read suggests that even outside of marriage, loving sex can point one toward God. As with many English writers, there is some attention to the rancor and pettiness engendered by class differences.

Although Read's imagination seems more dialectical than analogical, there is a sense of sacramentality in the way that physical realities insert themselves into people's spiritual lives in startling and substantial ways, turning them in a different direction. The concrete, physical entity that stimulates faith—a dying woman's message scrawled in her own blood, a criminal's disgust at the sight of his own face in a mirror—suggest the bodily, fleshly way in which God's grace so often enters a human life.

The point of these *psychomachiae* is the outcome of the battle in the human soul. The ultimate triumph is conversion. Like Graham Greene, to whom he has been compared, Read seems haunted by the theme of conversion, which, as Thomas Howard says in reference to *Brideshead Revisited*, "is one of the topics that is most intractable, and most inhospitable to any attempt to come at it narratively."[77] Although in a few of his novels Read treats conversion more explicitly than is common in contemporary Catholic novels, he still keeps a respectful distance from the interior process, preferring usually to suggest it by indirection or nuance rather than to give it explicit narrative treatment.

Read seems to be at pains to demonstrate that, although Catholicism may be clear and definitive, it need not be parochial or provincial.

Through the characters or the "Catholic" narrative voice, he sometimes tries to expand the Catholic consciousness. Like Greene and Bernanos, he knows the arguments of the skeptic and the atheist, and he knows the worst that can be said of the Catholic Church. These narrative voices are trying to contain their arguments—not really to deny or contradict them—because they include elements of truth. But the Catholic narrator is intent on exhibiting his awareness of these troubling facts to demonstrate that his Catholic faith remains solid in the face of such challenges. In accord with the root meaning of *Catholic* as universal, Read is stretching the capacity of Catholicism to encompass the truth about the world—even those "truths" that *seem* to contradict it. The polemical voice of the apologist does occasionally dissipate the vitality and energy of the narrative. In spite of Read's unquestioned ability to delineate the lives of skeptics and nonbelievers and even to articulate their arguments, he does not quite achieve a dialogical play of voices because all the other voices are subsumed into the Catholic one.[78]

Read has said that what interests him is "trying to express philosophical and moral ideas through fiction."[79] A novel of ideas that is at the same time lively and engaging is a rare achievement. Furthermore, in putting these ideas in dialogue with the large political and social movements of our time, juxtaposing them with war, revolution, displacement, and crime, Read is a counterforce to the romantic, the impressionistic, the overly subjective, and the playful and whimsical characteristic of much recent fiction. He supplies a certain gravitas. Read also speaks for a significant and growing number of Roman Catholics who see their religious tradition as the strongest source for clear moral direction in our chaotic age, but who fear that its power to provide that direction may have been seriously undermined by the liberalization of the Church after Vatican II. Most of all, what emerges from the fiction of Piers Paul Read is the conviction that *psychomachia* may not be a dead genre, that nothing is as dramatic as moral choice, and that conscience is the ultimate theater.

NOTES

1. Graham Greene, *The End of the Affair* (New York: Viking, 1961), 109.
2. Of the four writers treated in this study, Piers Paul Read conveys the strongest sense of the sinfulness of illicit sexual behavior.
3. Here again Piers Paul Read is most like the earlier Catholic novelists in his strong critique of the secular world, although it is stronger and more clearly dichotomous in his earlier work. Also, it is balanced by a critique of the Church as well.
4. Kellogg, *Vital Tradition*, 225.
5. Kellogg, *Vital Tradition*, 212.

6. Kellogg, *Vital Tradition*, 224–25.

7. For a thorough analysis of the way in which the ideas of Vatican II as well as those that precipitated much of the confusion and dissent that followed the Council, were present in the first half of the century, see Philip Trower, *Turmoil and Truth: The Historical Roots of the Modern Crisis in the Catholic Church* (San Francisco: Ignatius Press, 2003).

8. Kellogg, *Vital Tradition*, 227–28.

9. Sonnenfeld, foreward to *Crossroads*, vii.

10. Sonnenfeld, foreward to *Crossroads*, xii.

11. Sigrid Undset was a Norwegian novelist and Catholic convert who in 1928 won the Nobel prize for literature for *Kristin Lavransdatter*, a trilogy of medieval life in Norway.

12. Whitehouse, *Vertical Man*, 13.

13. David Lodge, interview by Bernard Bergonzi, *Alta: University of Birmingham Review* (No. 7, Winter 1968–1969), cited in Bernard Bergonzi, "The Decline and Fall of the Catholic Novel," in *The Myth of Modernism and Twentieth Century Literature* (New York: St. Martin's Press, 1986), 177.

14. There were also distinguished pre-Vatican II Catholic novelists in Norway (Sigrid Undset) and in Germany (Gertrude von Le Fort, Elisabeth Langgässer, Heinrich Böll). Undset and Böll each won the Nobel Prize for Literature.

15. Yet the fact that the Catholic Renaissance produced not just outstanding novelists, but philosophers and historians (Jacques Maritain, Gabriel Marcel, Étienne Gilson, Christopher Dawson), and poets and dramatists, (Paul Claudel, Charles Péguy, David Jones) suggests that there was indeed something about the social, cultural, and religious milieu that nurtured such a burgeoning of talent.

16. Sayers, "Being a Writer," 14.

17. Kellogg, *Vital Tradition*, 210.

18. Peter Hebblethwaite, "How Catholic Is the Catholic Novel?" *Times Literary Supplement*, 27 July 1967, 678–79.

19. Whitehouse, *Vertical Man*, 23.

20. Bergonzi, "Decline and Fall," 185.

21. Whitehouse, *Vertical Man*, 24.

22. Alice Thomas Ellis, *Serpent on the Rock* (London: Hodder and Stoughton, 1994), 20.

23. Although the doctors who examined her while she was in the convent said she would need surgery, her back healed on its own.

24. Peter Ackroyd, "Out of Sight," review of *The Sin Eater*, by Alice Thomas Ellis, *The Spectator*, December 24, 1977, 29.

25. John Nicholson, review of *The Other Side of the Fire*, by Alice Thomas Ellis, *Times* (London) December 1, 1983, 13.

26. Julia O'Faolain, review of *Unexplained Laughter*, by Alice Thomas Ellis, *Times Literary Supplement*, September 6, 1985, 972.

27. For this reason, in explicating her novels, I quote more extensively from Ellis than is customary in writing about fiction.

28. Nicholson, review of *The Other Side of the Fire*, 13.

29. James Mustich, Jr., afterward to *Unexplained Laughter*, by Alice Thomas Ellis (New York: Akadine Press, 1998), 158–59.

30. Ellis, *Serpent on the Rock*, 19.

31. Ellis, *Serpent on the Rock*, 22.

32. Ellis, *Serpent on the Rock*, 220.

33. Alice Thomas Ellis, *The Sin Eater* (Harmondsworth, England: Penguin, 1986), 98–99. Ellis says of her writing *The Sin Eater*, "I felt bereft and consequently resentful. . . . I put it in the form of a novel, since novels give better scope for ungoverned rage than more sober works and I had to do something rather than sink into despair." *Serpent on the Rock*, 24.

34. Ackroyd, "Out of Sight," 29.

35. Alice Thomas Ellis, interview by author, London, February 7, 2001.

36. Harriet Waugh, "A Modern Emma Woodhouse," review of *Unexplained Laughter*, by Alice Thomas Ellis, *The Spectator*, August 31, 1985, 24.

37. In an interview Lodge said, "I see that little eighth of Jewish blood in me as one possible source of this delight in comedy and the absurd. I like comedy as a genre, and shrink from heavy emotional drama in other media." John Haffenden, "David Lodge" in *Novelists in Interview* (London: Methuen, 1985), 165.

38. David Lodge, introduction to *The Picturegoers* (London: Penguin, 1993), ix.

39. The interview must have taken place in the early 1990s since Bergonzi refers to *Paradise News* (1991) as Lodge's "latest novel," and his next one, *Therapy*, would be published in 1995.

40. Bernard Bergonzi, "A Conversation with David Lodge," in *War Poets and Other Subjects* (Aldershot, U.K.: Ashgate, 1999), 203.

41. Bergonzi, "Decline and Fall," 180.

42. The novel was written at the time when Catholics were expecting a change in Vatican teaching on this practice.

43. David Lodge, "Memories of a Catholic Childhood," in *Write On: Occasional Essays: '65–'85* (London: Secker & Warburg, 1986), 31.

44. David Lodge, "My Joyce," in *Write On*, 60. Lodge says that although many young Catholics at the university lapsed from their faith, "the more interesting, challenging thing to do was to stay inside the ghetto—or, rather, to pass through its gates without renouncing its fundamental beliefs and values." 60.

45. Lodge, *The Picturegoers*, 173. Lodge here is reflecting a situation that is particularly acute in English Catholicism, also described by Evelyn Waugh:

Elsewhere a first interest in the Catholic Church is often kindled in the convert's imagination by the splendors of her worship in contrast with the bleakness and meanness of the Protestant sects. In England the pull is all the other way. The medieval cathedrals and churches, the rich ceremonies that surround the monarchy, the historic titles of Canterbury and York . . . all these are the property of the Church of England, while Catholics meet in modern buildings, often of deplorable design, and are usually served by simple Irish missionaries.

Evelyn Waugh, "Come Inside" in *The Road to Damascus: The Spiritual Pilgrimage of Fifteen Converts to Catholicism*, ed. John A. O'Brien (Garden City, N.Y.: Image Books, 1955), 6.

46. Woodman, *Faithful Fictions*, 70.

47. Bergonzi, "Decline and Fall," 180.

48. Lodge, *The Picturegoers*, 44.

49. Fraser, *Modern Catholic Novel*, 182.

50. Greeley, *Catholic Imagination*, 166.

51. Sara Maitland, interview by author, Austin, Tex., June 18, 1999.

52. Sally Cunneen, "Big Enough for God: The Fiction of Sara Maitland," *Logos* 6, no. 4 (fall 2003): 123.

53. Sara Maitland, *A Big-Enough God: A Feminist's Search for a Joyful Theology* (New York: Riverhead Books, 1995), 6.

54. Sara Maitland, *Novel Thoughts* (Notre Dame, Ind.: Erasmus Institute, 1999), 19.

55. Dillard, although she has published poetry and a novel, is primarily known for her nonfiction, a kind of prose-poetry that meditates on and celebrates the natural world. She is best known for her first book *A Pilgrim at Tinker Creek*. There is a serious theological strain in her work, and she gives sustained attention to the dark side of nature, which can create serious difficulties for belief in a purposeful creation by a benevolent God.

56. Maitland, *Big-Enough God*, 62.

57. Maitland, *Big-Enough God*, 189, 163. Maitland also states that she wants to see inclusive language used for the devil ("de-sexing Satan so to speak,") as well as for God.

58. Maitland, *Big-Enough God*, 189.

59. Maitland gives the following example of this mindset: The contemporary self "has a primary duty to its own self—'you can't love others until you love yourself,' they say—a notion that would seem bizarre to any mediaeval Christian." *Novel Thoughts*, 4.

60. Maitland, *Novel Thoughts*, 10. Of course, in another sense, belief in Christianity invites closure. The grand Christian narrative has the ultimate happy ending, when every tear will be wiped away (Revelation 21:4). Yet Maitland's attention to Christianity's requirement to undergo the desert or wilderness experience provides a refreshing and welcome balance to so many earlier Catholic novels that stressed Catholicism's neat and tidy answers.

61. Maitland suggests that one of the reasons for the incorporation of so much scientific fact into contemporary literary novels (including her own) is to give them "something solid, weighty, large, and self-authenticating" in the face of the postmodern assault on the meaning of the written word. *Novel Thoughts*, 15–16.

62. Maitland, *Novel Thoughts*, 19.

63. Sara Maitland, preface to *A Map of the New Country: Women and Christianity* (London: Routledge & Kegan Paul, 1983), xii–xiii.

64. I am grateful to Sally Cunneen ("Big-Enough for God," 130) for the insight that these voices function as a kind of chorus.

65. "The Languages of Love," review of *Daughter of Jerusalem*, *Publisher's Weekly*, 30 January 1981, 62; John Naughton, "Leavisites in Yorkshire," review of *Daughter of Jerusalem*, *The Listener* 100, no. 2586, (November 16, 1978): 659; Hermione Lee, "Marriage à la Mode," review of *Daughter of Jerusalem*, *The Observer*, October 22, 1978, 35.

66. When asked about her reason for including so many homosexual characters, Maitland said that it reflected her admiration for the feminists who were so strong and effective in the early days of the feminist movement, as well as for some homosexual friends that she has now. Interview by author.

67. Here and throughout this book, I use the word *catholic* with a lowercase *c* to refer to the broad sense of universal, all-inclusive, or as referring to those Christian churches, including the Anglican and Easter Orthodox, that claim to be part of the original, undivided church and to represent the fullness of the tradition. I use *Catholic* with an uppercase *C* to signify the Roman Catholic Church.

68. For example, Read says, " Seminars were spent discussing whether we could be sure of the existence of the chairs upon which we sat." Piers Paul Read, "A Confession," *Crisis*, September 1994, 15.

69. James Brockway, "Going Down Bravely," review of *Polonaise*, *Books and Bookmen*, February 1977, 23; Malcolm Bradbury, "A Case of Ilychitis," review of *A Married Man*, *New York Times Book Review*, December 30, 1979, 3.

70. Piers Paul Read, interview by author, London, April 11, 2001.

71. Actually, Read's first two novels, *Game in Heaven with Tussy Marx* and *The Junkers*, were highly experimental, showing that Read does have the ability to do something other than straightforward realistic fiction. However, with his third novel, *Monk Dawson*, he adopted the more traditional realistic mode of fiction writing, which he has followed ever since.

72. Paul Ableman, "Booted About," review of *A Married Man*, *The Spectator*, 24 November 1979, 21.

73. Piers Paul Read, "Screwtape Returns" in *Hell and Other Destinations*, 76–77.

74. Anne Janette Johnson, "Read, Piers Paul," vol. 36 of *Contemporary Authors*, New Revision Series (Detroit: Gale Research Inc., 1993), 354.

75. Piers Paul Read, *A Married Man* (London: Secker & Warburg, 1979), 241. This novel was made into a television drama starring Anthony Hopkins.

76. In an interview given in 1999, Read was asked his opinion about the Church's responsibility for the apparent collapse of religious belief in the Western world. He replied, "I believe that the Church lost the plot. Even Catholics do not like it when I go on about supernatural sanctions. If you study the earlier theologians, highly intelligent people like St Thomas More, St John Fisher, and St Francis de Sales, they really worried about people losing their souls. . . . One wonders whether even the most orthodox priests still believe in the likelihood of going to Hell. If you read the Gospels, however, that is what Jesus said. The gate is narrow which leads to salvation." Piers Paul Read, "Piers Paul Read on the Future of the Church," AD2000 November 1999. <http://www.ad2000.com.au/articles/1999/nov1999p8_286.html> (April 6, 2006).

77. Thomas Howard, "*Brideshead Revisited* Revisited," *Touchstone*, summer 1996, 32.

78. Russian critic Mikhail Bakhtin in his book *The Dialogic Imagination: Four Essays* developed the idea of the dialogic narrative. *The Harper Handbook to Literature* explains a dialogic narrative as one that involves "a number of voices in contrasting interplay, none clearly authoritative. In such a work, the knowledge and judgments of a narrator or focal character provide no final meaning but must be measured against the equally valid knowledge and judgments presented from other perspectives." *Harper Handbook to Literature*, 149.

79. From an interview Read gave to the *Washington Post*, quoted in Anne Janette Johnson's essay on Read, 254.

I

ALICE THOMAS ELLIS

4

In the Bleak Midwinter:
The Birds of the Air

*If the Incarnation of God is no longer understood as an event that directly con-
cerns the present lives of men, it becomes impossible, even absurd, to celebrate
Christmas festively.*

—Josef Pieper, *In Tune With the World: A Theory of Festivity*

*Even the sparrow finds a home, and the swallow a nest in which she puts her
young.*

—Psalm 84

The Birds of the Air (1980) is a Christmas story. In the Victorian era,
Christmas stories were a very popular genre of journalistic fiction,
Dickens's *A Christmas Carol* being the best-known example. Dickens's
story ends with the conversion of a mean-spirited miser, but Ellis's *The
Birds of the Air* lacks this uplifting conclusion. Instead it foregrounds the
irony that, in spite of all the sentimental rhetoric of good will, benevolence
and fellowship that characterizes this holiday, Christmas often intensifies
people's loneliness and depression, failing to deliver its promised good
cheer. The novel does, however, resemble the first part of *A Christmas
Carol* in establishing the need for conversion. Yet, whereas Dickens's story
focuses on the need for *one* man's regeneration, *The Birds of the Air* powerfully dramatizes the universal need for conversion. It is a Christmas
story where everyone is Scrooge.

The Birds of the Air has some echoes of another famous Christmas story,
although one not so well known as *A Christmas Carol: The Wakefield Second
Shepherds' Play*, a fifteenth-century mystery play.[1] In this drama some

shepherds complain about their grievous lot in a world where they suffer from the bitter cold, and are oppressed by insolent bailiffs, persecuted by scolding wives, and maltreated by the upper classes. "Thus hold they us under;/Thus they bring us in blunder./It were great wonder/If ever should we thrive."[2] They compound their misery by quarreling with each other. To make matters worse, a peasant steals one of their sheep and tries to pass it off as his newborn child. At the end of the play, however, farce, sarcasm, and ridicule give way to peace and awe as they all visit the newborn Christ child in the manger. Enmity, revenge, and envy are forgotten as they greet the child:

> Hail, darling dear, full of godhead!
> I pray thee be near when that I have need.
> Hail! Sweet is thy cheer! My heart would bleed
> To see thee sit here in so poor weed,
> With no pennies. (728–32)

In *The Birds of the Air* elements of *The Wakefield Second Shepherds' Play* and *A Christmas Carol* are transposed to late twentieth-century England. Parts of the novel share the farcical tone of *The Wakefield Second Shepherds' Play*. Although there is nothing so preposterous as trying to pass off a sheep as a baby, the ridiculous behavior of some of the characters comes fairly close to the shepherds' high jinks. Yet the somber, elegiac mood of *A Christmas Carol* is present as well. It is more pervasive than in Dickens's story, where the hardness of heart is concentrated in one person, perhaps reflecting that Ellis here is working from a conviction of the universality of Original Sin, whereas Dickens—at least in his earlier work—saw mean-spiritedness as more of an aberration.[3] In mood, tone, and theme *The Birds of the Air* could more appropriately be called an Advent story than a Christmas story.

The Birds of the Air opens a few days before Christmas in the home of Mrs. Marsh and her daughter Mary, an unmarried mother whose son has recently died. Deeply depressed, Mary has come home to live with her widowed mother. She feels "like someone for whom a marriage was being arranged by people who doubted the suitability of the match but who could think of no seemly way of retiring . . . treating her with an arch, considered and wholly unnatural care, whispering together and falling silent when they remembered her sitting by the window and possibly listening."[4] As in the *Wakefield Second Shepherds' Play*, where the shepherds complain, "these weathers are spiteful, and the winds full keen,/And the frosts so hideous, they water my eyes" (57–58), the wintry weather is emblematic of the spiritual state of the characters. "The wind had taken over the dark winter garden, growing wilder as the morning passed, rattling through the bluntly pruned twigs of the rose bushes, which clanked like an armoury, and arbitrarily redisposing the few remaining leaves of autumn, sweeping them past her gaze, lost and despairing—the unquiet dead taken by surprise" (7). The simile of the armoury accurately predicts the tone of much of what is to follow, for the characters' interactions are marked by spite, envy, rivalry, anger, and bitterness.

Mrs. Marsh, who considers herself a paragon of civility, politeness, and optimism, is in reality negative and captious. She glances around her daughter's room, "hoping to catch something in the process of untidying itself" (12). Later she brings her daughter lunch on a tray—an apparent act of kindness. Yet the reality is quite different. "'Why didn't you turn the light on?' she asked, though if it had been on she would have asked why Mary hadn't called her to do it, or remarked that too much light was bad for the eyes" (14). Mrs. Marsh's speech, replete with trite maxims, suggests the superficiality of her character. She likes "the human comfort of the cliché" (122). "'Look your best and you feel your best,'" she tells her daughter, urging her to wear make-up (45).

Mrs. Marsh has unbounded belief in her own power, rooted in her determination to outwit whatever forces have caused her pain or inconvenience. "Life had so treated her in recent years that she couldn't trust it to itself for a second. A solitary magpie—vain, god-cursed bird, clad in its eternal half-mourning—flew forever across her mind's eye and had to be propitiated or cunningly foiled with constant changing and rearranging. By questioning and vigilance fate might be deflected" (14). Her small house is crammed full of invited Christmas guests, and she spends most of her time worrying about where she will put them all and how she will feed them. She oversees the whole event with a manner both imperial and condescending. She greets one guest "in a sing-song voice as to a class of five-year olds," causing another guest to fear that "the nursery school atmosphere" would cause him to speak in "careful and toneless monosyllables" (103). She feels responsible for everyone and thoroughly resents it.

Mrs. Marsh's daughter Mary is characterized by her "refusal of comfort and love" (109). So infuriated is she by her mother's suggestion that she put on make-up that she thinks it would be diverting to put lipstick on her nose and eyeshadow on her teeth. Yet in addition to her self-indulgent grief, Mary has one other quality that sets her apart from the other characters—a brutal honesty about herself. "During the painstaking unravelling of feeling into thought, she had realised that she would have preferred Robin to live on, suffering, rather than herself suffer the anguish of loss. There's love, she said, astonished" (53). In another extraordinary moment of insight, when the guests are discussing the sinking of Venice into the sea, Mary realizes that she, in fact, is pleased by the prospect: "She thought that she herself must have that instinct of tyrants, who, when bereaved or upset, respond by demanding huge destruction, comparable to the loss they feel that they themselves have suffered. Sod Venice, she thought idly, imagining the splash, plop, suck, as palaces, churches, paintings, statues, the horses of St Mark sank unprotesting into the turgid flood" (122–23).

Before the Christmas "festivities" begin, the reader is introduced to Mrs. Marsh's other daughter, Barbara Lamb; her husband, Sebastian (Seb), a university professor; and their two children, Kate and Sam. When two of Seb's students are invited over for tea, Sam overhears one of them say, "'Old Lam looks shagged out. He probably spent the morning screwing the Thrush'" (16). Thus Sam learns of his father's affair with the wife of the Professor of Music, who is called "the Thrush." His mother intuits this knowledge at a holiday party she is hosting when she observes her husband feeding a piece of turkey to the Thrush. She sees it as a "playful, lascivious act," one that is so uncharacteristic of Sebastian that she comprehends its dreadful import and realizes what everyone else already knows (25). The devastated and humiliated Barbara can barely get through the rest of the party.

Browbeaten by her overbearing husband, intimidated by his academic colleagues, and mortified by his adultery, Barbara is a pathetic character, especially when she decides she will retaliate by having an affair with Hunter, her husband's editor, even though it should be obvious that he has absolutely no romantic interest in her. Unlike her sister Mary, she lacks both astuteness and self-knowledge. With the comment that Barbara "was unconscious that the reason why she had chosen these comestibles [as Christmas gifts] was that her native thrift rebelled against giving anything more durable to the aged or to one who might be terminally ill" (50), Ellis delivers a triple thrust: at Barbara's niggardliness, at her unawareness of her niggardliness, and at the hollowness that characterizes so much of that most prominent of Christmas customs: the exchange of gifts.

Sebastian, when he isn't feeding turkey to the Thrush, is pontificating to his academic colleagues or expressing irritation with his wife. He is so obsessed with his own interests, pleasures, and comfort that he resents having to go to his mother-in-law's house for Christmas (51). Mrs. Marsh's thoughts about her son-in-law's appearance capture iconically the impression he makes on people. "His head looked as though it had been lightly buttered—so sleek, so unguent and so slight. He made her think of hard roads under a film of rain, shallow and dangerous; of slugs and Nazis and the minister she sometimes met in the terminal ward of the cancer hospital when she was arranging the flowers" (71).

As for the other members of the Lamb family, daughter Kate, described as "formidable" (32), is fond of telling people that she has been writing poetry for years and doesn't hesitate to interrogate a party guest on

Wordsworth. Yet Barbara considers Kate "the child anyone would wish for" (23). Kate evidently agrees and works at being "determinedly winsome" (86) yet ends up being obnoxious. When she insists that her father's editor read her poetry, he reflects that "while this child already clearly had an ego like the liver of a Strasbourg goose it offered her no protection against rejection. Quite the contrary" (128).

Sam is a sullen and bad-tempered adolescent, who wears torn jeans and tennis shoes at his parents' party. Yet his appearance belies the astuteness with which he scrutinizes his parents' guests:

> They reminded Sam of his late peers at Mrs Bright's nursery school, to which all the university toddlers were despatched to be set off on the right foot. It would have been futile to deny that jealousy, ill-will and ambition were powerfully present; but just as Mrs Bright's firm and kindly eye kept the kiddies in check, so ancient usage and the edicts of extreme refinement kept the university from outright shows of pride and hostility. (21–22)

Sam is disgusted by the pretension, empty chattering, and posturing of the guests. "The Canon was nuts, his father was nuts, they were all nuts. The biggest brains in Britain—and all nuts" (27). To amuse himself, he goes among the guests, secretly recording bits of their conversation, and then as the party is beginning to wind down, plays the tape. The flustered guests hear fragments of their conversation: a Canon's fulsome declaration of his humble pride, a woman fawning over someone's "'lovely William-and-Maryish sort of house'" (36), and the Professor of Music telling a ribald joke. The horrified Barbara breaks down sobbing, but the reader's commiseration for her embarrassment is eclipsed by sheer delight at the embarrassment of the pretentious, conceited party guests. Sam struggles with the revelation about his father. Having just recently learned of his father's affair, he hopes to hear one of the party guests say something critical of the Thrush, for "Sam, in spite of his appearance and reputation, was, in matters of sex, an extremely proper, not to say prudish, child" (31).

The reader's heart warms to Sam's uncanny ability to identify vanity, hypocrisy, and self-promotion. When his mother greets a guest with "'How lovely to see you!'" Sam scowls, thinking that his mother "saw that woman nearly every day. It couldn't always be lovely" (21). He is repelled by his grandmother's eavesdropping on his private conversation with Mary.

"Surrounded by moral turpitude, he yet knew that any word of rebuke from him would be considered impertinent, naughty and asking for trouble" (77). It is probably no coincidence that Sam bears the name of a Hebrew prophet. Like most prophets, Sam is a bit eccentric and, like Moses

(Exodus 4:10), not an eloquent speaker, for Sam's conversation rarely consists of anything more than barely understandable muttering. "'No'gorr-acloff,'" he says to his mother when she asks him to wipe the frosted window (133). He wears scruffy clothes and dyes his hair green (in honor of Christmas?). He not only charms the reader, but, as his name suggests, becomes the moral center of the book.[5]

This is the little world awaiting Christmas: an arrogant, unfaithful husband; a humiliated wife; a vainglorious, narcissistic daughter; an embarrassed, perplexed son; a smug, manipulative, officious mother; and a deeply depressed daughter, in whom all emotion has died, except for "one desire—that she might see Robin again—and one fear—that she might not" (76).

The need for Christmas is established, not only through the characters, but through Ellis's pungent satire, which expands the theme to a moral commentary on the larger society.[6] The scene depicting the holiday party at Barbara and Sebastian's home includes some of the strongest satire, mostly directed at academics and literati. Sebastian's publisher Hunter, although himself connected with the intelligentsia through his work, seems to hold himself aloof from this culture and provides a stable, objective center for the satiric critique. He is nonplussed when Barbara, having just discovered Sebastian's infidelity and decided that she will have an affair with him, gives him "a slightly batty smile. . . . The smile alarmed Hunter. Being in the world of books he was familiar with lunacy in all its forms. He had last seen it, he remembered, on the face of an author who had written a book combining the basic principles of zoology with psychoanalysis which he believed beyond all doubt would change the course of the world. He shuddered" (41).

Barbara, although not so conscious of academics' intellectual vanity, is very conscious of their plain bad manners, as when someone puts out a cigar in a quarter of tomato. The wife of the Professor of Music (Sebastian's "Thrush") with "her embroidered ethnic evening bag, hung with tassels and studded with bits of mirror" (25), exemplifies those who express their "individuality" by slavishly following trendy, bohemian fashions. The satirizing of intellectuals continues through the novel, primarily directed at Sebastian, whose "insistence on ordinary language and absolute clarity of expression rendered his discourse entirely unintelligible to the ordinary person" (121).

When the scene shifts to Mrs. Marsh's home, the scope of the satire broadens. Planned retirement communities are satirized in Honeyman's Close, where Mrs. Marsh lives. The name "Honeyman's" is well chosen, considering the cloying language with which it is described. The Close boasts "the unique, inimitable cleanliness and warmth of the small, prosperous suburban home" and has "the well-appointed, walled, enfoliaged, grass-laid peace of modest but sufficient wealth—neater, more stable and more contained than great riches, and far more comfortable" (62). Ironically, the noun *close*, especially in England, refers to an enclosed piece of land surrounding or next to a cathedral. The Cathedral Close is frequently mentioned in Trollope's Barchester novels. Mrs. Marsh's Close, however, is designed, not as part of a sacred place, but to keep undesirables out: "There had been angry consternation when the Close heard that a policeman was to move in to the house next door to Mrs. Marsh's. The neighbours were relieved to learn that he was a Chief Inspector, but still they wished he'd chosen a different place of retirement" (58). Apparently, the undesirables also include children. Although it is nowhere stated that children are not allowed, "most of the neighbours were childless. . . . No tricycles lay about, no balls, no discarded garments" (58). There are no cats, and one family that had acquired a dog had given it away when they realized it didn't fit in. The Close is defined more by what it lacks than by what it has.

This passage on the Close also affords Ellis the opportunity to poke fun at the relationship of the English with animals. "The totem of the English was a small animal—furry, stuffed and articulate. Winnie the Pooh vied with the Queen (God trailing in the distance) for the forefront of the mind of the English middle class" (60). Mary wonders whether any other people "apart from Red Indians, make such a fuss of creatures which in reality they were in the habit of chasing, shooting, poisoning, trapping or beating to death with sticks" (60). The only real animal in the novel (aside from the birds, which will be discussed later), is a mangy kitten, which Mrs. Marsh's neighbor Evelyn has taken from the downs, tied a ribbon around its neck, and given to Mary as a Christmas present. Although Evelyn insists that the animal is very affectionate, it backs away from her, "its mouth open in silent loathing" (80).

There is also a sardonic allusion to British class consciousness. Mrs. Marsh is convinced that Barbara's father-in law, a judge, and mother-in-law, the daughter of a bishop, feel her daughter wasn't good enough for their son. The external markers of their class are their "living in the country, keeping dogs and getting mud on their boots" (54). The critique of these people goes beyond their living habits, for they never "in their whole lives, as far as anyone knew, had suffered any reversal of fortune" and they attribute the problems of the country to "the greed and sloth of the working classes and to something they called the 'politics of envy'" (55).

Mrs Marsh felt towards them the slight fear and hostility, mixed awkwardly with wondering respect, that each layer of the English class structure feels for the layer just above it. They were both, of course—Mrs Marsh and the in-laws—united in their admiration of the monarchy, since the royal succession was secure and no jumped-up entrepreneur or foreigner could aspire to it. The absence of possibility had a soothing effect on the caste system. (55)

For all the disorder and spite present at Mrs. Marsh's Christmas feast, it is still better than the Christmas dinner at Sebastian's parents' house. Sam has obviously experienced it before, for he imagines that "with dogs dribbling at their sides [they'd] be eating rotten pheasant with Smith's Crisps warmed up in the oven, and what his grandfather called 'bread poultice'" (115). For all of Mrs. Marsh's complaining, she does feed her guests a bountiful feast of turkey, stuffing, potatoes, gravy, sprouts, trifle, and Christmas pudding. A parting shot at class consciousness is made near the end of the novel when the next door neighbor Evelyn gives another neighbor her coat and urges her to go home. "Evelyn's father having been a bank manager, she was qualified in such extreme circumstances to give orders to a mere policeman's wife" (150).

There are also some jabs at American culture, called forth by the presence of Mr. Mauss, Sebastian's American publisher. Mary and Hunter laugh together over their image of the American Christmas—"riches, reconciliations, tears, snow, success, sentiment, furs and firs, the shop windows shining like Heaven and everything good for sale" (113–14). Mr. Mauss provides a further occasion for a jaundiced look at the American character when the intoxicated Barbara makes a spectacle of herself. Mr. Mauss is not only flustered, but also a bit angry, for being an American, he "liked all events and occasions—no matter how unfortunate or bloody—to end in sweetness and reconciliation, and it seemed most unlikely that these people would finish the evening in each others' arms singing" (150).

This strong satiric onslaught would be unbearable were it not countered by Sam's anger and candor, and by Mary's depression. Sam's typical adolescent behavior—his scruffy clothes, green hair, and idiosyncratic language—is diverting, and his ability to cut through the cant around him makes him endearing. He is ashamed of his parents and irritated with his pompous sister—all perfectly appropriate and honest reactions.

Mary's depression is the strongest counterforce to the satire. It is deep, pervasive, and terrifying. She is in a kind of living death, just waiting to die. "She supposed she must be dying, and wondered whether, if she touched the window pane with her cold finger, the cold would seep in from outside as though by osmosis" (7). The reader knows that Mary's depression is occasioned by the death of her son the previous summer, but the details are unclear. All we know is that one day two policemen came to her door to tell her of her son's death. Since then, she hates to hear a knock on the door. "Walls and windows too now possessed a strange ambivalence. Dangerous and circumscribing, they no longer represented safety or comfort but merely translated the wilderness into a view—into a humanised, rationalised vision of infinity, the measure of which it was impossible to formulate" (56). Instead of focusing on the human space of comfort, rationality, and imposed order signified by walls and windows, Mary sees a feeble human attempt to tame the wilderness by making it "a view." Yet the wilderness signifies infinity, which—not being subject to human measurement—is oppressive and disorienting.

Throughout much of the novel, Mary is positioned by a window, that "dangerous" place that frames the wilderness without. In the first scene of the novel, she is sitting "by the window, thinking of wilderness, of wastes of ice and sky, of the long wide light, cold beyond sensation or reflection" (9). In the very last scene of the novel, she goes into her room, opens the French windows (windows that are also a door), and steps into the garden:

> She could see the snow falling through the small rounded light from the downstairs lavatory window, a light as pure as from any cathedral clerestory. It fell with such soft determination in the still silence—soundless, weightless: gentle alien blossom that would melt, if she waited long enough, into familiar wetness, tears on the face: bathetic melting, mud in the garden, slush on the roads, useless tears.
>
> She lifted her face to the angelic descent in the muted darkness, to the movement compelled by something other than desire, the lifeless idle movement of the drowned, to the veil, grave cloths, the floating sinking cerements, untroubled by blood, by colour: the discrete, undeniable, intractable softness of the slow snow in the night and the silence. . . .
>
> 'Robin . . . ?' she said. (151–52)

This extraordinary passage ends the novel. The light that descends from above is both heavenly (as if from a cathedral) and human (from the lavatory), thus imaging the true meaning of the feast, a contrast to the sordid revelry inside the house. The light, which comes in quiet and darkness, allows itself to merge with the downward pull of matter, even death. It is appropriate that the book ends with a question, and an unfinished one at that. Although most of the action takes place on Christmas, this is really an Advent book. The mood, as filtered through Mary's consciousness, is interrogative, tentative, "in the dark"—yet attentive and expectant. The verb in this question, however, is *said*, not *asked*. Why? Because the sentence is both interrogative and declarative. It is interrogative because Mary is genuinely questioning what has happened to her adored son, wondering if he still exists, and if so, where and how. Yet at the same time it is a statement because, as symbolized by her stepping outside, she is opening herself up to that question, entering into it, allowing herself to face the emptiness.

In her book *Diving Deep and Surfacing*, Carol Christ says that a woman's spiritual quest, as described by women writers, "begins in an *experience of nothingness* . . . [which] often precedes an *awakening*, similar to a conversion experience, in which the powers of being are revealed."[7] Christ quotes Michael Novak, who argues that the experience of nothingness can, in fact, be liberating and that "a clear and troubling recognition of our fragility, our mortality, and our ignorance need not subvert our relation to the world in which we find ourselves."[8] This is not to argue that at the end of the novel Mary is clearly headed toward some sort of conversion experience. The ending is much more indeterminate than that. Yet she certainly seems more open to some kind of transformation, rebirth, conversion than any other character—and her name *is* Mary, and it *is* Christmas.

The vanity and pretension on display at Barbara and Sebastian's party, Mrs. Marsh's obtuseness about her own inner life, Sebastian's infidelity and callous treatment of his family, Barbara's pathetic attempt to initiate an affair with Hunter, Kate's self-promoting vanity, and Sam's disgust with the moral hypocrisy surrounding him all identify a world in need of Christmas—not the Christmas of artificial festivity concocted from too much alcohol, too many people in too small a space, too much food, and the insipid jokes in the crackers—but the penetration of humanity by divinity, the mystery of the Incarnation. Placing these examples of pettiness, spite, envy, rancor, and cruelty against the background of the holiday that, even for the secular world, celebrates peace, joy, and benevolence makes these failings seem even worse. These behaviors do not constitute a deliberate or conscious attempt to keep God away, but explicit reference to God does make these people uncomfortable:

> "Well, here's to God," said Mary, creating a diversion and pouring herself a whisky.
>
> They stared at her, uncomprehendingly.
>
> "It's his birthday," she said.
>
> Nearly everyone was shocked.
>
> Mrs Marsh felt a great desire to bang together the heads of her daughter and grandson. Christmas was bad enough without this sort of behaviour. (138)

The large number of people crowded into Mrs. Marsh's living room (the children have to sit on the stairs to eat their dinner) is emblematic of the way they clutter their spirits. A feast day, like the Sabbath, should be a clearing of space to spend time with the divine and to refresh the spirit. These people, however, are so befogged by alcohol, rich food, and too much of everything that there is no space for any kind of encounter with God. Josef Pieper suggests that at the heart of true festivity is a basic sense of the goodness of the world and of humanity's existence in it:

Underlying all festive joy kindled by a specific circumstance there has to be an absolutely universal affirmation extending to the world as a whole, to the reality of things and the existence of man himself. . . . By ultimate foundation I mean the conviction that the prime festive occasion, which alone can ultimately justify all celebration, really exists; that, to reduce it to the most concise phrase, at bottom *everything that is, is good, and it is good to exist.*[9]

Mary recognizes that "Christmas was like a storm washing people to and fro to end up, unwanted, in each other's homes: Kate lying like flotsam on the rug, the extraordinarily alien American, the policeman hopelessly out of place, Sebastian bored almost insensible and Barbara lost in unhappy fantasy. What was needed was an ebb tide" (137). Mary's anticipation of this yearly ritual calls forth this trenchant, if irreverent "prayer": "Forgive us our Christmasses . . . as we forgive them who have Christmassed against us" (33).[10]

The Christmas celebration that is the centerpiece of the novel is entirely secular. Sebastian is devoted to making language more precise, believing that it will "overturn all false, all mistaken structures of human thought—such as religious belief—and clear the ground for true human progress" (51). Sebastian disdains—not only religious faith—but even a serious concern with morality, as evidenced by Sam's observation of his father's look of contempt "when faced with an undergraduate trying to derive a moral principle from a set of factual premises" (28). Although Mrs. Marsh's deceased husband had been Catholic, she "avoided all mention of Catholicism in public, considering it, even after her years of marriage to her dear John, not quite nice" (138). She had allowed her daughters to be brought up Catholic, but she had never converted, and Barbara had lapsed after marrying Sebastian. In fact, neither Mary nor Barbara has been to church for ages, as their mother caustically reminds them. Although hardly traumatized by the death of her grandson, Mrs. Marsh *is* sensible to God's whimsical ways. Looking venomously at her peevish son-in-law, she feels "that death was blind or malevolent to take the beloved and leave the Sebastians" (127). Although the subject of Mrs. Marsh's thought is not God but death, it exemplifies the kind of confrontation with limits that, according to sociologist Peter Berger, can become a signal of transcendence—if it evolves into "death refusing hope."[11] Yet Mrs. Marsh's encounter with the intractable fact of death and its capricious ways seems to have produced only cynicism.

Mary, alone of all this group, *does* think about God. Although she is not an enthusiast, she is "resigned to faith, rather than a believer, having no doubts—no doubts, that is, as to the existence of God. Of his mood, his intentions, she wasn't sure. She saw no reason to suppose that he meant her well in the accepted meaning of that term" (85). It is common for people who have had a child die to be angry with God. But this is not Mary's re-action. "Her anger stopped short of God and was sustained by her hatred of death and the little demons in whom she saw herself reflected" (85). In fact, Mary *does* connect Robin's death with God, but in a remarkable, al-most bizarre way:

> Robin's death, the sudden absolute cessation of vaulting, joyful life, seemed to her quite as astonishing and worthy of remark as that other more widely acclaimed and admired miracle, birth. Despite her anger, she thought that God deserved more notice for this extraordinary trick. Even inclined as she was to side in rebellion with the Son of the Morning, she couldn't but praise God for his infinite invention. It was as funny, that sudden shocking silence, as Jack in the Box, a sleight-of-hand performed by a master. (67)

The death of her son has catapulted Mary into a state of astonishment that engenders—if not esteem or love—at least awe. She thinks that God is "beyond the wilderness" (85), which seems to be her way of conceptual-izing the gulf between humanity and God. This is the God of Job, who does not really answer Job's agonized questions, but simply asserts his power and majesty. "I will question you, and you tell me the answers! Where were you when I founded the earth? Tell me if you have under-standing. . . . Will we have arguing with the Almighty by the critic? Let him who would correct God give answer!" (Job 38:3–4; 40:2). Mary de-cides, however, that "God without Robin [is] not enough" and she is un-decided "whether to stay in life, where she had last seen her darling, or to set off in pursuit" (85–86). So Mary enters the Christmas season danger-ously close to suicidal depression.

The novel's title, *The Birds of the Air*, alludes to the bird imagery throughout the novel, from the sparrows hopping outside Mary's win-dow in the first scene, to the names of Sebastian's mistress ("the Thrush") and Mary's dead child, ("Robin") and "the birds of the air" she says should mourn for him (46), to the "quarrelsome birds, peaceful in the darkness, [that shift] their puffed and staring feathers" (149) at Barbara's shocking behavior at the end. For any reader familiar with the Christian gospels, the title echoes the passage from Matthew about God's provi-dential care for even the smallest and most insignificant of His creatures: "'Look at the birds of the air; they neither sow nor reap nor gather into barns, and yet your heavenly Father feeds them. Are you not of more value than they?'" (Matt. 6:26). Further on in the same gospel, Jesus again refers to the care God has for birds, this time in contrast to His own lack of comfort and security: "'Foxes have holes and birds of the air have nests; but the Son of Man has nowhere to lay his head'" (Matt. 8:20). Luke's gospel also records Jesus's use of birds to illustrate God's providential care for humans. "'Are not five sparrows sold for a few pennies? Yet not one of them is neglected by God. In very truth, even the hairs of your head are all counted! Fear nothing, then. You are worth more than a flock of sparrows'" (Luke 12:6–7), and later in the same chapter: "'Consider the ravens: they do not sow, they do not reap, they have neither cellar nor barn—yet God feeds them. How much more important you are than the birds!'" (Luke 12:24). These repeated references to the same idea indicate its importance in the teaching of Jesus.

Another analogy using birds appears in all three synoptic gospels: the comparison of the Kingdom of God to a mustard seed. According to Matthew, "'The kingdom of heaven is like a mustard seed that someone took and sowed in his field; it is the smallest of all the seeds, but when it has grown it is the greatest of shrubs and becomes a tree, so that the birds of the air come and make nests in its branches'" (Matt. 13:31). Almost identical versions of this analogy in Mark and Luke suggest that it encapsulates a central teaching of Jesus. These Biblical passages make Ellis's title richly evocative of God's protective, overarching love for His creatures and the kingdom of God as a sheltering home for them.

The biblical images of birds as lovingly sheltered and provided for are subverted by one of Barbara's childhood memories. When she and Mary were children and would quarrel, her mother would say, "'Birds in their little nests agree.'" Mary, however, cynical even at a young age, would deny it, "pointing out that birds in their little nests spend most of their time trying to shove the other birds over the edge" (52). The bird imagery takes on a sinister and menacing aspect when Mary remembers one summer when Robin had climbed a tree to poke down a crow's nest—not out of vandalism, but in order to prevent their getting down the chimney of the cottage:

> The careless structures of twigs in the chimney were a nuisance, causing damp grey yellow clouds of smoke to billow out when she first lit the fire, but it was worse to open up the silent cottage smelling of the wilderness, trapped, and see the sooty, perfect tracery of desperate wings on the whitewashed walls and know that somewhere there lay a corpse to be disposed of. Crows were stupid enough to fall down chimneys but too stupid to get up them again. (111)

These creatures, like humans, are quarrelsome with their closest relatives, ignorant of where they really belong (the tree/Kingdom of God), and foolish in making choices that endanger them.

The most extraordinary instance of bird imagery occurs when Mary thinks about the fact that all the ingredients in the stuffing for the turkey resemble humanity's confusion. It reminds her of the Second Law of

Thermodynamics, "which suggests that all construction, movement, en-
deavour merely hasten that time when the world and all its works will
be utterly undone, a whirling mass of dust in an infinite desolation" (89).
This thought reminds her of "another feast once, a long time ago . . . in
Melys y Bwyd" (89). Although the tale appears to be inserted into the
novel at this point for no reason, its relevance gradually becomes clear.

A group of ladies and gentlemen are about to enjoy their Christmas
feast when an old traveller, thought to be a holy pilgrim, comes in and is
invited to join the feast. He is dirty and infected with lice, and has a bony
head and a "cold grey gaze" (91). He startles the company by saying that
"'God's angels have a keen *nose* for prayer'" and "'*smell* prayers rising'"
(emphasis added) (93). He then offers to *show* them a story. This use of
synesthesia—angels *smell* rather than *hear* prayers, and he will *show* rather
than *tell* a story—puzzles the guests.[12] But he *does*, in fact, show them a
story. The centerpiece of the meal is a huge swan with several smaller
birds inside its belly. The old man stretches his hand over the table, stares
at the swan, and a strange thing happens. The swan begins to stir, and one
by one, the smaller birds—a wren, coot, pigeon, hen, duck, heron, wid-
geon, and crane—all come to life and fly out of the swan, some up into the
rafters, and some onto the table to drink water and splash in the ale. Then
the doors of the hall open, and the birds all fly out. Not only that, but all
the ingredients of the Christmas feast are miraculously returned to their
place of origin—onions to the earth, spices to Samarkand, honey back to
the honeycomb, almonds back to a tree in Spain, even the cook's spit back
into his mouth.

This bizarre tale has some parallels to the larger story of Mrs. Marsh's
family. Like her, the ladies and gentlemen offer hospitality on Christmas,
but do so grudgingly, fearing "that this holy person might well consume
more of the feast than the invited guests together" (90–91). One warrior,
like Mrs. Marsh's family, is preoccupied with his own troubles. "He was
already in a bad, nervous frame of mind because he feared that the Prince
of his district thought he was growing too powerful and was plotting his
destruction" (92). The tale, however, is also emblematic of the sacred story
celebrated at Christmas, the Incarnation. The unexpected guest at the
Christmas feast is poor and unattractive, and, like the Son of Man, has no
place to lay his head. Yet he is recognized by the company as a "holy, holy
person" (91). He tells/shows them something amazing, and as a result of
his coming, all creatures (primarily represented by *birds*) return to their
home and place of origin. Similarly, the inbreaking of the divine into our
world ultimately makes it possible for human creatures to return to their
heavenly home and their origin in God's creative love.

It is well known that the reason December 25 was chosen as the date for
Christmas was to appropriate pagan celebrations of the lengthening of

daylight after the winter solstice, thus promising the renewal of life in the spring. The feasting, singing, praying, and celebrating in the midst of a cold, dead world is humanity's defiant refusal to admit that death will have the last word. Death stalks Mrs. Marsh's Christmas celebration by the memory of physical death—of Mr. Marsh and Robin—and by the spiritual death evident in bitterness, rancor, spite, and vanity, and especially in the violations of married love in Sebastian's infidelity and Barbara's pathetic attempt at seduction.

Although most of the novel takes place on Christmas Eve and Christmas Day, it is most appropriate to see *The Birds of the Air* as an Advent story. In its poignant presentation of the emptiness at the center of the characters' lives and the hollowness of their forced festivity, it speaks by implication of the yearning that characterizes the Advent liturgy. The opening prayer for the Mass of the first Sunday of Advent begs,

> Father in heaven, our hearts desire the warmth of your love and our minds are searching for the light of your Word. Increase our longing for Christ our Savior and give us the strength to grow in love, that the dawn of his coming may find us rejoicing in his presence and welcoming the light of his truth.

Some reviewers have commented on the two aspects of the book—the witty and satiric attack on contemporary life, especially English Christmases, and its "deeper tonality," which conveys "the absurdity of possessing a soul in a diminished world,"—and conclude that the "philosophic mode is not always comfortable with the more sardonic one."[13] Rather than seeing this dissonance as a fault, however, I see it as contributing to Ellis's portrayal of an Advent world, a world on the brink of the Incarnation, yet so turned in on itself and mired in sin and joyless frivolity that it is unaware of the nearness of the object of its deepest longing. Mary may be determined never to "undergo another Christmas" (123), but she may be entering into a time of preparation for a different kind of Christmas that celebrates by "looking forward to spring, the thin clear light and the rains of hope" (74).

At one point early in the novel, Mary sees "Robin stencilled against her awareness like the geese against the Advent darkness, clear and preternaturally real, quite unlike her tweaked and harassed relations, and shining always with a radiance that graced the living only when they stood against the snow" (45). Her absent and longed for son shines with vitality and definitiveness, whereas her family members, mired in the physicality of their pagan Christmas celebration, lack that clarity. *The Birds of the Air* is about seeing the beloved that is longed for and giving oneself over to that hope. It is about making space for the Incarnation. It is about waiting, wanting, needing—but only Mary seems poised to recognize the approach of the divine.

NOTES

1. Mystery plays were medieval dramas depicting events from Biblical history. They developed from chanted dialogues for the Easter liturgy, and eventually moved outdoors, where they were performed on wagons or stages in city streets. *The Wakefield Second Shepherds' Play* is one of the best examples of this genre.

2. *The Wakefield Second Shepherds' Play*, in *An Anthology of English Drama Before Shakespeare*, ed. Robert B. Heilman (New York: Rinehart & Co., 1959), lines 24–27. All quotations are from this edition and will be cited in the text by line numbers.

3. Dickens published *A Christmas Carol* in 1843, when he was only thirty-one years old.

4. Alice Thomas Ellis, *The Birds of the Air* (London: Penguin, 1980), 7. All quotations are from this edition and will be cited in the text by page numbers.

5. One could argue that Hunter, who seems to be genuinely kind, and Mr. Mauss, who exemplifies a kind of American innocence, are also moral centers; but the novel really focuses on the family—Mrs. Marsh, her daughters, grandchildren and son-in-law—and within this context, Sam clearly has the strongest moral sense.

6. Dickens does the same thing in *A Christmas Carol*, for his tale is a critique, not only of Scrooge's own selfishness and greed, but of that of the larger society as well. This aspect of the story is often lost in dramatized versions but is very evident in the story as Dickens wrote it. Dickens, however, locates the evil in oppressive social systems and is more optimistic than Ellis about individual humans—at least at this stage of his career.

7. Carol P. Christ, *Diving Deep and Surfacing: Women Writers on Spiritual Quest* (Boston: Beacon Press, 1980), 13.

8. Michael Novak, *The Experience of Nothingness* (New York: Harper & Row, 1970), 15, quoted in Christ, *Diving Deep*, 14–15.

9. Josef Pieper, *In Tune With the World: A Theory of Festivity* (Chicago: Franciscan Herald Press, 1973), 20. (Emphasis in the original.)

10. This "prayer" is actually an old joke of Mary's mother that Mary thinks of as she is dreading the coming holiday. The sense of dread about the approach of Christmas thus is not peculiar to the depressed Mary, but on the contrary, is the norm. Certainly it is the experience of all the main characters (with the possible exception of Kate, for whom the holiday provides an opportunity to flaunt her poetic achievements).

11. Peter Berger, *A Rumor of Angels: Modern Society and the Rediscovery of the Supernatural* (Garden City, N.Y.: Doubleday Anchor, 1970), 64. The larger context of this phrase is as follows: "Man's 'no!' to death—be it in the frantic fear of his own annihilation, in moral outrage at the death of a loved other, or in death-defying acts of courage and self-sacrifice—appears to be an intrinsic constituent of his being. There seems to be a death-refusing hope at the very core of our *humanitas*. While empirical reason indicates that this hope is an illusion, there is something in us that, however shamefacedly in an age of triumphant rationality, goes on saying 'no!' and even says 'no!' to the ever so plausible explanations of empirical reason."

12. Synesthesia is the technique of transferring qualities of one sense to another.

13. Edith Milton, review of *The Birds of the Air*, *New York Magazine* 14, no. 35, (7 Sept. 1981): 64–65.

5

Strange Doings in Chelsea: *The 27th Kingdom*

The miracles in fact are a retelling in small letters of the very same story which is written across the whole world in letters too large for some of us to see.

—C. S. Lewis, "Miracles"

Nothing can save us that is possible:
We who must die demand a miracle.

—W. H. Auden

The 27th Kingdom (1982), which reviewer A. N. Wilson called "a brittle, anarchic theological fantasy," is a dark satiric comedy, with affinities to the fable and morality tale.[1] It was shortlisted for the Booker McConnell Prize, one of Britain's most prestigious literary honors. Set in London in 1954, it follows the adventures of a woman known as Aunt Irene and her nephew Kyril when a postulant at the convent where Irene's sister is the superior comes to stay with them for a while. Aunt Irene, whose ancestors were from the Ukraine, had gradually moved away, across twenty-seven lands (hence the title), and come to rest in London—in Chelsea to be exact. Aunt Irene has had two brief marriages but no children of her own. When Kyril's mother died at his birth, however, she inherited a child, who would become the center of her life. "It was as her nephew's aunt that she existed, and she was quite content that this should be so."[2] Aunt Irene enjoys her bohemian friends, her pleasures, such as parties and going to the races, and the antics of her nephew Kyril, although at times "Kyril could be exasperating" (11).

Valentine, the postulant whom Aunt Irene's sister asks her to take in, comes from an unnamed Caribbean island. Although Reverend Mother tells Aunt Irene that she is sending Valentine to her because the young woman must test her vocation in the world, Reverend Mother actually considers Valentine a very promising postulant. The real reason that Valentine must go is the apple in Reverend Mother's desk drawer. This apple, which Valentine picked when the nuns were harvesting apples, has been in her drawer for months, "a large bright flawless apple as crisp and fresh and gleaming as when it had been picked all those months ago" (86). Reverend Mother is waiting for the apple to wither.

> Until it did Valentine could not return, for there was nothing, absolutely nothing, as tiresome, exhausting and troublesome as a fully functioning thaumaturge in a small community. The more volatile nuns would get over-excited and the steadier ones worn out with coping with the vast crowds of sightseers who would jam the narrow lanes and ruin the crops of the neighbouring farms, and throw crisp packets and bottles into the river and the hedgerows, and strip the convent of stones and the orchard of wood for relics. There would be journalists and film cameras and charabancs and all manner of inconvenience. The bishop would be displeased, and no one would get any sensible work done at all. (86–87)

Valentine is very much an outsider: black, Caribbean, quiet, and devoutly religious. She is literally other-worldly. The injection of this alien into Aunt Irene's Chelsea stirs things up and provides the catalyst for many comic situations. Ellis, however, does not rely on her plot to provide humor. Simple descriptions are hilarious. A few examples: "[Michelangelo's] women were really men, cursorily emasculated, with breasts like poached eggs placed randomly on their chests" (22).

Then there is this description of Aunt Irene's cat, Focus.

> Focus was as white as frost. He had long floating fur and eyes the amber of the unclouded peat-stained streams of early spring bearing the late winter's floods—like whisky and water—as though to warm the pale mist of the fur that surrounded his Persian person. He had a flat, rather foolish, face, like a flower, which belied the intelligence and strength of purpose that lay behind it between his symmetrical ears. His appearance was against him, for it is difficult to take seriously something that looks like a down pillow turned inside out. (11–12)

or this description of Aunt Irene's charwoman:

> The bags under her eyes were being joined by other bags coming up in a flanking movement from the sides of her face, and she was grey-white under her pancake make-up, which stopped short of the hair line and in front

of her ears. The woman looked like something the Ancient Egyptians used to keep at their banquets to remind themselves that life wasn't just a bowl of dates and Osiris was hanging about at the end of the passage with his scales handy. (48)

Ellis's humor, however, goes beyond droll descriptions and often becomes trenchant satire. She satirizes the Bohemians of Chelsea with their quaint lace curtains and aspidistras. "At the corner a young couple had obtained building permission to restore a house to a single dwelling and were in the process of painting everything white. They were called Geoffrey and Jessica, or Julian and Jennifer, or something like that" (32).

Ellis ridicules the English obsession with class when Victor, who himself is from a very low class (his family deals in stolen goods), comments to Aunt Irene, who is troubled by repeated phone calls with nothing but silent breathing on the other end, "'It's the workin' classes. . . . They're ignorant, the 'ole lot of 'em'" (47). Aunt Irene tries to instruct Victor about the theory of evolution, although she doesn't really believe it herself. "It was suitable, she thought, for persons of her background and education to dismiss as potty as many theories as they liked, but it was very annoying when the unlettered did it" (83).

Aunt Irene delivers a comic thrust to the English love of horses, for she not only serves horsemeat at her parties, but actually prefers donkeys (as animals, not as food) to horses. "Donkeys were nice little things, but she'd never liked horses—with their barrel-like bodies stuck on those worryingly thin legs, biting at one end and kicking at the other. Thundering round race tracks with people bouncing about on top. No, the beauty of the living horse escaped Aunt Irene" (100). She tells Valentine about English women and horses:

> "People are very funny about horses," she went on. "English ladies fall in love with them at puberty."
> She stopped, realising that her conversation was about to take an indelicate turn. She wanted to explain that most girls progressed to preferring males of their own species—or at least their own species—by the time they grew up. If she had been talking to Kyril she would have wondered aloud why the Home Counties weren't full of little centaurs scowling from prams, trotting across lawns on their little hooves. (107)

Pride in one's lineage, a trait certainly not unique to the English, is also satirized. Aunt Irene's first husband, who was French, used to boast about his lineage, but once he had inadvertently revealed that he was of the house of David. At first she assumed that he was referring to the French painter of that name, but he explained "that he was descended from Jesus Christ and Mary Magdalene who had run away together, crossed many peninsulas and capes and arrived in a tiny town in France where they set up house and had lots of little babies who grew up to be Merovingian kings" (50–51).[3]

As for English cooking, Aunt Irene speculates on ways of being poisoned: "There was the slow but sure method known as English cookery, which meant white flour, white sugar, too much animal fat, too much salt, murdered vegetables, bicarbonate of soda, puddings and puddings and puddings, and salad once a year as a treat for Sunday tea—lettuce, tomato, cucumber and hard-boiled egg all layered together" (105).

Yet cutting through all this mirth is a dark strain. Reminders of death and violence are frequent, and there are grotesque, even macabre elements to the story. Valentine's sister has drowned in a boating accident (which her sister recklessly caused, killing two other people as well), and her father died of grief shortly thereafter. Mr. Sirocco, Aunt Irene's lodger, a painfully shy and timid man, is forced to leave to make room for Valentine and later hangs himself. Mrs. Mason, Aunt Irene's charwoman, is married to an irascible alcoholic. There are hints of violence among Aunt Irene's ancestors, as when she imagines she can hear the "doomed wails of beribboned brides flung from *troikas* to distract and temporarily assuage the ravening wolf packs roaming the steppes and forests in search of honeymoon couples" (8). Even Focus the cat has violence in his background. Because some humans had fondled the kittens, their mother was eating the litter, and Focus was rescued by a friend of Aunt Irene. This introduction of animal violence nudges the whole account toward farce. It teeters on the edge, but is pulled back by the underlying awareness of the predatory violence that is rampant throughout the animal kingdom and which is in such tension with belief in a benevolent creator God.

The most persistent and incisive example of evil in the novel, however, is not physical violence, but the selfishness, nihilism and cynicism of Aunt Irene's nephew, Kyril, who enjoys "drama and disaster and executions" (74). "Kyril resembled a dangerous baby to whom his own desires were of paramount importance and any denial of his wishes manifest of a cosmic outrage" (123). Hearing of Mr. Sirocco's death, he responds, "'Hooray'" (126). Yet even more chilling is his comfortable and unshaken belief in his own mental and moral superiority:

He saw himself as one of those unusual and fortunate men who were able to understand and fully exploit the new insights that were being developed in every field of human endeavor, both scientific and philosophical. Comte, Darwin, Freud, Einstein had, each in his own way, done his bit to soothe Kyril's conscience and smooth his path towards untroubled self-indulgence. Kyril now knew that there were no gods or ghosts, only taboos and neuroses and E=MC², and very nice too. The watches of the night held no terror for Kyril, for were not all things concrete and clear, and all mysteries explained? (110–11)

Christian novelists sometimes make their secular skeptical characters more likeable and ethical—the traditional virtuous pagan—than their religious ones.[4] Ellis, however, is more likely to depict obnoxious pagans. Although this practice can alienate secular readers and even annoy Christian ones, the nihilistic and amoral Kyril is so ridiculous and funny that the technique is more palatable than it is in some novels. Also, Ellis is almost as hard on Christians: Mrs. O'Connor, whose family are scavengers, looters, and thieves, is a Catholic, and Ellis gently ridicules Aunt Irene's use of religion as a palliative. When depressed, she goes to the Orthodox church, and "at the appropriate moments, she would beat her forehead on the floor, and her dessicated ears would swell with the splashing syllables and deep tones of the chanting priests, and she would emerge refreshed" (9). It can hardly be unintentional that Ellis has given Aunt Irene the same surname, Wojtyla, as the late Pope John Paul II, perhaps as a satiric comment on the shallowness of her religious life. The name (the surname of her second husband), is mentioned only once. She doesn't always recognize it as her name. "Nothing wrong with it—she just found it impossible to remember that it was her name too" (37).

Aunt Irene is "slothful and generally cheerful" (8). This phrase nicely encapsulates her character, for she is such an amalgam of endearing and dishonorable traits. She adores her nephew although she is certainly not blind to his faults. She is astute enough to recognize that her indulgence of him has done him no service. "She wished again she had been harder on Kyril, but she had always found it difficult to refuse anything to a beauty. . . . Well, there was nothing she could do about it now, short of dismantling him entirely and starting again, and she sighed" (122–23). Although not as wicked as Kyril, her ethics are questionable. She cheats on her taxes, serves horsemeat at her parties (without, of course, revealing what it is), and is not above lying when it suits her purposes. Still, she is kind to Valentine and solicitous of Mr. Sirocco. She exemplifies the nominal Christian—not depraved or malicious, but not particularly virtuous or honorable. She resorts to church or prayer when she is depressed or desperate, but most of the time forgets about it, keeping both feet firmly planted in the secular world, with only occasional forays into the religious.

Then there is Valentine, the postulant from across the sea. The name is that of a martyred saint, but one whose name has become transmuted and trivialized into that of a cherubic symbol of romantic love.[5] Valentine brings to London a clear, unclouded vision, and a lucid, penetrating, and discriminating sense of judgment.

> She had passed through London before but not noticed how full it was, how dirty: how impertinent the advertising hoardings with their exhortations to people to damage themselves and waste money on things to drink and smoke and put in their gravy. Everywhere there were invitations to commit foolish acts—Do this, Do that, Come here, Go there, Drink Blog's booze, Wear Gubbins's shoes. Unnecessary and intrusive when life was really so simple. It was sometimes extremely difficult, thought Valentine, not to be critical. (72)

The above passage, however, is the closest Valentine ever comes to being critical or judgmental. For the most part, her vision is transparent, limpid, and nonjudgmental. She is defined more by what she is not and what she doesn't do, than by what she is and does. She is unusual in finding Kyril "not irresistible" (23). She loves the convent, was sad to leave, and brings with her an aura of the cloister. Valentine is used to silence and to not seeing herself in a mirror. Even in the convent, she "had moved like a fish through water, accomplishedly, barely stirring the silence" (26). Again and again Valentine responds to comments and situations by saying nothing. Yet her silence assumes a power, a direction, and a meaning. To some extent, her silence was learned in the convent, where speech was forbidden except at certain times. "It was a trick nuns learned: to be very quiet in case of still small voices" (26).[6] Valentine practice of silence carried over to her life in the world. "She felt no need to talk. It seemed to Valentine that there was very little to say, and that what there was had mostly been said. As far as she was concerned, silence was a perfectly suitable medium for the existence of living organisms" (52).

This extraordinary range of characters in such a short novel gives it a fable-like quality, a kind of stretching that creates a full microcosm with just a few characters. Its incisive moral tone also aligns it with this genre. As if to give it a final nudge into this category, Ellis provides an animal character, Aunt Irene's cat, Focus.

> Under the stairs Focus was rolling about in catty paroxysms of delighted mirth. He'd never liked Aunt Irene's kitten, Kyril, who was always complaining about finding white cat hairs on his clothes and in his bread and butter; and he'd morosely witnessed Kyril's numberless conquests, comparing him with the neighourhood's dominant tom, a scratty looking object who stalked Cheyne Row. Focus had been made a eunuch for the sake of the sweetness of the air in Dancing Master House. He was glad, because it enabled him to take a removed and measured view of affairs—human, feline and, indeed, divine. (111)

While it is preposterous to relate the thoughts of a cat, which Ellis does in almost every chapter, she gets away with it without rendering the novel farcical or destroying the realism of her very palpable, albeit eccentric, residents of Chelsea. As the last sentence of the above passage suggests, Focus the cat not only provides humor, but enables Ellis to provide perspectives she may wish to include without being tiresomely moralistic. For example, when Aunt Irene tells an elaborate falsehood about how various important people wanted Valentine to study at Oxford or the Sorbonne or star in a movie, Focus bites her. "He was a straightforward and honourable cat, and his mistress's excesses always annoyed him" (68).

It is a measure of Ellis's skill that, despite the presence of a moralistic cat, bizarre situations and eccentric characters, *The 27th Kingdom* manages to be quite serious about the theme of holiness: its serenity and steadfastness, its affront to the secular world, its connection to the uncanny and the miraculous. Valentine, the prime exemplar of holiness and a life with God, has been living vowed religious life in a convent. The novel illustrates the disjunction between the way convent life is commonly thought of in the secular world and the way it is experienced by those who live it. Aunt Irene speaks for a common view when she tells Valentine, "'I think you and my sister are so clever to cut yourselves off from the cares of the world'" (31). However, Reverend Mother, Aunt Irene's sister, wonders "why people thought the conventual life so simple and straightforward. The problems of the world were as nothing compared with the problems of the Enclosure" (13). Even something as mundane as opening mail provokes an insightful comparison. Aunt Irene apologizes to Valentine for having opened her letter from Reverend Mother by mistake. Valentine, however is used to having her mail opened by the novice mistress and doesn't mind. "It was one of the things that scandalised outsiders, so Valentine didn't mention it. She found it seemly" (57). In Chelsea Valentine is struck by the difference between secular life and convent life, which was characterized by seemliness, order, and restraint. There time "was carefully measured and used, but here the hours and days fell in upon each other in a meaningless jumble, like dominoes pushed over by a drunken hand. There was never enough time, since it was squandered so. Space too was here all cluttered up with Aunt Irene's acquisitions" (66).

This convent/world dichotomy is sharpened when Cassandra, the granddaughter of Aunt Irene's friend Diana, decides she wants to become a nun. This decision infuriates her grandmother, for whom *nun* is "the dirtiest word in the lexicon" (127). Trying to talk her out of this resolve, Diana resorts to the standard cliché about the cloister: "that under every convent lay a tunnelled passage to the nearest monastery and that the younger nuns spent a great deal of time in hideous agony giving birth to illegitimate monklings who were then summarily strangled and flung into bottomless *oubliettes*" (143). Although this belief—the stuff of gothic novels—holds no real currency today, a residue of it lingers in the suspicion that there is something sexually dysfunctional and unhealthy about people who enter convents and monasteries and lead celibate lives.

This contrast between the secular perception of religious life and its lived reality is simply a more focused instance of the larger divergence between the world's view of religion and its essence. This point provides a delightfully comic moment when Kyril recounts an argument Cassandra had at Aunt Irene's party.

> "Well, someone said the monastic life was selfish. And she said yes, wasn't it marvelous how amazingly unselfish married people were—always giving things to beggars and tearing their coats in half and generally behaving in an altruistic and Christ-like fashion. . . ."
>
> "Then someone said religion was responsible for a vast amount of human unhappiness, and she said that in her experience it was sex that made people most unhappy, and she'd never met a girl who was buying six bottles of aspirins because God had got her into trouble and run away; and someone said 'What about the B.V.M.?' and she gave them a very old-fashioned look, and then she said she'd never come across a girl teetering on a window sill because God had left her for the blonde next door. And then she said God had never blacked anyone's eye for refusing his favours." (120)

Aunt Irene concludes that Cassandra must have been drunk to have said anything so outlandish. The conviction that religion entails sexual repression and causes wars and persecutions is a staple of secular thought, and Cassandra's challenges to this accepted wisdom hang in the air, unable to engage the other point of view. The two are simply incomprehensible to each other.

The most sustained comparison between the secular and the sacred is provided by the interaction of Aunt Irene and Valentine. This comparison is first rendered through the description of Aunt Irene's house. Whereas there were no mirrors at all in the convent, in Aunt Irene's house everything is mirrors—walls, ceiling, even the door. Finding this odd, Valentine naturally thinks of vanity, speculating how much Narcissus would have liked this bathroom, but also reflecting that the nuns do not need mirrors for evidence that they exist, thus implying that for the nonreligious mirrors may serve an ontological purpose as well as serving vanity. Aunt Irene's kitchen with its olive green walls, olive brown woodwork, copper pans and flowered kitchen china, a tasteful example of fashionable Chelsea décor, is contrasted in Valentine's mind with the convent refectory, which is "white as bone, the table long and bowed, not with the weight of viands, but with its own. The nuns ate very plain food and every last crumb" (26) whereas Aunt Irene disguises her horsemeat as an exotic stew, cooks aigrettes with fried parsley, and indulges in her favorite Danish pastries, which she calls *cream passionel.*

Aunt Irene is perplexed by Valentine's serene happiness. It is not just that Valentine is not sad, but that she is positively happy. Aunt Irene speculates that perhaps it is the sun that makes island people happy, whereas her own ancestors in cold Russia were morose. Happy or not, however, Valentine seems boring to Kyril and Victor, who like "sweet things, bright colours and loud noises" (44), but Aunt Irene finds herself enchanted by the prospect of simply sitting in stillness with the girl. Aunt Irene is struck by the fact that Valentine

> had nothing and yet had *hilaritas*, while she—with all her things and her people was suffering from *accidia,* that most debilitating malaise. . . . She was tempted to give all her goods to the poor and see what happened, but decided against it. There was no absolute guarantee that in return she would receive the contentment that characterised Valentine, and she'd feel pretty silly, shivering, naked in the world and *still* unhappy. (64)

Put in these mercantile terms, Aunt Irene's consideration of whether Christianity is a good bargain and can be guaranteed to deliver the goods (*hilaritas*) embodies the perennial question of whether Christianity is good because it is useful, or whether it is good because it is true and embodies the right relationship between creature and Creator. Her reasoning seems funny simply because it is put in such stark terms; but in reality, a defense of Christianity on utilitarian grounds is probably much more common—and more persuasive to many people—than one based on philosophical principles.

Another interesting difference between Aunt Irene and Valentine is their relationship to place, in particular, their place of origin, the place of their ancestors. Valentine has deep affection for her island home. She delights in telling Aunt Irene about the foods they eat there and, with "her eyes half-closed against remembered sunshine" describes the people who sell oranges and lemons (105). It annoys Aunt Irene that Valentine should love her country with its background of slavery and oppression. Like Valentine, she imagines the sun beating down on the island, but thinks of it as a place of "torment and grief" (105). Aunt Irene also speculates that it is best not to leave one's native place at all, but to stay rooted rather than risk estrangement, hostility, and harassment. Nor is it a good idea to welcome strangers, who may bring trouble or disease. Aunt Irene, with her "vast and seamless Siberian melancholy" (105), looks with suspicion on both home and distant lands, whereas Valentine is serenely and comfortably rooted in her homeland yet is able to carry that peace with her—even into Chelsea. Thus Valentine's perspective embodies one of the paradoxes of Christianity: the rooted stability (exemplified in religious and monastic life) coupled with the willingness and ability to carry that embedded peace into strange lands (exemplified in missionaries).

Valentine is certainly the moral center of the book, an embodiment of charity, faith, and an intimate relationship with God. As previously stated, her most conspicuous qualities are her quietness and her happiness, and Aunt Irene sees the happiness as foundational, concluding that quietness flows from happiness. This realization makes Aunt Irene want to touch her "as though she were a talisman" (28). It becomes increasingly evident that the foundation of Valentine's happiness is her relationship with God.

Ellis conveys the intimacy of Valentine's life with God in a delightful scene in which Valentine takes upon herself the task of arranging some tiles depicting scenes from the gospels that Aunt Irene has bought from Mrs. O'Connor. Because the gospel story is as familiar to her as her own family history, she recognizes that some important scenes are missing but still puts them in correct order.

> She looked like a girl assembling a family album, Aunt Irene realized suddenly. That loving care belonged to someone trying to remember whether that was the year George had measles, or whether the snapshot of Aunt Ethel in the bathing suit should come before or after the picnic on Beachy Head. She looked like a lover smiling at reminders of the beloved, dreaming of his babyhood, his first words, his last words. (44)

So caught up is Valentine in her intimacy with the Biblical characters that she speaks the words of Christ to Mary Magdalene on Easter morning: "'Noli me tangere'" (44). Why, of all the words of Jesus recorded in the gospels, would Ellis have Valentine say these? Perhaps because it gives Ellis an opportunity to interject this observation. "God was fenced about with prohibitions because he was dangerous and extremely strange" (44). Valentine may be intimate with God, but that intimacy does not imply a cozy, sentimental chumminess. At this point Kyril shatters the aura of respectful awe with the wry comment, "'There should be a sign in Aramaic . . . saying "Keep off the grass"'" (44). Rather than registering insult or amazement at his sacrilegious remark, Valentine, like an Old Testament prophet, delivers a short, incisive warning. "'You should be careful'" (44).

Several references to Valentine's dark skin demonstrate the racism of Aunt Irene's friends and associates. The charwoman, Mrs. Mason, tells Aunt Irene that she doesn't think it right for her to clean the bedroom of a half-caste. Yet Valentine's dark skin becomes for Aunt Irene a sign of health. "'I feel pale,' said Aunt Irene. 'Valentine makes me feel pale. She makes everyone look so unhealthy and maggot-like'" (125). Valentine's vibrant, robust color is a sign of spiritual vitality as well as physical health.

It would be unwarranted to claim that Valentine is a Christ-figure. She does, however, resonate with Christ-like qualities. She comes from another world. She is "vivid and alien—like a tropical angel, bright-winged in the forest darkness" (20). Aunt Irene, depressed by the violence in the world, calls for Valentine, "as though for an emissary from a world less mad" (145). Valentine also seems to have access to secret knowledge. After she tells Aunt Irene the secret of why Mrs. O'Connor is able to store her stolen goods in the parish presbytery, Aunt Irene asks her how she knows, and Valentine says "unsmiling. 'I just know'" (153). The lack of a smile is significant, for this kind of remark is almost always said with some kind of a smirk, a playful pretense of having specialized or privileged knowledge. But Valentine's deadpan manner here raises her ability to a higher level, insisting that her powers are not the stuff of jokes but a serious connection to the source of all knowledge.

Valentine's conjunction with the miraculous seems to be Ellis's way of stressing that Valentine's goodness goes beyond basic human decency or integrity. It is holiness. It is because of what happened during apple-picking at the convent that Reverend Mother sends her away to Aunt Irene's house. Valentine's basket was filled with the very best apples, which were at the top of the tallest and oldest tree and impossible for the nuns to reach, and one of the apples she picked shows absolutely no sign of aging even after many months. Before these facts are made known, however, the reader learns that Mrs. O'Connor, walking down the aisle of the church, sees "Valentine in the doorway facing the altar, dark as a painted saint against the gilded evening, and just for a moment the light that outlined her outlined her completely and Mrs. O'Connor could see light beneath her feet" (60).

The ending of the novel returns to this suggestion of Valentine's supernatural aura. "Thus it was that the Major was the last person to see Valentine fly" (156). The very next sentence, however, pulls the statement strongly in the direction of simple hyperbole. "A dark figure, treading air more lightly than any swimmer ever trod water, flew past his sober and astounded sight and dropped like a gull to the river, where a certain turbulence indicated that someone was drowning" (156–57). This culminating incident is perhaps the best example of the way that Valentine oscillates between the natural and the supernatural, between ordinary human goodness and extraordinary, miraculous sanctity.

Alice Thomas Ellis comes very close in this novel to succeeding what is so rarely achieved in fiction: a character that is both very good and very interesting. Virtuous characters, especially when they are girls or young women, are frequently cloying or sentimental, the archetypal example being Dickens's Little Nell from *The Old Curiosity Shop*. In *Pride and Prejudice* Jane Austen's heroine Elizabeth is attractive because of her sharp wit; her gentler and kinder sister, Jane, is much less interesting. Fanny Price, Austen's completely virtuous heroine of *Mansfield Park* is considered something of a bore by most readers. With Valentine, Ellis has managed to achieve, not so much an attractive, as an engaging character, by stressing what she is not. It is as if Ellis has taken the classical definition of evil as the absence of good, and inverted it, representing good as the absence of evil. Valentine doesn't talk much. When she does, her speech is short, plain, direct, and true. Allied to her scarcity of speech is her minimal movement, which contributes to the strong sense of her stability. The frenetic activity of the people around her seems futile to Valentine, for she is convinced that no people in flight "had ever been able to run fast enough. There was nowhere to keep running" (39). The world of London, as contrasted with convent life, appears wasteful, chaotic, and delusive.

Although Ellis has done a remarkable job of making a virtuous character attractive, some readers do find Valentine a bit dull. Nevertheless, her function as an island of steady serenity and spiritual peace in the midst of this cast of zany, eccentric characters gives her a certain allure. Valentine not only serves as a foil to the secular characters, but also demonstrates the effect that genuine confident goodness can have on evil when it is inserted into the middle of it. She certainly serves as a catalyst to Aunt Irene's musings about faith. "It had occurred to her the other day in church that possibly it was only the good who were *able* to believe in God—that the wicked, being hideously narcissistic, could see only themselves reflected in whatever they looked upon; could believe only in their own desires and inadequacies, were quite incapable of seeing the truth of a different person or deity" (132).

Two reasons suggest themselves as to why Ellis set *The 27th Kingdom* in 1954. The novel derives much of its thematic power from contrasts. Repeated references to the hardships the English endured during World War II are opposed to the self-indulgence and frivolity of Aunt Irene's set. Setting the novel nine years after the conclusion of the war allows for more conscious memories of that time of heroism and sacrifice. Also, religious life is juxtaposed to secular life. Valentine's memories of the convent and her inevitable comparison of her life there with the life she observes in Chelsea provides a striking critique of Aunt Irene's world. Religious life changed drastically, however, after the Second Vatican Council, and if Ellis had set this novel in a later time period, when religious women by and large left the convents to live in apartments, wear secular clothes, and choose their own work, this dichotomy between religious life and secular life would not have been so clear. In one of her nonfiction books, *Serpent on the Rock,* Ellis is candid about her dislike of the way the Second Vatican council changed the Catholic Church. "Nowhere have I found any evidence of Vatican II having had a beneficial influence. In place of the old rigours we have sentimentality, confusion, untruth, meaningless talk of 'renewal' and 'improvement,' and 'sharing,' and 'caring,' where once these were taken for granted and practised in a specifically and recognisably *Catholic* fashion."[7] She also has this to say about the influence of feminism on communities of religious women.

> The Roman Church permitted and encouraged women to form communities of their own, to live autonomously in convents and beguinages. They were allowed to reject men and marriage and the constraints of family life; to take a name other than their patronym and escape from the limitations and irritations of wedlock and a male-dominated society. They had freedom in its true sense, not anarchical but ordered. Now many have abandoned the simplicity of conventual discipline and emerged to demand the spurious freedom of the world.[8]

This is why Valentine has to come from a 1954 convent.

Why does the plot turn on an apple that refuses to age? The suggestion of Eden is unavoidable. Valentine's connection to the apple makes her an icon of a world untarnished by sin. She almost seems to have the preternatural gifts, which Adam and Eve are said to have lost through Original Sin.[9] She does have a kind of innocence, but a kind not to be confused with naiveté. After Mrs. Mason's insulting racist comments, "Valentine shrugged. She had seen evil before. She didn't like it, but it neither alarmed nor surprised her" (60). When Kyril suggests that Mr. Sirocco killed himself in despair because she rejected him, she informs him that the truth is that Mr. Sirocco had loved Kyril. So she is *not* really like the pre-lapsarian Adam and Eve, who fell when they tasted the fruit of the knowledge of good and evil. Valentine sees evil and names it for what it is. She does not, however, retaliate in any way. She belongs to the post-lapsarian world, but as a Christian who through grace is able to transcend the effects of the Fall—transcend, but not eradicate.

On the literal level, what drives Reverend Mother's determination to remove Valentine from the convent as long as the apple is miraculously preserved from the normal process of decay is simply a very pragmatic sense of the chaos that would be introduced into the convent if word were to get abroad that something miraculous is going on there. She is also convinced that "portents, prodigies and the untoward" are not only embarrassing, but are "quite beside the point" (87). On a deeper level, however, Reverend Mother's decision can be seen as an affirmation that one's salvation must be worked out in the muck and muddle of our very fallen world. It is a rejection of gnosticism, the Church's oldest heretical enemy,

which sees only spirit as good and repudiates matter as evil. The orthodox view is that matter, even in a fallen world, is good. The Church acknowledges the existence of miracles throughout Christian history, but
they are seen more as delightful embellishments rather than the substance
of the Christian life. No, miraculous apples simply will not do.

The next to the last paragraph of the novel returns to Reverend Mother
in the convent. She is delighted to notice evidence of decay in the apple.
"Miles away in Wales, the drawer of Reverend Mother's desk smelled like
a freshly tilled garden; of the dead who have finally returned, dust to
dust; of earth. How odd, thought Reverend Mother, that this smell should
fill the living with such hope" (159).

Perhaps not so odd for those who really understand what Christianity
is about. As G. K. Chesterton says in *Orthodoxy*, "The modern philosopher
had told me again and again that I was in the right place, and I had still
felt depressed even in acquiescence. But I had heard that I was in the
wrong place, and my soul sang for joy, like a bird in spring."[10] Valentine
knows that the wrong place—the earth outside of Eden, even with sin,
suffering, and death—*is* the right place. Despite her occasional miracle,
she has her feet firmly planted on the mucky earth and loves her position
as an embodied creature of God.

NOTES

1. A. N. Wilson, review of *The 27th Kingdom*, by Alice Thomas Ellis, *The Spectator*, December 31, 1983, 22.

2. Alice Thomas Ellis, *The 27th Kingdom* (Pleasantville, N.Y.: Akadine Press,
1999), 11. Hereafter cited in the text by page numbers.

3. This theory, of course, is not unique to Ellis. It is found in some of the gnostic gospels and was popularized in Dan Brown's best selling novel *The DaVinci
Code*.

4. A good example is Graham Greene's *The Power and the Glory*, where the
Lieutenant, an atheist, is in many ways a more admirable character than the
priest protagonist.

5. According to the *New Catholic Encyclopedia* (1967), the Roman Martyrology
commemorates two martyrs named Valentine on February 14. One, a priest, was
martyred in Rome, the other, a bishop, at Terni, sixty miles away. There is some
dispute about whether there were actually two different martyrs or simply two
different cults honoring the same person. At any rate, the custom of sending love
notes on St. Valentine's feast day developed in the late medieval period, possibly
because it was believed that it occurred at the same time as the mating season of
birds. s.v. "Valentine, St."

6. The phrase "still small voices" may be a reference to the story of the prophet
Elijah in the First Book of Kings. God told him to stand on the mountain and wait

for the Lord to pass by. There was a strong wind, an earthquake, and a fire, but the Lord was not in any of these. Instead, Elijah recognized the Lord in a still small voice. I Kings 19: 11–12.

7. Ellis, *Serpent on the Rock*, 214.

8. Ellis, *Serpent on the Rock*, 130.

9. Preternatural gifts is the term given to the gifts Adam and Eve enjoyed in the Garden of Eden before the Fall: superior knowledge, integrity, and bodily immortality.

10. Chesterton, *Orthodoxy*, 86.

6

A Cosmic Comedian:
Unexplained Laughter

*A man must sacrifice himself to the God of Laughter, who has stricken him with
a sacred madness.*

—G. K. Chesterton

*To take the Devil seriously is also to take seriously our total and spine-tingling
freedom. Lucifer was an angel who even in Paradise itself was free to get the
Hell out.*

—Frederick Buechner

Is anybody watching? Listen to me. What's so funny? These questions,
which occur so frequently in ordinary life, take on metaphysical dimensions in Alice Thomas Ellis's *Unexplained Laughter* (1985). In a small,
rural village in Wales, an attractive, witty, and sophisticated journalist re-
pairs to her vacation cottage to get over her latest love affair. An unseen
watcher observes the action. There are repeated demands to listen. A mysterious laughter is heard by some characters and not by others. In *Unexplained Laughter* a holiday in the Welsh countryside is the occasion for reflection on God, creaturely limits, mortality, betrayal, and faith, interlaced
with hints of transcendence.

How can a short, witty novel handle such weighty themes? In an afterward to an edition of this novel, James Mustich says of Ellis, "That she
manages to make light of the difficulty of dramatizing the preternatural is

127

one of the wonders of her work." Mustich's description of Ellis's technique bears repeating here:

> Matters of metaphysical moment that are often on the fringes of our awareness—but that seldom raise their heads in the commotion of everyday event [sic] because we are embarrassed by their ominous logic, and by the language, lore and even the liturgy of their superstitious legacies—are slipped into the conversation of Ellis's fictional gatherings with an only slightly disconcerting frankness, appearing (and disappearing) as quickly as a tray of exotic but alluring canapés. With the sleight of hand of a clever and accomplished hostess, the author invites deep themes into the room and lets them make themselves familiar.[1]

The protagonist of *Unexplained Laughter* is Lydia, a highly intelligent, sophisticated journalist with a razor sharp wit and candor that borders on brashness. She has recently suffered rejection by her latest lover, Finn, who has gone off to Greece with another woman. Some of Lydia's beliefs are in sharp contrast to her apparent secular worldliness. She believes in God although she acknowledges that she does not go to church. She insists that this God escapes all our efforts to capture Him in human categories. "'There's a limit to what you can think about God,'" she tells Betty, her houseguest.[2] Yet her lack of knowledge actually contributes to her faith. "'I know he's there because I can't imagine him. . . . If I could I should be extremely doubtful. He'd resemble Santa Claus or someone. Anyone I can imagine is quite unlikely to exist'" (50). Not only does she believe in God, she also believes in Satan, whom she calls Stan.

While drunk at an office party, Lydia has invited Betty, a colleague whom she dislikes, to stay with her at her cottage. Betty is a foil to Lydia: unattractive, unsophisticated, prosaic and dull. Yet she sometimes evinces a kind of common sense that can be refreshing. When Lydia declares, "'Fasting makes one mystical,'" Betty replies, "'It makes one dead after a while'" (24). When Lydia hears mysterious noises that sound like laughter, Betty tries to explain them away as wind, people out for a walk, or a problem with Lydia's hearing.

Lydia is intensely aware of how she looks, not in the sense of fashion, but in her uncanny ability to view her behavior from the outside—sometimes in terms of secular sophistication, other times in terms of her own evolving moral standards. Having Betty with her brings into sharper perspective Lydia's tendency to measure herself against some other standard. "'There was something spinsterish in Betty's plans for her salad, something intimate in her expectation that Lydia would collude with her, and something repellent in the prospect of two single women fussing over food in the kitchen. Lydia was damned if she'd play salads with Betty'" (15).

Betty's conversation is sprinkled with platitudes and moralizing. Yet she harkens back to the long lineage of literary characters that, though deficient in some way, are truth-tellers, such as Tiresias, the blind seer of Greek drama, who sees the truth to which the sighted are blind. More recent examples are some of the characters of Flannery O'Connor, who, though repellent as characters, articulate a reality that the other characters do not see.[3] Although she is constricted by her superficial and conventional mindset, Betty has "the glancing brutality of those with some intuition but not much intelligence" (19). She conveys with the delicacy of a sledgehammer some penetrating insights into Lydia's character.

> "You don't communicate really," said Betty. "You just like telling people things. You don't expect a response."
> "Of course I do," said Lydia. "I wouldn't fancy just standing there yelling into the void."
> "You like people to respond by telling you how clever you are," said Betty. "That's not actually a response. It's flattery." (28)

In addition to coming up with some distressingly accurate insights, Betty also confronts Lydia with disturbing facts. She says that everyone knows that Lydia was quarreling with Finn (Lydia's lover) in the street. Although Lydia insists that she was quarreling with someone else, she is startled to learn that her behavior is common knowledge. Furthermore, Betty's revelation forces Lydia to admit that her unseemly behavior was caused by her getting drunk in distress over Finn's departure, and as the narrative progresses, it becomes evident that Lydia does indeed have a problem with drinking. When she makes disparaging remarks about husbands and wives, Betty says, "'You'd have married Finn like a shot if he'd asked you,'" and Lydia cannot deny it (52). Although Betty appears superficial, she does have an uncanny ability to articulate insights that destabilize Lydia's tenuous sense of self-sufficiency and weaken her hold on her preferred vision of herself. Because Betty lacks Lydia's discriminating and subtle intelligence, she may not fully comprehend or analyze her own insights, but Lydia definitely gets the point.

Beuno is the brother of one of Lydia's neighbors and the only other character whom Lydia considers her equal. He is "the only friend she possessed who was worthy of respect and had reached a peak of maturity from which he would not stoop to tease" (151). Beuno intends to become a priest, and Lydia is pleased with him because it "was seldom she met someone with whom she was in religious accord" (49). He seems to live on a different plane, clear-seeing, intensely honest, and mystical. "'I want to comb God's hair,'" he says in reply to Lydia's question about whether he plans to marry.[4] "'If I married,'" he continues, "'I'd only end up cleaning his shoes. You can't love God and anyone else'" (52). Lydia sees him as "neat and elegant, like all wild animals, with an air of aristocratic insouciance and good breeding. The silly sheep, the witless pheasants, the dumb cows bred by man for his own purposes had lost all joy and definition" (47). Thus Beuno takes on a pre-lapsarian quality, uncontaminated by human society.

The other male characters—Beuno's brother Hywel, a sullen farmer who resents having other people in his home; Wyn, the doctor who seduces Hywel's wife and a neighbor's daughter; and Finn, Lydia's unfaithful lover—exemplify predatory, self-serving and duplicitous humanity. Other minor characters include Hywel's wife, Elizabeth, who has been carrying on a clandestine affair with Wyn; the Molesworths, a retired couple whose staid conventionality infuriates Lydia; and their daughter April, who is Wyn's latest sexual conquest.

Finally there is Angharad, Hywel's sister, who is "'not normal'" (38). Her incongruous statements begin and end the novel. These are the first lines of the book:

> *I think I am dead. I think I have been dead for a long time now. I am Angharad. Do you hear me?*
>   *Listen.* (7)

The last lines are these:

> *The silence is unbroken.*
>   *Listen.* (161)

Thus the novel is framed by commands to listen to a dead person and to listen to unbroken silence. Angharad's startling, poignant, and lyrical observations are interspersed throughout the novel, set off in italics from the rest of the narrative. Her odd phrasing and repeated references to herself as "dead" suggest a disordered personality, yet she has penetratingly clear insight into what is going on. Through her reflections the reader learns of Elizabeth's affair with Wyn. She functions as a transitory omniscient narrator, for she is often hiding and observes without being observed. No one seems to credit her with much intelligence or insight, thus allowing her a privileged place of observation. As she says, "'*they all think I am dead*'" (10).

This small Welsh community—provincial, circumscribed and inbred—leads Lydia to describe the valley as "'a sort of extended nut-house'" (58). Her sojourn here in a place she loves yet always feels she doesn't quite belong in, with a companion she would not have chosen if she had had her wits about her, is an analogue for the human situation. Not surprisingly, the novel includes reflection on and discussion of weighty subjects—death, creaturehood, spirituality, and God—although Ellis's pungent style and scintillating wit keep the discourse from getting ponderous. Lydia's wry but percipient insights, Beuno's candid faith, and the commentary of the narrative voice all serve to satirize fashionable but debased spiritualities, inadequate understandings of creaturehood, and flawed conceptions of God.

Betty embodies several contemporary pseudoreligions. Her approach to life is grounded in empiricism, hygiene, practicality, and politeness. Her empiricism is evident in her readiness to find a simple, rational explanation for whatever is puzzling or mysterious. She concludes, for example, that the reason Elizabeth has no children is her fear that genetic defects run in Hywel's family and would harm her child. Lydia, on the other hand, senses (correctly) something dark and mysterious in their marriage. Betty speaks in comfortable platitudes. "'You must get on with your life, and think about work, and not waste all your time in regrets'" (44). She speaks the language of self-help and positive thinking. Usually Lydia's witty rejoinders confound Betty's attempts at earnestness, yet this ploy does not always work, and Lydia is left confronting her own meanness or some unpleasant truth.

Betty's vegetarianism exemplifies a secular pseudo-spirituality. She explains to Lydia that she is progressing to the purer vegetarian practice of being a vegan, eating no meat or fish, eggs or milk products, and insists that this practice is healthier and not cruel. Lydia punctures Betty's self-righteousness with her pointed judgment: "'It sounds to me intensely cruel. If you forced someone to live on nuts and lentils they'd go roaring off to the European Court of Human Rights or something.'" As well as deflating the righteousness of vegetarians, this comment makes an oblique but sardonic comment on the pervasive "rights" dominance in contemporary ethical discourse. Lydia muses on the paradoxes in contemporary belief systems. She finds "it remarkable that the people who fussed most about their health with particular reference to diet and exercise seemed rather ill, just as those who enthused most warmly about sexual freedom were rather plain." At the same time, however, her finely honed sense of discrimination is not allowed to earn her moral status, for when she says she hates people who go to India, Betty responds with "'I sometimes think you hate everyone,'" and the reader is inclined to agree. When the narrator adds that Betty, who has been portrayed as dull and prosaic, "would have liked to go round India on a bicycle in an orange robe looking for an Enlightened One," a kind of aporia is opened up. (19) Trendy modern spiritualities are rendered silly, but Lydia's discriminating wit is seen as heartless.

When they ask Beuno about vegetarianism, the aspiring clergyman indulges in a classic, if a bit overstated, Christian response:

> "People turn to vegetarianism when the spirit fails. . . ."
> "They are in search of purity, perfection . . . the perfection of the body—while within the spirit rots and withers from neglect, and without the threat of doom trembles on the edge of possibility. Exercised, massaged, bathed and pampered, carefully fed as a prize marrow, the body is an empty shell flaunted in the face of catastrophe." (76)

Beuno's hyperbolic language is deflated by Lydia's asking if he is practicing sermons and by her own version of the same point—"'everyone's scared of cancer and/or the bomb, so they put their heads in the sand and take up jogging and unrefined bran'"—but the point holds (76). To Betty's insistence that people want to hear something "'encouraging and uplifting'" in sermons, Beuno responds, "'There isn't all that much on the bright side. Not if we're truthful.'" A metaphysical abyss hovers as he adds, "'Our only hope rests on the off-chance that God does exist.'" (77)

Sex and romantic love don't fare much better as alternative spiritualities. Lydia repeatedly tests herself to see whether she has recovered from being in love with Finn, as if he were smallpox. Against the background of her own love affairs, her promiscuous friends, the unfaithful Elizabeth, and the predatory Doctor Wyn, Lydia renders this judgment on what is often considered life's peak experience: "'All falling in love is infatuation. . . . Then if he marries you they say it's love. Then when you divorce him they say it's a tragedy because love has failed, when really it's all due to an eventual recovery from infatuation, which is a sort of brain disease'" (84). Lydia imagines that there is a god of love—not the conventional Cupid—but "'the little fat chap who laughs when people make love . . . much older, and oriental in appearance. He sits on a very smokey-looking cloud and he laughs and laughs at the sight of copulation. All his stomachs and his chins wobble'" (49–50).

Lydia's reflections on a dinner party mocks another modern spirituality: the cult of openness and instant intimacy:

> Now, many people as they retrieved their fingers from the handshake were likely to tell you that their husband had just fathered an illegitimate child and ask your advice on how to proceed, or offer to give you the telephone number of their analyst/acupuncturist/homeopath/hypnotist who had been so helpful over their drink problem. No one hesitated to tell you that their spouse was schizophrenic, they themselves alcoholic, homosexual or beastlily promiscuous (no, they were all rather proud of that one), or, of course, that they hated their mother. (48)

The final spirituality that is scrutinized is a pseudoreligion masquerading as genuine religion: the "religion" of some academic theologians. Betty, with her characteristic bluntness, has asked Beuno if he minds being in a Church that doesn't believe in God. "'It's only a few of them who don't believe,' explained Beuno. 'The academics. They get embarrassed at High Table if they think their peers imagine they do. They have to explain that although they're priests they're not really credulous nitwits, and then they feel they have to go further and they end up writing books about it and yapping away on the television'" (49).

These popular modern spiritualities are discussed against the background of the question of what it means to be a creature. Creaturehood means contingency, limits, and ultimately, death. Lighting a fire, Lydia thinks that "everything was composed of heat and corruption and water—that we live off death and water—and she resented her own blinding mortality" and says, "'I wonder what dreadful thing I did to end up as a human being?'" (59). One night she wakes up "with the fear of death upon her" (62). When Beuno asserts, "'The body without spirit is nothing but a carcase . . . a processor for food, stamped with mortality, instinct with corruption'" Lydia reminds him that this is true "'even when the spirit's living in it'" (76–77). The limits of creaturehood are inescapable, even if one has an authentic spirituality. The dead pheasant that Beuno brings to Lydia, and which she hangs outside her cottage until it is "high" is a poignant reminder of death. "There was only one way into life, one way through, and one way out, and it made Lydia mad. . . . Nevertheless she was subject, with all her kind, to the overall rules: chiefly to that most irritating of all which maintains 'You shall not know, you shall not wholly understand why it is this way. You shall just get on with it'" (70). Although humans have an advantage over other creatures in their ability to reason and communicate with language, they still remain largely isolated from their fellows, unable to understand one another. Beuno points out how many different points of view there are in the world:

> "People can be very unreasonable," explained Beuno. "Try and think for a moment how many points of view there are in the world and how seldom people really understand each other. There are those who practise ritual cannibalism and those like yourself [referring to Betty] who won't eat pheasants."
> "I don't understand why people want to climb mountains," said Lydia.
> "And I don't really understand the tenets of Islam," said Beuno.
> "I simply can't see how people can eat tripe," said Betty, shuddering. (78)

Intimations of creaturehood also include a sense of homelessness and a longing to be embedded in a place with roots and stability. Throughout her stay in the valley, Lydia, who has "never belonged to anything," has been keenly aware of her presence as an outsider (70). When she says that their neighbors do not like them, Betty reminds her that Elizabeth invited them to her dinner party. Lydia points out, however, that Elizabeth isn't really one of them, for she had moved there as an adult. "'If it wasn't for her we'd never have set foot in Farmhouse Grim. They don't like outsiders'" (59).

At the same time that Lydia's keen, analytic intelligence judges, categorizes and places all the inhabitants of the valley, she also claims the right of belonging there and refuses to see herself as a vulgar tourist, claiming that her ancestors came from the valley. She tells Betty that she wishes the tourists would all crash their cars and die and that the new house built by the Molesworths would burn down. Preparing to return to London, Lydia is desolate and says she doesn't know where she belongs. Beuno responds, "'With God . . . that sense of homelessness is a reminder of where you belong'" (148). She is determined to return, but as a "migrant bird . . . more like a swallow than an invader." She determines that when she dies, she will be buried in the local graveyard, and no one will be able to "distinguish her dust from the dust of the district" (154). Lydia's predicament reflects the experience of creaturehood: keenly aware of what separates her from others of her kind, angry at the limits that circumscribe human life, dejected at her helplessness in that face of those limits, longing to feel at home.[5]

Being endowed with self-consciousness, humans must choose how to act in the face of creaturely limits. Since satire is grounded in a critique of mores, this theme of creaturehood coalesces nicely with Ellis's deft satiric touch. Yet in this novel morality emerges as a more substantial theme than the book's comic tone would suggest. Reflecting on the adultery and seduction that she knows is going on in the valley, Lydia is struck by people's failure to own up to their behavior: "It was the weakness of humanity that it should disguise as strength—as sense and discretion and neighbourly feeling—an inability to recognise the more deplorable aspects of behaviour. Nice people didn't think about such things, which was why child-abuse and wife-beating went frequently unremarked" (75). Lydia is also struck by the complexity of morality, the fact that good and bad are not tidy, easily controlled categories, but elusive and volatile, escaping all attempts to finesse or manipulate them.

> It was strange how good and bad could run into each other, could appear as interchangeable: not the good of succouring the sick, nor the bad of shooting the helpless, but in the subtler regions of morality where things blended together and seemed to make the business of living easier. . . .
> . . . It was plainly much easier to join the legions of the wicked who weren't fussy and were rather more eager for recruits than the exclusive godfearing.

> Satan ran the sort of club that anyone could join. . . . Being good necessitated much thought and hard work, whereas any fool could be bad. (84)

Lydia's musings comment on human beings' frequent failure to see morality in its depth and complexity, and their preference to reduce it to a few easily agreed upon rules (killing is wrong). Her actions, however, illustrate another human failing—the disparity between what one *says* about morality and what one *does*. Not long after she has this insight, Lydia indulges in a piece of petty cruelty toward Betty. She and Beuno have been discussing the devil, and when Betty approaches them, Lydia can tell that Betty assumes they have been flirting with each other. Lydia knows that Betty is attracted to Beuno and is hurt by what she assumes to be intimacy between Lydia and Beuno. Yet she deliberately not only fails to correct this misapprehension, but kisses Beuno, thus demoting herself from wise moral analyst to conniver in mischief. "The bells of hell went ting-a-ling-a-ling." (94)

This playful comment ties in with the several references to Satan—or as Lydia prefers to call him, Stan. It has occurred to her that simply leaving out a letter "a" would result in this most prosaic of names, *Stan*. If Lydia's belief in God seems a bit eccentric for such a worldly sophisticate, her belief in Satan is truly exceptional. Her question to Beuno, as to whether it is "'altogether wise to be cheeky to the devil'" seems perfectly genuine (92). Their ensuing conversation is remarkable in its portrayal of two modern, intelligent people taking the devil seriously:

> "Do you think he knows we're talking about him?" asked Lydia, not nervously, but *truly* more out of curiosity. [emphasis added]
> "I don't think he's omnipresent," said Beuno, "and he isn't omniscient. He's not the opposite of God, which would mean he'd be as powerful. He has to keep going all the time—to and fro about the world and walking up and down in it. No, I don't think he's listening. His presence is unmistakable. . . ." [ellipsis in the original]
> . . . "Very occasionally I have strongly sensed his presence. *His* undoubted presence. But he doesn't need to attend to much personally. His hobgoblins can cause a lot of disruption, and simple ordinary people are remarkably good at being bad." (92)

This passage, like many in the novel, is a remarkable blend of frivolity and seriousness. Beginning with Lydia's question about being "'cheeky to the devil'" and Beuno's remark that "'I wouldn't seek him out, but if by mischance he should loom up before me I should waggle my fingers at him'" (92), the passage makes important theological points about the pervasiveness of human sin and the power of Satan before ending with another foray into the whimsical. "'I keep wondering what he'd do if I wandered up to the edge of the pit and leaned over and yelled, "Oi, you down there. Stan!"'" says Lydia. "'I expect he'd gnash his teeth in impotent rage,'" replies Beuno (93).

This dialogue beautifully illustrates one of Ellis's techniques for talking about religious themes to a secular readership. Even if one brings to the novel knowledge of her religious views, the playful tone, the witty repartee, the comical image of Lydia leaning over the edge of a pit and calling Stan, all keep the scene poised in a position of delicate ambiguity distanced by irony. The narrative voice shares Lydia's and Beuno's belief in the devil, making comments like "Satan, who finds work for idle hands to do, also fills idle minds with fruitless speculation" (73–74). Here, as with the reference to "the bells of hell," the narrator transcends Lydia's lack of insight into her own complicity with Stan. Although Lydia does recognize that her vindictive attitude toward Finn is wicked, she is quick to excuse it on the grounds that it is caused by another's sexual misbehavior. "Lydia felt strongly that the author of the universe probably thought much as she did about sexual matters. She really did have a long way to go, and she had not yet learned to recognise the precise lineaments, the demeanour and the shape of the shadow of Stan" (124).

Seeing oneself as creature implies a creator, and at least for Christians (and Lydia has identified herself as a Christian [50]), a relationship with the transcendent creator. This playful yet serious belief in Satan is the ballast for belief in God, a belief that, while much more common than belief in Satan, is almost as likely to be trivialized and mutated into something more comfortable and congenial to modern life. For Lydia, however, faith in God is anything but a comforting prop. "'I believe in God myself, . . . but on the whole this belief inconveniences rather than supports me. It makes me feel inadequate and toad-like when I would prefer to feel rather wonderful and extremely happy'" (148). Lydia's statements about God repeatedly contravene conventional sentimental notions of God as a comforting security blanket. She also attacks the popular notion that goodness is nonjudgmental and that therefore God, being all-good, must be totally nonjudgmental about human behavior. "It is only the virtuous who can be truly cruel" thinks Lydia. "Guilt and a sense of common humanity make people less harsh. It was the utterly excellent Yahweh who told the malefactors to go to hell" (84).

Beuno is Lydia's only real partner in dialogue about God. Finn, who has returned from Greece and turned up at Lydia's cottage, responds with cynicism when Lydia mentions God. She tries to explain to him that Beuno is "'in love with God,'" but his retort, "'What do *you* know about the love of God?'" shocks her into the realization that her normal discourse of wit, irony, and sarcasm will no longer serve. "Lydia had discovered, to her own surprise, that she found the matter too significant to quarrel about in a childish way. If she was going to quarrel about it at all she would have to do it seriously" (143). Betty typically lapses into sentimental clichés when the conversation veers toward the religious, but one of her observations is all too accurate. To Lydia's assertion that she likes God, Betty protests, "'You don't show much sign of it. . . . You never go to church and you're not very charitable.'" Lydia is forced to agree but adds, "'God makes me laugh.'"[6] Betty's pointed reply is, "'Perhaps you make *him* laugh. . . . Perhaps it's him you keep hearing'" (49).

These references to God as a kind of cosmic comedian relate to the overarching theme alluded to in the novel's title. Lydia's first words in the book are "'What was that?'" in reference to a strange noise she hears as she and Betty are wading across a stream to get to her cottage. Betty has a ready explanation: "'It's an owl'" (7). From that point on there are repeated references to a mysterious noise that Lydia insists is laughing. Betty is usually ready with naturalistic explanations like animals or wind or a problem with Lydia's hearing. At one point she halfheartedly suggests ghosts but quickly recants, adding "'There's no such thing as ghosts'" (35). At one point Lydia acquiesces to Betty's suggestion of tourists out for a walk, but "she somehow knew it wasn't" (36). Allusions to this mysterious laughter punctuate the narrative, and no proffered explanation is really conclusive: hence the title, *Unexplained Laughter*.

When Elizabeth, who is Angharad's main caregiver, is told about the mysterious laughter, she fears that the visitors will suspect Angharad, noting that the girl sometimes frightens people without meaning to. The implication that Angharad might be the source of the noise persists, for she is an unseen presence, often hiding, overlooking the action far more—and understanding far more—than anybody imagines. Angharad is fully cognizant of Elizabeth's affair with Wyn, and she intuitively understands Elizabeth's feeling for her. *"Elizabeth does not love me, but she does not always hate me, and when she brushes my hair perhaps she means to be kind"* (90). Elizabeth often worries that Angharad is out on the hills, so the suggestion lingers that the girl may be the source of this mysterious noise, especially since no other explanation is on offer. James Mustich evidently accepts this explanation when he writes in his afterward to the novel that Angharad "teases this visitor with the uncanny laughter that disturbs the comprehensive silence, both real and figurative, in which the valley dwells."[7] Yet such an explanation does not fully satisfy. Not everyone hears the laughter that Lydia does. Betty sometimes hears something, but finds some reassuring naturalistic explanation. At her suggestion of wind down the valley, Lydia insists it is someone laughing. "'Roars of laughter'" (118). Beuno is able to hear it and agrees that it is laughter, but he can't tell where it is coming from. Lydia insists that "'It's all over. . . . It comes from everywhere'" (118). Beuno believes that the important question is not how but why. "'*How* is a question asked by the foolish and answered by the trivial'" (119). Their ensuing dialogue takes up the suggestion that this laughter may be connected with God. Beuno tells Lydia she should not be frightened.

> Beuno went on. "Laughter and evil can't coexist. There's nothing funny in hell."
> "It's not just evil that frightens people.'" Lydia reminded him. "Jehovah was wont to scare the pants off the Israelites—or whatever it was they girded up their loins with."
> "Only when they were naughty," said Beuno comfortingly. (120)

Beuno's playful riposte does not negate Lydia's important point that throughout history, gods have more often been scary than loving.[8] Fear of the Lord is still one of the seven gifts of the Holy Spirit, however uncongenial that may be to contemporary religious temperaments. This desire to dispense with the angry Jehovah of the Old Testament has a history as long as Christianity. Marcion in the second century was excommunicated because he wanted to exclude all of the Old Testament from the Christian Bible, for he was convinced that such a fearsome deity could have no relation to the God of love revealed by Jesus.[9] Certainly the laughter that Lydia and Beuno hear is more eerie than jovial, suggesting that if it is somehow connected with the divine, it is more akin to the God of transcendent mystery than to the God we address as *Abba* (Daddy).

Lydia makes the important distinction that not everything that produces laughter is true humor. Slapstick, which can make people laugh, is based on chaos; but Lydia, who hates mess, believes that real humor "'comes out of precision, not chaos'" (120). Beuno, however, considers the second law of thermodynamics "'extremely funny because all the things we are all so busy doing only hasten the inevitable end. Earnest misapprehension is very funny'"(120). Beuno's point suggests that humor emerges from a God's eye view of human life. Lydia is quite right to point out that laughter is not necessarily a sign of harmony or good will. Laughter can also be sinister and—when the source is not known—downright threatening.

Although Lydia is frightened when she first hears the laughter, she later tells Beuno that she is *not* frightened. Indeed, she seems to have taken a kind of ownership of it. At the end of the novel, the laughter seems to have disappeared, and Lydia wonders what has happened to it. Beuno says he has exorcised it. The possibility of Beuno having really exorcised the laughter both discounts the idea of a purely naturalistic explanation for it, and also problematizes its association with the holy, for exorcism refers to driving out an evil spirit, not a good one. At any rate, Lydia is annoyed. "'It was *my* laughter. . . . You might've asked'" (149). Beuno says he did it because of the same instinct that causes one to turn off a dripping tap, no matter whose it is, and Lydia understands. "'Yes, I know,' said Lydia. 'Like things out of place. The secret behind surrealism. It gives you a bit of a turn, but then you realise how essentially childish it is, and somehow dangerous'" (140).

Thus the laughter is not so much evil as "out of place." Like a dripping tap, it may be a sign that something is wrong; but *unlike* a dripping tap, it is dangerously seductive. The temptation to get swept up into the surreal, the miraculous, the extraordinary must be resisted. Beuno's reminder that "'Children have a sense of order, of propriety, but haven't yet understood quite where things should be'" (149) applies to all humans, who are in one sense children, living in a world they don't understand and cannot control. Intimations of transcendence through extraordinary phenomena can be titillating, but may also, as Beuno suggests, distract one from the more important task of seeing God in the ordinary events of everyday life. As Beuno says to Lydia when she asked him about where to find God, "'Here, of course. . . . But no more here than anywhere else. You'll find him just as easily on Paddington Station if you happen to be looking'" (116–117).

The laughter is associated more with Lydia than with any other character—not only because she is the one who *always* hears it, and who hears it as *laughter*—but also because she herself laughs often. Very early in the novel Angharad reports that she had seen "*the woman*" (obviously Lydia) and heard her laugh. "*She lay on her back and laughed up at the sky*" (18). Lydia's own humor is witty and cynical and is frequently her way of dealing with the "'extended nut-house'" of the valley, and of life in general. For example, as soon as Lydia conjectures that Betty has come to the cottage to make sure that she doesn't harm herself as a result of depression because Finn has left her, she emits "a sudden giggle, helpless to prevent it" and thinks how amusing it would be "to make a big splash and drowning noises" (22). Throughout the novel, Lydia's wit is refreshing and bracing, cutting through cant and hypocrisy and silliness, although it often has a mean streak to it. At the end of the novel as she heads back to London, Lydia thinks she will give a party "and have a good laugh" (155).

Perhaps this laugh will be "good" in a sense that goes beyond the usual meaning of "hearty" in this familiar phrase. For the haunting laughter in this novel is connected with Lydia's coming to a greater sense of herself as a creature. Her very reason for being at the cottage exemplifies the constraints that define humanity. She is struggling to get over a disappointing love affair that ended in rejection and betrayal. Everywhere she is reminded of the finiteness of humans' abilities to transcend selfishness and the short reach of their attempts at generosity. From Beuno's characterization of the human body as "'nothing but a carcase'" (76) to the treachery of Doctor Wyn, the deceit of Elizabeth, and the misanthropy of Hywel, Lydia is repeatedly confronted with humans' mean estate. She tells Beuno that when she was a child, she used to wonder what her pet bunnies did when she wasn't watching and that sometimes they were eating their babies. Beuno remarks that in case Lydia is wondering what will happen to the people of the valley when she leaves, "'They will go on eating their babies'" (146). Death, predation, and cruelty are everywhere in nature and in human life, however much contemporary urban people try to hide or camouflage them. During this holiday in Wales, however, Lydia cannot avoid seeing them. Linked to her awareness of human limitations and mortality is her continuing sense of homelessness. "But the sorrow was there still, the sorrow of not belonging." The valley may be "an extended nut-house" but she is "almost in tears with the misery of departure" (58, 154).

Lydia's awareness of mortality and human limits as well as the mysterious laughter have brought her to a heightened sense of herself as not only a creature, but a flawed, or—in Christian terms—a sinful creature. In addition to her vanity and her tendency to drink too much, on this holiday she must confront her own inclination to cruelty. She is condescending to Betty and taunts her. She revels in her own sense of superiority to the local people and deliberately plans a picnic near a place where she knows there are drawings on a rock that will embarrass Doctor Wyn. She is, however, usually aware of these failings. "She knew the recent conversation had been fantastical, with faint cruel undertones, and that it had excluded Betty, who was a good little thing." Even more impressive is the image that concretizes this insight. "She now felt herself to be like the squirrel, staring with bright inimical eyes at a sad domestic beast" (53). Lydia has enough honesty and self-awareness to realize that in some ways Betty is her superior. "Lydia had to admit that Betty's eagerness to admire and approve of people, while annoying, was a good characteristic and one that she herself lacked" (79).

Although she is more intelligent, witty, and perceptive than all the other characters except Beuno, what distinguishes Lydia is her openness to transcendence. She hears the laughter. She believes in God and resists the temptation to anthropomorphize, contain, or tame Him. Furthermore, she believes in Satan and takes him seriously. Although Lydia had these traits before this holiday in Wales, they have been strengthened. Her conversations with Beuno have crystallized and enhanced her belief in God.

Beuno, of course, does share her openness to transcendence, and a more conventional or more romantic novel might have Lydia and Beuno falling in love and planning a life together at the end of the novel. Surely Lydia is attractive enough to make Beuno change his mind about celibacy. From the beginning of the novel, they have communicated and connected in a way that no other two characters do. Yet Lydia from the beginning sees that Beuno could not be a candidate for a new romance.

> His quality of ruthless innocence rendered him unsuitable for most human intercourse. While neither a saint nor a psychopath, he clearly had some of the characteristics of both—chiefly what Lydia could only think of as a sort of selfless solipsism. He was a person of disinterested good will and he wanted no return from humankind. These people are fortunately few and far between because they are extremely odd and have a way of upsetting apple-carts. Lydia could quite see Beuno maddeningly getting himself martyred on some trivial point of principle, or overturning a regime with his angelic intransigence. (82)

Yet as Lydia's partner in God-talk, Beuno has contributed to the emotional health she has been seeking far better than would a new romantic interest. One reviewer speaks of "their attraction of minds" that "allows her to glimpse the possibility that goodness might be worth having and even obtainable. They have a love affair of the spirit."[10] It is not insignificant that Beuno is named for the seventh century missionary and monk who evangelized much of North Wales. There is a legend that when his niece was beheaded by a jilted suitor, Saint Beuno placed the severed head back on her body and she lived. There were also miraculous healings reported at his tomb. Like his patron saint, Beuno helps to put Lydia back together and heal her spirit.[11]

Whatever has happened to Lydia during this holiday, Angharad has played an important part. Who or what is she? What does she represent? Literally, of course, she is a mentally handicapped girl, incapable of speech, but with a rich inner life and acute powers of observation. Lydia has seen her in the graveyard and thinks she doesn't "look quite human" and that "the girl might have lacked an umbilicus; might have come straight from the hand of God, who having finished making the mountains had picked a bit of clay from under his thumbnail and fashioned just one more sort of person, perhaps as an experiment" (32). Although largely unseen, Angharad affects others' lives, but most of all, she watches—and watches other people watching.

> *I have watched him before, watched him watching Elizabeth as he puts his arm around a girl. He watches her face and he smiles the way he smiled when I broke my bones. No one but me knows he is smiling because his mouth does not move. But I know. I have seen him with his girls in the fields and when he knows I am watching he kisses them. (90)*

All of this emphasis on watching goes beyond the common human experience of feeling that someone out of sight is watching you to a sense of wonder about what Mustich calls "a watching in the world—a wakefulness—attentive to our thoughts and deeds."

> Silence can seem so alert. We could assign our sensitivity to mere anxiety, but there are times, I'm certain, when our anxiety is summoned by an unseen audience. In the shadow of its vigilance (whatever its meaning, intention, or intelligence), the very idea of the holy takes root, as the world urges us to repay its watchfulness in kind.[12]

As previously noted, the last words in the novel are Angharad's.

> *They have gone. The winter will come soon. I wish I was flying now. The silence is unbroken.*
>   *Listen.* (155)

These few phrases gather up several themes of the book: the sense of homelessness and transience, the chill of mortality, humanity's reckless desires, and most striking of all, the paradoxical command to listen to the silence.

As Lydia drives back to London, her spirits are rising as she plans to have a party and a *"good* laugh [emphasis added]" (155). She may have a sense that, as clever and perceptive as she is, she is watched by a presence much more discerning and that, even as she is listened to, she must take greater care to listen—and to continue to watch out for Stan.

NOTES

1. Mustich, afterward to *Unexplained Laughter*, 158–59.
2. Alice Thomas Ellis, *Unexplained Laughter* (Pleasantville, N.Y.: Akadine Press, 1998), 49. Hereafter cited in the text by page number.
3. Examples are Manley Pointer in "Good Country People" and Mary Grace in "Revelation." Flannery O'Connor, *The Complete Stories* (New York: Garrar, Straus and Giroux, 1971), 271–91; 488–509.
4. This passage which indicates that celibacy is an option—not a requirement for the priesthood he seeks—clarifies that Beuno is planning to become an Anglican—and not a Roman Catholic—priest.
5. In Mary Shelly's novel *Frankenstein*, the artificially created human being constructed by Dr. Frankenstein, although commonly referred to in popular culture as a *monster*, is actually designated throughout the novel by the term "the Creature." He is tormented by the same feelings and perplexities that beset Lydia: a sense of separation from other humans, astonishment at their ill treatment of one another, and frustration at the limitations—despite his extraordinary brute

strength—that impede his efforts to achieve the community and harmony he desires. The Creature's anger at his creator's failure to love and care for him is not reflected in Lydia's experience, although, like the Creature, she *knows* she has been created and cannot help but wonder about the Creator's curious ways.

6. G. K. Chesterton also associated mirth with God: "There was some one thing that was too great for God to show us when He walked upon our earth; and I have sometimes fancied that it was His mirth." *Orthodoxy*, 168.

7. Mustich, afterward to *Unexplained Laughter*, 159.

8. In his classic *The Idea of the Holy*, Rudolf Otto says human beings experience the numinous as *"mysterium tremendum"* (tremendous mystery). Religious experience arouses creature-consciousness, "the emotion of a creature, submerged and overwhelmed by its own nothingness in contrast to that which is supreme above all creatures." Rudolf Otto, *The Idea of the Holy*, trans. John W. Harvey (New York: Oxford Univ. Press, 1958), 12, 10.

9. Marcion wanted to include in the Bible only a shortened version of Luke's gospel and ten of Paul's epistles.

10. Harriet Waugh, "A Modern Emma Woodhouse," 25.

11. <http://www.saintpatrickdc.org/ss/0421.htm> (July 31, 2006).

12. Mustich, afterward to *Unexplained Laughter*, 157–58.

II

DAVID LODGE

7

✝

Re-inventing Catholicism:
How Far Can You Go?

A good novel about a few people merely trying to get by may seem a rather small achievement. If so, then perhaps we have lost sign of the value and purpose of fiction.

—John Podhoretz, Review of *How Far Can You Go?*

The more thoroughly we can revise the liturgy, the more thoroughly we can revise the church's images of God and teachings on morality.

—R. R. Reno, *In the Ruins of the Church.*

How far can an unmarried Catholic go in kissing, hugging, or petting before falling into mortal sin? This perplexing question of moral theology provides the title of David Lodge's sixth novel, *How Far Can You Go?* (1980).[1] Lodge makes the reference explicit four pages into the novel when he explains that "a favorite device of the bolder spirits in the sixth form to enliven Religious Instruction was to tease the old priest who took them for this lesson with casuistical questions of sexual morality, especially the question of How Far You Could Go with the opposite sex. *'Please, Father, how far can you go with a girl, Father?'*"[2]

In his earlier novels *The British Museum Is Falling Down* (1965) and *Out of the Shelter* (1970), Lodge had used Catholic material primarily for sociological background and comedic possibilities.[3] In *How Far Can You Go?* (1980), not only does Lodge adopt a more critical tone, but Catholicism is not just the background or context, but the sum and substance of the subject matter. The novel chronicles the changes that have taken place in the Catholic Church since the 1950s. As with *The British Museum Is Falling*

Down, the Catholic material is rich fodder for comedic possibilities, what with the problems of chastity before marriage, dissident priests and nuns, liturgical high jinks, and of course, birth control. Nevertheless, a new note of theological depth and seriousness enters in, aptly expressed in the question that forms the title, "How far can you go?" Older Catholics immediately recognize the question with which young Catholics have traditionally sought to learn how far they could go sexually without falling into mortal sin. On a deeper level, however, the title raises a more philosophical question—one with no easy or definitive answer.

The more complex and profound question at the heart of the novel is how far can you go in changing the forms—liturgy, traditional devotional practices, and language that embody and express religious beliefs—without undermining the theology and faith for whose sake those forms exist? According to Catholic historian Eamon Duffy, "Lodge's point . . . is that the Catholic metaphysic was inseparable from the tight web of Catholic practice."[4] Mary Ann Glendon has said "all the most divisive controversies of the post-conciliar years were about how far Catholics can go in adapting to the prevailing culture while remaining Catholic."[5] One critic has also suggested "the title refers not only to morality but to Lodge's fascination with the games of fiction."[6] The semantic richness of the title is unfortunately lost in the American edition, which was published as *Souls and Bodies.*

The main character in *How Far Can You Go?* is the Catholic Church itself. The institutional Church is integral to many Catholic novels, but primarily as background—looming, mysterious, monolithic—against which the drama of an individual Catholic's spiritual struggle is played out. In others, such as Graham Greene's *The End of the Affair* or Evelyn Waugh's *Brideshead Revisited,* the whole thrust of the narrative is to bring the protagonist to the point of entering the Church. In *How Far Can You Go?,* however, the Church itself is really the main character. The novel has many characters but no single protagonist, for it follows the lives of eight young Catholics, their spouses, and a priest. What is extraordinary about these characters is that they are so ordinary.[7] They are middle class; most of them marry and have children, work at ordinary professions, and face the same problems and frustrations as most of their readers. The theme is the experience of being an average Catholic in the two-thousand-year-old Roman Catholic Church in the latter half of the twentieth century. What gives the tale piquancy is that these ordinary Catholics find themselves in a hierarchical and authoritarian institution that, with the Second Vatican Council, the sexual revolution, and other social upheavals of the 1960s, finds itself propelled into turbulent change.

The novel is much more, though, than a well-researched, realistic novel about an interesting era in religious history, although it is all of that. It also explores in a poignant and sensitive way some central questions about religious experience and the capacity of an institutional church to give structure and coherence to that experience, particularly in the world of the late twentieth century when innovation, evolution, and flux have accelerated to a degree previously unimaginable.

The novel contains many metaphors for the Church. The first one is the dismal interior of the church of Our Lady and St. Jude, where in the opening chapter the university students are attending a weekday mass. The weather and the setting establish the tone: "An atmospheric depression has combined with the coal smoke from a million chimneys to cast a pall over London. A cold drizzle is falling on the narrow nondescript streets north of Soho" (1). Inside the church the atmosphere is not much better:

> Inside the church of Our Lady and St Jude, a greystone, neo-gothic edifice squeezed between a bank and a furniture warehouse, it might still be night. The winter daybreak is too feeble to penetrate the stained-glass windows, doubly and trebly stained by soot and bird droppings, that depict scenes from the life of Our Lady, with St Jude, patron of lost causes, prominent in the foreground of her Coronation in Heaven. In alcoves along the side walls votive candles fitfully illuminate the plaster figures of saints paralysed in attitudes of prayer or exhortation. There are electric lights in here, dangling from the dark roof on immensely long leads, like lamps lowered down a well or pit-shaft; but, for economy's sake, only a few have been switched on, above the altar and over the front central pews where the sparse congregation is gathered. (1)

This description can be read as an icon of one view of pre-Vatican II Catholicism.[8] The language—*greystone, squeezed, feeble, stained, soot, bird droppings, lost causes, fitfully, paralysed, dangling, pit-shaft, for economy's sake, sparse*—create an impression of weakness, infirmity, ugliness, and decay. The church is being squeezed by a bank and warehouse, symbols of the modern secular and commercial world. The traditional stained-glass windows admit little light, partly because the light itself is dim, and partly because of dirt and stains (perhaps the Church's own shameful past—worldly and corrupt clergy, the Crusades, Inquisition, condemnation of Galileo and so forth). The Church is associated with lost causes. The saints depicted in the statues seem to be paralyzed, suggesting that *all* they can do is pray or exhort, but not really live and interact in the modern world. The last sentence, with its reference to "dangling from the dark roof" unavoidably suggests a hanging. The literal reference, of course, is to lamps, which *could* conceivably light up a dark space, but "only a few have been switched on" even though Christ exhorts his disciples in Matthew 5:15 not to put one's light under a bushel basket. Is it a false economy that keeps the light feeble and ensures a sparse congregation? This is an image of the Church on the eve of the Second Vatican Council, which, in an attempt to modernize, to "open the windows and let in fresh air," as Pope John XXIII said, would shake and unsettle that ancient institution to a degree probably unforeseen by anyone.

In addition to this powerful opening image, the meaning of the Church is explored with some analogies. Lodge uses the analogy of a children's board game to describe the metaphysical worldview of the young college students attending this weekday mass.

> Up there was Heaven; down there was Hell. The name of the game was Salvation, the object to get to Heaven and avoid Hell. It was like Snakes and Ladders: sin sent you plummeting down towards the Pit; the sacraments, good deeds, acts of self-mortification, enabled you to climb back towards the light. Everything you did or thought was subject to spiritual accounting. It was either good, bad or indifferent. Those who succeeded in the game eliminated the bad and converted as much of the indifferent as possible into the good.... On the whole, a safe rule of thumb was that anything you positively disliked doing was probably Good, and anything you liked doing was probably Bad, or potentially bad—an "occasion of sin." (6–7)

The analogy is elaborately extended. Venial sins were "little sins which only slightly retarded your progress across the board. Mortal sins were huge snakes that sent you slithering back to square one" (7). Purgatory was a "kind of penitential transit camp on the way to the gates of Heaven" (7). An indulgence was a "kind of spiritual voucher"(7) while a plenary indulgence is a "kind of jackpot" (8). Lodge's comic effect here can probably be fully enjoyed only by Catholics old enough to have been taught this worldview in the days before Vatican II when Catholic catechesis stressed definitions, categories, and terminology, and when sin and the afterlife featured much more prominently in religious instruction than they do now.[9] Nevertheless, all readers can appreciate the jarring disjunction between the metaphysical seriousness of such matters as the ultimate meaning of life, morality, the afterlife, salvation, and damnation, and the trivial amusements of a children's board game. The convoluted discussion of the "Catch-22" nature of indulgences increases the darkly comic effect: "But there was a catch: you had to have a 'right disposition' for the indulgence to be valid, and a spirit of calculating self-interest was scarcely that. In fact, you could never be quite sure that you had the right disposition and might spend your entire life collecting invalid indulgences" (8).

The board game analogy accentuates the fact that the Catholic faith functions as a kind of insurance policy, which is the second analogy. This game of spiritual Snakes and Ladders is not played for fun, but out of self-interest. The young people are attending this weekday Mass (when they are not obliged to) because "they believe it will stand them in good stead in the next world. . . . Religion is their insurance—the Catholic Church offering the very best, the most comprehensive cover—and weekday mass is by way of being an extra premium, enhancing the value of the policy" (16–17).

Early in the novel Lodge interjects a reminder that religion is not just a collection of rules to order sexual behavior, but is tied to the most fundamental questions of human life: Is there any purpose to our lives? Is there ultimate justice? Is there a life after death? Is there a God who loves us? After describing each of the students attending the early morning mass, with particular attention to their sexual experience and inclinations—and in some cases the lack thereof—Lodge shifts his attention to the only other members of the congregation, two pious old ladies. They are "Good women, pious women, but of no interest" (15). Pointing out that the old ladies "are certain to die in the near future," the narrator wonders why the young people are not "curious to determine whether a lifetime's practice of the Catholic faith and the regular reception of its sacraments has in any way mitigated the terrors of that journey, imparted serenity and confidence to these travellers, made the imminent parting of the spirit and its fleshly garments any less dreaded. But no, it has not occurred to any of them to scrutinize or interrogate the old ladies in this way" (16). Thus Lodge slips in the disquieting notion that, although certain aspects of religion may be ridiculous, it does claim to offer answers to the most basic human questions, consolation in suffering, and order and meaning in what seems to be a random and chaotic world.

Yet the two old ladies, the reference point for these concerns, are described as unattractive, pathetic, even slightly ridiculous. Going to communion, they shuffle "forward with painful slowness on their swollen feet," and kneel at the altar rail, their "heads nodding gently like toys on the parcel shelf of a moving car, their eyes watery and myopic, their facial skin hanging from their skulls like folds of dingy cloth" (15). As they receive the host, the acolyte is disgusted by their "trembling discoloured tongues and loosely fitting dentures" (16). Not only are they physically repellent, but their inner life is feeble and desiccated. When the priest hears their confessions of "trivial peccadilloes," he has to prompt them with some suggestions of venial sins, for they are increasingly incapable of envy, anger, and covetousness, let alone lust, gluttony, or sloth (16). Their failure to sin is not an achievement; it is a deficiency. They are noteworthy—not for a surplus of grace—but for a lack of vitality. They truly belong in this gloomy church.

Why are these representatives of traditional piety described as so repellent? The congregation in the church—the attractive but shallow students and the pathetic if earnest old women—personify a tension at the heart of religion. The larger questions of meaning and mortality are of little interest to the young and vibrant, for as Lodge says of his young Catholics, "none of them actually believes he or she is going to die" (16). Instead, their attention is focused on how their religion regulates and constricts their sexual lives. Of course, they are greatly interested in knowing "how far they can go" without committing mortal sin; but this concern springs from a shallow desire to avoid hell, rather than from any serious interest in the philosophical or moral questions religion purports to answer. The old ladies, on the other hand, do take the big questions seriously. Yet their life of faith seems to have left them—if not spiritually dead—at least lacking any kind of robust inner life. The students have vitality, but are shallow and self-calculating. The old ladies are spiritually anemic and pathetic. What we do *not* see is an exemplar of a spiritual life that is serious *and* vigorous, mature *and* dynamic.

For the young students the strongest feature of the Catholic Church is its identification with sexual repression. It is a kind of moral Gestapo, making sure that eros is kept at bay, lest people enjoy themselves too much. Although most religions impose some kind of discipline to contain the chaotic and powerful force of sexuality, at least in terms of contemporary religions, Catholicism has the reputation of being particularly harsh and repressive in its sexual morality. In the first chapter the young people attend a St. Valentine's Day party sponsored by their Catholic student group. They perform a skit portraying a couple making passionate love on a sofa. However, the back of the sofa is to the audience, and it "is all done, rather cleverly, by Polly alone, using her four limbs and a collection of male and female attire" (27). When their chaplain Father Brierley observes this display, he is horrified and scolds them severely. "The Catechism, he reminds them, explicitly forbade attendance at immodest shows and dances as an offence against the sixth commandment. . . . He was surprised, he was shocked, he was disappointed" (27–28).

The young people are embarrassed and disgruntled. Polly ends up in tears. The reader's sympathy is definitely with the students and against the puritanical priest, who has ruined a little innocent and harmless fun. But Lodge adds a note of interest to this rather stereotypical scenario of the mean-spirited clergyman ruining other people's fun when he reveals Father Brierley's conflicted feelings after the incident. After a night of being "tormented by the memory of Polly's stockinged leg waving in the air above the back of the sofa" (29), he tells his pastor that he is having impure thoughts about this girl. The scene dissolves in comedy when the pastor ingenuously asks him, "Have you tried ejaculations?" (29).[10]

This early scene inaugurates a major theme of the novel: the tension between Catholicism and eroticism. The two pillars of Catholic sexual morality (at least in the minds of the students)—sexual abstinence before marriage and no artificial contraception after marriage—continuously militate against a spontaneous, unabashed, exuberant expression of their sexuality. The frustration of their erotic energy plagues them all in different ways, but plague them it does—at least as long as they remain connected to Catholicism. Polly, the one character who seems most immune to suffering from scruples, who gives up her virginity easily and with a certain joyful abandon, also drifts away from the Church, marries a divorced man, and leads a completely secular life. There are some hilarious scenes where engaged couples struggle with the temptation to "go all the way." Ironically, one of the couples gives in to this temptation when they go on a retreat for engaged couples, where by some mistake they have turned up at a retreat for married couples and been given one room. Once having enjoyed the bliss of sexual delight, the couple is unable to restrain themselves further, and the bride is pregnant on her wedding day.

This theme reaches its culmination about halfway through the book when Lodge breaks the spell of realism, leaves behind the narrative voice, and gives a rather extended analysis of the Church's teaching on artificial contraception, Pope Paul's encyclical *Humanae Vitae*, which reaffirmed the ban, and Catholics' widespread dissent from it. Rather than slide unobtrusively into this other voice, however, Lodge forcibly calls our attention to his shift. "The omniscience of novelists has its limits, and we shall not attempt to trace here the process of cogitation, debate, intrigue, fear, anxious prayer and unconscious motivation which finally produced that document" (114).

> Thus it came about that the first important test of the unity of the Catholic Church after Vatican II, of the relative power and influence of conservatives and progressives, laity and clergy, priests and bishops, national Churches and the Holy See, was a great debate about—not, say, the nature of Christ and the meaning of his teaching in the light of modern knowledge—but about the precise conditions under which a man was permitted to introduce his penis and ejaculate his semen into the vagina of his lawfully wedded wife, a question on which Jesus Christ himself had left no recorded opinion. (115)

This trenchant satire is fascinating because it refuses to indulge in easy answers. Lodge points out that this "was not, however, such a daft development as it seems on first consideration, for the issue of contraception was in fact one which drew in its train a host of more profound questions and implications, especially about the pleasure principle and its place in the Christian scheme of salvation" (115). Not only was contraception the crack in the dam that would lead to a general lowering of sexual moral standards, but it also called into question the credibility of the Church as a reliable moral teacher.[11] If the Church had been wrong on contraception all along, one could only wonder on how many other points she had been mistaken?[12]

This ongoing theme of sexual repression and the teaching on contraception is imbedded in a matrix of larger religious questions, exemplified by the early scene with the two old ladies attending mass. This dimension of the novel gives it a weightier substance and keeps it from being just one more amusing diatribe on a repressive Catholic upbringing. As the novel proceeds, it interjects reminders that although faith may provide a system of meaning and answers to important questions, it also requires faith that sometimes strains and cracks under the pressure of lived experience.

One of the students, Michael, becomes engaged to Miriam, a non-Catholic. Although she converts to Catholicism at the time of her marriage, Miriam is troubled by doctrines such as the Immaculate Conception and the Assumption. "'Christianity is hard enough to believe in without adding all these unnecessary extras,'" (58) she complains. Michael, in fact, is also "uneasy about the Assumption, for which there didn't seem to be one jot or tittle of Scriptural evidence" (58). Miriam also has trouble with the Catholic doctrine of the mediation of saints, especially Mary. "'Do you mean,' she asked, her tulip-cut of glossy copper-coloured hair thrust forward with the urgency of her question, 'that if *A* prays to Jesus via Mary, and *B* prays direct to Jesus, *A* has a better chance of being heard than *B*, other things being equal? And if not, then why bother going through Mary?' Neither Michael nor Father Conway had a satisfactory answer to that one" (59). Miriam is discovering that Catholicism is what C. S. Lewis refers to as "thick" as opposed to "clear" religion.[13] Unlike a clear religion that is clear, rational, and demystified, a thick religion is one that gives a prominent place to mysticism, ritual, and ceremony, has an elaborate and complex belief system, and includes metaphysical and miraculous elements that are an affront to enlightenment rationality.

Problems with faith are not limited to the laity, however. When Father Brierley becomes disgruntled with parish work, especially with his pastor who seems to care only about money, he is given the opportunity to take a refresher course in Biblical Studies. He is shocked at what he learns there:

> It came as something of a shock to discover that views mentioned formerly only to be dismissed as the irresponsible speculations of German Protestants and Anglican divines who could hardly be considered seriously as Christians at all, were now accepted as commonplace by many Catholic scholars in the field. The infancy stories about Jesus, for instance, were almost certainly legendary, it seemed, late literary accretions to the earliest and most reliable account of Jesus's life in Mark. . . . And the Virgin Birth itself, then—was that a fiction? . . . And the Resurrection. . . ? Well, here even the most adventurous demythologizers hesitated (it was another kind of How Far Could You Go?) but a few were certainly prepared to say that the Resurrection story was a

symbolization of the faith found by the disciples through Jesus's death, that death itself was not to be feared, that death was not the end. (88–89)

Furthermore, not only are these ideas shocking in themselves, but Father Brierley sees a disturbing fissure in what used to be seen as solid, homogeneous Catholic orthodoxy. "It seemed to him that a dangerous gap was opening up between the sophisticated, progressive theologians and exegetes on the one hand, and ordinary parochial Catholics on the other" (90). Father Brierley sees it as his mission to educate the laity in these new ideas about the Bible, to try to close the gap.

Father Brierley gets his chance to startle the complacent laity when there is a terrible mudslide in a mining village in South Wales, burying an infant school with some hundred and fifty children and teachers. Lodge meticulously articulates the theological dilemma: "The school was due to break up at midday that Friday to begin the half-term holiday, and had the landslide occurred a few hours later, and destroyed an empty building, it would have been called a miracle in the popular press; but as it did not, it was called a tragedy, the part, if any, played in it by God being passed over in tactful silence" (106).

Here Lodge dramatizes a common, but seldom acknowledged, inconsistency in Christians' behavior. When they are spared in a disaster or accident that harms or kills other people, they thank God for watching out for them, neglecting to mention the obvious corollary: that God evidently was *not* watching out for the others. In response to this tragedy, Father Brierley, now back doing parish work, chooses to preach on the book of Job. He argues that the appropriate response to such an event is neither to see it as punishment for sin nor to accept it as the will of God, but rather, like Job in the Old Testament, to complain and speak of one's bitterness. Job did this and was rewarded with a theophany, an overwhelming manifestation of God's presence and power. Father Brierley, expecting his congregation to be somewhat shocked by his message, is disappointed to see only "blank, bored faces" in the congregation (107). His pastor questions whether "making people doubt the goodness of God" does any good, but Father Brierley's fierce response is, "What are we, then, his priests or his public relations officers?" (108). The parishioners' boredom may be a form of resistance to Father Brierley's formidable challenge to develop a more honest, if less comforting, kind of belief and their reluctance to give up the consolations of a childlike faith.

The confrontation of simplistic faith with the problems posed for belief by life in the modern world takes on cosmic proportions when Father Brierley (now referred to by his first name, Austin)[14] is visiting Miriam and Michael and joins their son Martin in the back garden to look through his telescope. Pondering the immensity of space and the enormous age of the universe, Austin wonders how to reconcile this data with the Christian story:

> Had other Christs died on other Calvaries in other galaxies at different times in the last twenty billion years? Under the night sky, the questions that pre-occupied philosophers and theologians seemed to reduce down to two very simple ones: how did it all start, and where is it all going? The idea that God, sitting on his throne in a timeless heaven, decided one day to create the Universe, and started the human race going on one little bit of it, and watched with interest to see how each human being behaved himself; that when the last day came and God closed down the Universe, gathering in the stars and galaxies like a croupier raking in chips, He would reward the righteous by letting them live with Him for ever in Heaven—that obviously wouldn't do, as modern theologians admitted, and indeed took some satisfaction in demonstrating. On the other hand, it was much easier to dispose of the old mythology than to come with anything more convincing. When pushed to say what happened after death, the most ruthless demythologizers tended to become suddenly tentative and to waffle on about Mystery and Spirit and Ultimately Personal Love. There was now something called Process Theology which identified God with the history of the Universe itself, but as far as Austin could understand it, the only immortality it offered was that of being stored in a kind of cosmic memory bank.
>   "I'm going in," he said to Martin. "I'm getting cold." (171)

Father Brierley may be talking about the temperature of the air, but his re-mark suggests a metaphysical chill as well. The universe seen through the eyes of modern science and technology seems forbidding, heartless, and chilling.

As soon as Austin comes in the house, Michael asks for Austin's advice about his son's indifference to religion. Austin's answer: "'I should leave him alone, if I were you'" (171). But Michael entreats him to speak to Mar-tin, complaining that his son's religion classes "'seem to be all about be-ing nice to immigrants and collecting tights for Mother Teresa'" (171–72). This little scene, so familiar to Catholic parents, reveals a tension at the heart of contemporary Catholicism.[15] Under the pressures of scientific dis-coveries about the world and modern Biblical scholarship, it has become increasingly difficult to affirm the seminal Christian doctrines of Original Sin, the Incarnation, the Atonement, and the resurrection of the body in any way that harmonizes with a contemporary worldview. Miracles, vi-sions and other metaphysical aspects of the religion are de-emphasized to the point of disappearing. The part of Christianity that is palatable to modernity is social justice and interpersonal ethics, so that is what is mostly preached and taught. Catholicism is becoming more of a "clear" religion and less of a "thick" one.

The result, however, is that Catholicism comes to seem little different from benevolent, secular humanism.[16] More importantly, it offers little reassurance in the face of the terrors of a cold, empty universe, random evolution, and materialistic determinism. When Michael suggests that Austin have a chat with Martin, Austin replies, "I have already. . . . I'm learning quite a lot" (172). The irony of the priest, who is expected to be the teacher, becoming the pupil of the adolescent boy points up how the ancient Church, which used to be confident that it had all the answers, is experiencing a metaphysical upheaval. The carefully crafted formulas and definitions that emerged from the Council of Trent in the sixteenth century will no longer serve. They certainly will not do for the young people like Martin, who find Christian dogmas—not so much irrational—as simply irrelevant. Whereas their parents' only real problems with Catholicism had been its restrictions on their sexual lives, the younger generation is just indifferent to religion.

The new emphasis on ethics and social justice absorbs some of the religious energy that can no longer confidently embrace the central Christian mysteries, but not all of it. As scientific and other kinds of knowledge exert enormous strain on religious belief, other types of nonintellectual religious experience come to the fore. The emotional component of faith is attracted to the charismatic revival, which simply sidesteps the vexing scientific, historical, and anthropological issues and concentrates on intensely emotional and personal religious experience.

Ruth, who has joined an order of religious sisters, gets caught up in this spiritual movement while visiting the United States. She participates in emotional prayer meetings where people speak in tongues, sing exuberant music, practice the laying on of hands, and pray for healing. Although Ruth is at first repelled by this behavior, she eventually finds herself profoundly moved and decides that her previous faith had been desiccated and inadequate: "'All my life as a nun there's been one thing missing, the one thing that gives it any point or sense, and that's, well, real faith in God. It sounds ridiculous, but I don't think I ever had it before. I mean, I believed in Him with my head, and I believed with my heart in doing good works, but the two never came together, I never believed in Him with my heart.'" (179)

Back in England Ruth prays over Edward, who suffers from a back problem, and the next day the pain is gone. The following day, however, the pain is back. Tessa, Edward's wife, thinks, "I shall never be a real Catholic. . . . I don't really believe in the power of prayer" (189). Although Tessa is a convert, whose "conversion" was mainly to accommodate Edward when they married, her comment about miracles probably expresses the sincere feelings of many Catholics, as reluctant as they might be to admit it. Miracles, until recently an integral part of being a Catholic,

now seem to many the stuff of legends and medieval paintings and irrelevant to the more urgent claims of social justice or the thorny questions of
sexual morality.

Another way of coping with the chaos and fragmentation of religious
beliefs is to embrace fundamentalism. Violet, who is emotionally unsta-
ble, is addicted to tranquilizers and eventually spends time in a psychiatric hospital. She becomes a Jehovah's Witness and is convinced that the
Catholic Church is the Whore of Babylon, that celebrating Christmas is
un-Christian, that Adam was created in 4026 BC, and that the 1,000 year
reign of Christ on earth is about to begin.

These fundamentalist "facts" and the histrionic enthusiasm of the
Charismatics can seem funny, as did the students' convoluted struggles
to remain sexually pure. They can also seem trivial compared to the major philosophical religious questions that weave through the novel, but
Lodge has an uncanny way of linking the comic and the philosophical.
In the middle of a scene with comic (and often sexual) ambience, he will
introduce a reminder of the big questions. At one point Tessa has bought
a facts-of-life book for children for an acquaintance who had mentioned
needing something like this for his child. When she attempts to deliver
it, however, she spies through his window the man locked in an embrace
with his child's babysitter, his head "clenched between her fat thighs"
(188). Tessa flees and offers the book to her taxi driver to use with his
own children or to give to someone else. The title of the book is *How Did
I Get Here Anyway?* The driver comments, "'A good question . . . I've often wondered myself'" (188). The statement immediately takes on a
metaphysical resonance since the adult taxi driver obviously knows the
biological facts of life. Juxtaposing the ludicrous sexual scene Tessa has
just witnessed with the metaphysical wonder that often initiates the
search for God yokes the two realms together in a way that is both jarring and thought provoking.

A similar technique is used in the scene where Ruth, having wandered
away from her first charismatic prayer meeting after being put off by the
"strange noises, keening and coaxing and crooning sounds," ends up in
Disneyland (176). She enters "a world of appearances, of pastiche and
parody and pretense. Nothing was real except the people who perambu-
lated its broad avenues" (177).

It struck Ruth that Disneyland was indeed a place of pilgrimage. The cus-
tomers had an air about them of believers who had finally made it to Mecca,
to the Holy Places. They had come to celebrate their own myths of origin and
salvation. . . . For all their superficial amiability and decency they were *be-
nighted*, glutted with unreality. Ruth began to recite to herself the words of
Isaiah: *"For the heart of this nation has grown coarse, their ears are dull of hearing,*

and they have shut their eyes, for fear they should see with their eyes, hear with their
ears, understand with their hearts, and be converted and healed by me." (178)

The startling juxtaposition of this haunting passage from the prophet Isaiah with the tawdry, vulgar, fake—albeit technically remarkable—theme
park, an icon of our technically advanced but shallow contemporary civilization, which is not so much void of deeper spiritual meaning as simply uninterested in it, yokes together the transcendent and the mundane.
The invocation of the sacred upon this vulgarity can infuse it with the
possibility of grace—or dissipate the hint of the sacred in laughter—or do
both simultaneously.

In addition to the previously mentioned difficulties with the faith—
Miriam's resistance to the miraculous, Austin's advanced Scripture studies, natural calamities, the immensity of the apparently indifferent universe seen through Martin's telescope—there is also the crisis of faith
brought on by personal tragedies and suffering. Although they no longer
struggle with premarital lust or contraception, some of the former university students experience the sorrow of sexual infidelity. Dennis has an
affair with his secretary, and both Violet's and Polly's husbands are unfaithful. Even more poignant are their encounters with mortality as they
approach middle age. Michael, who has been trying to introduce more variety into his sex life with Miriam, begins "to shit blood, and quickly
[loses] interest in sex altogether" (153). His disorder proves to be nothing
more alarming than colitis, which can be treated with cortisone and diet,
but the experience of carrying to London a parcel of his excrement, the
smell of which is embarrassingly obvious, not only provides a comic
scene, but also lays bare his humiliating and fearful feelings at facing his
own mortality. Not only is the odor of his excrement embarrassing, but
with "the prospect of a painful and undignified rectal examination at the
hospital, and the constant obsessive fear of being told that he had cancer
of the bowel," he reads in the newspaper a column entitled "Is Death The
Dirty Little Secret Of The Permissive Society?" (159). No sooner does
Michael return home than he finds out that Angela's father has been taken
ill, and he is subsequently diagnosed with lung cancer. As Angela is trying to adjust to her father's impending death, she learns that her brother
Tom, a priest, is planning to leave the priesthood and marry. Austin Brierley, the priest who had been the students' chaplain, also leaves the priesthood and marries.

So the former students have to contend with all kinds of death: the
death of marital fidelity, of priestly celibacy, and of life itself. In her discussion with her brother Tom, Angela tries to be positive, arguing that
being Christians means "'we shouldn't be afraid of, well, death?'" She
describes a family who, after the death of their mother, had a kind of

party. Tom, however, thinks that is "'rather affected'" (166). Angela speaks for the new Church, advocating joy, celebration, and the love of God. Her upbeat attitude may have displaced the older traditional piety that found death fearsome—faith or no faith—and decorated its churches with devils, hellfire, and the specter of death the reaper, but her focus on the positive seems inadequate to deal with the terrors of mortality.

Of all the kinds of suffering that descend on the characters, however, none is more moving than that of Angela and Dennis when their fourth child is born with Down's Syndrome. At the baby's baptism, godfather Edward, who is a physician, is suspicious of the infant's extremely placid behavior and some markings on her hands. He tells his wife he is "'ninety-nine per cent sure'" the baby has Down's Syndrome (111). Lodge's comment: "I did say this wasn't a comic novel, exactly" (112).

The situation is given added poignancy by the suggestion that the birth defect may have been caused, at least in part, by the fact that Angela and Dennis followed the Church's teaching on birth control. Edward recalls that after having encouraged his patients to use rhythm in their family planning, he had made a disturbing discovery:

> There had been four babies born in the practice with non-hereditary congenital abnormalities since he had joined it, and three of them had been born to his family-planning clients. Somewhere in the medical journals he had come across the hypothesis that genetic defects were more likely to occur when the ovum was fertilized towards the end of its brief life-span, and this was obviously more likely to occur with couples who were deliberately restricting their intercourse to the post-ovulatory period. (78)

Thus, this personal tragedy is linked back to the contraception debacle and the whole thorny issue of Catholic sexual morality. The former students eventually come to see their earlier acquiescence as immature, wondering why they had persisted so long: "They wondered themselves, years later, when they had all given it up. 'It was conditioning,' said Adrian, 'it was the projection of the celibate clergy's own repressions on to the laity.' 'It was guilt,' said Dorothy, 'guilt about sex. Sex was dirty enough without going into birth control, that was the general feeling'" (79).

Yet their adherence to "this frustrating, undignified, ineffective, anxiety-creating system of family planning" (78) is not the only thing they have given up. They have also given up hell.

> At some point in the nineteen-sixties, Hell disappeared. No one could say for certain when this happened. First it was there, then it wasn't. Different people became aware of the disappearance of Hell at different times. Some realized that they had been living for years as though Hell did not exist,

without having consciously registered its disappearance. Others realized that they had been behaving, out of habit, as though Hell were still there, though in fact they had ceased to believe in its existence long ago. By Hell we mean, of course, the traditional Hell of Roman Catholics, a place where you would burn for all eternity if you were unlucky enough to die in a state of mortal sin.

On the whole, the disappearance of Hell was a great relief, though it brought new problems. (113)

The students' metaphysical world has changed.[17] Thus to see *How Far Can You Go?* as simply a farcical satire on the Catholic Church's teaching on contraception would be a superficial reading. It is not simply that these immature, intimidated young people finally grow up and decide to take responsibility for their own sexual lives. The big problems for faith that are presented in the novel—the inability to believe in the miraculous, the tendency to see the Bible more as a human book and less as a divine one, natural calamities, the immensity of the apparently indifferent universe— whirl around in a metaphysical universe which has lost its moorings. The clear definitive architecture of the "Snakes and Ladders" universe is gone; the scaffolding holding it up has disappeared.

Yet the basic human needs and longings remain, and the big questions still cry out for answers. Furthermore, the attenuation of sexual anxiety and guilt does not address the fears that plague those too old, too sick, or otherwise disadvantaged to distract themselves with erotic joy: "The good news about sexual satisfaction has little to offer those who are crippled, chronically sick, mad, ugly, impotent—or old, which all of us will be in due course, unless we are dead already. Death, after all, is the overwhelming question to which sex provides no answer, only an occasional brief respite from thinking about it" (121).

The students have lost not only creed and code, but also cult.[18] Although it would be inaccurate to say that they have no forms for worship, they are living in a time when Catholic liturgy, forms, ceremonies, and popular piety, much of it little changed from the Middle Ages is undergoing rapid and chaotic change. Not only have rites, ceremonies, and prayers changed, but the very language itself. The mass is now "Eucharist," not Mass; it is "celebrated," rather than "said" or "offered." "Confession" is "Reconciliation."[19]

The last chapter, entitled "How It Is," is in the form of a transcript of a television documentary, "Easter with the New Catholics" produced in April 1975. The first statement is that of former priest Austin, saying, "We can't be sure that the Resurrection actually happened" (228). One of the original group of university students—now about twenty years older than they were at the beginning of the novel—asserts that probably no

pope will ever again try to make an infallible pronouncement; another
says she would consider having an abortion, and another that she sees no
reason why nuns shouldn't dance. The day includes a forum entitled "Towards a new theology of sex" (231). The sacrament of Confession is administered, not one to one in a dark closet-like confessional, but to people
who "sit around and talk about [their] personal failures and hangups,"
and at the end a priest gives general absolution (233). The dawn of Easter
is celebrated by a dance of two women in "flowing robes of saffron and
blue" accompanied by flute music (229).

Although parts of the Easter Mass are familiar, they are interspersed
with voices over that break any illusion of the permanence or stability
conveyed by traditional rituals. In the traditional Easter Vigil the entire
congregation renews their baptismal promises by answering questions,
one of which is "Do you reject Satan?" to which they answer, "I do." But
now the promise is followed by the words of Ruth, who as a Charismatic,
asserts that she definitely believes in evil spirits that can cause frightening
experiences, whereas Miriam says she doesn't believe in Satan as an actual being. "'The Devil I think is a sort of personification of the evil in all
of us, the potential evil'" (237). The difference between the two responses
reflects different ways of believing and of reformulating traditional doctrine: emotional personal experience or demythologized symbolism. Similarly, Michael sees the Eucharist as a kind of "archetypal symbolism" that
"goes back to primitive ritual," whereas Edward insists that he is old fashioned on this point and believes "Jesus Christ is really and truly present
in the Eucharist" (238). The idea that being a Catholic means a unity in
faith is shattered.

As for the liturgy, Polly, who has been away from the Church for many
years, says of the new mass, "It's certainly more comprehensible, but
rather flat, somehow. Like a room that's too brightly lit. I think you have
to have shadows in religion. Bits of mystery and magic" (238). The phrase
"too brightly lit" recalls by contrast the opening chapter's early morning
Mass in 1952, where inside the church "it might still be night" for the
"winter daybreak is too feeble to penetrate the stained-glass windows" (1).

Midway in the novel, as the new ideas unleashed by Vatican II are
swirling around the former students, their former chaplain, Father Brierley had

> prophesied a time when the whole elaborate structure of bishops and priests
> and dioceses and parishes would melt away, house-eucharists would replace
> the huge anonymous crush of the parochial Sunday mass, and mutual coun-
> selling and consciousness-raising groups would replace Confession and
> Confirmation.

So they stood upon the shores of Faith and felt the old dogmas and certainties ebbing away rapidly under their feet and between their toes, sapping the foundations upon which they stood, a sensation both agreeably stimulating and slightly unnerving. (142–43)

Stimulating and *unnerving* are the right words to express the experience of Catholics in the decades following Vatican II. The positive connotation of the first word and the negative one of the second convey that sense of simultaneous optimistic excitement and disorienting loss that afflicted so many Catholics at this time. On the other hand, readers familiar with Matthew Arnold's famous poem "Dover Beach," in which the poet laments the Victorians' loss of belief, cannot fail to notice the similarity to Lodge's image:

> The Sea of Faith
> Was once, too, at the full, and round earth's shore
> Lay like the folds of a bright girdle furl'd.
> But now I only hear
> Its melancholy, long, withdrawing roar,
> Retreating, to the breath
> Of the night-wind, down the vast edges drear
> And naked shingles of the world.[20]

Lodge then makes a striking comparison to metafiction. "For we all like to believe, do we not, if only in stories? People who find religious belief absurd are often upset if a novelist breaks the illusion of reality he has created" (143). Breaking the pleasure of narrativity, the comfort of stories, which imposes meaning on the ongoing random events of life, is both a pleasure and a pain. Earlier in the novel Lodge had subjected his readers to just such an unnerving reading experience in referring to the death of Dennis and Angela's child Anne in a van accident.

> I have avoided a direct presentation of this incident because frankly I find it too painful to contemplate. Of course, Dennis and Angela and Anne are fictional characters, they cannot bleed or weep, but they stand here for all the real people to whom such disasters happen with no apparent reason or justice. One does not kill off characters lightly, I assure you, even ones like Anne, evoked solely for that purpose. (125)

Readers may find the breaking of the narrative spell diverting and exhilarating, even as they feel the security of the fictional world slipping away beneath them. They may also be feeling something analogous to the experience of Catholics in the years after Vatican II. The shock of the new, the thrill of being *avant-garde*, the joy of throwing off the dead weight of burdensome no-longer relevant traditions in order to make room for something more authentic and vibrant, followed by a sobering reassessment of what was being lost—all of this can seem familiar to Catholics.

But not to all Catholics. Some see the changes wrought by Vatican II as simply destructive and wish nothing more than the return of the Church of the 1950s with its Latin masses and full seminaries. Others see the pre-Vatican II church as all bad and attribute all the current chaos, low morale, and diminishing numbers of clergy and religious to the failure of the Church hierarchy to implement the reforms quickly and fully enough and to cultivate the egalitarian church that Vatican II promised. Both of these groups would probably fail to respond to or to even fully understand Lodge's extraordinary achievement in this novel. His ability to turn a steady eye on both the failings *and* the strengths of both the old and the new Church is remarkable. Furthermore, the title *How Far Can You Go?* attests to the fact that the liturgical changes and other innovations that resulted from Vatican II—mass in the vernacular, the abandonment of religious habits and clerical dress, lay lectors and eucharistic ministers, guitars and folk groups instead of organs and choirs, greatly diminished use of religious art in churches—are much more than simply matters of taste and style in worship "fashions." For embodied creatures, the "packaging" of religion is more than packaging. Outward forms are the conduits through which believers apprehend, absorb, and express the core beliefs of their religion.[21] Lodge doesn't minimize or ignore the difficulties for faith in the modern age, and the novel suggests that these difficulties do not disappear with a more contemporary Mass and trendy liturgical music. At the same time, he insists on the perennial urgency of the basic questions that religious belief purports to answer and foregrounds the need for a language and symbolism for articulating those questions and answers that avoid the twin dangers of being either rigid, lifeless, and formulaic; or trendy, trivializing, and ephemeral.

That is why his use of some postmodern metafictional techniques in this novel is so fitting. A self-consciously fictional narrative—a story aware of its own fictionality—is an ideal vehicle to explore the life of faith in our time. As G. K. Chesterton points out, Christianity is primarily a story.[22] Does that mean that Lodge's novel is suggesting that Christian faith is a simply a bedtime story we tell ourselves because we are afraid of the dark, knowing deep down that it is only a story? Not quite. One of the characteristics of metafiction is its open-endedness, its refusal to provide comfortable closure. It invokes possibility. Chesterton emphasizes that the point about a story is that it "may end up in *any* way [emphasis added]. . . . All Christianity concentrates on the man at the cross-roads."[23] Certain characteristics of metafiction—tentativeness, ambiguity, openness—make it an ideal vehicle for talking about faith. Lodge's novel makes it clear that unexamined assertions and formulaic answers are not adequate vehicles for a contemporary faith. Yet a religion that claims to be based on more than a private revelation, that purports to be a historic faith rooted in real past events, handed down by an authoritative tradition, and expressed in inherited symbols and rituals, needs to be cautious of changing too much too fast. As the narrator of *How Far Can You Go?* puts it, "in matters of belief (as of literary convention) it is a nice question how far you can go in this process without throwing out something vital" (143).

NOTES

1. I quote from the American edition of the novel, which was published under the title *Souls and Bodies*. For reasons that will be explained, I much prefer the English title *How Far Can You Go?* and will refer to the novel by that title.

2. David Lodge, *Souls and Bodies* [American edition of *How Far Can You Go?*] (New York: Penguin, 1980), 4. Hereafter cited in the text by page number.

3. Lodge has referred to *The British Museum is Falling Down* as "essentially conservative . . . the conflicts and misunderstandings it deals with being resolved without fundamentally disturbing the system which provoked them." Haffenden, "David Lodge," 146.

4. Eamon Duffy, *Faith of our Fathers: Reflections on Catholic Tradition* (London: Continuum, 2004), 141.

5. Mary Ann Glendon, "The Hour of the Laity," *First Things*, Nov. 2002, 25.

6. Mark Lawson, "How Far Did He Go?" *The Tablet*, 4 Sept. 2004, 12.

7. This point becomes clearer when one considers the protagonists of other famous Catholic novels: the nameless "whiskey priest" of Greene's *the Power and the Glory*, Charles Ryder of Waugh's *Brideshead Revisited*, Francis Marion Tarwater of O'Connor's *The Violent Bear It Away*. Also, many of these novels, especially Greene's, have exotic settings, while Waugh's are set among the privileged upper classes. My point is that few of them take as their material the experience of ordinary, middle-class married Catholics trying to work and raise a family in a typical urban environment in Western Europe or America. Indeed, it is almost as if writing about religious experience militates against using such ordinary material, as if one could speak of divine or supernatural things only by using exotic settings or elite or eccentric characters.

8. This negative view of pre-Vatican II Catholicism is challenged by those who argue that it overlooks many of the strengths of the pre-Vatican II Church and raises the question of why it was attractive to so many highly intellectual and cultured converts who entered the Church during those years, whereas after Vatican II the Church failed to attract such distinguished converts. See Sheridan Gilley, "A Tradition and Culture Lost, To Be Regained?" in Hornsby-Smith, *Catholics in England*, 42–45.

9. Lodge's later novel *Paradise News* emphasizes the fact that contemporary Christianity has de-emphasized or even marginalized the issue of the afterlife,

and therefore, of salvation or damnation, an aspect of Christian doctrine that in previous times was seen as central and pivotal.

10. Ejaculations are short prayers like "My Jesus mercy!" that are repeated many times. In the days before Vatican II, when Catholic children were taught many traditional prayers and forms of piety, the double meaning of this term was the occasion of much mirth in religion classes where the instructor, often a religious sister, either tried to ignore or did not seem to be aware of the sexual meaning.

11. Lodge has this to say about the results of the acceptance of contraception:

> The availability of effective contraception was the thin end of a wedge of modern hedonism that had already turned Protestantism into a parody of itself and was now challenging the Roman Catholic ethos. Conservatives in the Church who predicted that approval of contraception for married couples would inevitably lead sooner or later to a general relaxation of traditional moral standards and indirectly encourage promiscuity, marital infidelity, sexual experiment and deviation of every kind, were essentially correct, and it was disingenuous of liberal Catholics to deny it. *Souls and Bodies,* 115.

12. Thomas Aquinas articulated this problem in the thirteenth century. Discussing indulgences he wrote, "In like manner, if any error were to be found in the Church's preaching, her doctrine would have no authority in settling questions of faith." (from "On Whether Indulgences are as Effective as they claim to be," in *S. Bonaventura.* Sent. IV., D. 20, quoted in Ronald Knox & Arnold Lunn, *Difficulties.* London: Eyre & Spottiswoode Ltd., 1932) 269.

13. William Kilpatrick explains Lewis's distinction this way:

> Thick religions are associated with smoky altars, sacrifice, deep mysteries, blood ties, mystical bonds, and communion with the gods. Clear religions, on the other hand, are demystified. They are tidy and rational, and claim to be based on principles of enlightenment and harmony. They promise illumination rather than salvation. . . . As Lewis saw it, the problem with a clear or "minimal" religion is that it has "no power to touch any of the deepest chords in our nature, or to evoke any response which will raise us even to a higher secular level." They promise illumination rather than salvation.

The Emperor's New Clothes (Westchester, Ill.: Crossway, 1985), 75. See also C. S. Lewis, "Religion Without Dogma?" in *God in the Dock,* ed. Walter Hooper (Grand Rapids: Eerdmans, 1970), 142–43.

14. After Vatican II it became quite common for priests to insist on being called by their first names, rather than the traditional "Father" and their surnames.

15. This tension is evident in all Christian sects, not just Roman Catholicism; but the extent of the change from an emphasis on personal piety and salvation to one of concern with social justice seems more extreme in Catholicism.

16. *Young Adult Catholics* by Dean Hoge describes the current situation as follows: "This conflation of religion with ethics and disconnectedness from specific Catholic social teachings implicitly demotes a distinct Catholic identity. Being religious simply means being a 'good person,' doing good deeds." Dean Hoge et al., *Young Adult Catholics: Religion in the Culture of Choice* (Notre Dame, Ind.: University of Notre Dame Press, 2001), 224.

17. Ronald Knox clarifies the significance of the loss of this belief:

I think I see that if you discount the idea of eternal punishment, and so rob Christianity of its sharp issues and severe outlines, you alter its character radically; it is no longer the same religion. I do not mean that there is no Christian motive left for holiness if you leave eternal punishment out of sight: that would obviously be untrue. But I mean that the whole thing is built to scale; the doctrine of the Atonement, for instance derives its force from the tremendousness of the issues involved; and the power of the keys becomes meaningless, or at least alters its meaning, if we are to suppose it is impossible for a soul to put itself, even temporarily, outside the covenant of God's mercy. The whole of Christianity, whether in the New Testament or in Church history, or in the history of those non-Catholic sects which have preserved a virile tradition of piety, is always framed against a background of finality, of despairing urgency, of claims and duties *absolutely* imperative. Knox, *Difficulties*, 58.

18. The three C's of a religion are 1) *creed*—a set of beliefs about God, the universe, and human beings, 2) *code*—a set of moral rules and guidelines, and 3) *cult*—rites, forms, ceremonies, prayers for the worship of God.

19. James Demers puts it this way:

The mutilation of the language of the faith began in earnest at the Second Vatican Council with the dusting-off of the word "liturgy." The "sacrifice of the mass" became "the celebration of the eucharist," "confession" became "reconciliation," and that was just the beginning. The word "mass" was all but banned from use in seminaries, colleges and schools. The "table of the Lord," "spiritual banquet" and "community of believers" appeared. *The Last Roman Catholic* (Carp, Ontario: Creative Bound Inc., 1991), 74–75.

20. Matthew Arnold, "Dover Beach," in *Victorian Poetry and Poetics*, 2nd ed., ed. Walter E. Houghton and F. Robert Stange (Boston: Houghton Mifflin), 1968, 484.

21. Louis Tarsitano, writing in *Touchstone*, describes the effect of these changes:

Where the strongest traditions of liturgy and piety had once prevailed, priests relaxing in their "presidential chairs" while laymen administered the Holy Communion to people forbidden to kneel made nonsense of the sacramental reverence once shared by prelates and scrub ladies alike. Experiments in feminism at the altar and in the home sought to obliterate the created and revealed order of the sexes that is the necessary foundation for a moral sexual order. The forced remodeling of church buildings, while played out like domestic farce ("Put the altar over there. No, how about here? No, let's try it again back there"), in its removal of beauty and transcendence would have made a Roundhead soldier blush. Louis Tarsitano, "Passing On True Religion," *Touchstone*, Dec. 2001, 15–17.

22. "To the Buddhist or the eastern fatalist existence is a science or a plan, which must end up in a certain way. But to a Christian existence is a *story*, which may end up in any way." Chesterton, *Orthodoxy*, 143.

23. Chesterton, Orthodoxy, 143.

8

✝

Intimations of Immortality:
Paradise News

Even for those who believe in the Christian possibility of eternal life, death is still a reality and still stings.

—Daniel Callahan, "Visions of Eternity"

I suspect that our conception of Heaven as merely a state of mind is not unconnected with the fact that the specifically Christian virtue of Hope has in our time grown so languid.

—C. S. Lewis, *Miracles*

"'The question facing the theologian today is, therefore, what can be salvaged from the eschatological wreckage?'"[1] This question, which begins the last chapter of David Lodge's *Paradise News* (1991), is taken from a lecture given by Bernard Walshe, the novel's protagonist. Bernard, a former priest, has lost his religious faith, but being untrained for any other kind of work, he is teaching part time at an ecumenical theological college. The segment of his lecture that begins the last chapter is a candid and poignant analysis of the dilemma facing Christianity at the end of the twentieth century. Bernard argues that although belief in an afterlife remains a central tenet of Christianity, being the culmination of its "linear plot" of salvation history and a staple of Christian teaching, it has little credibility for many educated people. Furthermore, many of the major theologians of the twentieth century have regarded the idea of an afterlife for individual human beings "with scepticism and embarrassment" or "silently ignored" it (280). Noting that fundamentalism, which *does* continue to promote belief in an anthropomorphic afterlife, is flourishing

169

"'precisely on the eschatological scepticism of responsible theology'" (281), Bernard is reminded of W. B. Yeats's lines:

The best lack all conviction, while the worst
Are full of passionate intensity.[2]

But can Christianity afford to marginalize what has been one of its most motivating and inspirational beliefs? As Bernard puts it to his students, "'if you purge Christianity of the promise of eternal life (and, let us be honest, the threat of eternal punishment) which traditionally underpinned it, are you left with anything that is distinguishable from secular humanism?'" (282).

Bernard's question and his keen analysis of the dilemma facing Christianity in our time—the inability of sophisticated and intellectual Christians to emphasize and propound belief in an afterlife at the same time that human longing persists for what has always been a foundational dogma—marks *Paradise News* as a new stage in David Lodge's use of Catholicism in his fiction. Although the novel remains ambivalent on the question of an afterlife, the serious exploration of the possibilities for faith in a postmodern age and a sense of sacramentality in everyday life make *Paradise News* a more nuanced, complex, and theologically interesting novel than any of Lodge's earlier work. Just as the title *How Far Can You Go?* refers to both an adolescent approach to sexual morality and profound theological questions, the *Paradise* in *Paradise News*, refers both to Hawaii and to heaven.

In *Paradise News* Lodge is less concerned with Catholicism as sociological data and the day to day life of ordinary Catholics and is more focused on philosophical questions, especially that of an afterlife, that central Christian belief, which is being de-emphasized by theologians and intellectuals but remains of vital importance for ordinary Christians. In this sense, then, Lodge's theme in this novel is more Christian than specifically Catholic. Nevertheless, with the protagonist a former priest and his father and aunt practicing Catholics, a substantial amount of Catholic material is used. But *Paradise News* is different from Lodge's earlier Catholic novels, not only in its theme and subject matter, but also in its tone. Although critic Bernard Bergonzi found *How Far Can You Go?* bitter in places and marked by a "cold Voltairean irony," I suspect that he, like most readers, finds *Paradise News* more genial, tender, and affirmative.[3]

Lodge describes himself as "by temperament tentative, sceptical, ironic," so it is not surprising that the novel refrains from speaking strongly or authoritatively on the question of religious belief in general and an afterlife in particular.[4] Certain aspects of the novel—some postmodernist narrative techniques, and cynicism associated with the central metaphor of Hawaii as paradise—tend to erode the possibility of any grand philosophical ideal, any absolute. Expectations, preconceptions, and hopes are subverted. Other forces in the novel, however, pull it toward affirmation. The central metaphor, which at first seems to destabilize the possibility of belief, ultimately allows for transformation and life out of death. Although initially described with cynicism and irony, Hawaii at times not only lives up to its promise of paradisaical, unearthly beauty, but also offers transformative possibilities to the characters. Furthermore, the sense of sacramentality that suffuses the novel suggests that God's transforming presence is active, not only in the institutional sacraments of the Church, but in unexpected ways as well.

The "paradise" of the novel's title is both the eschatological goal—heaven—referred to in Bernard's lecture, and Honolulu, Hawaii, where Bernard goes to visit his dying Aunt Ursula, and which is the setting for most of the novel. Bernard articulates the central metaphor when he reflects on his life as a priest: "The Good News is news of eternal life, Paradise news. For my parishioners, I was a kind of travel agent, issuing tickets, insurance, brochures, guaranteeing them ultimate happiness" (153).

The primary meanings of *paradise* are the Garden of Eden and heaven, but the word is also so commonly used to refer to desirable vacation destinations like Hawaii or Tahiti that it is a dead metaphor. In this novel, however, the metaphor is *not* dead. Lodge repeatedly reminds the reader of Hawaii's association with paradise, as one of the tourists, anthropologist Roger Sheldrake, makes a point of noting down every instance of the word's use in Honolulu business:

Paradise Bakery
Paradise Dental
Paradise Jet Ski (191)

Paradise Finance Inc.
Paradise Sportswear
Paradise Beauty Supply Inc. (195)

This continual reminder of Hawaii's metaphorical link to paradise foregrounds the word, conflates the three meanings together, and seems to diminish the significance of any of them. Tourists are like pilgrims looking for an Eden-like terrestrial paradise. Christians are spiritual tourists hoping for a heavenly paradise. Both are beset by frustration, disappointment, thwarted expectations, and misleading promises.

For the most part, cynicism, artificiality, and disappointment characterize the presentation of Hawaii. This paradise is tacky. Although the airport is a pleasant surprise—walkways open to the "warm and velvety" air and a "kind of tropical garden . . . next to the terminal building, with artificial ponds and streams, and naked torches burning amid the foliage" (67)—Bernard is disappointed by the drive into the city:

> A melange of amplified music, traffic noise and human voices penetrated the car windows. It reminded Bernard of the crush around Victoria Station, except that everything looked much cleaner. There were even familiar names on the shopfronts—MacDonalds [sic], Kentucky Fried Chicken, Woolworths. . . .
> "It's not quite what I imagined," said Bernard. "It's very built-up, isn't it? I had a mental picture of sand, and sea and palm trees." (73)

Nor does the reality of this tropical "paradise" live up to its reputation:

> Two bosomy blondes in brassières and skirts made of what looked like shiny blue plastic ribbon were gyrating to a kind of Hawaiian rock music. Their fixed, enamelled smiles raked the audience like searchlights. . . .
> "It doesn't look very authentic," said Bernard.
> "It's rubbish," said Dee. "I've seen more authentic hula dancing at the London Palladium." (106)

The reason that Bernard's traveling companion, anthropologist Roger Sheldrake, is compiling a list of Hawaiian businesses with the word *paradise* in them is that he sees a parallel between tourism and religion: "'You see, I don't think people really want to go on holiday, any more than they really want to go to church. They've been brainwashed into thinking it will do them good, or make them happy. In fact surveys show the holidays cause incredible amounts of stress'" (62). Tour companies sell "paradise" just as churches sell heaven. But the product is phony. Pulling out a Travelwise brochure with a picture of an idyllic, near-empty beach, Sheldrake points out that it "'bears no resemblance to reality,'" that almost no tourists find "'a beach as deserted as this one'" (63). He later refines his schema into two types of tourism, both based on religious metaphors. One is the tour as pilgrimage, where the traveller visits famous places—museums, monuments, cities. The other is the tour as paradise, "in which the subject strives to get back to a state of nature, or prelapsarian innocence" (192). Whether paradise is seen as the goal of a religious pilgrimage, which medieval people devoutly believed could help them earn heaven, or the Garden of Eden, which was heaven on earth, Sheldrake's travelers have taken the energy formerly channeled into religious activities and redirected it into vacation travel—the modern path to paradise. According to Sheldrake, however, both religion and tourism proffer empty promises.

The narrative technique also undermines the possibility of an affirmative or comforting answer to eschatological anxiety. Lodge, who is a prolific literary critic, as well as a novelist, has written extensively about postmodern literary techniques, sometimes illustrating his theory with examples from his own fiction.[5] In *Paradise News* he employs several techniques that disrupt the mostly straightforward, realistic narrative, to push it into the self-conscious narrativity of metafiction, thus destabilizing the reader and refusing to allow him or her to stay in the comfortable space of a traditional story. Lodge is fond of switching into the mode of a script, usually near the end of his novels, as he does with the televised Easter celebration at the end of *How Far Can You Go?* The final chapter of *Changing Places* is also in the form of a film script. In *The Art of Fiction* Lodge explains that part of his purpose in *Changing Places* was a formal one: since he had employed so many other kinds of stylistic shifts in earlier chapters—shifts in tense, interpolations of newspaper accounts, letters, and other documents—he needed to provide something even more striking so that the conclusion would not be anticlimactic. He also states that he wished to end the novel on a note of "radical indeterminacy."[6]

Lodge follows a similar course in *Paradise News*. Part of the narrative is in the form of Bernard's journal. Part is a series of postcards sent by various members of Bernard's tour group. Part is a long letter to Bernard from Yolande, a woman he becomes romantically involved with during his stay in Hawaii. In the penultimate chapter, in which Bernard attends a cocktail party to mark the end of the Travelwise tour, narrative techniques include a newspaper article, an advertising video, and a videotape made by one of the Travelwise tourists, titled *Everthorpes in Paradise*. Much of this chapter consists of conversations of the various tour members overlaid with descriptions of what is going on in the videotape. Two sequences are taking place simultaneously: the past-tense events of the trip and the present tense conversation. The tourists intermittently ignore, or are surprised, amused, or embarrassed by what they see on the television screen. Lodge's narration of the video sequence includes details that mark this narrative as an artificial construct.

> The film began with a picture of two teenage boys and an elderly lady waving goodbye from the porch of a mock-Jacobean house with leaded windows and integral garage. "Our boys and my mother," Beryl explained. There followed a long static close-up of a notice board saying *"East Midlands Airport,"* and then a jerky sequence with a painfully high-pitched whine on the soundtrack showing Beryl, in her red and yellow dress and gold bangles, climbing a steep flight of mobile steps into the cabin of a propeller plane. She stopped suddenly at the top and swept round to wave at the camera, causing the passengers behind and beneath her to cannon into each other and bury their faces in each other's bottoms. (267)

A random sequence of events, it is arranged and "posed" by its creator in such a way as to render it a story of "paradise"; but that *meaning* is clearly at odds with the actual facts. Its artificiality is emphasized. Apologizing that he has not had time to "edit this properly, or dub any music on," Everthorpe asks for patience with his "rough cut" (266). The bored viewers begin to show interest as they recognize themselves and others, saluting themselves "with hoots of laughter, cheers and jeers" (268). The delight of seeing oneself in another story, living two dimensions at once, begins to pale, however, as the artificiality of the film obtrudes:

> The voice of Brian Everthorpe was heard crying, "Cut!" Beryl stopped sauntering and turned to frown at the camera. Then she appeared to get back into bed and to wake up all over again.
> "Had to do two takes of this, because of the ambulance," said Brian Everthorpe. "I'll cut the first one out of the finished film, of course." (268)

As the film becomes more tedious, Everthorpe speeds it up to provide humor. The viewers are denied the pleasure of satisfying closure, however, as Everthorpe suddenly switches off the video machine when he is paged with the news that he must meet an unwelcome guest. If this novel is about the way that the life of faith enjoins living on two parallel tracks at once, drawn toward, tantalized by, in some senses even misled by, the hope of reaching some kind of "paradise," then metafiction makes an appropriate analogue for that life.

Another destabilizing factor is the narrator's ambivalence about tensions within contemporary Roman Catholicism. Although the novel is saturated with Catholicism, one is hard-pressed to align the narrative voice with one particular perspective. Indeed, the novel reflects attitudes that characterize both liberal and conservative Catholics.

One area of tension in contemporary Catholicism is liturgy: traditionalists favoring ceremony, restraint, formality, and in some cases, Latin; reformists favoring flexibility, spontaneity, exuberance, and the vernacular. There are two celebrations of the Eucharist in the novel: Bernard's father receives Holy Communion in the hospital, and Yolande attends a Mass on Waikiki beach. Both events disclose a tension with regard to modes of celebration: formal versus informal, pre-Vatican II versus post-Vatican II, traditional or charismatic. The novel refuses, however, to speak univocally on this issue. Yolande finds the beach Mass refreshingly natural and authentic, especially in contrast to the ostentatious formality of the only other Mass she has ever attended "in an Italian church . . . stuffed with hideous statuary. . . . like a TV spectacular, with the altar-boys in their red robes, and the priest in his brocade get-up, parading in and out" (287). But this Mass on the beach impresses Yolande with its simplicity and naturalness, the altar "just a simple table set up on the beach, and the congregation sitting or standing around in a loose circle on the sand" (287).

Bernard's father, however, is uncomfortable with a casual approach to the sacraments. When he receives Holy Communion in the hospital, he insists on receiving the host on the tongue in the pre-Vatican II manner and is discomfited and shakes his head "like a startled horse" when the charismatic priest puts his hand on his head to pray for his recovery (134). Aunt Ursula is also discomfited by changes in the Church. Telling Bernard about her return to the Church after years away from it, she says that she "hardly recognized the service" (135). "There was a bunch of kids up at the altar, with tambourines and guitars, and they were singing jolly camp-fire type songs, not the good old hymns I remember. . . . And the mass was in English, not Latin, and there was a *woman* on the altar reading the epistle, and the priest said the mass facing the people—I was quite embarrassed watching him chewing the host" (135). Although Bernard appears patronizing and dismissive of the old people's views, the narrative voice behind Bernard seems to have some sympathy with their distress. There is a disjunction between the fashionable contemporary and the cherished familiar.

As with *How Far Can You Go?*, the aspect of Lodge's portrayal of Catholicism that probably engenders the most sympathy is its critique of Catholic attitudes toward sex. Bernard's Catholic childhood has badly distorted his sexuality. "I was troubled by the things that were happening to my body, and the thoughts that were straying into my mind. I was very worried about sin, about how easily you could commit it, and what the consequences would be if you died in a state of it. That's what Catholic education does for you—did for you in my day, anyway. Basically I was paralysed with fear of hell and ignorance of sex" (145). Bernard's priestly life is described as artificial, self-indulgent, and disconnected from the pulse of real life. For part of his priestly career he was an academic theologian, where he spent most of his time "insulated from the realities and concerns of modern secular society. It was rather like the life of a mid-Victorian Oxford don: celibate, male-centered, high-minded, not exactly ascetic" (146). When he gets into parish work, a woman he has been counseling impulsively kisses him, and Bernard realizes how deprived he has been "of human physical contact, of the animal comfort of touch, during all the long years of [his] training and work as a priest" (166). He also realizes that after the kiss and his decision to leave the priesthood, he feels more alive than he has felt for years and believes that he "was never a more effective confessor than [he] was that evening—compassionate, caring, encouraging" (167). The implicit causal link between the affection and Bernard's more effective ministry prepares the reader for Bernard's transformation into a more generous, warm, and sensitive human being after he becomes sexually involved with Yolande in the second part of the novel.

The harmful effects of the Church's methods of promoting sexual morality, its engendering of fear and shame in order to enforce its strict standards, and the dehumanizing effects of mandatory celibacy for the clergy all tend to erode confidence in the Church as a reliable spiritual guide, a mediator between God and humanity in this life, and a guarantor of eternal salvation in the next. It would be natural and tempting, therefore, to categorize the novel as polemical, a pointed, satiric argument as to why the Church has to modernize and adapt itself to the mores of contemporary, secular society. Such a stance, however, not only would be simplistic, but would fail to acknowledge other parts of the novel. Lodge denies us such easy closure.

Other features of the novel critique aspects of liberal theology. The theological college where Bernard has been teaching is one of those that have adapted to "the more ecumenical spirit of modern times by opening their doors to all denominations, indeed all faiths, and to laypeople as well as to clerics" (28). Bernard compares the wide variety of courses and beliefs to the variety of products available in a modern supermarket. "On its shelves you could find everything you needed, conveniently stored and attractively packaged. But the very ease of the shopping process brought with it the risk of a certain satiety, a certain boredom. If there was so much choice, perhaps nothing mattered very much" (29).

The promise of the ecumenical movement—a deepening and enhancement of one's own religious tradition through a greater understanding of other faiths—has, in fact, eroded clarity, diminished meaning, and reduced the urgency involved in the life of faith. Bernard notes how the language of contemporary religious discourse has become vacuous and elusive. In a book on process theology, which he is reviewing, he reads a description of God as a cosmic lover: "*His transcendence is in His sheer faithfulness to Himself in love, in His inexhaustibility as lover, and in His capacity for endless adaptation to circumstances in which His love may be active*" (29). Bernard wonders who, apart from theologians, possibly cares about such formulations. "It often seemed to Bernard that the discourse of much modern radical theology was just as implausible and unfounded as the orthodoxy it had displaced" (29). Thus the contemporary Christian is in a kind of no-man's land, straddling two territories: the old orthodoxy—crippled by shame, repression, fear, superstition—but colorful, dramatic, and compelling; and the new ecumenism—enlightened, humane, benevolent—but abstract, boring, and vacuous.

This critique of "advanced" religion strains against the critique of traditional religion, opening up a kind of aporia in religious life. Although the old ways crippled the spirit and distorted one's sensual and emotional maturity, the new way starves the hunger for religious experience and the desire for meaningful answers to ultimate questions. Thus Lodge opens up a kind of postmodernist religious space, in which the old certainties have fallen away to leave the would-be Christian religiously destabilized.

The cynicism and instability, however, are countered by a reconsideration of faith in terms suitable for a postmodern age and by a sense of sacramentality. Although Bernard no longer believes in Christianity, his loss of faith recounted in his diary may be the prelude to a more genuine adult faith, for his early religious "faith" is shown to be largely derivative, immature, and fear-driven.[7] If Bernard is moving toward some new kind of faith, one suspects that it may be similar to the present theological perspective of the author, which, it will be recalled, Lodge himself described as "demythologized, provisional, and in many ways agnostic."[8] It is also a faith that resonates with St. Paul's description of faith as "confident assurance concerning what we hope for, and conviction about things we do not see" (Hebrews 11:1). Although "assurance" (*hupostasis*) and "conviction" (*elegchos*) sound positive, they are yoked with "hope" and "things we do not see," thus linking presence with absence and giving the term a destabilizing, oxymoronic ambience: an appropriate faith for our postmodern age. Furthermore, an element of doubt is seen by some contemporary theologians as essential for a healthy faith. Kenneth Leech in *Experiencing God: Theology as Spirituality* asserts that without "creative doubt, religion becomes hard and cruel, degenerating into the spurious security which breeds intolerance and persecution. . . . But to the eyes of conventional religion, this mingling of faith and doubt appears as atheism."[9]

This idea of creative doubt is further emphasized at the very end of the novel when Yolande includes in her letter to Bernard the following quotation from Miguel de Unamuno's *The Tragic Sense of Life*, which she has photocopied from the *Reader's Digest*:

In the most secret recess of the spirit of the man who believes that death will put an end to his personal consciousness and even to his memory forever, in that inner recess, even without his knowing it perhaps, a shadow hovers, a vague shadow lurks, a shadow of a shadow of uncertainty, and while he tells himself: "There is nothing for it but to live this passing life, for there is no other!" at the same time he hears, in this most secret recess, his own doubt murmur: "Who knows? . . . " He is not sure he hears aright, but he hears. Likewise, in some recess of the soul of the true believer who has faith in the future life, a muffled voice the voice of uncertainty, murmurs in his spirit's ear: "Who knows?. . . ." Perhaps these voices are no louder than the buzzing of mosquitoes when the wind roars through the trees in the woods; we scarcely make out the humming, and yet, mingled with the roar of the storm, it can be heard. How, without this uncertainty, could we ever live? (293)[10]

Not only is "creative doubt" healthy; according to Unamuno, it is essential to life itself. The novel suggests that it is also essential to a healthy and realistic religious faith at the end of the twentieth century. Furthermore, although contemporary theologians may de-emphasize it, belief in an afterlife is an important part of such a faith, yet it is as much hope as faith.

In addition to its articulation of a contemporary faith which incorporates doubt in a potentially fruitful way, the novel also offers an approach to God through sacramentality. Sacramentality is prominent in *Paradise News* as incident, image, and theme, imparting to the story a sense of completeness, efficacy, and direction. According to the Catechism, sacraments are "efficacious signs of grace, instituted by Christ and entrusted to the Church, by which divine life is dispensed to us."[11] The principle of sacramentality insists that matter can be a vehicle for spirit, that God's grace comes through material things, that God is still present in the world. Thus the images and reminders of sacramentality, while not providing any definitive answer to the question of an afterlife, provide a sense of connection with the divine and a context for hope that that connection survives bodily death.

Bernard Walshe's contemporary "pilgrimage" includes all seven sacraments in some form. The sacraments of Holy Eucharist and Anointing of the Sick are explicitly celebrated according to the rite of the Catholic Church. Some are present in memory or expectation, others allusively or symbolically. The Holy Eucharist appears in the novel when Bernard's father receives Communion in the hospital, where he is recovering from a minor auto accident, and later at a Hawaiian folk Mass on Waikiki Beach. The hospital chaplain explains to Bernard that he likes bringing the Eucharist to the hospitalized because they seem "to appreciate the Eucharist so much more than parishioners at an ordinary Sunday mass" (134). When Ursula, who is in a different hospital, is told about her brother's receiving Communion, she is envious, wishing that her health plan allowed her to be in a Catholic hospital. This incident leads to Bernard's giving Ursula a quasi-academic lecture on contemporary Eucharistic theology. Annoyed by some of Ursula's remarks, he feels frustrated and impatient with what he perceives as her reductionistic, childish, and naive theology; yet it is clear that for both Ursula and her brother, participating in the ancient rite of the Eucharist provides some kind of spiritual anchor.

After Bernard returns to England, Yolande describes in a letter to him the Mass she has attended on Waikiki Beach. After Aunt Ursula's death, Father McPhee, in accordance with her wishes, takes her ashes to the beach to scatter them in the ocean. He times it to coincide with a Hawaiian folk Mass regularly held on the beach on summer Saturdays. Yolande, who has always considered herself an atheist, has attended only one other Mass, the wedding Mass referred to above that seemed to her like a TV spectacular. This folk Mass on the beach incorporates Hawaiian singing and hula dancing, which amazingly, in the hothouse artificiality of Honolulu, seems genuine and human:

> Even the authentic demonstrations they put on at the Bishop Museum are essentially theatrical, while the hula you see in Waikiki is halfway between belly-dancing and burlesque. So it was quite a shock to see hula dancing at a Mass. But it worked. I think it worked because the girls weren't particularly good at it, and not particularly good-looking. I mean, they were OK, on both counts, but they were nothing special. . . . And of course they didn't have that fixed, gooey smile that you associate with pro hula girls. They looked serious and reverent. (288)

This sacrament is transformative. Honolulu now looks different. "I was looking back at the shore, and I must say Oahu was doing its stuff that evening. Even Waikiki was a thing of beauty. The tall buildings were catching the light of the setting sun as if floodlit, thrown into relief against the hills in the background, which were dark with raincloud" (289). Although the phrase "Oahu was doing its stuff" suggests that this beauty is routine in Honolulu, in fact, throughout the novel, Honolulu has been described as vulgar and artificial. The emphasis on sun, sky, and light suggest a connection with the transcendent; and the image of the rainbow not only recalls God's covenant with Noah to preserve the human race but reinforces the yoking together of contrasting realms: the illuminated buildings against the dark, stormy hills, and the human, artificial world set against the God-given natural world. "There was a rainbow over one of the hills, behind the tower block in the Hilton Hawaiian Village with the rainbow mural. . . . I suppose that just about sums up Hawaii: the real rainbow cosying up to the artificial one" (289). This is an image of a sacramental world, the intersection of two realms, the heavenly and the earthly, the natural and the supernatural. Paradise now looks like paradise.

The Anointing of the Sick (formerly known as Extreme Unction) is the sacrament given to those in danger of death from sickness or old age. It consists of anointing with sacred oil, scripture readings, laying on of hands, and prayers. According to the *Catechism*, "The first grace of this sacrament is one of strengthening, peace and courage to overcome the difficulties that go with the condition of serious illness or the frailty of old age."[12] Ursula asks for this sacrament on the day before her meeting with her brother, Bernard's father. This is a decisive moment because it is for this meeting that Bernard and his father have come to Hawaii.

> "One more thing," Ursula said, as they were preparing to leave. "I think maybe I should receive the Last Sacrament."

"That's a good idea," said Tess [Bernard's sister]. "Only we don't call it that any more. Or Extreme Unction. It's called the Sacrament of the Sick."

"Well, whatever it's called, I think I could use it," said Ursula drily. (243)

It is agreed that she will receive the sacrament at the hospital when they go there for the meeting between Ursula and her brother. Father McPhee, the friendly, charismatic chaplain will be able to celebrate the sacrament when, as Tess says, they are all together as a family.

The sacrament of Holy Orders is present both through Bernard's failed priestly vocation and Father McPhee's apparently successful one. During his stay in Hawaii, Bernard writes a journal/autobiography, in which he writes about his vocation to the priesthood:

> I couldn't talk to my parents: they never mentioned the subject of sex. I was too shy to ask my elder brother. . . . I was astonishingly ignorant, and afraid. I suppose I thought that by committing myself to the priesthood, I would solve all my problems at a stroke: sex, education, career, and eternal salvation. As long as I fixed my aim on becoming a priest I couldn't, as they say, "go wrong." (145–46)

Not surprisingly, a vocation based on such motives (and never, apparently, strengthened by any nobler ones) ultimately fails. In contrast, Father McPhee, the priest who attends Bernard's father in the hospital and who conducts Aunt Ursula's funeral, is human and approachable, "a youngish, plumpish man, with a short haircut, wearing the stole over a grey clerical shirt and black trousers" (133). He places his hand on the patient's head and prays spontaneously for his recovery (an action one can never imagine the old Bernard doing). Although Father McPhee's ministerial competence is stressed, the language also stresses that he is *priest*, not simply minister. He stands in the line of the ordained that Catholics believe stretches back to the apostles and that validates their special connection to Christ. The language of the passage—"wearing a stole," "acolyte," "host," "ciborium"—connects Father McPhee's ministry to the ordained priesthood in a church where the priest offers the *sacrifice* of the mass and stands *in persona Christi*.

Matrimony is present in a dark ironic way, as the novel is replete with failed and troubled marriages: Ursula's, Yolande's, Bernard's sister's and even a young honeymoon couple on the tour who aren't speaking. Yet the prospect of Bernard and Yolande's eventual marriage, which is a distinct possibility at the end of the novel, suggests that past failures can still be redeemed. Refusing her husband's offer of a reconciliation, Yolande explains to Bernard that, although "Nothing is fixed, nothing is definite," marriage is a possibility. Referring to her husband, she says, "Lewis is all right, but he's not an honest man. Now that I've met one, I can't be content with anything less" (292). Yolande also tells Bernard that although she is not yet sure whether she wants to marry him, she intends "to find out, by getting to know [him] better" (292), thus raising the possibility that a relationship based on carefully acquired knowledge of the other and a love founded on honesty, respect, and integrity might actually stand a chance of being a sacramental marriage.

Confession and Confirmation function more as overarching themes than as discrete entities. Ursula's need to be reconciled with her brother is seminal for the plot. Although Bernard at first appears to be simply the mediator and facilitator for this meeting, it becomes apparent that he also has to "confess" to himself and to another human being the sins of his past life: his inauthentic vocation, his ineffective ministry, his masquerade as an "atheist" priest (154), his failed relationship with a woman at the time he left the priesthood, the falsehood involved in his role as a non-believing "theologian," his desiccated emotional life, and his failure to relate to people.[13] Bernard makes his "confession" in the form of the journal that he writes and lets Yolande read.

Since the sacrament of Confirmation is the celebration of a mature, adult commitment to the faith, it is unwarranted to see the unbelieving Bernard's Hawaiian experience as a sacramental Confirmation. Certainly there is no explicit indication that he has renounced atheism and is moving back toward theism, nor does he give even a hint or suggestion that he will return to Catholic belief and practice. However, the primary meaning of the verb *to confirm*, coming from its Latin roots (*cum*, with + *firmare*, to make firm), is to strengthen, and in this sense accurately describes Bernard's experience. According to Thomistic theology, grace builds on nature; until Bernard is mature on the natural human level, he cannot be a mature Christian. There is no question that in Hawaii he becomes a more mature person and thus is laying the groundwork for the possibility of a mature relationship to God.

Perhaps the most powerful sacramental image in the novel is Bernard's symbolic baptism. About halfway through the novel Bernard has been trying to find an affordable nursing home for his Aunt Ursula when, hot and tired, he decides to go for a swim. The experience is idyllic, almost a kind of bracketed space lifted out of terrestrial, mundane time:

> It was a perfect hour for a swim. The sun was low in the sky and had lost its fierce daytime heat, but the sea was warm and the air balmy. I swam vigorously for about a hundred yards in the general direction of Australia, then floated on my back and gazed up at the overarching sky. Long shreds of mauve-tinted cloud, edged with gold, streamed like banners from the west. . . . Occasionally a bigger wave surged past, swamping me or lifting me into the air like a matchstick, leaving me spluttering in its wake, laughing like a boy. I decided I would do this more often. (162)

Several elements lift this experience into a supernatural, liturgical realm: the "perfect" hour, the establishment of direction in terms of another continent (the fact that swimming to another continent is a preposterous notion establishes bigger than life parameters for this experience), the "overarching sky," a mauve and gold natural world (instead of the more "natural" colors of blue and green), elevation into the air, the intense joy. Most importantly, the experience is transformative. When Bernard comes out of the water and sees the silhouettes of boats against "a backdrop of shimmering gold," he understands for "perhaps the first time . . . how Hawaii could cast a spell upon the visitor" (163).

He discovers to his horror, however, that his keys are lost, most probably buried somewhere in the sand. His momentary panic and despair is dissipated, however, when he notices that the beams of the sun, which is almost touching the horizon, are "level with the surface of the ocean." He walks "in a perfectly straight line" to the water's edge. "I stopped, turned, and squatted on my heels. I looked back up the gently sloping beach to the spot where I had changed for my swim, and there, a yard or two to the right of my towel, something gleamed and glinted, something reflected back the light of the setting sun, like a tiny star in the immensity of space" (165). Again, the language—"perfectly straight line," "gleamed and glinted," "sun," "star," "immensity of space"—suggests transcendence, and is reminiscent of Dante's imagery in the *Paradiso*, the continual references to the sun recalling Dante's primary symbol for God. From his new angle of vision, keeping his "eyes fixed on the spot where the spark of light had gleamed," Bernard is able to locate the all-essential keys. Thrilled with his newly found competence, he feels "light-hearted and gleeful." Just as Catholicism has traditionally taught that Baptism leaves an indelible mark on the soul, Bernard notes that he clutched the newfound keys so tightly that "the indentations in [his] palms have not yet faded" (165). The found keys, like any car keys, not only open a door but also give Bernard the ability to harness energy from a powerful force and to use it to move in the direction of his choice. From this point on in the novel, Bernard displays new competence, self-confidence, and vitality.

The theology of sacramentality affirms presence, efficacy, and transformation; and the sacramentality in the novel counters the negativist tendencies of the cynicism, fragmentation, and destabilizing narrative techniques, creating a context for affirmation and possibility in the face of the "eschatological wreckage."

When Ursula asks him if he believes in an afterlife, Bernard answers, "'I don't know,'" (205) thereby articulating, not only his personal agnosticism, but the novel's reluctance to speak definitively on the point. However, Ursula's rejoinder, "I don't see the point of religion if there's no heaven" (205), articulates what the average Christian (as opposed to theologians)

knows to be a fact: that Christianity cannot afford to marginalize or trivi-
alize this essential doctrine. Part of the problem in trying to answer questions about the afterlife is the lack of any adequate language, either to
frame the question or articulate an answer. As Bernard tells Ursula about
the ideas of modern theologians, such as the appropriation of the Buddhist
idea of "'the extinction of the individual ego, its assimilation into the eternal spirit of the universe,'" Ursula probably speaks for many people when
she responds, "'I don't think I like the sound of that'" (206). Bernard sees
a difficulty in speaking of heaven as a place. "'A garden. A city. Happy
Hunting Grounds. Such solid things'" (206). Yet he himself had written in
his journal that when he read a liberal theologian who argued that there is
"no god but the religious requirement, the choice of it, the acceptance of its
demands, and the liberating self-transcendence it brings about in us," he
had to admit that he felt no "liberating self-transcendence" and that this
language left him feeling "lonely, hollow, unfulfilled" (154). Against this
kind of language, Lodge sets Aunt Ursula's unsophisticated but sensible
question, "'Why not be bad, if you're not going to be punished in the long
run?'" To Bernard's suggestion that "'virtue is its own reward,'" Ursula's
rejoinder is, "'The hell with that'" (205). Thus language presses upon language, leaving us with the alternatives of formulations that are childish,
naive, and overly-literal; and others that are vague, lifeless, unconnected
to lived experience. Any formulation of that belief/hope is bound to be, in
some sense, oxymoronic: "confident assurance concerning what we hope
for, and conviction about things we do not see," presence and absence.

Significantly, the term used in the title and throughout the book is primarily *paradise*, not *heaven*. Colleen McDannell and Bernhard Lang point
out in their book *Heaven: A History* that the term *paradise* has more earthly,
human connotations than *heaven*. Not only is its primary meaning the
Garden of Eden, but when used to refer to heaven, it usually indicates a
kind of heaven where the joys are more human and terrestrial.[14] Since the
paradise that Bernard discovers is, in effect, a completely terrestrial one—
one that any good secular humanist could affirm—does the novel imply
that that is the only paradise there is? Does Yolande speak with the authority of the narrative voice when she says, "'I think we have to make
our own heaven on this earth'" (220)?

Such an interpretation is inadequate. The tension and paradox running
through all the discourse about faith—Bernard's account of his loss of
faith, Ursula's explanation of her return to it, the eloquent musings of Unamuno—are simply a realistic account of the nature of faith in today's
world. Mostly what allows for affirmation, transformation, and possibility are those qualities that make *Paradise News* different from Lodge's earlier Catholic novels: a more sustained and serious engagement with the
basic issues of faith, rather than its externals, a more nuanced view of

Catholicism, and a sense of both the Church and the world as sacramental, offering a possibility of a connection with the transcendent.

Although Bernard's first impression of Hawaii's pseudoparadise is that it is tacky, tawdry, and downright uncomfortable, gradually it rises to its promise. Bernard has glimpses of transcendence in its natural beauty—especially the ocean. In it he reconnects with his family and acts as peacemaker, intercessor, comforter, and aide, thus confirming that even during his dry, academic, ecclesiastical life, he was growing in virtue. His surprising discovery that he is, in fact, a very good man may be his most precious gift in Hawaii, one indispensable to his ability to re-find his faith and connect to God. He also discovers erotic love, which orients him toward a richer, more fully human life. The Hawaiian "paradise," which originally seemed to betray its promise, ends by living up to it in an unexpected and unforeseen way. Human love, growth in virtue, forgiveness, intimations of transcendence through the natural world all suggest that, though we are denied certainty, we have grounds for believing/hoping that God touches us sacramentally and is drawing us toward a paradise beyond all imagining. The first sentence in the novel is a question: "'What do they see in it, eh?'" (3). The last sentence in the novel is an answer to a question: "'Very good news'" (294).

NOTES

1. David Lodge, *Paradise News* (New York: Penguin, 1991), 280. Hereafter cited in the text by page number.
2. The lines, which are quoted on p. 281, are from Yeats's "The Second Coming."
3. Bergonzi, "Decline and Fall," 183.
4. Haffenden, "David Lodge," 152.
5. See, for example, his *The Art of Fiction*, chapters 8 and 50.
6. David Lodge, *Art of Fiction*, 227–28.
7. French theologian François Varone makes the point that a conversion to mature Christianity means leaving behind "the false God pleased-by-duty and by fear, the facile and useful God of efficacious rites" and discovering the God "who exists so that I may exist, who gives an overall meaning to my life so that I can fill out that meaning for myself and for others, the One who gives meaning to my responsibility, searching, doubts and plans. One has to exist in order to be a believer." François Varone, *Ce Dieu absent qui fait problème* (Paris: Cerf, 1981), 62, quoted in Michael Paul Gallagher, S. J., *What Are They Saying About Unbelief?* (New York: Paulist Press, 1995), 64.
8. Lodge, introduction to *The Picturegoers*, ix. One might question whether a theological perspective described in these terms is really deserving of the name *faith*, or whether it is rather a form of hope. What kind of faith can be described as "agnostic"? Yet in the face of the serious challenges posed by contemporary sci-

ence and Biblical criticism, one might also argue that as much as a robust, unquestioning faith might be desirable, that described by Lodge is probably an accurate and honest description of the faith of many serious, thoughtful contemporary Christians.

9. Kenneth Leech, *Experiencing God: Theology as Sprituality* (San Francisco: Harper and Row, 1985), 25. It will be recalled that I previously made the point that the best Catholic novels leave room for doubt.

10. The passage is found in Miguel de Unamuno, *The Tragic Sense of Life*, vol. 7 of *Selected Works of Miguel de Unamuno*, trans. Anthony Kerrigan (Princeton: Princeton Univ. Press, 1972), 131.

11. *Catechism*, 1131.

12. *Catechism*, 1520.

13. The importance of confession *to another human being* is key in the Catholic understanding of this sacrament. Protestants often wonder why they cannot simply confess their sins to God in private. As explained in the *HarperCollins Encyclopedia of Catholicism*, confession is necessary because of the social nature of sin, which is "an offense against both God and the community. Consequently, Reconciliation is reconciliation with both God and the community. Since every sin has a social dimension, every confession of sin or act of Reconciliation must also have a social dimension" (344).

14. Colleen McDannell and Bernhard Lang. *Heaven: A History* (New York: Random House, Vintage Books, 1990). For example, the happiness of the blessed would consist primarily in the company of loved ones and in aesthetic, intellectual, and in some accounts, even physical pleasures—rather than in the Beatific Vision.

9

Angst Meets Comedy: *Therapy*

Kierkegaard is for the young, but he is also for grownups who have attained the wisdom of knowing how fragile and partial is our knowing in the face of the absolute.

—Richard John Neuhaus, "Kierkegaard for Grownups"

There was never a pilgrim, "who did not come back to his village with one less prejudice and one more idea."

—Chateaubriand

That a television comedy writer would become captivated by the austere philosophy of Søren Kierkegaard may seem unlikely, but that is exactly what happens in David Lodge's *Therapy* (1995). Laurence Passmore, known as "Tubby" to his friends and relatives, is the very successful scriptwriter of a popular television situation comedy, *The People Next Door*. He is married to an attractive, talented university professor, has a grown son and daughter, a lovely home, and a flat in London, and enjoys the benefits of a large income. Yet, in spite of a life which most people would envy, Tubby is plagued by an inexplicable malaise. One day a friend kiddingly asks him how his *angst* is. Not knowing what the word means, he looks it up in his dictionary, which leads him to reference books to look up Existentialism, which leads him to look up Kierkegaard—and he is off on an experience that transforms his life.

As he begins reading Kierkegaard, Tubby discovers that the philosopher's concepts of dread and despair, his theory about repetition, the role of choice in creating an authentic self, and especially his analysis of the three stages of life—the aesthetic, the ethical, and the religious—begin to play themselves out in his own life. Kierkegaard provides more questions than answers, but when Tubby's comfortable life is suddenly turned upside down, he faces his own existential crisis, which leads him all the way to the shrine of Santiago de Compostela in Spain.

The relevance of the title is evident early in the novel, for the first section is largely taken up with Tubby's descriptions of the various therapies he utilizes to alleviate his pain. He goes to Roland for physiotherapy, to Alexandra, a psychiatrist, for cognitive behaviour therapy, to Dudley for aromatherapy, and to Miss Wu for acupuncture. Tubby also considers his meetings with Amy, his platonic mistress in London, as "a sort of therapy."[1] Apart from his general despondency, the only reason given for these therapies is a knee operation to correct some sudden mysterious attacks of pain. The operation is not successful, nor is there any really satisfying explanation for the pain. Roland tells him that it is "Internal Derangement of the Knee," or as doctors sometimes refer to it I.D.K. Roland wryly suggests that the letters really stand for "I don't know" (13).

Tubby is not really miserable but just continually feels an inexplicable discontent. His emotional state is given farcical concreteness in the form of a solicitation from an organization called MIND, which comes in the form of an envelope with a balloon and a letter inside. When he blows up the balloon, it shows a profile of a man's head (which Tubby thinks resembles him) and the words: "BEREAVED, UNEMPLOYED, MONEY, SEPARATED, MORTGAGE, DIVORCED, HEALTH." The letter says, "'to you . . . the words on the balloon may seem just that—words. But the events they describe are at the heart of someone's nervous breakdown'" (61). This experience makes Tubby feel guilty because he cannot claim any of these factors as the cause for his unhappiness. He has no good reason to be unhappy, but he is.

Looking up the name *Kierkegaard* in a biographical dictionary, Tubby is transfixed by the titles of his books:

I can't describe how I felt as I read the titles. If the hairs on the back of my neck were shorter, they would have lifted. *Fear and Trembling, The Sickness Unto Death, The Concept of Dread*—they didn't sound like titles of philosophy books, they seemed to name my condition like arrows thudding into a target. Even the ones I couldn't understand, or guess at the contents of, like *Either/ Or* and *Repetition*, seemed pregnant with hidden meaning designed especially for me. (64–65)

Tubby starts reading *The Concept of Dread*. Kierkegaard defines *dread* as a "*sympathetic antipathy and an antipathetic sympathy*."[2] Historian of philoso-

phy Frederick Copleston explains the term this way: "Attraction and re-
pulsion, sympathy and antipathy are interwoven." Dread is different
from fear, which has as its object something "quite definite, real or imagined, a snake under the bed, a wasp threatening to sting, whereas dread
is concerned with the as yet unknown and indefinite."[3] For Kierkegaard
dread also refers to the state of a person who is both attracted to the good
and repelled by it. It can also, however, refer to the anxiety one feels at the
prospect of freedom. Kierkegaard uses Adam as an example: God's command not to eat the fruit awakens in him "the possibility of freedom."
Adam experiences "the alarming possibility of *being able*. What it is he is
able to do, of that he has no conception."[4] Adam is both attracted to the
possibility of freedom yet also repelled because it involves sin.

Kierkegaard thinks that this state of dread often precedes a transition to
another mode of living. His notion of the three stages of life is developed
in *Either/Or*, one of the other books Tubby borrows from the library, along
with *The Concept of Dread*.[5] The first stage is the aesthetic. Although the
name suggests that a person at this stage is primarily concerned with
beauty, what Kierkegaard means is actually closer to what is commonly
understood by the word *hedonism*, a devotion to pleasure. The pleasures
may be those of gross sensuality, but they can also be the refined pleasures
of the intellect or of the fine arts, the emotional pleasure of human relationships (such as the Bloomsbury Group advocated), or the romantic idealization of nature (as with Wordsworth). The aesthetic person's highest
goal is to enjoy the fullest range of experience, unencumbered by any objective moral norms, ethical principles, or religious faith.

Tubby at the beginning of the novel is a Kierkegaardian aesthete, who
certainly enjoys the pleasures of the senses. He relishes good food, particularly at Gabrielli's, the Italian restaurant he frequents with his platonic
mistress, Amy; as well as the homemade dishes she sometimes brings to
the flat, "*moussaka*, or beef with olives or *coq au vin*" (42). He is fond of the
pleasures of sport. "I don't know anything like that glowing, aching tired-
ness you feel after a keen game of squash or eighteen holes of gold or five
sets of tennis" (24). He also enjoys a satisfying sex life with his "sexy wife
at home" (31). Furthermore, he enjoys it with comfort and security. "One
thing I've never worried about, though, is Sally's fidelity. We've had our
ups and downs, of course, in nearly thirty years of marriage, but we've always been faithful to each other. . . . To enjoy sex you need comfort—clean
sheets, firm mattresses, warm bedrooms—and continuity" (28).

Tubby is not a bad man. He is not a lecher or a gross sensualist. He is a
faithful husband and responsible father. He feels sorry for the squatter
who has bedded down in the entryway to his London flat and invites him
up rather than have him taken away by the police. He makes people

laugh. He is endearing at times, as in his self-description, which he is directed to write by his psychotherapist:

> My stomach was all muscle in those days, . . . but as I got older, in spite of regular exercise, the muscle turned to flab and then spread to my hips and bum, so now I'm more pear-shaped than barrel-shaped. They say that inside every fat man there's a thin man struggling to get out, and I hear his stifled groans every time I look into the bathroom mirror. It's not just the shape of my torso that bothers me, either, and it's not just the torso, come to that. My chest is covered with what looks like a doormat-sized Brillo pad that grows right up to my Adam's apple. (19)

Although he is a rich, successful television writer, Tubby suffers from the same nagging self doubts and self criticism as most people. His psychotherapist is quick to diagnose his problem as guilt and lack of self-esteem, those ubiquitous whipping boys of the therapeutic culture. Tubby admits that he lacks self-esteem and craves the respect of others. Yet that doesn't seem an adequate explanation of his unhappiness, given all the positives in his life. Tubby's preoccupation with his unhappiness is causing him to be distracted. He sometimes simply fails to hear what people are saying to him.

It may seem hyperbolic to suggest that Tubby is suffering from Kierkegaardian dread or despair—what Amy calls *angst*—but Tubby finds the titles *Fear and Trembling, The Sickness Unto Death,* and *The Concept of Dread* compelling. He does seem to be experiencing the emotion that usually precedes the transition from one stage to another. As one historian of philosophy puts it, "an individual on the aesthetic level is aware, notwithstanding his variety of sense experiences, that his life consists, or *ought* to consist, of more than his emotive and sense experiences."[6] Such a person inevitably suffers from boredom, and his life comes to seem empty and meaningless.

Tubby is puzzled because he cannot identify any reason for his unhappiness. He does mention some annoyances: occasional sleeplessness, his inability to have a climax when he had sex with his wife recently, a predicament about how to write the female star out of the television show when her contract expires. None of these problems, however, seems an adequate explanation.

Reflecting and amplifying his personal unhappiness is Tubby's growing awareness of the pain and violence of the world at large, imaging, as it were, his own sadness writ large. A two-year-old boy is lured away from a butcher shop by two older boys and is later found murdered. Two ten-year-old boys are charged with the crime. Vulgar and sterile new buildings and shopping plazas proliferate, homeless people bed down on London sidewalks, (including one who sleeps in the doorway to Tubby's

London flat), bomb alerts are frequent. He learns that the wife of one of his tennis partners has had a sexual fling with the son of the Club's golf pro; and his friend Jake, married less than two years, asks to borrow Tubby's flat to have a rendezvous with a woman. Tubby is further disillusioned when he spots his physician, Dr. Nizar, with a young woman he knows is not his wife. Even the royal family is misbehaving sexually— "Internal Derangement of the Monarchy" (92). The evening news reports the death from cancer of Bobby Moore, hero of Britain's victory in the 1966 World Cup Final. The poor response of a studio audience for the filming of *The People Next Door* is explained by the fact that they have just received notice that the plant where they work is going to shut down and they will all lose their jobs (79). Kierkegaard gives Tubby the vocabulary to describe his emotional state. "Dread is what I feel when I wake in the small hours in a cold sweat. Acute but unspecific Dread" (64).

Tubby resists the idea that what he feels is Kierkegaardian despair, writing in his journal that what he feels is "nothing as dramatic as that" (111), yet he comes to understand that Kierkegaard does not mean despair over some particular thing or event, but a more generalized, diffuse despair. In *The Sickness Unto Death* Kierkegaard writes, "So to despair over something is not yet properly despair. It is the beginning, or it is as when the physician says of a sickness that it has not yet declared itself."[7]

Tubby's vague, unfocused despair suddenly becomes very focused when his wife Sally tells him that she wants a separation. The disease has declared itself.

For the reader, who has been drawn into Tubby's account of his problems with the television show, his various therapy sessions, his discussions with his platonic mistress, and his lavish lifestyle, this development is almost as much of a shock as it is to Tubby. Like him, the reader may have failed to notice some clues that all was not well with the marriage: his remark that these days sex is almost always at Sally's instigation, his admission that he sometimes fails to listen to what Sally is saying to him, his impulsively running off to the filming session of *The People Next Door* when he expressly told Sally that he was not going to go, in consequence of which she had invited the neighbors in for a drink.

This shock propels Tubby into a spate of wild, erratic behavior, including spying on his wife's tennis coach, taking his platonic mistress to Tenerife, and flying to California to try to have a second chance with a woman whose advances he had declined several years before. Sally's announcement is followed by a series of first-person narratives by other characters, giving their version of what has happened. The first one is testimony by Brett Sutton, Sally's handsome tennis coach, relating how someone had tried to break into his house, how he found his ladder outside leaned up against his bedroom window, and how finally he was awakened one night to find Tubby in his bedroom with a torch (flashlight), staring at him. Tubby's first reaction to Sally's request for a separation had been to assume she had a lover and to suspect her virile tennis coach.

Brett's account is followed by Amy's, a description of Tubby's pathetic attempt to turn his platonic relationship with Amy into a sexual one. Amy's story, however, also sheds light on Tubby's marriage and separation: that Sally had told Laurence (as Amy calls him) that "he was like a zombie" (137), that he had spent the whole weekend trying to talk her out of it, that he had asked her if there was someone else and she said there wasn't, and that Sally had once walked out and stayed away for a weekend, and when she returned insisted on marriage counseling, thus explaining how Tubby happened to be going to psychotherapy in the first place. Amy's account is followed by similar narratives by Louise, an executive with a television production company in Hollywood who had once tried to seduce Tubby when he was in California to advise on the American version of *The People Next Door*; Ollie, the producer of *The People Next Door*; Samantha, a beautiful young script director whom Tubby takes along on a weekend in Copenhagen; and finally, Sally herself, who gives an extended account of their courtship, marriage, and the reason why she wants to end the marriage.

Telling the same story from different points of view naturally provides a much fuller and more richly textured view of Tubby, his marital situation, and his fascination with Kierkegaard. Multiple viewpoints are not uncommon in contemporary fiction, but *Therapy* provides a tour de force when Tubby again becomes the narrator and reveals that he has written all of the previous accounts by imagining himself into the psyche of those people. This experiment was done at the direction of his psychotherapist. Tubby recognizes that Alexandra thinks the exercise will help to raise his self-esteem because it should help him to realize that people really do not hate him, but actually like and respect him. The project does not, however, have the intended effect. "Being the sort of writer I am, I couldn't just summarize other people's views of me, I had to let them speak their thoughts in their own voices. And what they said wasn't very flattering" (212). When Alexandra accuses him of having been very hard on himself, he says he had tried to see himself "truthfully from other people's points of view" (212).

The writing of these accounts is a pivotal event in Tubby's moral growth. Kierkegaard's stress on the *individual*—as opposed to generic or abstract *humanity*—is what is distinctive about his philosophy. It is the individual in his or her particularity that is all important, not generic *humanity* or *mankind*, which is the subject of so much philosophy.[8] Tubby's writing of these various accounts, each of which so perfectly captures the personality, outlook, and even style of speech of each "author," indicates an extraordinary capacity to enter into the particularity of those persons. Although the ability to capture the idiosyncratic flavor of each of the character's speech could be attributed simply to the talent of a practiced scriptwriter, Tubby's ability to enter into other people's mind-set and vicariously live their experience goes beyond a good ear for dialogue to an ability to appreciate the uniqueness of those individuals and suggests the beginning of real moral growth. Recall that in the classic conversion story, *A Christmas Carol*, Scrooge's reformation is accomplished through his opportunity to see life through other people's eyes—in particular their views of him.

Tubby's keen awareness of these people as individuals suggests that he is poised to make a transition to Kierkegaard's second stage, the ethical. In *Concluding Unscientific Postscript*, Kierkegaard says, "The ethical is concerned with particular human beings, and with each and everyone of them by himself. If God knows how many hairs there are on a man's head, the ethical knows how many human beings there are; and its enumeration is not in the interest of a total sum, but for the sake of each individual."[9] Historian of philosophy Samuel Stumpf summarizes Kierkegaard's notion of the ethical man:

> Unlike the aesthetic man, who has no universal standards but only his own taste, the ethical man does recognize and accept rules of conduct that reason formulates. Moral rules give the ethical man's life the elements of form and consistency. Moreover, the ethical man accepts the limitations upon his life that moral responsibility imposes. Kierkegaard illustrates the contrast between the aesthetic man and the ethical man in their attitude toward sexual behavior, saying that whereas the former yields to his impulses wherever there is an attraction, the ethical man accepts the obligations of marriage as an expression of reason, the universal reason of man.[10]

It may seem ironic to suggest that Tubby is moving into the ethical stage, considering that previously (when he was apparently an aesthete) he was faithful to his wife during a long marriage, whereas now his greatest desire is to go to bed with other women as soon as possible. Yet his fidelity to Sally was not, in fact, based on strong ethical principles as much as on his penchant for comfort and convenience. It is in the context of explaining why he and Sally have been faithful to each other that he makes the remark about needing "clean sheets, firm mattresses, warm bedrooms—and continuity" to have enjoyable sex (28). Furthermore, in explaining why he and Amy do not have sex, he says, "Amy doesn't really want it and I don't really need it. I get plenty of sex at home" (31). He again appeals to comfort as the reason that he values monogamy over the philandering indulged in by so many of his friends: "What's so wonderful about married sex (and especially middle-aged, post-menopausal sex, when the birth-control business is over and done with) is that you don't have to be thinking about it all the time." Furthermore, Tubby finds that this sense of routine spills over into all aspects of married life so that you "need to speak to each other less and less" (128). So Tubby's "fidelity" does not really qualify him as "ethical" in Kierkegaard's terms.

There are some indications that Tubby has been moving toward the ethical sphere even before the shock of his wife's asking for a separation. Early in the novel, he has written some dialogue for *The People Next Door* that refers to abortion. One of the couples on the show suspects that their unmarried daughter may be pregnant and mentions the possibility of her having a "termination" (57). His producer feels the reference is "too controversial, and too upsetting" (58). Tubby, however, feels that it is unrealistic to expect that an "educated, middle class" couple would not even mention the possibility of abortion in such a situation. To the objection that the lines are not "'absolutely essential'" to the story, Tubby replies, "'Not absolutely essential. . . . Just a little moment of truth'" (58). Although seeing abortion as an option in a problem pregnancy may seem anything but ethical to some readers, it is important to remember that for Kierkegaard the word *ethical* does not mean adherence to any *particular* set of moral proscriptions or religious teachings, but simply the fact that one *does* order one's life by duty and principle, rather than simply by a devotion to pleasure. Tubby here is risking offending segments of his audience in order to depict honestly current thinking on a controversial subject.

Other indications that Tubby is developing some kind of an ethical sensibility are his refusal to let Jake use his London flat for one of his sexual trysts and his reluctance to turn over to the police the young squatter who has taken up residence in his entryway. It is conceivable that in each case Tubby bases his action more on an emotion than on any clearly and consciously held moral principle. He tells Jake that if he allowed him to use his flat for a sexual assignation, he would "'never be able to look Rhoda [Jake's wife] straight in the eye again.'" (48). As for the squatter, Tubby says, "I surprised in myself a strange reluctance to hand the youth over to the power of the law" (115). He invites him upstairs for a cup of tea and gives him fifteen pounds to rent a room for the night. Admittedly, in taking these actions Tubby does not demonstrate the clear adherence to duty and principle that is characteristic of Kierkegaard's ethical man. Yet, he seems to be moving toward a stronger sense of the rights and dignity of other people than he had as the callow youth and television writer presented in the flashbacks. In a stumbling and half-hearted way, Tubby is moving *toward* the ethical.

Kierkegaard's influence in nudging him toward the ethical is most dramatically shown when Tubby takes Samantha, a voluptuous script editor, along with him on a trip to Copenhagen ostensibly to do some research, but, in fact, to see the hallowed places associated with the Danish philosopher. He also has every intention of seducing Samantha, which is why he invites her. Yet when the delectable young woman, who is perfectly aware of his intentions, offers herself to him, he declines. When Samantha says she thought he brought her to Copenhagen to sleep with her, he replies, "'You're quite right, that was why I asked you to come, but when I got here I found I couldn't do it. . . . Because of Kierkegaard'" (190). Furthermore, he confides that Kierkegaard has become a kind of "'spirit or a good angel, saying, "Don't exploit this young girl."'" (190). In fact, what started out to be a sexual escapade ends up being a kind of pilgrimage as Tubby stands in reverence before Kierkegaard's possessions in the Kierkegaard room of the City Museum "as if they were sacred relics" (184). Kierkegaard has metamorphosed into a kind of guardian angel "hovering at [his] shoulder" (209).

If Tubby's Copenhagen trip can be considered a pseudopilgrimage, his next strategy for coping with the pain of the end of his marriage involves him in a very real—if not exactly traditional—pilgrimage. It begins when he starts looking for his first girlfriend, Maureen Kavanagh. Memories of Maureen start popping into his mind even before Sally asks for a separation. Thinking of his expensive car, which he is so proud of, Tubby wonders what Maureen would think of it, given that she considered it such a treat to ride in even an old car when they were dating in the 1950s. When he encounters Kierkegaard's religious ideas, he again thinks of Maureen, whose parents were strict Catholics, who would only allow him to see Maureen at the Catholic Youth Club at her parish. Although a nominal Anglican, Tubby had feigned interest in Catholicism in order to be allowed to attend the meetings and social events. When the lavender that Tubby's aromatherapist uses on him reminds him of the lavender scented stationery Maureen used to send him letters, it brings back "Maureen in all her specificity. Maureen. My first love. My first breast" (221). He mentions that memories of Maureen have been flitting through his mind ever since he have been writing a journal, as his psychotherapist had directed him to do. He then decides to write a full-fledged memoir of Maureen.

Tubby recounts their meeting at the corner where they each caught different trams going to their different schools. His account of their long, drawn-out, strictly chaperoned courtship, is not only nostalgic but amazingly erotic. He sees and admires her for months without ever speaking a word to her. They finally become acquainted when he helps her pick up her books after she falls when running for her tram. He summons up his nerve to ask her to go to the movies with him, only to be called a "'young blackguard'" by her stern father and gruffly told, "'My daughter's a respectable girl. I won't have her talkin' to strange fellas on street corners, understand?'" (230). Tubby attends every Catholic Youth Club function in order to have some time with her, and at the dances, he actually gets to touch her. The older, memoir-writing Tubby makes an amusing contrast between the dancing of today and the dancing of the 1950s:

> When, nowadays, I put my head inside a discothèque or nightclub patronized by young people, I'm struck by the contrast between the eroticism of the ambience—the dim, lurid lighting, the orgasmic throb of the music, the tight-fitting, provocative clothes—and the tactile impoverishment of the actual dancing. I suppose they have so much physical contact afterwards that they don't miss it on the dance floor, but for us it was the other way round. Dancing meant that, even in a church youth club, you were actually allowed to hold a girl in your arms in public, perhaps a girl you'd never even met before you asked her to dance, feel her thighs brush against yours under her rustling petticoats, sense the warmth of her bosom against your chest, inhale the scent behind her ears or the smell of shampoo from her freshly washed hair as it tickled your cheek. (235)

Tubby says that they "advanced in physical intimacy slowly, and by infinitesimal degrees" (238). The contrast to the blatantly open and free sexuality of the first part of the novel is striking: the casual philandering of Jake and Tubby's other friends, the eagerness of two young women in Hollywood to go to bed with a man they hardly know, the way that Samantha, aroused by a pornographic film, almost begs Tubby to have sex with her. Looking back, the older Tubby recognizes that Maureen's upbringing and restricted social environment allowed her to have a combination of traits almost unheard of today.

> She had a naturally pure mind, pure without being prudish. Dirty jokes left her looking genuinely blank. She talked about wanting to get married and have children when she grew up, but she didn't seem to connect this with sexuality. Yet she loved to be kissed and cuddled. She purred in my arms like a kitten. Such sensuality and innocence could hardly co-exist nowadays, I believe, when teenagers are exposed to so much sexual information and imagery. (241)

Yet the scene where Tubby first holds Maureen's breast is more erotic than many explicit descriptions of sexual intercourse that are such a staple of contemporary fiction.[11]

> Holding my breath I gently released a breast, the left one, from its cup. It rolled into my palm like a ripe fruit. God! I've never felt a sensation like it, before or since, like the first feel of Maureen's young breast—so soft, so smooth, so tender, so firm, so elastic, so mysteriously gravity-defying. I lifted the breast a centimetre, and weighed it in my cupped palm, then gently low-

ered my hand again until it just fitted the shape without supporting it. That her breast should still hang there, proud and firm, seemed as miraculous a phenomenon as the Earth itself floating in space. I took the weight again and gently squeezed the breast as it lolled in my palm like a naked cherub. (246)

Tubby goes on to recount how Maureen's growing sense of guilt about the liberties she is allowing him led him to end their relationship in a way that he now sees was hurtful and cruel. "I realized *for the first time* what an appalling thing I had done all those years ago. I broke a young girl's heart, callously, selfishly, wantonly" (261). In fact, the writing of this memoir has dramatically changed the way he thinks of Maureen. Whereas in the past, if he thought of her at all, it was just as a nice, naïve kid, he now seems overwhelmed, as he was in his youth, by her extraordinary beauty and her warm, affectionate nature.

This development in Tubby's life is important in three ways. First, it connects him more strongly with Kierkegaard, initiating an experience that resonates with the philosopher's ideas in *Repetition*. Second, it signifies a growth in character that is moving him closer to be the ethical sphere. Third, it sets him on the road of pilgrimage.

Ever since Tubby has discovered Kierkegaard, he is as fascinated with the story of the philosopher's relationship with a woman named Regine, as he is with his philosophy. Kierkegaard became engaged to Regine but soon afterward, broke it off quite suddenly. He still loved her, but was convinced that the difference in their temperaments—her lighthearted gaiety and his melancholy, introspection and seriousness—did not bode well for a happy marriage. Furthermore, he was convinced that Regine was "unreflective and unspiritual" and "could never accompany him along the ways of critical reflection."[12] Regine begged him to reconsider, but he would not.

Tubby is impressed with the parallels between Kierkegaard's break with Regine and his own with Maureen so many years ago. He even notes that their names almost rhyme—Regine-Maureen. Also, just as Regine, begging Kierkegaard to change his mind, asked him to kiss her, similarly, Maureen, after telling Tubby that they would have to refrain from kissing as long as she was playing the Virgin Mary in the Nativity play, told him that he could kiss her once before the moratorium and lifted her face. Tubby's response was, "'Oh, grow up, Maureen,'" and he walked away (253). His extended reflection on this era of his life makes him determined to find his old photographs of her and then to find Maureen herself. He feels an urgent need to make up to her for his cruelty.

Kierkegaard's book *Repetition* was written right after his parting from Regine and is to some extent based on it. The narrator is an older gentleman who has become the confidante of a young man who, like

Kierkegaard, had become engaged to a young woman he loves, but who decides to break it off for rather complicated reasons. Two views about repetition are expressed in this work. The first is that of the narrator, an aesthete, who believes that it might be possible to retrieve past events by calling them forth from the eternal present where they all reside. In a humorous account of his visit to Berlin in order to test this thesis by staying in the same lodgings and attending the same theater as he had done previously, he learns that this is not possible, partly because he has tried so hard to bring it about. The young man, on the other hand, is obsessed with the story of Job, particularly the way in which Job received back from God everything he had lost and more. The young man considers this a *"repetition."*[13] He admires Job—not for his patience—but because "the disputes at the boundaries of faith are fought out in him, [and] the colossal revolt of the wild and aggressive powers of passion are presented here."[14] God effected a repetition that the young man compares to a thunderstorm. "When everything has stalled, when thought is immobilized, when language is silent, when explanation returns home in despair—then there has to be a thunderstorm. . . . When did it occur for Job? When every *thinkable* human certainty and probability were impossible."[15] Job's ordeal "places him in a purely personal relationship of opposition to God, in a relationship such that he cannot allow himself to be satisfied with any explanation at second hand."[16]

When the young man finds out that his former fiancée has married someone else, he considers that such a thunderstorm heralds a repetition in his own life. He has been "given back" his freedom but without resorting to the strategy suggested by his confidante: that he pretend that he has a mistress. He compares himself with Job. "Is there not, then, a repetition? Did I not get everything double? Did I not get myself again and precisely in such a way that I might have a double sense of its meaning?"[17] The young man is convinced that there is repetition after all although it does not mean literal replication. Even though Job got new children, his original beloved children are still lost to him. True repetition is "repetition of the spirit," not material duplication.[18] Furthermore, this repetition contrasts the attempt of the aesthete to recreate his earlier Berlin experience. According to one Kierkegaard scholar, "his attempt suffers the fate of all repetition pursued on an aesthetic basis: it fails just because it is an *attempt* and because it is *pursued."*[19] "Repetition of the spirit," on the other hand, is a gift from God and comes with the violence and surprise of a thunderstorm. "How beneficent a thunderstorm is! How blessed it is to be rebuked by God!"[20]

Given that Kierkegaard's young man believes that Job's repetition occurs only after "everything has stalled, when thought is immobilized, when language is silent, when explanation returns home in despair," one could argue that the end of Tubby's marriage constitutes a "thunder-storm" in his life.[21] When his comfortable and routinized life is shattered, Tubby starts thinking of different kinds of repetition.

Aside from his ridiculous antics trying to discover Sally's lover—the only explanation Tubby can think of as to why she would want to leave him—his first response is to think of all the opportunities he has had for extramarital sex, opportunities that he has declined. He now wants to make up for lost time by recreating the opportunity but this time going ahead and enjoying the delights of unmarried sex. First he decides to turn his relationship with his platonic mistress into a nonplatonic one. Although he and Amy do, in fact, have sexual intercourse, the whole experience is far from the romantic idyll Tubby envisions, partly because of the vulgarity, commercialism, and downright ugliness of Tenerife, the island where they go for their tryst, ("essentially an enormous lump of coke, and the beaches are made of powdered coke"), and partly because the sex itself is so unsatisfying (152). In trying to go back and remake his relationship with Amy into something else, he ends up spoiling what had been a mutually satisfying friendship.

Tubby's next attempt at remaking the past more closely approximates the attempt of Kierkegaard's narrator when he tries to repeat his theater experience in Berlin. Tubby wants to re-create an experience exactly—only he wants it to end differently. He remembers that when he was in Los Angeles as a consultant for the American version of *The People Next Door,* Louise, an attractive, young television executive, had been very forthright about her willingness to sleep with him. Now that his wife has left him, he wants to go back and accept the offer. He sees it as a possible Kierkegaardian repetition. "It was the lure of Repetition, the idea of having Louise offer herself to me again, making possession doubly sweet, that impelled me to travel all those thousands of miles" (207). Tubby is obsessed with the idea of replicating every detail about the experience he remembers but is continually frustrated. At first Louise doesn't even remember him, although she finally does when Tubby refreshes her memory. When she agrees to have dinner with him, Tubby insists that they eat at the same fish restaurant in Venice that he remembers. It turns out, however, that the fish restaurant is now a Thai eatery. He wants to eat outside and watch a glorious sunset like they did before, but now it is chilly and overcast. He remembers that she had liked whiskey sours and is disappointed when she wants only mineral water. He even orders the same kind of wine, Napa Valley Chardonnay. As Louise says in her memoir (actually written by Tubby), "He was trying to recreate the exact circumstances of that evening four years ago as far as possible in every detail. . . . I guess in his head I was forever sitting at that table beside the ocean, gazing wistfully out to sea and waiting for him to reappear, released from his matrimonial vows, to sweep me into his arms" (167–68). The ultimate disappointment, though, is that Louise will not go to bed with him because she now has a steady boyfriend (by whom she is trying to get pregnant) and only agreed to the dinner date because her boyfriend was out of town.

As Tubby's plans to recapture his lost sexual opportunities are all foiled, he begins thinking more and more of Maureen. He decides to try and find her and returns to Hatchford, the neighborhood where they had lived. He finds it an "eerie" experience, "a dreamlike mixture of the familiar and the unfamiliar" (264) Although the streets and main buildings are familiar, the area is now inhabited mostly by Caribbean and Asian families. Tubby finds the house he lived in has been improved: sealed aluminum units replacing the old sash windows and the wall dividing the two small parlors into one "bright and pleasantly proportioned living-room" (265). Tubby immediately wonders why his family hadn't done that. Maureen's house, however, has not simply been changed, it has been demolished. Through inquiries at the parish church, he finds a record of Maureen's marriage—to Bede Harrington, who had been an officious, pompous, and unattractive member of the Catholic Youth Club. Finding Bede's number in the London phone book, Tubby calls and then goes to see him. From him he learns that Maureen is in Spain on a pilgrimage.

Impulsively, Tubby decides to go and find her in Spain. His enthusiasm for this daft project is heightened when, after he tells Bede that his wife has left him, Bede responds, "'Then that makes two of us'" (277). Is Tubby's decision to seek Maureen in Spain a Kierkegaardian "leap" or just another impulsive attempt of a newly separated man to ease his pain? Perhaps a little of both. Kierkegaard is clear about his conviction that significant moral growth—from the aesthetic sphere to the ethical and from the ethical to the religious—occurs, not as a slow and gradual process, but as a leap. Tubby's decision to seek Maureen in Spain is such a bold and radical decision that it can be considered a "leap." Having made this decision, his whole focus and attitude change. He stops fighting the divorce, telling Sally's lawyer that he "wouldn't obstruct divorce proceedings any longer, and would agree to appropriate maintenance and a reasonable financial settlement" (278). The terms he offers are deemed by Sally's lawyer to be not only fair but generous.

Whereas his earlier forays to Tenerife and Los Angeles were undertaken with a clear goal in mind (sex!), Tubby does not really know what he wants or expects from Maureen. "I don't really know what I want from Maureen. Not her love back, obviously—it's too late for a Repetition" (278). He is opening himself to the unknown, and in that sense too this action is a leap. In the introduction to the last section of the book, which is a revised memoir of his experience in Spain, Tubby says, "I do feel I've reached the end of something. And, hopefully, a new beginning" (286).

The tone and ambiance of this section are in sharp contrast with the rest of the novel. Nature comes more to the fore, and the accoutrements of living are much more austere and simple than those of Tubby's tennis club, London flat, fine restaurants, and various therapeutic venues. His expensive car, which he has ferried over to the continent, ("the Richmobile," as his daughter calls it) is his only link with his former life. After he crosses the Pyrenees, the weather is fine, and Tubby notes in his journal that "the scenery was spectacular: mountains green to their peaks, valleys smiling in the sunshine, caramel-coloured cows with clinking bells, flocks of mountain sheep, vultures hang-gliding at eye level" (288). The contrast with the earlier descriptions of the ugliness of Tenerife or the congestion of London are obvious. Just as in *Paradise News* the early descriptions of a tawdry, commercialized Hawaii give way to a sensitive rendition of its natural beauty as the protagonist grows into greater spiritual maturity, so here Tubby seems to become sensitive to the natural world for the first time.[22]

Even before Tubby actually finds Maureen, he is drawing close to her world by his encounter with Catholic Spain. When he attends a Catholic Mass at the monastery of Roncesvalles, he likes "the idea of doing something Maureen would certainly have done a few weeks earlier" (290). As in *How Far Can You Go?* and *Paradise News*, Lodge depicts the surprise of someone who hasn't attended Mass in many years and encounters the post-Vatican II liturgy. Tubby notes that "the pilgrim mass didn't bear much resemblance to anything I remembered from the repertory of the Immaculate Conception in the old days. There were several priests saying the mass at the same time and they stood in a semi-circle behind a plain table-style altar . . . facing the congregation" (290–91). Yet there is a sense of connection with the past as well, "the liturgy echoing round the pillars and vaults of the ancient church, as it had for centuries" (291).

Therapy is the only one of Lodge's Catholic novels whose protagonist is not a cradle Catholic, lapsed Catholic, or convert. Approaching Catholicism from the outside, Tubby describes the appearance of this religion to one who, though acquainted with it through Maureen and the Catholic Youth Club, is not conditioned by early indoctrination, fear of hell, or moral guilt. His description of Benediction from his adolescent point of view is classic example of an outsider's view:

Suddenly there was a clamour of highpitched bells, and I peeped through the doorway, looking down the aisle to the altar. It was quite a sight, ablaze with dozens of tall, thin lighted candles. The priest, dressed in a heavy embroidered robe of white and gold, was holding up something that flashed and glinted with reflected light, a white disc in a glass case, with golden rays sticking out all round it like a sunburst. (232)

The exotic strangeness of Catholicism, which was such a strong characteristic of the pre-Vatican II Church, is much attenuated in the Catholicism that Tubby encounters in the 1990s; yet it is there, especially in Spain, for Catholicism drags its long and picturesque, if sometimes tortured, history behind it. In the village of Cebrero, the church "contains relics of some gruesome mediaeval miracle, when the communion bread and wine turned into real flesh and blood, and the place is also said to be associated with the legend of the Holy Grail" (293).

Through patient questioning and searching, Tubby finally does find Maureen. As in Hatchford, he is struck by the changes wrought by the intervening years. The beautiful young girl has become "a plump, solitary woman in baggy cotton trousers and a broadbrimmed straw hat" (293–94). "In truth she looked a wreck . . . her neck was creased like an old garment; and her figure had gone soft and shapeless, with no perceptible waistline between the cushiony mounds of her bosom and the broad beam of her hips" (296). Not only does she look different, but the site of their meeting is far from the idyllic spot he had imagined. "As it was, we met on the edge of an ugly main road in one of the least attractive bits of Castile, deafened by the noise of tyres and engines, choked by exhaust fumes, and buffeted by gusts of gritty air displaced by passing juggernauts" (294).

The biggest shock of all, however, comes one night when Tubby hears Maureen crying in her room in the inn where they have stopped. He goes to her room to comfort her, gets in bed with her, and discovers that where one of her breasts should be, there is a "plateau of skin and bone" and "the erratic line of a scar" (307). Although startled, he is not repulsed. In fact, he kisses the puckered flesh. Maureen says "'that's the nicest thing anybody ever did to me'" (307), a remark that takes on added poignancy when it is later revealed that her husband has had no sexual relations with her since her mastectomy.

Once he and Maureen actually get to Santiago, the cathedral itself is a kind of icon of Catholicism, a montage of its colorful, grotesque, troubled, and romantic past. Tubby describes it as follows:

> The Cathedral is a bit of a dog's breakfast architecturally but, as we say in television, it works. The elaborately decorated façade is eighteenth-century baroque, with a grand staircase between the two towers and spires. Behind it is the portico of the earlier romanesque building, the Portico de la Gloria, carved by a mediaeval genius called Maestro Matteo. It depicts in amazing, often humorous, detail, some two hundred figures, including Jesus, Adam and Eve, Matthew, Mark, Luke and John, twenty-four old codgers with musical instruments from the Book of Revelations, and a selection of the saved and the damned at the Last Judgement. St. James has pride of place, sitting on top of a pillar just under the feet of Jesus. (309)

The sense of exuberance, bordering on burlesque, and the tumultuous variety of this building capture an aspect of Catholicism that can be as off-putting as it is attractive. The juxtaposition of Tubby's earthy colloquialisms ("dog's breakfast," "old codgers") with the language of high art ("façade," "portico," "baroque," "romanesque") is a linguistic icon of the rich texture of Catholicism that is both awe-inspiring and comic.

Catholicism's insistence on the material as a valid conduit for the spirit is evident in the pillar supporting the statue of St. James, where the custom is for pilgrims to place their fingers into the hollow spaces that have been worn into the marble by previous pilgrims. Maureen does so and closes her eyes in prayer. Behind the main altar pilgrims climb up on a platform behind the statue of St. James and embrace it, the traditional "'hug for St. James'" (310). Even Tubby is swept up in the enthusiasm and, like the other pilgrims, knocks his head against the forehead of the bust of the sculptor, Maestro Matteo, the tradition being that doing so will enable one to acquire something of his wisdom. Tubby is still a comedy writer at heart. "Every now and again somebody would bang their head against the pillar under the statue of St. James as they put their fingers in the holes, and then everybody in the line behind them would follow suit. I was tempted to try slapping my buttocks like a Bavarian folkdancer as I paid homage, just to see if it caught on" (310).

Tubby's droll comments about this spectacle come close to rendering it satire—if not farce. Yet that doesn't quite happen because it is overlaid with a genuine respect for Maureen's faith. When he had stopped at the abbey of Roncesvalles, where all the pilgrims are asked to complete a questionnaire, he had found Maureen's. Under *"Motives for journey"* the pilgrims could check one or more of the following: *"1. Religious 2. Spiritual 3. Recreational 4. Cultural 5. Sporting"* (290). Maureen has checked only *"Spiritual."* When they arrive in Santiago, Tubby wants to find accommodations, but Maureen wants to go immediately to the Cathedral. Kneeling at the foot of the pillar, she closes her eyes in prayer. When to Tubby's surprise, she reveals that she had booked a room at the most elegant hotel in the city before she had left home, he asks how she could be sure she would arrive on that very day. Her reply: "'I had faith'" (312).

Yet it is not only piety that has inspired Maureen to make this pilgrimage. She is trying to get over the death of her son Damien, who was killed while doing volunteer work in Africa. As she tells Tubby:

I read an article about the pilgrimage in a magazine, and it seemed just what I needed. Something quite challenging and clearly defined, something that would occupy your whole self, body and soul, for two or three months. I read a book about the history of it, and was completely fascinated. Literally millions of pilgrims went along this road, when the only way of doing it was on foot or on horseback. They must have got something tremendous out of it, I thought to myself, or people wouldn't have kept on going. (302–3).

Anyone who has ever read Chaucer's *Canterbury Tales* knows that motives for making pilgrimages have always been mixed. The worldly friar, the wife of Bath, and the crude miller have their counterparts in present day Spain.

> The most numerous were young Spaniards for whom the pilgrimage was obviously an impeccable excuse to get out of the parental home and meet other young Spaniards of the opposite sex. The *refugios* [inns built to accommodate pilgrims] are unsegregated. . . . Then there were the more sophisticated young backpackers from other countries, bronzed and muscular, attracted by the buzz on the international grapevine that Santiago was a really cool trip, with great scenery, cheap wine and free space to spread your bedroll. (292)

Others have more serious motivations, although they might not be specifically religious. Some are walking for charity, some to celebrate a turning point in their lives, others to step back from their lives and think about their future. Yet rather than dividing into neat categories of religious and nonreligious, the categories merge and blend. Like Maureen, many of the pilgrims would define their motives as "spiritual."

In his determination to find Maureen, Tubby actually becomes a pilgrim himself. When his agent objects to Tubby's taking a holiday in Spain at a critical time, Tubby retorts, "'It's not a holiday. . . it's a pilgrimage'" (280). At one point he and Maureen come upon a television crew filming a documentary about the pilgrimage. They ask to interview Tubby, but he insists, "'I'm not a true pilgrim.'" "'Ah! Who is a true pilgrim?'" asks the director. "'Someone for whom it's an existential act of self-definition,'" proclaims Tubby. "'A leap into the absurd, in Kierkegaard's sense'" (304). Tubby goes on to deliver his existentialist interpretation of pilgrimage to the television audience.[23]

Tubby may not consider himself a true pilgrim, but his Kierkegaardian overlay certainly renders his journey serious and spiritual, if not religious. In Kierkegaard's schema of the three stages, a person reaches the religious stage when, conscious of his own sins, his alienation from God, and his inability to fulfill the moral law by his own efforts, he makes a leap of faith which brings him into relationship with God. He knows God—not as an object—but intimately as a subject. The religious man is not free of suffering; indeed the truly religious person may suffer greatly, but like Job, is rewarded with an intimacy with God.

Tubby has worked out a schema for pilgrims corresponding to Kierkegaard's three stages of personal development. The aesthetic pilgrim is "mainly interested in having a good time," the ethical sees the pilgrimage "as essentially a test of stamina and self-discipline" (304–5). The true pilgrim, the religious one, makes the pilgrimage as a kind of leap into the absurd:

> To Kierkegaard, Christianity was "absurd": if it were entirely rational, there would be no merit in believing it. The whole point was that you chose to believe without rational compulsion—you made a leap into the void and in the process chose yourself. Walking a thousand miles to the shrine of Santiago without knowing whether there was anybody actually buried there was such a leap.[24] (305)

In fact, however, Tubby's participation in the pilgrimage goes beyond his moral support of Maureen and his endorsement of pilgrimage in the Kierkegaardian sense. He physically joins in. Because Maureen is suffering from strained ligaments, Tubby arranges to drive with her pack to each day's destination, arrange for accommodations, and then walk back, meet Maureen, and walk the rest of the way with her. Amazingly, Tubby's problem knee gives him no trouble. Maureen attributes this "miracle" to St. James: "'It's a well-known phenomenon. He helps you. I'd never have got this far without him. I remember when I was climbing the pass through the Pyrenees . . . feeling I couldn't go any further and would just roll into a ditch and die, I felt a force like a hand in the small of the back pushing me on, and before I knew where I was, I found myself at the top'" (300). Maureen also attributes to St. James the fact that Tubby turned up just when she was feeling hopeless. "'It was like a miracle. St. James again'" (302). At the end Tubby walks the whole last stage of the pilgrimage with Maureen and says that he is very glad he did. "You notice much more on foot than you do in a car, and the slowness of walking itself creates a kind of dramatic tension, delaying the consummation of your journey" (309).

Although it is the very premise of a television comedy writer named Tubby suffering from *angst* that makes the novel so delightfully comic, it may be straining credulity to see him in the process of "leaping" into another Kierkegaardian sphere. Is he in any meaningful sense a pilgrim? Two factors about Tubby suggest that it is not preposterous to see him as a serious pilgrim: his curiosity, and his determination to take a good honest look at himself.

His curiosity is one of the first traits revealed about Tubby. Only three paragraphs into the novel, Tubby has written in his journal, "Gingerly I got to my feet" (4). Immediately he wonders if the word should be *gingerlyly*, and he looks it up and finds that "adjective and adverb both have the same form." (4). Tubby often looks up words for their correct spelling or definition, and this penchant not only individualizes his character, but

indicates a fundamental curiosity about things and a desire to understand. He is always going to "look it up" (49), and looking up *angst* is
what leads him to read Kierkegaard. Joseph Conrad wrote in *The Secret
Agent*, "Curiosity being one of the forms of self-revelation, a systemati-
cally incurious person remains always partly mysterious."[25] Conrad's link
between curiosity and self-revelation is intriguing. The incurious person
is mysterious because he himself is not open to mystery. Self-revelation
and curiosity both stem from the same source: a desire to know and to understand. The curious person reveals himself because in doing so, he
learns more about himself. Tubby's curiosity is linked to his determination to see himself honestly, such as his attempt to see himself "truthfully
from other people's points of view" (212) when he writes the accounts as
if he were other people and his realization of the callousness with which
he had broken off his relationship with Maureen.

Pilgrimage not only provides the central narrative framework for the
last part of the novel, but also functions as an image of individual spiritual growth and of the Church itself. The phrase "pilgrim church" is one
of the key metaphors from the documents of Vatican II that has become a
staple of Catholic discourse about the Church.[26] It is often invoked to support the model of a church that is less rigid and hierarchical, and more
flexible and porous; less concerned with immutability and more concerned with spiritual growth and responsiveness to a changing world.

The pilgrim church in this novel is clearly a seasoned traveler, weighed
down with baggage, with bruised and sore feet, feeling at times, as Maureen says of herself, "'almost at the end of [her] tether'" (302). The pilgrimage experience—the ancient churches, the cult of martyrs, relics, and
miracles, the enormous outpouring of piety that can result from a scribal
error[27]—is a visible manifestation of the Church's long history, which is
both an inspiration and an encumbrance, indeed, at times, an embarrassment. Yet, as Maureen says, people "'must have got something tremendous out of it'" (303).

Like Maureen, the pilgrim church in this novel shows signs of aging;
like her she is scarred and disfigured by struggles and has lost her youthful beauty. Like Maureen, when Tubby catches up with her in Spain, the
Church sometimes looks "a wreck" (296). Her efforts to maintain integrity
and fidelity have led to strategies (the Inquisition, the Crusades) that,
though well-intentioned, now seem inhumane. As in Lodge's other
Catholic novels, the Church's traditional sexual morality comes under
critical scrutiny, especially in the chapters where the young people's burgeoning sexual feeling is crushed, Maureen is burdened by guilt, and
Tubby's frustration leads him to end the relationship. Yet Maureen's puritanical upbringing and overprotective father do not seem to have irre-
trievably warped her burgeoning sexuality. Tubby imagines that she was

devastated after he broke off their relationship. Yet when he apologizes to her for his treatment, she admits she cried herself to sleep for ages, but adds, "'young girls are always doing that. You were the first boy I cried over, but not the last.'" In fact, she went on to fall hopelessly in love with a "'wildly handsome registrar'" and have an affair with a houseman in the hospital where she worked (297). It was when she was on the rebound from this affair—not from Tubby—that she married Bede. Tubby is hurt to find that she hasn't thought about him in years.

Although the dour Bede may seem a disappointing and unworthy beneficiary of the erotic energy of such a lovely young woman, there is something solid, even sustaining, about the home and family they have established.[28] Not stylish or sophisticated—"ordinary large inter-war semi, with a long back garden," curtains that match the loose covers in the sitting room, family photographs on display (272–74)—there is, nevertheless, something welcoming here, in spite of the disturbing fact of twin beds in the master bedroom. Just as Maureen's father was presented as *both* overprotective *and* a benevolent guardian (like the Church), so also Bede's effort to shield his children from the worst aspects of modern popular culture by intermittently banning television from their home when his children were growing up is seen, on the one hand, as an unrealistic attempt to shelter them from the real world and, on the other, as a careful attempt to keep harmful influences at bay. Bede himself admits to Tubby that his daughter became completely addicted to television as soon as she left home and had a set of her own and concludes that "'all effort to control other people's lives is completely futile'" (273). Although Bede is undoubtedly right that an effort to control people (even one's own children) is doomed to failure, his exclusion of television very likely contributed to the serious tone in their home that produced children like their son Damien, who was killed in Angola while working for a Catholic aid organization.[29] Similarly Maureen's growing up in the strict, overprotective environment provided by her church and family did not make her into a cold, repressed woman. In fact, so positive does she feel about sex, that she tells Tubby she hopes Damien had sex with his girlfriend before he was killed (302). Maureen's upbringing is certainly not beyond criticism, but especially when she is compared with some of the products of the overly sexualized secular society like Louise and Samantha, her upbringing does not seem all that bad.

Bede and Maureen have stayed connected to their Catholic roots. When Bede tells Tubby that Maureen does a lot of volunteer work for the Church, Tubby asks, "'You both still go to church, then?'" Bede answers curtly, "'Yes'" and with his next breath asks Tubby if he wants milk or sugar with his coffee (274). It is as if their still going to church is just an ordinary fact of life, to be taken for granted, hardly something to explain or defend. Bede and Maureen represent the resilient and tenacious Catholic faith that survives in some people who lived through the tumultuous upheavals of the post-Vatican II years. Sociologist Andrew Greeley attributes such faith to the Catholic sacramental imagination nurtured in "a pervasive religious culture that had been shaped by it and continued to be supported by it."[30] Maureen's belief in St. James, miracles, and prayer, and the importance she attaches to the traditional rites associated with the pilgrimage are evidence of a connection to "the imaginative tradition and the spirituality of the lay folk," which Greeley sees as such a wellspring for faith.[31]

If pilgrimage has functioned in this novel as a useful metaphor for Catholicism—both the institution and the individual Catholic—and provided visual icons of the "dog's breakfast" of Catholicism, the Kierkegaardian themes have further enriched the depiction of religious experience. As we have seen, Kierkegaard believes that one achieves genuine religious faith only through a "leap." Kierkegaard's concept of the "leap" was partly a reaction against the theories of the philosopher Hegel, who proposed that significant change was accomplished through the gradual process of thesis, antithesis, and synthesis. Although Kierkegaard preferred instead the figure of the sudden leap into a higher sphere, the truth, of course, is that growth involves both kinds of movement: gradual Hegelian development and Kierkegaardian leaps, just as the physical development of species (at least according to some biologists) involved long periods of slow, steady evolutionary growth, spurred on by "leaps" of punctuated equilibrium. Frederick Copleston believes that Kierkegaard gives insufficient credit to the part that reason plays in the movement to faith: "As Kierkegaard's dialectic is one of discontinuity, in the sense that the transition from one stage to another is made by choice, by self-commitment, and not through a continuous process of conceptual mediation, he not unnaturally plays down the role of reason and emphasizes that of will when he is treating of religious faith." Copleston goes on to point out that although he finds the analogy of the leap insufficient to describe coming to faith, the life of faith does partake of Kierkegaard's notion of repetition. "And this act of faith is not something which can be performed once and for all. It has to be constantly repeated."[32] One thinks of how much repetition is at the heart of the Christian life and particularly Catholic life: the repetition of scriptural passages, liturgical rites and forms, devotions like the rosary and litanies, and in all the various traditions which have become part of the pilgrimage to Santiago de Compostela.

The use of the pilgrimage theme, with its rich sacramental sense of the sacred conveyed through matter, and the Kierkegaard theme, with its strong "either-or" mode, enables Lodge to achieve something quite remarkable. Andrew Greeley says of this novel, "Combing the two imaginations, analogical and dialectical, in the same 'therapy' is a deft touch, evidence that the two imaginations need not exclude one another."[33]

On their last day together in Spain, Maureen and Tubby drive to Finisterre, which means "end of the world" in Latin. Once again nature is foregrounded in its elemental and primitive beauty, as in those earlier sections of the book in France, as Tubby began his pilgrimage, and in *Paradise News* where the true beauty of Hawaii was revealed in contrast to the vulgar commercialized version presented earlier. These settings feature the characters either alone in a moment of profound self awareness or with another in a moment of genuine intimacy.

> The rolling wooded hills of the country around Santiago gave way to a more rugged, heath-like terrain of windblown grass broken by great slabs of grey rock and the occasional stubborn, slanting tree. As we approached the tip of the peninsula the land seemed to tilt upwards like a ramp, beyond which we could see nothing but sky. You really felt as if you were coming to the end of the world; the end of something, anyway. We parked the car beside a lighthouse, followed a path round to the other side of the building, and there was the ocean spread out beneath us, calm and blue, shading almost imperceptibly into the sky at the hazy horizon. We sat down on a warm, flat rock, amid coarse grass and wildflowers, and watched the sun, like a huge communion wafer behind a thin veil of cloud, slowly decline towards the wrinkled surface of the sea. (315)

Although Tubby wants Maureen to divorce Bede and marry him, she says she cannot do that. When he asks how she can stay in a loveless marriage, she responds that her marriage may have been sexless, "'but not loveless. . . . And I did marry him, after all, for better or for worse'" (316). So strong, in fact, is Maureen's faith in the permanence of marriage, that she encourages Tubby to try to reconcile with his wife.

As they drive back to Santiago that evening, Tubby stops the car, and they get out to look at the Milky Way, "a pale, glimmering canopy of light." Tubby remarks that the "'ancient Greeks thought it was the way to heaven'" and Maureen says, "'I'm not surprised.'" This exchange, together with the earlier eucharistic imagery and the fact that their dinner that evening had been fresh fish that "they grilled . . . for us over charcoal" reminiscent of the disciples' post Resurrection supper with Jesus by the sea of Tiberius (John 21:9–14) overlays the scene with a shimmer of transcendence (317). As Tubby and Maureen face each other with tenderness, affection and deep honesty, but with profound awareness of the contingency of their lives and their ongoing responsibility for the choices they have made, and as they situate their lives within the mystery and beauty of the larger universe, they brush up against the sacred.

Tubby has been reborn into a new life. Refurnishing the flat, which was robbed while he was in Spain, is "like starting a new life from scratch" (320). His knee pain, the original reason for all his therapies, has mysteriously disappeared, and he handily beats his old tennis partner "rushing the net after every serve and scampering back to the baseline when he tried to lob me" (320). His marriage is over, but Maureen will not leave Bede. Instead the three of them are the best of friends and are planning to go to Copenhagen in the autumn. Tubby and Maureen occasionally "have a siesta" in his London flat. The ending, of course, is not "neat." How could it be? Tubby is still very much on a pilgrimage—perhaps preparing to make another leap?

Therapy, along with *How Far Can You Go?* and *Paradise News* is distinguished by Lodge's remarkable ability to imbue his comic novel with a seriousness that gives it added richness. What keeps Tubby's story from being simply another amusing satire is—not only the poignancy of his divorce, a pain familiar to so many contemporary people—but the fact that the story of this likeable scriptwriter draws in and reflects the pain of the wider world. The MIND balloon with its reminder of all the reasons for depression, the studio audience of workers who have all just lost their jobs, the description of Tubby's father working as a tram driver standing at the controls in the cold for eight hours, the London homeless shelter shown to Tubby by the homeless man camped out in his entryway all keep the narrative from being focused too exclusively on the troubles of one very privileged member of the middle class. It is more than a reminder of the ubiquitous nature of human suffering. There is also a suggestion that larger structures of government, finance, industry, and the military promote pain and unhappiness. Even something intended to promote well-being, like the Rummidge City Centre ends up being ill suited to provide either comfort or visual pleasure. "Now the new buildings, with their stainless steel escalators and glass lifts and piped music, stand expectant and almost empty, like a theme park before opening day, or like some utopian capital city of a third-world country, built for ideological reasons in the middle of the jungle, an object of wonder to the natives but seldom visited by foreigners" (85). After spending a week doing little other than writing his memoir of Maureen, Tubby buys a paper and reads mostly bad news. "Nothing much has changed in the big wide world. Eleven people were killed when the Bosnian Serbs lobbed mortar shells into a football stadium in Sarajevo. Twenty-five UN soldiers were killed in an ambush by General Aidid's troops in Somalia. John Major has the lowest popularity rating of any British Prime Minister since polling began" (259).

This saga of a comedy writer's postdivorce adventure is definitively situated in a broken world, suffering from what Christianity calls original sin. Many secular novelists depict powerfully the pain of the larger world, yet they often do so at the cost of cynical pessimism, and if they use a comic mode, it tends toward irony and dark satire. Lodge's comic tone, however, remains buoyant and optimistic. His Catholic sensibility, I would argue, is partly responsible for his remarkable ability to integrate such a robust comic vision with an uncompromising account of a world which is, at best, disappointing, and at worst, sordid and corrupt.[34]

Kierkegaard's theory of comedy, as explained by Eastern Orthodox theologian David Hart, provides one of the best accounts of what David Lodge achieves in *Therapy* and his other novels.

> The special logic of this theory, after all, is that the *Christian* philosopher [or novelist]—having surmounted the "aesthetic," "ethical," and even in a sense "religious" stages of human existence—is uniquely able to enact a return, back to the things of earth, back to finitude, back to the aesthetic; having found the highest rationality of being in God's *kenosis*—his self-outpouring—in the Incarnation, the Christian philosopher [novelist] is reconciled to the particularity of flesh and form, recognizes all of creation as a purely gratuitous gift of a God of infinite love, and is able to rejoice in the levity of a world created and redeemed purely out of God's "pleasure."[35]

In affirming heaven, Lodge is gaining the earth.

NOTES

1. David Lodge, *Therapy* (New York: Penguin, 1995), 14. Hereafter cited in the text by page number.
2. Søren Kierkegaard, *The Concept of Dread*, trans. Walter Lowrie (Princeton: Princeton University Press, 1957), 38. Italics in the original.
3. Frederick Copleston, S. J., *Modern Philosophy: Schopenhauer to Nietzsche*, vol. 7, part 2 of *A History of Philosophy* (Garden City, N.Y.: Doubleday, Image Books, 1965), 120.
4. Kierkegaard, *Concept of Dread*, 40. Italics in the original.
5. Kierkegaard developed his ideas of the three stages in several of his other books, especially *Stages on Life's Way* and *Concluding Unscientific Postscript*. *Either/ Or*, however, the book Tubby borrows, is devoted primarily to a description of the first two stages, the ones that most pertain to Tubby's life.
6. Stumpf, *Socrates to Sartre*, 448.
7. Quoted in Robert Bretall, ed., *A Kierkegaard Anthology* (Princeton: Princeton University Press, 1946), 343.
8. According to Copleston, "Existence . . . was for Kierkegaard a category relating to the free individual. In his use of the term, to exist means realizing oneself through free choice between alternatives, through self-commitment. To exist, therefore, means becoming more and more an individual and less and less a mere

member of a group. It means, one can say, transcending universality in favour of individuality." Copleston, *Modern Philosophy*, 105–6.

9. Bretall, *A Kierkegaard Anthology*, 226.

10. Stumpf, *Socrates to Sartre*, 449.

11. The same point is often made about films: that older films where sex was conveyed by innuendo or suggestion are more erotic—certainly more romantic—than contemporary ones where sexual acts are explicitly portrayed with full nudity.

12. James Daniel Collins, *The Mind Of Kierkegaard* (Chicago: Henry Regnery, 1953), 9.

13. Søren Kierkegaard, *Fear and Trembling & Repetition* eds. and trans., Howard V. Hong and Edna H. Hong (Princeton: Princeton University Press, 1983), 212.

14. Kierkegaard, *Fear and Trembling & Repetition*, 210.

15. Kierkegaard, *Fear and Trembling & Repetition*, 212.

16. Kierkegaard, *Fear and Trembling & Repetition*, 210.

17. Kierkegaard, *Fear and Trembling & Repetition*, 220–21.

18. Kierkegaard, *Fear and Trembling & Repetition*, 221.

19. Bretall, *A Kierkegaard Anthology*, 136.

20. Kierkegaard, *Fear and Trembling & Repetition*, 212.

21. Kierkegaard, *Fear and Trembling & Repetition*, 212.

22. Actually, the very first paragraph of the novel has Tubby describing squirrels playing in the leafless trees in his garden. However, although the scene is natural, its barren wintry setting and the frenetic activity of the squirrels seem descriptive of the London/Rummidge life depicted in the first two thirds of the novel:

> I watched two playing tag in the chestnuts just outside my study window: spiralling up a trunk, dodging and feinting among the branches, then scampering along a bough and leaping to the next tree, then zooming down the side of its trunk headfirst, freezing halfway, claws sticking like Velcro to the corrugated bark, then streaking across the grass, one trying to shake off the other by jinking and swerving and turning on a sixpence till he reached the bole of a Canadian poplar and they both rocketed up its side into the thin elastic branches and balanced there, swaying gently and blinking contentedly at each other. Pure play—no question. (3)

If this is play, it is play London-style. The natural scenes of the last third of the novel, however, are much more peaceful, pastoral, and verdant.

23. According to the *HarperCollins Encyclopedia of Catholicism*, there are three requisites for an authentic pilgrimage: "(1) the belief that God responds to prayer, (2) the conviction that God is present at holy sites, and (3) the desire to make a sacred journey to a holy site." "Pilgrimage," *HarperCollins Encyclopedia of Catholicism*, 1001.

24. Earlier Tubby had pointed out to Maureen that the tradition that St. James is buried in Santiago is believed by many to be due to the error of a scribe, who wrote "Hispaniam" (Spain) for "Hierusalem" (Jerusalem). Such rational quibbles carry no weight with Maureen. "'I think he's around the place somewhere'" she replies. "'With so many people walking to Santiago to pay him homage, he could hardly stay away, could he?'" (300–1).

25. Joseph Conrad, *The Secret Agent: A Simple Tale* (Cambridge and New York: Cambridge University Press, 1990), 179.

26. The metaphor is used in *Lumen Gentium*, the Constitution on the Church.

27. See endnote 24.

28. This is also true of Maureen's working class home, which Tubby used to visit while her father was at work. "Mrs. Kavanagh gave me a cup of tea and a slice of home-made soda bread in her big, dark, chaotic basement kitchen, and burped a baby over her shoulder as she assessed me" (231).

29. The name Damien is one with a particular Catholic resonance, being the name of a nineteenth-century French priest, recently beatified, who spent his life serving the lepers on the Hawaiian island of Molokai until he himself contracted the disease and died. The name of Maureen and Bede's son and the fact that he was working for a Catholic aid organization suggest that he has absorbed and retained something of the faith tradition of his parents.

30. Greeley, *Catholic Revolution*, 146.

31. Greeley, *Catholic Revolution*, 118.

32. Copleston, *Modern Philosophy*, 115.

33. Greeley, *Catholic Imagination*, 50.

34. David Hart explains how Kierkegaard saw the profound difference between humor and irony:

> Irony can certainly recognize that the incongruities that throng human experience typically frustrate the quest for truth; but, having seen as much, irony is then impotent to do anything more than unveil failure and vanquish pretense. Humor, on the other hand, is born from an altogether higher recognition: that tragic contradiction is not absolute, that finitude is not only pain and folly, and that the absurdity of our human contradictions can even be a cause for joy. Humor is able to receive finitude as a gift, conscious of the suffering intrinsic to human existence, but capable of transcending despair through jest. And this is why the power of humor is most intense in the "religious" sphere: Christianity, seeing all things from the perspective of the Incarnation (that most unexpected of peripeties), is the "most comic" vision of things: it encompasses the greatest contradictions and tragedies of all, but does so in such a way as to take the suffering of existence into the unanticipated absurdity of our redemption. David Hart, "The Laughter of the Philosophers," *First Things*, Jan. 2005, 32.

35. Hart, "Laughter of the Philosophers," 36.

III

SARA MAITLAND

10

✛

Women of Faith:
Daughter of Jerusalem

Maitland does not write about religion but attempts to illuminate the potential mystery and sacredness within the lives of individuals—most often women— in transformation.

—Sally Cunneen, *"Big Enough for God: The Fiction of Sara Maitland"*

Women's experience brings into view a dimension of personhood which the theological tradition has ignored, distorted or falsely characterized in its construal of the normatively human.

—Susan L. Secker, "Human Experience and Women's Experience: Resources for Catholic Ethics"

Why include Sara Maitland's *Daughter of Jerusalem* (1978) in a study of contemporary Catholic novels? Not only was the author not a Catholic when she wrote the novel, but none of the main characters is a Catholic, nor do any of them exhibit the slightest indication of searching for God or having any religious faith. Although Maitland did convert to Catholicism in 1993, *Daughter of Jerusalem* was published in 1978 and thus predates her conversion. Yet I need to remind the reader that Maitland explained in *A Big-Enough God* that her conversion to Catholicism represented a repositioning with regard to authority rather than a substantial change in her philosophical and doctrinal religious views.

I will first focus on the novel in its singularity: its emphasis on the very personal and particular experience of one individual struggling with the heartbreak of infertility.[1] Then I will open it out to its more universal meanings in terms of Christianity and Catholicism.

Many couples suffer the disappointment of infertility. Yet from the beginning, Maitland stresses the particularity of this couple's experience. Liz and Ian are not a typical married couple. Ian is an ex-gay. He and Liz had lived together for ten months without having sex, but gradually he began to feel heterosexual desire, and they began a sexual life, which eventually led to their marrying. Liz, on the other hand, had indulged a lusty heterosexual appetite during her student years at Oxford:

> There had been mornings when she had woken in a bed and looked at the sleeper beside her and thought, "Who is this?" But sex was good that way, no danger, no need to have regard for the feelings of the other. There was no safety in love. And she would clamber out of the bed, leave a cheerful kiss or witty note and wander off into the dawn. . . . If you sleep with Liz she'll give you a good time, witty and clever as well as sexy, fun to be with, and she won't lay anything on you: no tears, no demands, not even an abortion, because she'll be somewhere else tomorrow.[2]

In addition to reversing the typical pattern by having the female be the more promiscuous one of the couple and by portraying a former homosexual in an apparently happy heterosexual relationship, Maitland concretizes their oddness by making Liz bigger, heavier, and stronger than Ian. She also earns more money than he.

Infertility in itself creates an odd situation for a couple. As Liz's best friend puts it, "'Here is everyone else I know trying to lose weight and not get pregnant; while you won't eat and can't'" (15). Liz's infertility is rendered even stranger, however, in that her doctor has been unable to determine any physical cause for it. More precisely, he can find a cause, but not a *physical* cause. Liz simply mysteriously fails to ovulate—except when her husband is away. At the beginning of the novel, Dr. Marshall has speculated that perhaps Liz is confused about her femininity and is suppressing ovulation. He suggests that she consider psychotherapy. This abnormality of Liz's physiology is contrasted by the extreme regularity of her menstrual periods: every fourth Sunday. "An exemplary working model: one hundred and forty-four repeat performances, the envy of her friends, the admiration of her doctors" (43).

In addition to being a story of a woman's struggle with infertility, the novel chronicles the painstaking journey to greater maturity of a sensitive, honest young woman. Liz's ego is fairly frail, suffering from a strained relationship with her mother, guilt because of her alienation from her adored father at the time of his death, some tensions within her commitment to feminism, her dislike of but dependence on arrogant doctors, and her fear of Ian's leaving her. But Liz brings great resources to her struggles: she is extremely intelligent, brutally honest with herself, and supported by a sisterhood of good friends. "It helped to have told Nancy, and know she had a claim on her sympathy and attention, despite two pre-school children, a husband, half a job, and a thousand other concerns" (17); and it helps being married to a man she deeply loves and who loves her. As Liz presses on in her determination to have a child, it is as if she has to do more than regularize her ovulation in order to become a mother; she also has to grow in self-knowledge, nourish her genuine yet still insecure love for Ian, and mend her relationship with her mother.

As a child Liz had adored her father and had a distant relationship with her competent, but critical, mother. Because of complications of Liz's birth, her mother had not been able to have other children, thus depriving Liz's father of the son he always wanted and Liz's mother of the additional children for whom she longed. Naturally, Liz feels responsible for these disappointments. Her father was the "first great love affair of her life" (41). "Her father had found her bouncy attentions charming as long as they were directed at him. When she was fifteen she started to read books he had not read, have friends he did not know, ideas he did not share. He withdrew his approval: she had betrayed him" (61). The night when Liz, now a student at Oxford, was having her first sexual encounter, she neglected to return a phone call, which was her mother calling to tell her that her father had been taken to the hospital after suffering a massive heart attack. Although he had lived two weeks before his death, he had never regained sufficient consciousness to recognize her. Now Liz is haunted by guilt and fears that her conflicted relationship with her father still affects her relationship with men. "Now she still wanted the approval of fathers. She tried to beguile this man [a friend at a party] into approving her, briefly creating herself as a child with the admiration of an older man. Not much older, actually, but powerful, male, and finding her charming" (61).

Liz's mother, although a competent caregiver, was somewhat cold and distant. As a child, Liz had taken particular joy in her favored status with her father and the special times they shared together, without her mother. Now as an adult, Liz's relationship with her mother, as well as with her deceased father, is encumbered with guilt. "Her relationship with her mother was so tied up in guilt: she had betrayed her from the start, gone over to the enemy, sold herself to the highest bidder. She had prevented her mother from having the son by the accidental ferocity with which she had torn her way into the world. She had killed her mother's husband" (93).

One of Liz's greatest sources of strength is her identity as a feminist and her sense of sisterhood with a group of women with shared values, with whom she meets weekly. "This was her family. This was where she was both nurtured and disciplined. This was where she was at home: if there were tensions, anger, spites, it was only to be expected in family life" (217). And there are tensions. Liz desperately longs to have a child, and even though two members of the group are mothers, and even though they claim that, as feminists, they support every woman's choice, Liz still feels that "feminists do not feel guilty about having abortions, only about wanting to have babies" (27). Matters come to a crisis when the group insists that Liz join in a mass demonstration in favor of abortion rights. Although Liz still intellectually supports abortion rights, her longing for pregnancy creates an emotional revulsion toward the idea of participating in the demonstration. "'I just don't want to, I can't, I . . . I've spent the last year telling you . . . Christ, I'm just not into abortion, right now, okay?'" (47). But her friends insist that she take part, arguing that she is betraying her feminist principles if she does not. Liz feels that this pressure is curiously akin to that wielded by men in positions of power and authority: "It was an old, old pressure. Be a good child and Daddy will love you. Be a good woman, giving and giving and giving, having no needs of your own except making your man feel good and James will love you. Now, support this march and we will love you and listen to you. Don't and we won't. Moral blackmail" (48). There are tensions, jealousies, rivalries among the women that demonstrate that Maitland has no illusions that feminist sisterhood is idyllic or free from the strife and frustration that plague all human societies.

Furthermore, Liz finds herself in the uncomfortable position of being dependent on the expertise of the medical profession, which is mostly male, arrogant, and patronizing. This power structure is embodied in Dr. Marshall, the head of the fertility clinic where Liz seeks help. As Liz's friend Nancy says: "If you were a bright young doctor and wanted power, where could you better seek it? No wonder so many men want to go into obstetrics and paediatrics and gynaecology. They can pretend there it is all kindliness; but you've got already submissive people and you claim to give them what they want, so they do exactly what you say and are grateful afterwards" (219–20).

Liz's greatest fear is her fear of losing Ian. It is bound up with her failure to produce the child that Ian also desires, perhaps as much as she. "If he was late home, was it because he wanted to avoid her, needed to escape from the pain and intimacy of her demands and her failure? Would he stop loving her because she could not have his child?" (110–11) Liz's fear of abandonment merges with her sense of the withdrawal of the love of all the "mothers" in her life.

> All mothers go away in the end. Her own mother. Her father. Ian. Nancy. The baby is used to waking the mother with the smallest whimper in the night. Now the mother does not come: the baby rolls on to its back to project its voice louder into that infinite space, and sees the shadowy shape of the mo-

bile hung over the bed. . . . Now the mother had withdrawn, gone away, did
not respond to the wailing in the dark. (111–12)

Liz craves approval and is burdened by a sense of failure. These are common human experiences, but her exceptional intelligence, acute sensitivity, and residual hurts from her conflicts with her parents and earlier relationships with men make her feel them more intensely than most.
"'Everything I put my hand to I turn into a mess. Maybe the doctor's
right, maybe I'm just fucked up'" (99). She is reprimanded by Dr. Marshall for taking part in the abortion demonstration, and she is scolded by
her women friends for her initial reluctance to do so. After a terrible fight
with Ian, she allows herself to be seduced by her boss. "She cries because
the failure in her body is spreading to her whole person" (103). In fact, Liz
comes to feel that her inadequacy is such a fundamental part of her being
that it is actually what does earn her such meager love and approval as
she does manage to gain: "she bought love by being inadequate as a
woman. Perhaps that bloody doctor was right: she did not want the baby
because she had noticed, subconsciously of course, that it was precisely
her failure that earned her that loving concern on which she depended for
attention" (179).

Because of her searching moral scrutiny of herself, Liz grows in self-
knowledge and maturity. Her relentless pursuit of greater honesty is a
key element in this struggle. When confiding in Tim, a gay friend, about
the tensions between Ian and herself, she is distressed to learn that Ian
had told Tim about their early sexual difficulties, whereas she had been
careful to "protect" Ian by saying nothing about them. Yet she cannot allow herself to take credit for this discretion. "She knew that she was dishonest, that it had not just been for his sake that she had refused to talk
about his impotence, that it had been for her own, because of her own
shame and lack of confidence" (97). In another instance, Liz and Ian
have taken to the circus the daughter of Liz's best friend and the daughter of one of Ian's colleagues. The two children are of different races, and
when they are going home on the tube Liz realizes that she is glad that
she and Ian have not actually adopted an Asian child, as they had once
talked of doing. "She was ashamed of herself for being glad, ashamed
for even noticing the curious glances they got with two different
coloured children in tow" (225).

One major challenge for Liz is her relationship with her mother. Shortly
before she and Ian are to leave on a much-anticipated holiday in Italy, her
mother has an auto accident and asks Liz to come and nurse her at home
so that she can leave the hospital. Liz agrees to do so, urging Ian to go on
holiday without her. She finds the situation difficult: "She hated cooking
in her mother's kitchen, hated the feeling that she was intruding, feared

all the time that her mother was about to criticise, to scold, to tell her the
Right Way to do something that she did her Own Way every day" (125).
Yet Liz also gains some interesting insight into what it might actually be
like to be a parent.

> Her mother did not need nursing, she needed tending to. . . . She needed
> amusing and shopping for, and help getting dressed and undressed. She
> would call suddenly when Liz was in the middle of something else and she
> would have to stop and answer. Her mother was not demanding, but she was
> dependent.
>   Like having a child, Liz thought, and hated it. She did not find it amus-
> ing to have to give up the shape of her own day into the keeping of another.
> (125–26).

During her stay with her mother, Liz begins to see her in a more human
light, rather than simply as the cold, distant parent and rival for her father's affection. She begins to feel faint stirrings of liking for her mother
and to have some empathy for her: "Her father must have been intolera-
ble to her mother. Even the fact that she had been able to pick up bits of
foreign languages on trips abroad—a skill that any small child has—had
been used to put her mother down. The endless jokes about Liz's brains
being from his side of the family" (128). As her mother shares with Liz her
plans to sell her house and share a smaller house with a woman friend,
Liz gains new respect for her.

Their improved relationship culminates with her mother's gift to Liz of
a large sum of money, a surplus from the sale of her house, which she feels
she will not need for her new life. She hopes that Liz and Ian will use it to
buy a house of their own, although she does not make it a condition for
the gift. At the end of the novel Liz and Ian have arranged for the pur-
chase of an old Victorian house they love, are painting and fixing it up,
and preparing to move in shortly after Christmas. They have also offered
a home in the big house to their friend Alice, who has recently become a
single mother.

Embedded in the distinct particularity of Liz's struggle with infertility
and her efforts to forgive herself for past failures and to hold onto Ian's
love are the more universal stories of the societal and familial pressures
on women, the empowerment of sisterhood, and the long, painstaking
growth toward maturity and self-knowledge. In addition, the novel offers
a poignant portrait of a marriage of two wounded healers, who in spite
of, or perhaps because of, their own failures are able to provide a safe, affirming and nurturing love for each other.

Daughter of Jerusalem is a moving story rich in insight into these aspects
of contemporary life, in particular, the heartbreak of infertility. But in

what sense can this book be considered a Catholic novel? As mentioned above, none of the main characters is at all religious, although Liz's memories of her father suggest that he was either a Catholic or a high Anglican, since she remembers church services with incense and vestments. Liz's story as sketched here certainly does not seem to be the material of a Catholic novel. That story, however, is *not* the complete novel. Each chapter ends with an epilogue, a retelling of an incident in the life of a Biblical woman. No explicit connection is made between Liz's story and the Biblical narrative, but careful analysis reveals that the two are indeed thematically related. Although the two sections do not explicitly "speak" to each other, they are, in fact, in dialogue.

The first chapter "April"[3] recounts Liz's appointment with Dr. Marshall when he suggests that her infertility might have a psychological basis, that she resists being a truly adult woman, and that she should consider psychotherapy. Liz visits her friend Nancy, who is supportive. She also tells her women's group and Ian about Dr. Marshall's theory. The epilogue for this chapter depicts Mary after the Annunciation, focusing on her act of assent. "So assent becomes the moment of conception. The assent with full knowledge, without even the hidden, subterranean doubt" (32). Whereas Dr. Marshall's hypothesis about Liz's infertility is that she does not really assent to her femininity, specifically to the challenge of being an adult woman, the epilogue stresses Mary's assent as the very essence of what happened at the Annunciation. Yet what is to be the nature of Liz's assent is not yet clear. Whereas Mary's is "an assent to the totality of herself, to a womanhood so vital and empowered that it could break free of biology and submission," it is not at all clear that Dr. Marshall's Freudian-esque analysis of Liz's rejection of her femininity is correct. Yet Liz does need to affirm something and accept a mysterious challenge, which she cannot even begin to fathom.

The epilogue is also remarkable for the way in which it pulls the figure of Mary, who has been so idealized and etherealized in Christian art and traditional piety, into the realm of the physical: "Here she is, a Semitic Arab adolescent, in the northern backwater of the minor Roman province of Palestine, some time after the annexation but before the destruction of the temple in A.D. 70. Probably vitamin and iron deficient; small dark, devout Jew. Almost certainly illiterate, destined by custom of time and place to be given in marriage while still pubescent" (33).

So we have these two very particular women: Liz, "'a women's libber with a reputation for gross immorality . . . married [to] a gay guy'" (98), and this illiterate "Semitic Arab adolescent," who, like Liz, is an "unconventional girl" (33). both of whom find themselves at odds with their surrounding culture and for both of whom assent is the path to the realization of their full womanhood.

The second chapter, "May," focuses on Liz and other women. Liz suggests to Dr. Marshall that they try to form some type of discussion group or group therapy for the women who come to the clinic. Dr. Marshall scolds her for elitist feminist ideas:

> "Don't you think that perhaps it is rather a middle-class, or to use your vocabulary, rather an élitist notion? For most of the women who come here, it is hard enough for them to talk to me, or other members of my team. . . . It is all right for you small minority of articulate women, educated, practised in tearing up your personal lives for the edification of your friends, but most of the women here would be too embarrassed, too private, to gain anything from such a conversation." (37)

At another meeting of her women's group, there is talk about patronizing rules that dis-empower women while ostensibly "protecting" them. Liz feels warm contentment among her friends. "The discussion was gentle, not strongly directed; but in her sense of passivity she liked that. She was happy. She felt that the others were very warm to her tonight too, although she was not sure why" (45). She later realizes why. Jane, an unmarried member of the group, is pregnant. All the others already knew, but sensitive to the hurt this news would cause Liz, who so badly wants to be pregnant, had been apprehensive about telling her. Later the meeting becomes adversarial as her friends all assume that Liz will take part in the upcoming abortion demonstration and don't understand her reluctance. After the meeting Nancy assures Liz that she understands the "emotional content" of Liz's reaction and accepts it as valid. Nevertheless, she asks her to put her personal feeling aside for the greater good of women's freedom, urging her, "'analyse that ambivalence, don't privatise it'" (52). To retreat to the private is to fall into other peoples' hands, allowing them to "'split up issues and women, accepting their control'" (53). Although Liz is still ambivalent about the abortion demonstration, she feels "warmed all through" and realizes that she does "not want their sympathy. . . . She [wants] their strength. And their love." (53)

This chapter ends with an epilogue describing the Visitation, the episode in the gospel of Luke where the newly pregnant Mary, having been informed by the angel that her aged cousin Elizabeth is also expecting a child, goes to visit her. "Thereupon Mary set out, proceeding in haste into the hill country to a town of Judah, where she entered Zechariah's house and greeted Elizabeth. When Elizabeth heard Mary's greeting, the baby leapt in her womb" (Luke 1: 39–41). Once again, the epilogue emphasizes the physical particularity of the women, lifting them up out of the realms of idealized myth and Italian Renaissance art and plunking them down firmly on *terra firma*. Elizabeth is now in her fifties.

"And menopause has not treated her kindly; her complexion has collapsed quickly and her breasts are withering, while round the hips she is putting on weight" (54). Maitland stresses Mary's need for another woman. "It is impossible for her to be alone" (54). Women, especially women linked by kinship or common experience, can provide for each other what no one else can. "But there in one another's arms, and only there, they are affirmed, encouraged, borne up, freed" (55). Although they do "strengthen one another, explain to one another" (54), it is not just that these two marginalized women need to prop each other up in the face of others' disapproval. Their mutual empowerment goes beyond that.

> And in the arms of her friend, her sister, within the strength of another woman Mary conceives again: the flowering of the great song of praise and power and triumph, the love song that unites her not just to Elizabeth but to all the other difficult women everywhere and everywhen. The mighty are cast down, the humble exalted. . . . But the women hold one another, empowered by one another they declare for the new order, together they feel and sing and love themselves towards the new Jerusalem. (55)

This Visitation episode provides a fitting epilogue to the chapter focusing on Liz and her friends. Like Mary and Elizabeth, they share some commonalties, but they also have some potentially divisive experiences. Although all committed feminists, the group includes a married mother, a divorced mother, a single soon-to-be mother, as well as a lesbian and a promiscuous heterosexual. They contradict the stereotype that all feminists are cut from the same mold. Their interests also go beyond concern for their own freedom and welfare, for they are genuinely committed to socialist ideals that they believe will build a better world for everyone. Like Mary in the Magnificat, they have a vision of a world where the poor will be lifted up and the hungry given every good thing.

The third chapter, "June," concerns the societal pressure on women to have children. Liz is repeatedly urged by her mother and other women to have a baby, all of them mistakenly assuming that Liz is childless by choice and that she is too selfish or career-oriented to take on motherhood. Moreover, Liz feels that she is failing Ian, who also longs for a baby. In desperation she conceives the wild notion that Ian should father a child by another woman. The epilogue for this chapter features Sarah, the wife of the Jewish patriarch Abraham. Sarah was sterile and urged her husband to have a child with the slave girl Hagar. Whereas the Biblical account does say that it was Sarah's idea for her husband to have a child by Hagar, Maitland goes farther than that, insisting that Sarah genuinely loves Hagar, whereas she feels only disgust for her husband. "She loves Hagar: the energy that once went out to her husband is now redirected.

Some evenings when Hagar is brushing her hair, tenderly back away from her face, brushing it admiringly up from the nape of the neck, sending shivers down Sarah's spine, Sarah reaches up a single hand and touches the younger woman's wrist" (81). Describing how Sarah actually lures the two of them to bed, Maitland overturns the conventional stereotype of the jealous, shrewish old wife who detests her husband's concubine. She makes the familiar biblical story even more peculiar when she indicates that Sarah has no use for her husband's God and considers him a malicious trickster. "Although she does not believe that Abraham's God listens to or cares about her, she has doubt that he exists and that her husband and his God plot together to get the best of all possible worlds for Abraham" (82). Thus Maitland sunders the archetypal faithful couple that traditionally stand as the fountainhead of Judeo-Christian religion. The beginning of the great religious tradition is not in unified amity, but in quarrelsome divisiveness. Furthermore, Maitland intensifies the dissonance because, not only does Sarah not love her husband, she resents her own God-given surprising pregnancy and dislikes her own baby son, Isaac, after he is born. "She hates him. He is not her son, she did not consent to him. Isaac looks like his father from birth. He is not beautiful and spoiled like Ishmael" (82). Sarah adores her husband's son by his concubine, and despises her own child!

There seems to be no basis in Scripture for Maitland's portrayal of Sarah's unnatural response to her own son. Perhaps Maitland wants to emphasize the issue of autonomy and choice. Even in the Biblical version, it *was* Sarah's choice to have Hagar bear Abraham's child, thus giving her vicarious motherhood, whereas her own pregnancy was ordained by God. Thus Ishmael reflects her own initiative and choice, whereas Isaac reflects the power of God. There is also no basis in Scripture for Sarah's fondness for Hagar. In the Biblical story Sarah is so abusive to her that Hagar runs away. Although Maitland's version allows her to integrate the theme of women's friendship and support, its tension with the Biblical narrative is problematic.

Chapter 4, "July," foregrounds Liz's complicated and conflicted relationships with men. She tries to defend her participation in the abortion demonstration in the face of Dr. Marshall's criticism. She also relives her conflicted relationship with her father, in particular, her knowledge of how much he wanted a son, a hope that was dashed when Liz's complicated birth rendered it impossible for her mother to have more children. She recalls a trip to Spain and her father praying before the Black Madonna at Monserrat. Liz speculates that he was praying for the miracle of a birth of a son. This chapter also introduces tension between Liz and Ian. She confides in Tim, their mutual friend, about Ian's recent aloofness. She also recalls the night when she made a conscious decision to lose her virginity and refused to take a phone call, which was her mother trying to inform Liz of her father's massive heart attack.

Liz wants her men to be strong. The adoration of her father, which she felt as a little girl, persisted although it became mixed with anger when she tried to break away as an independent adult. Dr. Marshall has the "magic" that seems to be her only hope for obtaining the longed for child, yet he infuriates her with his patronizing attitude. Ian genuinely loves and cherishes her, yet he is also a mystery to her, and his emotional withdrawal hurts her. "They were not exactly fighting though: they were just very separate" (94). She is angered when she learns from their mutual friend Tim that Ian had told him about his sexual impotence, which persisted for months, when he and Liz began their relationship.

The epilogue for this chapter depicts Delilah from the book of Judges (16:1–31). It takes up where the Biblical story leaves off. Samson is dead, and Delilah is wondering why she betrayed him to the Philistines. "She cannot tell now why she did it. He was a lovely man, and he had loved her" (107). This statement also resonates with Liz's feelings about Ian, which are the focus of this chapter. The novel emphasizes how Ian really loves Liz, how she *knows* that he does, that he is the only man ever to love her with such a pure, self-giving love. Her father and James, her former boyfriend, had proffered a "love" that had a large admixture of self-interest. Delilah denies that she betrayed Samson for financial gain, although she did accept silver from the Philistines. She concludes that there "was a softness in him which she did not love, which she despised, which made her want to destroy him. . . . She pestered him for the secret of his strength, because she could not bear the knowledge that he would tell her" (108). Delilah has internalized her society's glorification of the warrior. "She had been brought up among real men, who killed in the army and came home at night to kill again on the bodies of their women, who had been hard brutal men without softness" (108). Yet eventually she overturns her conclusion (much as Liz does when her honesty forces her to see deeper into her own motive for her reticence about Ian's impotence) and realizes she has been wrong:

That his softness, his willingness to share everything with her, even his weakness, his passions, his uncertainties: those were the things that a man should have, those were the things that were better than battle honours, which he had too. She had been given the chance to give her love to someone worthy of love and she had turned it down. . . .

. . . It was herself she had betrayed . . . because she had not been woman enough to meet the new and gentle man in him. (109)

Liz knows that in Ian she has a real treasure, a man of sensitivity and gentleness; and yet part of her is still in thrall to that old programming, the primeval lure of power. Whereas Dr. Marshall suggests that Liz is not woman enough to accept the feminine role of motherhood, Liz fears that, like Delilah, she has "not been woman enough to meet the new and gentle man" in Ian.

In chapter 5, "August," Liz continues to sense Ian's distance from her. It is at this time that Liz's mother asks her to stay with her after her hospitalization. Two important things happen during Liz's sojourn with her mother. First, she comes to like and respect her mother. Secondly, as if in support of Dr. Marshall's theory that Liz's failure to ovulate might be psychologically based, her thermometer tells her that she has ovulated, and like the only other time this has happened, it is when she is away from her husband. In desperation Liz calls their flat in London, hoping that if Ian has not yet left for Italy, they would still have time to have intercourse while she is fertile and produce the baby they both long for. Her attempt is in vain, however; no one answers the phone. When she later gets her period, she sees her menstrual blood as a sign that she is "cursed from within. . . . What had she done that her body would do this to her?" (134).

The epilogue to this chapter features a peripheral character from the New Testament, the woman with the "issue of blood" (sometimes translated as "hemorrhage"). Although this woman does not even have a name, the story of her encounter with Jesus is found in all three synoptic gospels. With all the crowds pressing around Jesus, the woman thinks that if she can only touch his garment, she will be cured of her affliction. She manages to do so and immediately feels that she is healed. Jesus asks who has touched him, for he is "conscious at once that healing power had gone out from him" (Mark 5:30). The woman identifies herself and falls at his feet. Jesus assures her that it is her faith that has saved her and tells her to be at peace. Like this woman, Liz has an "issue of blood," her monthly menstrual period that announces that once more she has failed to conceive. Like the woman in the gospel, Liz is humiliated and pained by her inability to be a normal, healthy woman. Perhaps she too can be "saved" through faith and through some sort of encounter. But faith in what? There is no indication that Liz even believes in God, in spite of the fact that her father was in some sense religious.

Chapter 6, "September," brings to a head the tension that has been developing between Liz and Ian. On the night that she and Ian are supposed to make love because, according to her temperature, this is the time when she might be fertile, he chooses to go out with a friend they meet in the pub instead of going home with her. When he finally does come in late, drunk and stoned, they get into a terrible argument. Ian hits her. She leaves the flat and walks around until morning. When she goes into work, she confides in her boss Tony. His comforting hug turns into a sexual embrace, and they end up having sex. In spite of agonizing over her infidelity to Ian, she derives great physical pleasure from Tony's strong, forceful male sexuality. Although she goes home to Ian that night and they both apologize profusely, she does not tell him about her infidelity. When she realizes that she has ovulated, she is horrified at the thought that she might be pregnant by Tony.

During this time Liz comes as close as she ever does to prayer. She is talking to her friend Nancy who is compared to a madonna, but not one "enthroned in gold, distanced by jewels. A friendly madonna who will carry the silly little messages of foolish girls to her almighty son. Liz cannot approach Him, only supplicate with the mother for the favours the father and son can give. Holy Mary Mother of God, I have sinned exceedingly, please help me, please show me what I can do to regain that love and security that you have eternally" (158). Although the passage says that Liz *can* supplicate the mother in this way, the reader is given no assurance that she actually does so. This "prayer" hangs suspended in the narrative space, pregnant with possibility.

The last scene before this chapter's epilogue is an extremely interesting conversation between Liz and Nancy, in which the two friends explore the convoluted and tangled intersections of love and fear, service and domination, peace and violence in relationships between men and women. Although feminist Nancy appears to have an almost ideal marriage, she admits that sometimes she is frightened of her husband. "'He doesn't even need to hit me; just this force, this will to win'" (159). She speculates that some of the energy she directs into the women's movement is redirected anger at Edward, which she does not feel free to express. This chapter is a sobering look at the undercurrent of hostility that simmers below the surface of any relationships between men and women and is especially disconcerting when it is discovered lurking even in what seems to be an almost ideal instance of married love.

The epilogue to this chapter tells the story of Debra and Jael from the book of Judges (4:1–5:31). Once again we see two women bonded, but this episode is like the shadow side of the Visitation. Instead of the two women celebrating their fertility and drawing together in love and support, Debra and Jael are united in violence and killing. What brings them together is a battle between the Israelites and the Canaanites. Debra, a prophetess and a judge, summons Barak to lead the Israelites and oversees the battle. The Israelites prevail, and Sisera, the general of the opposing army, flees to the tent of Kenite the Heber. Kenite's wife Jael welcomes him, but then as he sleeps, she proceeds to murder him by driving a peg through his head. In the Biblical text the actions of the two women are presented separately, but Maitland's rendition takes the story further, depicting Debra coming to Jael's tent after the murder. "Debra and Jael look at each other, they smile at each other—they are friends. They look at the smashed head of Sisera, the tent peg still firmly standing in the bloody remains, and they grin. They reach out hands almost shy with excitement and touch each other very gently. They know their husbands will not want to touch them, they know they are the enemy" (162).

In showing women, not only capable of, but even enjoying pleasure in violence, in feeling empowered by it, Maitland overturns conventional gender stereotyping. If her women are men's equals in terms of intelligence and other positive traits, they also share males' propensity to lust for power and to use violence to achieve their ends. Furthermore, it bonds them in a kind of sisterhood. Whereas the Visitation ends with Mary singing the Magnificat, which celebrates God's bountiful goodness and His empowering of the poor and the weak, Debra's canticle (not included in the epilogue) praises the Lord for the Israelites' conquest, and while clearly giving the Lord the glory, also takes unabashed delight in the slaughter and mayhem. Most disturbing are these verses: "From the window peered down and wailed the mother of Sisera, from the lattice: 'Why is his chariot so long in coming? why are the hoofbeats of his chariots delayed?'" (Judges 5:28). Maitland's account zeroes in on the way women, as well as men, need to feel powerful and can be exhilarated by the use of violence to achieve dominance and engender fear in others. The end of the epilogue asks, "What is the source of the joy that lights up these two women?" but does not answer it. It does, however, note that "men cannot help seeing the women, they cannot help feeling the hatred, and the joy. They are sick with fear" (162).

In chapter 7, "October," Liz is relieved to learn that she is not pregnant from her sexual encounter with Tony. Her mother reveals her plan to give Liz money to buy a house, and Liz and Ian set about looking for one. A new sense of happiness and peace enters Liz and Ian's life together as they set about preparing a nest for themselves and an enlarged family. That family will include, not only their hoped for baby, but also the pregnant Alice and her soon-to-be-born child, whom they invite to live with them in the big old Victorian house they buy. The experience prompts Liz to remember an elaborate dollhouse her parents gave her one Christmas, which was made to look as much as possible like the house Liz lived in. This section of the novel is replete with the joy, security, and delight that can be part of family life and that is symbolized by the family home. However, the fact that Liz and Ian stretch the definition of *family* to include an unmarried single mother and her baby attests to the fact that Liz and Ian's home will be a blend of the traditional and the innovative, flexible enough to accommodate new ways of being family.

In her relief that she is not pregnant by Tony, Liz more than ever cherishes Ian's gentle way of loving her. "She wanted to remember the playful tenderness, the sense of control and completeness she could feel with Ian which was worth a thousand hysterical orgasms. She wanted the intensity of care and attention they had to pay to each other. She could not use Ian's body and he would not use hers. She would deny completely that heady and unthinking lust. She knew too well where it led" (166). They return to childhood amusements: they swing in the park, and Liz buys Ian a skateboard.

Two important developments in this chapter are Liz's decision to go into therapy and her growing self-confidence. Her desire for a child has by now become so overwhelming that she is even willing to consider Dr. Marshall's conjecture that had so horrified her in the first chapter. Secondly, she vividly remembers an early visit to the clinic when there had been a microscopic examination of her cervical mucus. When Dr. Marshall left the room for a few minutes, the young student doctor invited her to come and see "'something pretty'" under the microscope. There she saw the "most beautiful pattern: elegant like ice on a window-pane; irregular fernish fronds crystallised on the glass plate" (181). Liz was overwhelmed by the beauty and intricacy inside her body. In a sense she fell in love with her reproductive system. The chapter ends with Liz feeling more confident about her body, remembering this incident and Dr. Marshall's recently seeing signs of ovulation, happy anticipation of moving into the new (old) house, and her decision to take the risk of going into therapy. She speculates that, like that unexpected peek at the interior of her body, a closer look into her psyche might also reveal unexpected beauty. Most important of all, she feels that the fact that she is not pregnant by Tony holds out the possibility that she can really be forgiven by Ian. She is desperately determined to hold on to his love.

The epilogue is narrated by Mary Magdalene. Maitland follows the traditional view that conflates Mary Magdalene and the prostitute who anointed Jesus feet with ointment and dried them with her hair.[4] Maitland brings her identity as a prostitute front and center, suggesting that her motive in going to the dinner party, where she washed Jesus' feet, is originally to tease him and shake his composure. But the joke backfires when Jesus gives her a gentle smile. The tears she cries are more tears of joy than of repentance, for Jesus has taken away her shame and called her a "loving woman" (185). Accentuating the root meaning of the word *redemption*, she informs us that Jesus "had bought her back, paid her price to her pimp, paid for the doctor that dosed her for the foul disease that clogged her gut" (185). Other additions to the gospel story include Jesus's introducing her to his mother and asking "her to take care of his own mother who was often confused by the noise and the movement and the late nights and the mixed company" (185); and her speculation that Jesus was a virgin, noting that "he lacked a certain animal roughness" (186). Mary Magdalene takes pleasure in the novel experience of liking him for himself rather than out of sexual desire or as a paying customer. Recalling the morning of his Resurrection, she notes that when she recognized him in the garden, "it was a meeting of friends" (187). This epilogue resonates with the strong need for forgiveness that Liz has felt in this chapter, together with her renewed sense of reverence for her own body.

Chapter 8, "November," is centered on the birth of Alice's child. Alice comes to Liz and Ian's flat when she thinks she is in labor, and her water breaks there. Their friend Jane, who has agreed to be with Alice at the hospital during the labor and birth, arrives and takes her to the hospital. Liz feels a sense of exclusion, intensified because of Ian's fascination with the process of Alice's labor. In fact, after they have left, Liz even gets down on her knees, rubbing her finger into the damp stain on the carpet left by the amniotic fluid when Alice's water broke. The incident provokes a memory of being at church with her father during the Easter season when the priest sprinkled the congregation with healing, cleansing holy water. Liz conflates this memory with the stain on the carpet. "This was the water from the inner temple; she would be purged, healed, would obtain the powerful magic from Alice, would glut herself on the water and say Alleluia, Alleluia" (199). So thoroughly does she believe this that she "raises the finger to her mouth and sucks greedily" and continues to taste her finger throughout the day (200). The next morning they learn that Alice has given birth to a baby girl, Miranda. A subsequent visit to Alice and the new baby in the hospital strengthens Liz's determination to find some way to have a baby of her own.

The epilogue to this chapter reinforces the theme of the barren woman's desperate desire for a child and her willingness to resort to "magic" to achieve it. It features Rachel and Leah, the two wives of the patriarch Jacob. Rachel, the one Jacob truly loves, is barren; whereas Leah, the ugly sister, whom Jacob had been tricked into marrying, bears many children. There is bitter rivalry and animosity between the two sisters, thus demonstrating that Maitland is well aware that all is not sisterhood among women—even (or especially?) between biological sisters. "Leah, ugly and unloved, mocked at her in the evenings; mocked her and took greedy delight in her barrenness" (210). Leah's hatred turns to disgust when Rachel begs her to sell her the mandrake roots her children have found, for it is widely believed that mandrake roots have the magical power to bring about pregnancy. "She only cared that she should get her hands on some magic powerful enough to fill her belly and her breasts with meat and milk, and make her feel like a woman" (212).

The last chapter, "December," centers on the celebration of Christmas. This is the ninth chapter, thus the novel covers nine months, the period of human gestation. Liz and Ian fret over where to spend the Christmas holiday. Neither going to Liz's mother nor going to Ian's family is a pleasant prospect. They finally decide to spend the day with their friends Nancy and Edward. Like most of the other chapters, this one includes a memory from Liz's childhood. When Ian begins a sentence with "when you get pregnant"—not "*if* you get pregnant," Liz realizes how important it is both for him and for her to hold on to hope, not to give in to despair. This incident provokes a memory of a fight in the school playground when she had refused to give up:

> "Do you surrender, do you surrender?" One of the few fights she had had as a child. She had been beaten. In the playground of her primary school, down on the hard tarmac, with the victor crowing over her, banging her head up and down on the hardness, forcing her wrists harder and harder, and chanting "Do you surrender, do you surrender?" The victory was obvious. . . . But until she surrendered, until she admitted it in her own words, the victory would not exist, would have no reality. . . . Liz believed in the power of silence. She would not name her fear, she would rather drown in the waters of chaos than name even the possibility of despair even secretly, because then it would exist. (220–21)

Liz refuses to give in to the temptation to despair. Although she is tempted by the thought that naming her fear and facing it might help her come to terms with the truth, she resists this temptation. Jesus's words, "Get thee behind me Satan," Jesus's rebuke to Peter, who rejected Jesus's prediction of his Passion and death (Mark 8:33), are inserted into the passage, perhaps as a residual, almost unconscious memory from Liz's childhood Bible lessons. The words emphasize the vehemence with which Liz repels the temptation to surrender. Whereas Leah turned to the magic of mandrake roots, Liz resorts to "white magic." She decides to conjure—not with dark words—but with the good words: "Mother, sister, lover, child, friend. Solidarity, love, delight, friendship. Hope" (221).

Liz and Ian are playful and happy decorating and furnishing the new house. They take two children of friends to the circus and enthusiastically enter into a childlike sense of fun and excitement. On Christmas Day at Nancy and Edward's, Ian gives her a puppy. Although at first she is distraught at thinking it is meant as a substitute baby for a barren woman, she is delighted with it.

At one point, Liz realizes that she has not started her period. "She counted weeks again, she must have got it wrong, she must have got it wrong. She knew she had not. Eight or ten hours. Only eight or ten hours. That was nonsense, she was being silly" (231). She is not being so silly, however, since it was revealed in the second chapter that Liz's menstrual periods are incredibly regular. By the time she and Ian walk home from Nancy's, Liz calculates that her period is twelve hours late. She will not say anything to Ian yet, but "she holds on to her minute ray of hope" (234).

As Liz clings tenaciously to this budding hope, she remembers an Anglican nun who visited them when Liz was a child. The nun had watched Liz's father holding her on his lap and suddenly admitted that she was guilty of the sin of envy. Liz's father replied with a condescending platitude, "'Dear sister, I'm sure there are the most glorious compensations.'" The angry nun retorted, "'Don't be so stained-glass sentimental. Of course there are no compensations. There are good things in my life, and I love it, but they are never compensations for that. You have to grow up and grow strong and grow loving with a great big hole in the centre of you'" (235). The phrase "There are no compensations" runs through Liz's mind as she and Ian talk about their complicated motives for wanting a child. Ian feels it will prove him a real man. Liz feels it will make her a real woman. They both feel it will keep the other from leaving him or her. Liz holds on to hope and love. She believes that "out of [Ian's] gentleness will come fruitfulness. She demands it. She refuses to articulate fear or despair; instead she articulates hope and belief. She says, "'We are going to have a baby.' She does not dare to believe it, but she believes it" (237). The narrative (exclusive of the epilogues) ends with these words: "It is over twelve hours now. She hopes" (238).

The last epilogue returns to the subject of the first two: Mary. The setting is shortly after the birth of Jesus. From the perspective of Joseph, Maitland stresses the physicality of the birth. "He sees the blood, the exhaustion, the damp head plunging out into the world from between her legs; he sees the eagerness of the scarlet child to reach his mother's breast" (238). As with the other epilogues, Maitland takes this Biblical, overly-spiritualized woman and makes her human and earthy. From Mary's perspective, she also emphasizes the physicality of the birth. "The pelvic ring is smaller than the baby's head; the biological facts remain even after their meaning is destroyed. The immaculate flesh is flesh still" (238). Even more important than what has happened to her body, however, is Mary's growing realization of the implications of her assent to this motherhood.

> In the glorious moment of her assent, in the rich song of praise that flowed from her in the arms of her cousin Elizabeth, in that moment she had thought to end it all. Had thought the moment would be total. . . . Once was enough. No more pleasures of the flesh; no more needing and wanting in the body. It was done: the circle was completed.

But the spiral was started: she was returned to where she had begun. Virginal, alone, complete, she was now bound inextricably to the product of that perfection—and on what strange routes would this boy child drag her? With what sword would he pierce her heart? (239)

Mary realizes what every mother discovers. No matter how much she may think about motherhood before she gets pregnant, no matter how much she observes, analyzes, or scrutinizes the interactions of mothers and children, a mother learns after the birth of her baby, that she is vulnerable in a way she could never have imagined. She will never again have the control of her life that she once had. "She had started what she could not control; what she could not name or finish" (239). The last words of the novel are, "This was the beginning of the end" (240). It is the beginning of the end—not only of Mary's motherhood, of her earthly life—it is also the end—in the sense of final destination, ultimate goal—of all human life. It is the beginning of the redemption of humanity.

The novel's epilogues, featuring Biblical women, who are often overlooked or marginalized in a book in which all the major roles are played by men, foreground women's religious experience and their essential role in salvation history. In addition to investing these women of Scripture with vivid, palpable humanity, these epilogues also add a deeper layer of meaning to Liz's experience. More broadly, they suggest that sexuality, power struggles, and the longing for children are all intricately bound up with a woman's life with God.

Although Sara Maitland was not a Catholic when she wrote this novel, its themes express a Catholic vision of life. It powerfully conveys the goodness of the material world, in particular, the marvelous and intricate female body, the locus of the engendering of new life, expressed beautifully when Liz observes her own cervical mucus through the microscope. This aspect of the novel anticipates what Maitland would say years later in *A Big-Enough God*: "We have gained a universe so extraordinary that it should stun us into awe."[5]

Liz's desire for a baby goes beyond the instinctual urge for reproduction and society's tendency to ascribe worth to women primarily as providers of children. Rather, Liz's longing is emblematic of humanity's need to extend itself in the service and nurturing of others. Some of Liz's conflicted feelings about sex reflect Catholicism's troubled history of trying to achieve a healthy and balanced attitude toward sexuality. The Church inherited from the ancient world in which it was born a deep suspicion of sex and a tendency to associate it with sin and evil. Yet it strongly resisted the gnostic temptation to see matter as evil. Children were seen as the good that "baptized" sex and made it allowable in the Christian life. Although the Church remained suspicious and wary of the tremendous power of sexuality, it reflected its Judaic roots in wanting to claim it as a blessing from God, even insisting that marriage is a sacrament.

Maitland's own view reflects both ends of this polarity. She does not idealize or romanticize sex. She is clear about the ways in which it can be used for power, self-aggrandizement, and selfish pleasure. Liz's relationship with her former boyfriend James illustrates this: "The insult that James had used with most power against her had been 'hysterical': he had pounded at her personality, just as, riding the waves of desire, he had pounded at her body. With his mind and his body he had made her acquiescent, had reduced her to a simple heap of quivering need" (72). Yet Liz's relationship with Ian models another kind of sex: gentle, tender, and considerate. Ian, who had experienced only homosexual sex before taking up with Liz, is at first unable to have intercourse. Finally, after ten months of living together, they finally achieve it:

> It was hardly an act of passion for either of them, paler, more fragile; from Ian it was a gift of confidence in her, a movement towards her achieved with so much doubt and confusion, but still a movement. . . .
>   . . . Her tough, thin body felt soft and other to her, curved and contoured in new ways, as though he had transformed her. A body coming into her, not saying, "It is safe? Are you careful?" but saying instead, "What can we do with this? Where can we go from here?" She had known, startled, at once, that she would never leave him, that they were bound together. (29–30)

What is so noteworthy about this gentle, tender lovemaking is that it is so connecting. It is the opposite of a solipsistic activity; it is a bonding, a ligature. One wonders if Maitland chose to make Liz's husband a former homosexual to allow her to portray a more tender, feminized kind of sexuality. Maitland's nuanced account of sex, while a far cry from associating sex with sin, does see the way in which it is bound up with humanity's fallen condition. It is clearly not the glorious and liberating acme of experience that our culture tries to make of it. In this way, Maitland articulates a vision that resonates with Catholicism's own struggle to achieve an honest and balanced understanding of sexuality.

The novel not only is concerned with attitudes toward sexuality in general, but also touches on the controversial issues of homosexuality and abortion. While the novel avoids taking any clear-cut position on either of these questions, it does generate some sympathy for the Catholic view. Although homosexual people are sympathetically portrayed (as they are in all of Maitland's novels), Ian's learning to be a happy and successful heterosexual lover suggests that sexual orientation can sometimes be unlearned and redirected.[6] Furthermore, as the novel depicts this man and woman working to achieve the wholeness of heterosexual love, their very struggles suggest that for no one is the fullness of heterosexual love simply a given; it must be worked for, learned, and practiced. Although Ian has strong feminine qualities and Liz has strong masculine ones, their sexual complementarity is evident.

As for abortion, Liz's conflicted feelings about taking part in the demonstration is an interesting comment on this difficult issue. Liz has no rational reasons for not demonstrating in support of abortion rights. Intellectually, she defends a woman's right to make this choice. Yet, her own longing for a baby creates a wave of emotional revulsion toward the idea of destroying nascent human life. The novel could be suggesting that rational argument should not be the only factor in this question, that an emotional response may be keyed to a deeper truth that is not amenable to rational critique. At any rate, few novels communicate a stronger sense of the phenomenal miracle of a baby.

Hope is the overarching theme of Daughter of Jerusalem. "Hope binds them painfully together; flickers in the darkness when they are honest enough to try and stamp it out; crops up again whatever means she tries to kill it with" (238). Liz's refusal to give in to despair and her determination that she will do whatever it takes to have a baby recall the definition of faith in the Epistle to the Hebrews: "Faith is confident assurance concerning what we hope for, and conviction about things we do not see" (Hebrews 11:1). The understanding of Christian faith as an amalgam of hope, conviction, and determination informs this novel. Furthermore, the fact that her name is a form of Elizabeth, suggests that, as with her Biblical foremother, her barrenness will ultimately bear fruit.

At the end of the novel, the reader does not know whether or not Liz is pregnant. Many signs, however, point to that possibility. The period of time covered in the novel is nine months, the time of a human pregnancy. The epilogues begin with the annunciation and end with the birth of Jesus. Most telling of all, perhaps, is the two-word sentence that ends Liz's story: "She hopes" (240).

NOTES

1. One could argue that it is the couple, rather than an individual, that is struggling with this disappointment, for surely Ian, Liz's husband, also suffers. Yet, although Ian is portrayed sensitively and sympathetically, the narrative focus is clearly on Liz.

2. Sara Maitland, *Daughter of Jerusalem* (New York: Henry Holt & Co., 1978), 20. Hereafter cited in the text by page number.

3. All the chapters are named for a month, the last chapter being "December"; thus the novel covers nine months, the gestation period.

4. According to Philip Jenkins,

The image of Mary Magdalene as a prostitute comes from the image of her that develops in the later church, where she is portrayed as a reformed prostitute. This image arises from the merger of several female figures in the New Testament, including the penitent woman who wipes Jesus' feet with her hair, and even the woman taken in adultery whom Jesus saves from stoning. Historically, though, there is no suggestion in the New Testament that Mary was originally portrayed in either role.

Philip Jenkins, *Hidden Gospels: How the Search for Jesus Lost Its Way* (Oxford: Oxford Univ. Press, 2001), 135.

5. Maitland, *Big-Enough God*, 62

6. The Catholic Church has no official position on whether homosexual orientation can be changed to heterosexuality. Courage, the officially approved support group for Catholic homosexuals who wish to live lives faithful to Church teaching, claims that although there are some instances of successful reorientation, the numbers are small.

11

Through Wilderness to Freedom: *Virgin Territory*

The virgin martyrs expose a nerve, a central paradox of Christian history: that while the religion has often justified the restricting of women to subservient roles, it has also inspired women to break through such restrictions, often in astonishingly radical ways.

—Kathleen Norris, *The Cloister Walk*

I am aware how much many women do not feel or do deny their very proper anger.

—Sara Maitland, *A Big-Enough God*

Virgin Territory (1984), Sara Maitland's novel about virginity, begins with the rape of a nun.[1] This act of violence, in which sexuality, brute force, and consecrated religious virginity are conjoined, initiates a story that explores the meaning of virginity for contemporary women in general and for Catholic women in particular. *Virgin Territory* reflects on the way the meaning of virginity has sometimes been distorted and institutionalized in the Church in order to disempower, regulate, and limit women. The novel also argues, however, that an authentic and mature virginity—encompassing sisterhood, generosity, fruitfulness, and autonomy—is a viable and mature mode of living Christianity. It also challenges the stereotypical idea that celibate communities are inherently opposed to individuality, personal growth, and emotional maturity.

In order to understand what Maitland is doing in this novel, it is necessary to reflect on Christianity's conflicted relationship with women and sexuality, and the Catholic Church's exaltation of virginity. The link between

sex and reproduction has been seminal in the development of sexual morality in all societies, not only Christian ones. Anthropologists and social historians explain that the religious proscription against premarital sex for
women in almost all cultures came about because of male insecurity about
their inability to have certainty about the paternity of the children born of
their partner. Andrew Delbanco in *The Death of Satan* argues that "Sin and
sexuality . . . will never be reconnected as they once were because the original linkage doubtless arose as a means of establishing social stability at a
time when sex could not be separated from pregnancy."[2] Some of the statements in the Pauline epistles reinforced this natural human tendency to discipline sexuality and also led the early Christian community to see
women's role as one of subservience and obedience.

Although most societies have prized virginity in brides and many religions have established codes to regulate and discipline sexuality, the
Catholic Church's relationship with sex has been particularly problematic.[3] According to John Marshall, counselor and medical adviser with the
Catholic Marriage Advisory Council in England, "the Roman Catholic
Church has prescribed the sexual behavior of its members in a way that
no other religious group has ever attempted. In traditional textbooks of
moral theology, for every page dealing with sins against social justice as
many as one hundred were devoted to sexual sins."[4] Most of the saints
commemorated in the liturgical year were either virgins or martyrs. If not
virgins, they repented after a sinful youth, turned from their evil ways,
and embraced chastity for the rest of their lives. Not surprisingly, then,
virginity is an *institution* of the Catholic Church—in the sense that Robert
Bellah uses the term *institution* in *The Good Society*: "Institutions are normative patterns embedded in and enforced by laws and mores (informal
customs and practices)."[5] In Catholicism, virginity has been associated
with, often even identified with the good, the pure, and the holy—to the
point that marriage was often seen as a state of life inferior to consecrated
virginity. Not that marriage was ever considered sinful, though some theologians thought that sex—even sex between married partners—was suspect and could be justified only by the conscious intention to have children. If one experienced pleasure as a byproduct, that was only venially
sinful—as long as one did not freely will the pleasure.[6]

For most of the twenty centuries of its existence Catholicism exalted
virginity and tolerated sexuality primarily for the purpose of procreation.
The Church's ban on extramarital sex was palatable to society because it
was obvious that children need committed parents and a stable family.
The arrival of a technology that separated sex and reproduction removed
or reduced much of the underpinning for society's condemnation of extramarital sex. What has changed in the contraceptive age is not only the
ability to sever the connection between sex and pregnancy by means of

chemistry and technology. The concomitant development—at least as important, if not more so—is the breaking of the philosophical link between sex and pregnancy, the sense that because sex is the means of engendering life, it is therefore sacred. Without that link to the sacred, sex has come to seem more and more simply a personal pleasure, hedged about by a zealously guarded right to privacy. Furthermore, if the ancient proscription against premarital sex, which has for so long been overlain with transcendent authority, is shown to be a purely natural construct, now no longer needed (not only because of the pill, but because of DNA testing), then the dissolution of this boundary opens up uncharted territory for moral behavior that can be both exhilarating and terrifying. The new situation does not mean that traditional orthodox sexual morality is to be jettisoned and a new one reinvented. But it does mean that the old rules can no longer be seen with such simplistic clarity. Everything is much more complicated now.

These new challenges to contemporary sexual morality are reflected in the novel's title. Just as the discovery of the "virgin territories" of the Americas, revealing the existence of huge numbers of people who had lived and died without ever having heard of Christ, raised profoundly vexing questions for evangelization and the doctrine of no salvation apart from Christ, so also the discovery of the new land of Christian morality after the pill requires re-drawing our moral maps.[7] Furthermore, this new territory has sent shock waves through the whole authoritarian structure that for so long has framed the Christian worldview and moral theology. This structure was in some respects rigid and oppressive; yet it had the familiarity of home. Now we are in new territory and have to make our way.

The title *Virgin Territory* is richly evocative. The phrase typically denotes land that is newly discovered, untouched, and pure. It connotes pristine, unpolluted nature, freedom from the contamination that comes with civilization, and the richness of untapped resources. It suggests limitless possibility. The "virgin territory" in this novel is the spiritual landscape in this new time, when an understanding of the moral uses of sexuality and the meaning of virginity, which had remained fairly consistent and coherent for almost twenty centuries, are now being called into question. The idealization of virginity has not only profoundly shaped Catholic moral teaching, but also contributed to the cult of the Virgin Mary, impacted who was chosen for canonization as a saint, and—for much of its history—caused the Church to devalue the holiness of the vocation of marriage. In his book *Making Saints,* a study of the canonization process, Kenneth Woodward asks, "What is it about the passionate life of the body which the church finds unbecoming in a saint? Why, in particular, are there no examples of happily married saints?"[8] As Maitland herself points out in *A Map of the New Country: Women and Christianity*, "contemplative and virginal life was presented as the best, and at times the only way for women to achieve holiness and respect within the Christian community; and from this women's own sexuality was devalued and with it the work and calling of the majority of women."[9]

After the Reformation, when the Protestant churches adopted the practice of having married clergy and, with few exceptions, repudiated monasteries, convents, and all forms of vowed religious life, they did much to regain esteem for the married state, in fact, to see it as the *ideal* state for Christians. Counter-Reformation Catholicism reacted by reaffirming the holiness of virginity. Just as it reacted to the Puritans' attack on religious images with the extravagant and ornate religious art of the Baroque, so it reacted to this attack on virginity with renewed emphasis on its sanctity. After the Reformation, Catholicism came to be more and more defined by its *difference* from Protestantism: thus to be Catholic was to believe in the authority of the Pope, the Real Presence of Christ in the Eucharist, seven sacraments, and the holiness of the celibate vocation.

Maitland argues, however, that even though marriage and sexuality have been more highly regarded in the Protestant tradition, the suspicion and fear of passionate sexuality and of the feminine are not exclusive to Roman Catholicism, but are only most clearly and explicitly expressed in it.

> It is important to realise that it is not that the Roman Catholic Church is more sexist than other denominations—it just has the unique and valuable talent for making visible what other denominations attempt to deny. The prejudices of Christianity are made plainest in the Roman Catholic Church. The logical and theological inconsistencies at the heart of their position are only a clear statement of what all the denominations actually practise.[10]

Thus it is important to read Maitland's analysis as not simply directed at Roman Catholicism, but at the larger Christian tradition. This exaltation of virginity and devaluation of female experience, which became intensified in Catholicism due to the Protestant challenge, remained standard for the better part of four hundred years. Then the 1960s brought the Second Vatican Council, the sexual revolution, and the women's movement. Suddenly the old way of thinking about virginity just didn't make sense.

To understand why the meaning and value of virginity was called into question, it is instructive to consider why the Church exalted and idealized virginity so much and regarded sex, even married sex, with such suspicion and fear. Although the gospels record few explicit teachings of Jesus about sex or virginity, Christianity was born in a culture that was already highly suspicious of sex. Uta Ranke-Heinemann in her book *Eu-*

nuchs for the Kingdom of Heaven: Women, Sexuality, and the Catholic Church points out that it is *"not true* [emphasis in the original] that Christianity brought self-control and asceticism to a pagan world that delighted in pleasure and the body. Rather, hostility to pleasure and the body are a legacy of Antiquity that has been singularly preserved to this day in Christianity."[11] The ancients, however, praised sexual continence primarily for its health benefits and its avoidance of the tumultuous passions which interfered with the goal of a tranquil life, rather than seeing it as sin or moral transgression. Stoicism, a widespread philosophy during the first two centuries of Christianity, was identified with "stolid, passionless behavior."[12] In such a culture celibacy was seen by many Christians as preferable to marriage.

According to the gospels, Jesus said little about sex, but one saying is recorded in the gospel of Matthew 19:12: "Some men are incapable of sexual activity from birth; some have been deliberately made so; and some there are who have freely renounced sex for the sake of God's reign. Let him accept this teaching who can." This text was seized on by Christians who sought an authoritative justification for their preference for virginity and their desire to elevate it to the ideal. Ranke-Heinemann, however, argues that this text has been misused. She points out that it follows immediately upon Jesus' teaching on the indissolubility of marriage: "I now say to you, whoever divorces his wife (lewd conduct is a separate case) and marries another commits adultery, and the man who marries a divorced woman commits adultery." When Jesus' disciples reply that in that case, it would be better not to marry at all, Jesus replies, "Not everyone can accept this teaching, only those to whom it is given to do so" (Matthew 19:9–11). He then makes the statement quoted above. According to Ranke-Heinemann, "whatever one's response to it, [this text] deals not with the incapacity for marriage or the principled rejection of it . . . , but with renouncing adultery; and hence it has nothing to do with celibacy. . . . Thus Jesus is repudiating adultery and divorce."[13] In other words, the "it" that only few can accept refers to the teaching on marriage and divorce—not the ideal of celibacy. Even with such a tenuous scriptural basis, the exaltation of virginity as the highest state for a Christian soon became part of the Christian mindset. As Maitland points out, "Since St Monica, in the fourth century, . . . the Roman Church has not declared any woman a saint who was not a nun or a queen—with a few exceptions for virgins who came to painful ends."[14]

The women's movement and the sexual revolution taught women to value their own sexual experience—not only heterosexual intercourse, which had been legitimate at least within marriage—but also lesbian sexuality and the physical processes of menstruation, pregnancy, and childbirth, processes that in the male mind connected women with the sickness, decay, and suffering inherent in matter and flesh.[15] Feminism's revaluation of women's bodies and sexuality inevitably called into question the traditional meaning of virginity. Does it have any meaning now other than a negative one: a lack of sexual experience, a dormant period before sexual activity begins? Are there significant reasons to abstain, now that pregnancy can be prevented and paternity proved in other ways? Does virginity have any real meaning as a part of mature adult religious experience?

Virgin Territory does more than delineate the undermining of the old rationale for virginity. It is fully aware of the positive meanings virginity has had for women in all cultures—not only Christian ones. It has been seen as conferring a degree of autonomy and power upon women and as giving them a special connection to the divine. In *The Cloister Walk* Kathleen Norris quotes a Benedictine sister who explains that "'virginity is centered in the heart and could be named "singleness of heart." . . . Virginity is a state that returns to God in wholeness. This wholeness is not that of having experienced all experiences, but of something reserved, preserved, or reclaimed for what it was made for. Virginity is the ability to stay centered, with oneness of purpose.'"[16] Maitland does not want to simply jettison virginity as irrelevant in the modern age. Rather, the novel struggles to see how it can be understood as a key element in the spiritual maturity of all women—not just consecrated celibates.

When the Reformation challenged the Roman Catholic insistence on virginity as superior to marriage and celibacy as a requirement for priesthood, Protestant novelists produced a stream of fiction purporting to expose the perversion and corruption within convents, monasteries, and rectories, all supporting a view of virginity as unnatural and unhealthy.[17] What makes *Virgin Territory* so much more engaging than the old "I Leapt Over the Wall" variety (which continues to be written) is its much more nuanced, complicated, and interesting investigation of the meaning of virginity than that presented in those novels. In no sense is Maitland's book an exposure of the "horrors" of the nunnery. On the contrary, the sisters are portrayed as exceptionally intelligent, generous, warm women. They are not paragons of virtue, and some struggle to reconcile themselves with certain aspects of their vocation or hitherto unexplored parts of their personalities; but on the other hand, so do other characters in the novel. The sisters have no corner on dysfunction.

The rape which disrupts the sisters' life is announced in the very first—and very dispassionate—sentence of the book: "At 8:45 one night, on the pitted track which led from the shanty-town to the house above it where the nuns lived, Sister Katherine Elizabeth was raped by two men, (probably) members of, or paid by, the National Security Forces."[18] The contrast between the violence and the bald, journalistic language in which it is related is striking. The rape victim is a missionary sister working in an un-named South American country. Ironically, however, she is only a periph-eral character in the novel. The narrative focuses on Sister Anna, the one who at first seems to be most controlled and least upset by the rape. Her closest friend, Sister Kate, reacts with a powerful and consuming anger—anger that eventually causes her to leave the convent and join a group of guerilla fighters. The novel is not so much about the rape itself as about the chain of events it sets in motion, especially in Sister Anna.

Although Sister Anna is the main character, Sister Katherine Elizabeth, the rape victim, frames the book. The first and last sentence both refer to her. The opening sentence is the one quoted above, and the last is, "But she knows that her sisters would worry enormously, especially, if she were late for Compline, so she trudges on up the hill towards the women's house where she lives" (210). Her response to the rape had not been the quiescent passivity of Anna nor the tumultuous, seething anger of Sister Kate. Rather, her response had been something in between—con-fusion, a sense of violation, worry about being pregnant. When it was clear that she was not pregnant, she set about processing her anger. In the final paragraphs of the book, she is still "in process," but it is clear she has come a long way:

> She has still not entirely worked out how to forgive the rapists without min-imising the rape, not just her rape but the possibility of the rape of all women everywhere. But for herself, gradually, something has happened. Rather two things have happened, closely connected but different. Her protection has been stripped away, her privilege and her protection, and that she cannot en-tirely regret. She has something in common with all women everywhere, and something in common with her friend and brother on the cross. (209)

Sister Katherine Elizabeth thinks of Anna and Kate and prays for them. Of the three, she is the only one to stay in the order and remain in Santa Vir-gine. She knows that she still needs to grow through the pain of the rape, but she is clear about what she needs to do.

> But something else has been stripped away too, her purity and choice made clearer by losing its symbol; the Church, the western civilisation which is meaningless here [in South America] had given her her virginity, but she has given herself back her purity, has reclaimed her chastity, and it is all her own. . . . For herself she knows that she still has to wrestle not with her anger which is legitimate, fierce and right, but with her guilt which is pointless, de-structive and wrong. (209).

It is this clarity that is denied to Kate and to Anna, which is probably why Sister Katherine Elizabeth—although the one who was actually raped—is able to continue her life as a sister at Santa Virgine, whereas Kate and Anna are not. Furthermore, it makes the important observation that although her virginity (in a physical sense) could be taken away from her, her *chastity* is under her control. Thus the word *chastity* is appropriated to mean a kind of virginity that is linked to autonomy and empowerment.[19]

Virgin Territory, however, focuses—not on Sister Katherine Elizabeth—but on Anna, who initially feels "nothing at all; she [sits] detached and distant" (7). It becomes clear, though, that on some deep level Anna has been deeply affected when she suffers an emotional breakdown. "Five weeks later in the middle of her adult literacy class Sr. Anna burst into tears. No one could have been more surprised about this than she was and there was nothing she could do about it. In front of the weary, patient, harshly determined women who sacrificed their little leisure to try and learn a skill that Sr. Anna took for granted, she could not stop crying" (7). She also cannot eat, becoming nauseated at the sight of food.

Anna's breakdown is related to her sense of powerlessness, which is a central theme of *Virgin Territory*. The rape which initiates the narrative causes frustration and anger among the sisters primarily because there is nothing they can *do* about it. Although they feel certain that the rape had been perpetrated by the Security Forces, they knew they could not report it:

> If the sisters reported the rape the Security Forces would move in and arrest someone, anyone, would punish randomly, would take the excuse to deal with a community leader, a suspected opposition member, with someone they wanted removed. . . . To expose themselves as needing the protection of the State would both undermine their credibility within the local community and put a question mark not only over just the one little house in Santa Virgine, but over the whole US-based Roman Catholic justice work in the country. (6)

The sisters' helplessness fuels their anger.

At first Anna seems to be the only one of the sisters who is not angry. "Only Sister Anna felt nothing at all; she sat detached and distant; her eyes were sharpened by her feeling of distance and she knew all about the agony the others lived with—she watched it with something akin to distaste" (7). But Anna's apparent tranquility masks a repressed anger fueled by an impassioned power struggle. Her antagonists, however, are not the perpetrators of the rape; rather, the rapists are merely one expression of her oppressors, who are referred to throughout the novel as "the Fathers." The Fathers embody the oppressive patriarchal power that has been bearing down on Anna all her life. The reason for her apparent lack of response to the rape is that this outrageous instance of male violence and brutality makes it difficult for her to continue to ignore her repressed anger at "the Fathers." Her struggle leads to her bouts of crying and her inability to eat. Her superior decides Anna needs a leave of absence and sends her to the Mother House in New York to reconsider her future. There Anna accepts the Mother Superior's suggestion that she spend a year in London doing historical research at the British Museum.

After Anna leaves Santa Virgine, she begins to encounter the Fathers in the form of disembodied voices she hears after she comes to London. They "ranted in her head, in her dreams and in her private spaces" (23). At first they seem to be simply an expression of a kind of Freudian super-ego. "'Behave yourself,'" said the voices of the Fathers. "'Pull yourself together. It is all right, we will not desert you. Keep the rules and we will take care of you. . . . You are not making enough effort. You must listen to us. You must not listen to anyone else. You must not weep in public. We do not like scenes. You have failed us, you are failing us. You will have to be punished. We will punish you'" (23).

Yet the super-ego does not adequately explain who these "Fathers" are for Anna. They are called "the Fathers" because in them is subsumed—not only her own biological father—but the harsh and demanding God revealed in parts of the Bible, the patriarchs of the Old Testament, the early theologians known as the Fathers of the Church, the Holy Father (the pope), priests, who are called "Father," the conquistadors, who raped the "virgin territory" of the newly discovered lands, and the European missionaries who brought Christianity to the New World but, in so doing, sometimes abused and brutalized the native inhabitants. Anna's research forces her to face an unsavoury chapter in the Church's history.

> The flourishing complex networks of tribes that had once inhabited the Amazon, maintaining a level of population never since reached again, had been destroyed, blotted out of history and material reality in the name of Jesus Christ.
> . . . They, the Catholic Church, had battered and impoverished an entire continent, a land rich in resources, in culture and in dreams; and then they had won sanctity by ministering to their own victims. (32)

The perpetrators of this "rape," although dead for centuries, merge in Anna's psyche with her tormentors. "The Holy Father, the Pope, had in the name of that God divided the whole New World between his two most favoured sons, Spain and Portugal. . . . The Holy Father was infallible, he had power over the distant seas and oceans, with his words he authorised the killing of people, the rape of women, the armed robbery of the Indian cultures. That was the power of the Fathers" (60). Anna comes to see a disjunction between the ideals of her faith and the appalling record of its historical reality. "Anna could not face the meaning; that so much power, dominating so much of history, drew its authority from the belly of a peasant woman, a curious inspired child bride who had believed that her pregnancy would set the captives free. The Mayans were enslaved, technically for refusing the gospel." (61).

The voices of the Fathers continue to torment Anna, becoming more and more vindictive. Their most frightening threat is to unloose chaos, thus inverting the work of the benevolent Father God of Genesis who blessed the cosmos with light and order and life.

> "Our wrath is very dreadful. Just remember, in the beginning there was not; and we were when there was not. Our goodwill created all things, and we hold it in being. If we are angry it will all go, fall, explode, implode, there will be no more light, no more matter, no anything, nothing real, no ground, no time. . . . The centre will not hold. We can blow the nucleus out of the atom. This is called Hiroshima and fall-out and megadeath. It is called void, and we own and control it." (76)

The Fathers urge her to return to her convent, "where the good women are: there alone you may be safe. Shall we tell you some names for our anger. It is called desecration and violence and Holocaust and rape" (77).

The depiction of the Fathers is disturbing—and is undoubtedly meant to be, for the narrative voice seriously believes that this coercive force has done serious damage—and not only to women. Yet readers are likely to find these passages overwrought, strident, and even brutal. Also, one sometimes wishes for some acknowledgement of the positive side of these authority figures, for their ability to bring order, stability, clarity; to hold in check the dark chaotic forces. A Father can bring the serenity and rational clarity of Apollo as well as the thunderbolts of Zeus.

Anna's keen sense of persecution by males—males whom she sees primarily as fathers—suggests that her own father may have been particularly severe. Yet he seems to be a kindly man with a warm and affectionate relationship with his daughter. He is proud of her and supportive of her religious vocation. "He liked the idea of one of his daughters becoming a religious; and especially Anna, his baby. It justified him. It contradicted all those voices which had told him that you could not bring up children like that, particularly daughters, and expect them to turn out stable and well-adjusted, good. He had been pleased with Anna, and had demonstrated his pleasure to her" (20). Yet it gradually becomes clear that, although he is kind and indulgent in some ways, Anna's father can also be overbearing and controlling. When Anna was a baby, her mother had left her husband and five young daughters. One can only wonder what would have led a mother to take such a drastic step. Late in the novel Anna realizes that her father did not want his daughters to search for their mother. This insight is linked to Anna's growing awareness of her own longing for mother love and her awareness that a mother can provide something that a father cannot.

During her time in London it becomes clear that, although Anna is in a modern, liberalized religious order, she is alienated from her physical self. In traditional Catholic piety, the decision to renounce sex has often been bound up with an outright rejection of physical pleasure altogether, sometimes, in fact, coupled with a deliberate infliction of physical pain, such as self-laceration or sleeping on the floor. St. Francis is reputed to have thrown dirt in his lentils, lest he enjoy the taste of them too much. Anna, although not inclined to practice medieval style penitential disciplines, does need to learn how to allow herself physical enjoyment, the pleasure of new clothes, of domestic fellowship, of friendship, of touch, and of eros.

Although she is living in a convent in London, Anna begins to live a more private and secular life than she ever has since she became a nun. Instead of doing pastoral work or community service, she does solitary scholarship in the British Museum. Two things, however, draw her out of her cerebral and spiritual life and into a closer connection to bodily life, specifically to her own female body with its desires and fears. One important factor is her involvement with a young family whom she helps with their handicapped child. A second catalyst is her relationship to Karen, a young woman she meets in the British Museum.

Feeling guilty that she isn't engaged in any service work, Anna responds to a request at Sunday Mass for volunteers to help with therapy for a severely handicapped child. Her offer to help leads to a close involvement with Stephen and Fiona, a young married couple who are struggling to cope with Caro, their severely brain-damaged daughter, and need volunteers to help with her exercise therapy. Stephen and Fiona's marriage is a solid friendship—warm, affectionate, humane, reciprocal. Anna begins to feel almost like a member of the family and basks in the healthful glow that emanates from their home, in spite of the stress of coping with a severely handicapped child. When the couple makes the courageous decision to risk another pregnancy, something of their courage and willingness to risk is imparted to Anna.

The awkward work of doing physical therapy with Caro leads Anna to start wearing secular clothes instead of her habit. (It is not insignificant that the secular clothing she wears—a gift from one of the other volunteers—is a track suit, clothing specifically designed for building up one's body.) At first this is difficult for Anna, for "the habit had become something to cling to, a sign that she was a nun, a bride of Christ. Without it she was lost, nothing clear or defined any more" (63).

Anna's involvement in this project draws her into the warmth and intimacy of Stephen's and Fiona's domestic life. Her very first visit to their home inaugurates Anna into this pleasure. "Soon Fiona brought a bottle of wine from the kitchen. She pulled the curtains and a few moments later went out again and returned with bread and cheese and a large earthenware bowl of fruit. She did not ask if Anna would stay and eat, she did not interrupt the easy flow between her husband and this nun. Anna was soothed by the ease of it, the warm offhand hospitality, and the comfort of home" (48).

Gradually, Anna's involvement with the family leads her to discover more about her own needs.

> Fiona did not want . . . Anna's generalised charity; she wanted companion-ship, pleasure, relationship. Anna found this alarming and realised how well she had been trained in detachment, in distance, in depersonalisation. They had been trained to love, but also to protect themselves against the demands of love, against loss and vulnerability at the personal level. . . .
>
> Overwhelmingly, as she recognised this she envied Caro. She wanted for herself the constant nourishing nurturing that Caro could demand as a right from Fiona. Anna felt herself orphaned, although she was furious with her-self for so feeling. God was not enough, she wanted something more physi-cal, a place where she would be held, be held even when she vomited and convulsed and retched, as Fiona held Caro. (58–59)

As important as Stephen and Fiona are for Anna's growth in self-know-ledge, her relationship with Caro is even more important. This is an ex-traordinary statement to make about a child who was born nine weeks premature, suffered brain damage at birth, and cannot speak. Yet it is not just that Anna feels compassion and love for the child, which she does, but she finds her beautiful and is moved by her "ferocity and power" (52). Caro is tremendously strong; she is "physical, all body" (63).

Anna feels such a deep connection with her that she seems to hear Caro's voice coming from deep within her. In these monologues Caro ex-presses her anger at not being accepted the way she is, at the attempt to make her into a normal child. "They don't love me, said this voice, they don't love me. Me. ME. They want me to be something different. They want a dear good little girl: they don't want this angry one, this fierce dark one" (53). These words may be projections of Anna's own repressed feelings; perhaps the anger and defiance she sees expressed in Caro is vi-olent enough to breach the barrier behind which Anna has kept feelings too painful to acknowledge. Caro seems to express Anna's own longing. "It was too true that they had something in common, but something that Anna had destroyed in herself early in its life. An abortionist, a back-street abortionist, she had aborted the child inside herself. The child who would allow her to play, to be cuddled and be loved" (53). Caro's monologues are some of the most powerful and original parts of the novel.

Love, ha ha, said Caro from her heaped self on the carpet. Truth, pah, forget it. There are no promises. This is the place where there are no promises. Resurrection, blah. There are no ministering angels down here, only the roaring wind of forsakenness and bitter vinegar against the raging thirst. I don't make terms; the sides of the chrysalis are not stable. Who says it is a safe place, the rocking belly. The walls of the cellar may well collapse and crush and bury you forever. You have to risk it. You have to come into the dark unprotected, without a thread to lead you back again. You have to leave your protection and come down where there are no words; where words don't work and all sense is broken down into guttural noises. Syllables like the Sybil spoke, which had to be interpreted. There is no interpreter. You are alone. (57)

The imagery in this extraordinary passage links Anna's struggle with Christ's passion and underscores the way in which Anna's struggle must include a letting go of the rational structures and promises which until now have provided the foundation and purpose of her life. Caro's words here suggest that Anna must be configured to the Jesus of Mark's gospel, who is "filled with fear and distress" (Mark 14:34), who cries out, "My God, my God, why have you forsaken me?" (Mark 15:34), rather than to the Jesus of John's gospel, who is calm and in control throughout his whole ordeal.

Caro insists that she must be loved for herself—as she is. "Come and get me. Love me enough. Love me who I am. Come and get me, come and love me. Let me make the terms. I will show you my dark castle and you will never want to go away again. But don't cheat me. Love me or I will fight you and kill you. Kill joy. Kill hope. Kill love" (69). The last three phrases portend that in order to tap into the reservoir of tremendous energy and passion deep in the psyche, one must be willing to love that which is strange and frightening. Furthermore, one risks losing even the tamer pleasures of ordinary love, joy, and hope if one is unwilling to embrace this alien presence.[20]

Anna's hunger for nurturing, mothering, and friendship have been awakened by her involvement with Fiona, Stephen, and Caro. These needs are even more strongly aroused by her relationship with Karen, a writer and lesbian, whom Anna meets in the library of the British Museum. Karen asks Anna for some help with a Spanish text. At first Karen is "not above a little nun-baiting" but soon finds herself caught up, first in a warm friendship, and then in an overwhelming erotic attraction (77). With Karen Anna goes to her first pub, relaxes in the warm and affectionate domesticity of the household of women with whom Karen lives, and enjoys the pleasures of a massage. It is not insignificant that Anna's first encounter with Karen is initiated when "an absolutely *material* voice [breaks] the silent shouts of the Fathers with a whisper [emphasis added]"

(77), for Karen is Anna's guide into a deeper experience of physicality. Karen deepens and extends the experience of female friendship that Anna had enjoyed with Sister Kate, providing intellectual stimulation and the invigorating challenge of her aggressive feminism. She introduces Anna to simple quotidian pleasures like lunch in a pub and acquaints Anna with a new kind of sisterhood. Having lived most of her adult life as a nun, Anna should know all about sisterhood. Yet Karen's community of women is both like and unlike the convent life that Anna has known. Karen lives in "a big shabby house in Hackney with five other women" (116). Their home is comfortable and yet has a certain casual elegance:

> Their social life centred on an enormous kitchen which they had created for themselves in what had once been the front sitting-room; a lovely well-lit space with bow windows, the original elaborate plaster mouldings still on the ceiling and an old carved and tiled fireplace. One wall was covered with cork board on which the complexities of their daily lives were pinned up. . . .
> In the middle of the room was a large battered table, around which they gathered generally but casually most evenings. Elsewhere they had more private space; it was a house where privacy was respected and where it was perfectly acceptable to take one's food and friends and eat elsewhere. (116)

This might almost be an idealized vision of convent life—without the required prayers or deference to a Mother Superior. This home is Anna's transitional "convent," a stepping-stone from religious life to secular life. Her convent had felt safe and comfortable. The structure and ordered hierarchy had been part of that comfort. The sisterhood in Hackney, on the other hand, has a home that seems to run without hierarchies; it is based on mutuality, reciprocity, and democracy. Although such an informal system probably would not work in a society that included hundreds of religious women staffing schools and hospitals, it is a model that infuses new vision into Anna's conception of sisterhood.

By far the most important result of Anna's relationship with Karen is that it instigates her discovery of her own sexuality. Anna's entrée into sexual love is sudden and violent. She has enjoyed Karen's friendship for several weeks. Karen is very conscious of her own erotic feelings for Anna, but Anna is blind to her own feelings until one of Karen's roommates, out of concern for Karen, tells Anna of Karen's feelings. To Sybil's question, "'Do you fancy her then?'" Anna first answers, "'Certainly not,'" but then, to her own amazement, blurts out "'Yes, . . . Yes I do.'" (123). "She had named her evil desire, and naming it had loosed it from its prison. It was alive and free; it had lived unfed in its dungeon for too long, now it was ravenous and devouring. . . . What she experienced now was a driving force of desire, a great fierce demanding thing which she did not like and could not control" (124–25).

Anna has begun to find her way out of the domination of the Fathers through pleasure—the pleasure of having a physical body, the pleasure of being a woman. First she has the pleasure of giving up the habit, wearing comfortable clothes that enhance her femininity. Then she enjoys the warm domesticity of Stephen and Fiona's home and experiences vicariously the comfortable intimacy of their marriage. Finally she discovers her own sexuality by falling in love with Karen. Her bond with Caro has also helped her to clarify her struggle against the rational, controlling world of the Fathers. From the beginning Anna had "sensed that Caro was on her side; or at least not on the Fathers' side" (61). In fact, Caro is fighting them over Anna. She stands for freedom and play and anarchy. "My play is delightful anarchy. Not for learning, for taming, for training, for ordering, not for decorum and deportment. But for joy and kaleidoscopic light shattering and reforming in the depths of the unmade stars. . . . Anna, the battle field is your flesh, and the Fathers and I will fight over it" (132).

Anna's growing ability to confront the Fathers comes to a climax when she is caring for Caro while Fiona gives birth to a baby son. Caro screams for four hours. Eventually Anna begins to scream too, her own anger being incited by Caro's and somehow giving her the courage to defy the Fathers.

> "OK," she shouted, "come here. By the power of the Holy Virgins I summon you; by my own power I command you. I gave up my magical powers for you. Of course I am afraid, but I shall chew on the energy of that fear and it will nourish me. . . ."
> ". . . I have been a good child of the Fathers for thirty-six years, three years longer than Christ put up with it, and what have I got out of it? You don't deal straight do you? What have you given me? . . ."
> ". . . Your voices are mine. You have no more power over me than the power I have given you. And I have given you a lot of power, the power of my fears and frailties, my weakness, my stupidities, my evasions and dishonesties. . . . I will not, I do not pay any more." (188–89)

In her mounting fury Anna even invokes the memories of women who have resorted to violence to resist male brutality—Jael, Medea, and the Theban women who tore Pentheus apart. Although she is temporarily cowed when the Fathers remind her of how her own father taught her that loss of control would be punished, she reasserts her defiance in a "No" that is as insistent and powerful as Molly Bloom's "Yes" at the end of *Ulysses*.

> "No, I will not consent any more. No, I reject your lousy rewards for my so-called good behaviour. No, I don't know what I want instead. No, I can't

answer all your hurtful questions. No, I don't know how I will live without you. But I don't care. I don't bloody care anymore. You've pushed too far. . . . But I won't tolerate this way of living any more. I've had it. I won't. I won't. I won't." (191)

Something else that enables Anna to confront the Fathers is her fish tattoo. Shortly before her defiance of the Fathers, she has gone to the tattooist who had engraved a leopard on one of Karen's housemates. Anna asks for a crucifix between her breasts. He talks her into accepting instead a fish as a Christ symbol. He convinces her by reading a passage from Annie Dillard's *Pilgrim at Tinker Creek*, reflecting on the abundance of fish and yet the difficulty of seeing them: "'To say holiness is a fish is a statement of the abundance of grace; it is the equivalent of affirming in a purely materialistic culture that money does indeed grow on trees. "Not as the world gives do I give unto you"; these fish are spirit food. . . . They are there, they are certainly there, free food and wholly fleeting. You can see them if you want to; catch them if you can.'" (177).[21] In her argument with the Fathers, Anna says, "'I have chosen another: the mark of the fish is upon me, I am branded in his love'" (188).

Not only does Anna defy the Fathers, but she also gently declines Caro's invitation to retreat with her into the anarchy, chaos, and play of infantilism. "I do want to be a grown-up, you see, that is what I have chosen. You have given me a love gift, a new part of myself, a new way, but I don't have to come all the way down with you. I love you but we are not the same." (199).

Anna's close association with Stephen and Fiona during this pregnancy, culminating in the birth of a healthy child, underscores an important theme of the novel: Anna's need to give birth to a more mature self and to acknowledge her own relationship to her mother. Caro asks Anna to "Birth me again in water and the word" (133), but it is really to herself that Anna must give birth, not only to her own inner child that she had aborted, but to the grown up woman that she can now become. At the end of the novel Anna decides to leave her religious order since it "doesn't seem like a place where a child should grow up" (207) and return to South America to decide how to "best use the second half of [her] life" (205). She is not bitter or resentful about her time in the order, assuring the Mother Superior that "I want you to know how much I love you all and how precious to me my time in the order has been" (206). Although she feels "frail, vulnerable and cold" (209) Anna "has stepped freshly outside her own conditioning, out of her carefully constructed skin" and is "laying claim to new possibility" (208–9).

In tentatively feeling her way to maturity, Anna knows that she needs the power of the mothers. When she tells Fiona about her family, Fiona is

surprised by Anna's apparent lack of interest in her mother. Anna somewhat defensively explains that as the youngest she hardly knew her
mother. It is clear, however, that her father's attitude is an obstacle to her
feeling, let alone revealing, any interest in or affection for her mother.

> "He's deeply devout, you see, in his own style. But legalistic. I don't know
> what went on between them. But in his eyes she had left—she was a Bad
> Mother, a Bad Wife. He saw himself as guiltless, I'm sure, because whatever
> had happened before, by running off she had sinned, sinned against the
> sacraments. Claudia tried to find her once actually, soon after she was mar-
> ried, but not very hard because it hurt him so much. It made him sad, so it
> didn't seem worth it." (65)

Anna thinks not only of daughters looking for mothers, but of mothers
looking for daughters—Demeter looking for Persephone—and of Mary
looking for the child Jesus in the temple. One of the strongest images for
her though is that of the Amazons. In her research she has read about
Francisco de Orellana, who discovered, not only the Amazon River, but a
tribe of fiercely energetic Indians led by women. "These, the adventurers
learned, were the great mothers, the women who ruled the interior and
lived entirely without men, rounding them up for insemination and returning all boy children to their care. . . . This was the land of the mothers, the warrior women" (159).

Although the common notion of Amazons is that they were warriors,
Anna thinks of them primarily as mothers. She realizes that in becoming
a nun and entering a *Mother House*, she was looking for a mother, and now
as she prepares to leave the order, she looks more to the Amazons than to
nuns for the mothers she needs. "But now she would have to go travel-
ling unprotected, commit herself to the great river and float down into the
dark interior; she had to go and seek the country of the Mothers" (203).

The image of the journey down the river into the heart of the jungle is
galvanizing for Anna—not only as the context for the discovery of the
Amazons by Francisco de Orellana, but because of a vacation that she and
Kate had taken together when they too floated down the Amazon into the
"dark sweaty jungle." It had proved to be more than the "tame exploration" they expected.

"They were devastated by the profusion of the jungle, by its excesses
and extravagances; a steamy langour had attacked them, held them in its
arms, rocked them like a mother and they had not been able to struggle
against it. . . . The rules were held in soft abeyance, all mental precision
seemed eaten away, all the hard clarities and certainties gone" (10). This
imagery of lethargy and disorientation not only links Anna's experience
with that of the explorers but also delineates the nature of her present

struggle to bring her more mature self to birth. The old clarities and the old precision had been held in place by Anna's submission to the Fathers, and to fully escape from them she must be willing to enter the chaos of profuse, tangled, and undisciplined life that is imaged by the jungle, the darkness and physicality into which Caro had invited her. There, if she is lucky, she will find the mothers she seeks.

Mothers and virgins: these are the two images of woman, which Anna sees as sources of nurturance and power. Yet—except for the Virgin Mary—they seem to be contradictions, unable to coexist in the same woman. This paradox returns us to the central theme of the novel (according to the author)—virginity. What is the meaning of virginity in the age of "the pill" when women's lack of sexual experience is not the only way of preventing pregnancy or of assuring men of their paternity? In particular, how do we make sense of the Church's long-standing exaltation of virginity and its yoking together of virginity and holiness? Although the traditional view has always existed that consecrated virgins could be "spiritual mothers," that concept seems inadequate to encompass what Maitland is trying to claim for virginity here.

One day in London Anna has a sudden insight about her apparent lack of anger at the time of the rape:

> She knew absolutely that she minded passionately about the rape; and she knew why. In the brilliance of the knowing she even knew why she had not been able understand [sic] before. If God was not going to protect his holy virgins, what the hell was the point of becoming one?
>
> The purpose of the Fathers is to protect the daughters. Of the man to protect his woman. That was their justification for everything. That was what the whole deal was. If they weren't going to do it, if they could not do it, then who needed them? (95–96)

Anna learns that virginity that is bartered in exchange for protection, safety, and security, not only fails to protect one, but also keeps one a spiritual child. Although Anna does not explicitly connect her experience with that of Sister Katherine Elizabeth, the sister who had been raped and technically deprived of her virginity, the novel does so by juxtaposing with no transition Anna's final thoughts and the thoughts of Sister Katherine Elizabeth, who realizes that her "protection has been stripped away, her privilege and her protection, and that she cannot entirely regret" (209).

A quotation that Kate had given to Anna after their trip down the Amazon clarifies this paradox of fruitful virginity and is probably the best expression of what Maitland means to convey by her title: "The virgin forest is not barren or unfertilised, but rather a place that is specially fruitful and has multiplied because it has taken life into itself and transformed it, giving birth naturally and taking dead things back to be re-cycled. It is virgin because it is unexploited, not in man's control" (14). This imagery supports the idea that Maitland strongly connects virginity with a certain rebelliousness against "man's control," a view espoused by Kathleen Norris, who sees the virginity of the virgin martyrs as "anything but passive; it was a state of being, of powerful potential, a *point vierge* [virginal point] from which they could act in radical resistance to authority." Norris also points out that these women exhibited "a defiance that their belief in Christ made possible. Knowing that they were loved by Christ gave them the strength to risk a way of life that was punishable by death."[22]

It is also clear, however, that Maitland's connection of virginity with women's empowerment does not confront merely *male* authority, but the human proclivity for self-indulgence and possessiveness. Christopher West, who explicates Pope John Paul II's theology of the body, says that virginity should be understood as the integrity of body and soul untouched by the rupture of sin. Drawing largely on the Genesis creation story, he suggests that virginity approximates the pure sexuality of Adam and Eve before the fall, a sexuality that was fully self-gift, uncontaminated by selfishness, domination, or exploitation.[23]

As Anna prepares to take up her new life, she is heading off into uncharted "virgin territory." Her challenge is not only to become an adult woman, but also to explore and come to understand the meaning of virginity in her own life and in the life of the Church. Although she decides to leave the order, she wants "to remain within the charity of the Church" (205) and so makes an official application for dispensation from her vows. She is not prepared to discard virginity as a useless archaic ideal; but she can subscribe only to a virginity that is not ethereal, escapist, or sterile. On the contrary, it must be rooted in a profound affirmation of the goodness of the flesh; it must be supported by sisterhood; it must be powerful, generous, and fruitful.[24]

NOTES

1. Maitland described *Virgin Territory* as a novel about virginity in a conversation with the author. Interview by author. Strictly speaking, the word *nun* refers to religious women who are cloistered; those who teach, care for the sick, or do other kinds of work in the world are referred to as *sisters*. In fact, however, people generally use the word *nun* to refer to both, as Maitland does in this novel.

2. Delbanco, *Death of Satan*, 16.

3. See Uta Ranke-Heinemann, *Eunuchs for the Kingdom of Heaven: Women, Sexuality and the Catholic Church*, trans. Peter Heinegg (New York: Doubleday, 1990).

4. John Marshall, "Catholic Family Life," in *Catholics in England: 1950–2000: Historical and Sociological Perspectives*, ed. Michael P. Hornsby-Smith (London: Cassell, 1999), 67.

5. Robert Bellah, *The Good Society* (New York: Vintage Books, 1991), 10–11.

6. According to John Marshall:

The official church [the Pope and Curia] adopted the Augustinian view that the enjoyment of sexual pleasure in intercourse between husband and wife was only justified by the intention to have a child. Excluding conception from intercourse was a mortal sin. Even when conception was not deliberately excluded, sexual intercourse for any other reason than to have a child was venially sinful. Pope Gregory the Great went even further and said that even when conception was intended, sexual intercourse was venially sinful because the pleasure it aroused was immoderate. Marshall, "Catholic Family Life," 68.

7. This imperative does not mean that we must discard all our moral principles. The European discoverers knew Europe very well, but when they explored more of Asia and Africa, not to mention entire new continents, they had to see Europe in a different context. Similarly, our understanding of chastity and virginity, as well as sexual morality, must take account of our changing views of sex, due to developments in the biological and social sciences and technology.

8. Kenneth Woodward, *Making Saints: How the Catholic Church Determines Who Becomes a Saint, Who Doesn't and Why* (New York: Simon and Schuster, 1990), 337.

9. Maitland, *Map of the New Country*, 53.

10. Maitland, *Map of the New Country*, 117–18.

11. Ranke-Heinemann, *Eunuchs for the Kingdom of Heaven*, 9.

12. Ranke-Heinemann, *Eunuchs for the Kingdom of Heaven*, 11.

13. Ranke-Heinemann, *Eunuchs for the Kingdom of Heaven*, 33

14. Maitland, *Map of the New Country*, 10. Although Maitland's assertion is perhaps a bit overstated, it is difficult to find a woman canonized before the twentieth century who does not fall into the category of nun, queen, or virgin who suffered a horrific death (Joan of Arc). St. Monica is an exception that proves the rule.

15. Ranke-Heinemann points out that "The idea of a menstruating woman's receiving Holy Communion was consistently frowned upon all the way into the Middle Ages, although more severely in the Eastern Church than in the West." *Eunuchs for the Kingdom of Heaven*, 24.

16. Kathleen Norris, *The Cloister Walk* (New York: Riverhead, 1996), 200–1.

17. Matthew Lewis's *The Monk* (1795) is one of the most famous examples of this genre. The novel's protagonist is a thoroughly corrupt and decadent monk, who rapes and murders. The novel was extremely popular in its day.

18. Sara Maitland, *Virgin Territory* (New York: Beaufort Books, 1984), 1. Hereafter cited in the text by page number.

19. Technically, the word virginity is "the condition of never having had sexual relations" and *chastity* means "the virtue by which human sexuality is ordered to its proper purpose." *HarperCollins Encyclopedia of Catholicism*, 1315, 302. Thus even married people are called to practice chastity. In fact, however, the two words are often used interchangeably. *Chastity*, however, has a more positive connotation—especially since Vatican II—and it is clear why Sister Katherine Elizabeth would use it to express her sense of her own sexual purity and integrity.

20. It is significant that the name *Caro* is also the masculine form of the Italian adjective meaning, *dear, beloved*. Caro does represent Anna's beloved inner child,

especially in its more masculine manifestations of self-assertion, strength, anger, and ferocity. Anna must come to know her own inner child, for only when that inner child is known and truly beloved, can she be tamed.

21. Maitland quotes from an edition of *Pilgrim at Tinker Creek* published by Picador Press, New York.

22. Norris, *The Cloister Walk*, 190, 198.

23. West makes this point in a set of audiotapes explicating John Paul II's theology of the body, *A Crash Course in the Theology of the Body*, 2d. ed. (Carpentersville, Il.: The Gift Foundation, 2002.) Sound cassette, tape 3.

24. The two things Anna seeks—fruitful virginity and a loving mother—would seem to constitute an oxymoron, at least in terms of existing within the same woman at the same time. Yet in Catholicism they exist together in the Virgin Mother, Mary.

12

Holding on to the Good:
Brittle Joys

The fantasist, whether he uses the ancient archetypes of myth and legend or the younger ones of science and technology, may be talking as seriously as any sociologist—and a good deal more directly—about human life as it is lived, and as it might be lived, and as it ought to be lived.

—Ursula LeGuin, National Book Award Acceptance Speech

For in life we must struggle to hold on to brittle joys.

—St. Augustine

Brittle Joys (1999) is the first novel Sara Maitland wrote after her conversion to Roman Catholicism in 1993. As with *Virgin Territory*, the main character is a Catholic, and there is some explicit use of Catholicism. Although Maitland herself has said, "I think of myself, and always have since my conversion to Christianity nearly a quarter of a century ago, as deeply orthodox, in the catholic tradition,"[1] it is not surprising that *Brittle Joys*, written after her conversion, would reflect a broader use of the Roman Catholic tradition, including a literal belief in a guardian angel, concern for proper liturgical vessels, the importance of religious art, and the power of the Mass to quiet the spirit.

This novel treats many of the subjects and themes that predominated in Maitland's earlier work: feminism, homosexuality, power struggles—especially with regard to gender—and tensions within families. This novel, however, is distinctive for its attempt to recover a sense of the transcendent and supernatural in religious experience, a problem much discussed within the Catholic community. In *A Big-Enough God* Maitland says:

> Demythologizers have a rather arid understanding of what it is to be a human being and of what it is to tell the truth. The high-tech world and well-sanitized faith in which they apparently want us to live may be cleaner and safer than the scruffy old one, but it is not very joyful . . . yet I do believe that demythologizing has now gone far enough, has in fact gone too far. We are in urgent need of a bit of re-mythologizing.[2]

Thus we have a novel in which an angel is a central character and miraculous things happen. *Brittle Joys* is in many ways a narrative unfolding of many of the key ideas in *A Big-Enough God*. In particular, it expresses the importance of risk, the exuberance of creation, the rejection of matter-spirit dualism, the need for artful theology, the retrieval of the mythical and transcendent, and perhaps most important—as signified by the title—the brittleness and preciousness of human joy.

The protagonist, Ellie (also called Héloïse and Nelly), is an internationally known glassmaker. She was brought up in Scotland, in a stern and joyless Presbyterian home: "Her mother and father would never have allowed an angelic visitor in their home. They scarcely allowed dreams. Time-wasting rubbish. A joyful angel would have been told to wipe its feet on the doormat, keep its wings tucked in so as not to break the china, if it had not been expelled on the spot for popish idolatry."[3] While still an adolescent, Ellie ran away from home, moved to England, learned the art of glass making and become a successful artist. She enjoys her work in her studio and camaraderie with her three handpicked female assistants. She has an apparently stable and satisfying marriage to Henry Landsdown, a psychiatrist eighteen years older than she. Her only child, a grown daughter, is estranged from her and has vanished somewhere in southeast Asia. Ellie enjoys lunches with her best friend, Judith, who is a lesbian, as well as the company of gay male friends. Her world is turned upside down, however, when Henry asks for a divorce because he wants to marry another woman. The remainder of the novel follows Ellie's attempt to cope with this traumatic development, as well as with the death of her mother, her fear of her gay friends dying from AIDS, and her painful estrangement from her daughter. All of this is frequently punctuated by conversations with an angel.

Is Maitland serious about this angel? It seems that she is, for she says in *A Big-Enough God*, "I really do believe in angels and I am glad that I do. They and other imaginative constructs of mind and heart are sources of joy, the joy that I am completely certain makes the shape and meaning of the creation."[4] Does Maitland believe that angels exist *only* as figments of our imagination, or do they have an independent, objective existence? Although the phrase "imaginative constructs of mind," though provocative and maddeningly ambiguous, renders her account of angels acceptable to a skeptical mind, it also leaves open the possibility that angels are *real* beings that communicate with us *via* our imaginations. Risk is an important theme in this novel; and Maitland herself was taking a real risk in making an angel a character. It led to problems with her publishers and opens her to the charge of lack of seriousness.[5] The fad of angels in pop culture that swept through the United States in the 1990s only increased this possibility.

Her first conversation with Angel (capitalized as the angel's name) occurs toward the end of the first chapter. It begins, as such colloquies always do, with "the all too familiar twitchy sensation just above her coccyx, followed by the odd warm glow up her spinal column and there was Angel manifesting somewhere in the region of her *corpus callosum*. Ellie found it slightly sinister that Angel located herself just there so that she could never be quite sure if she was dealing with a rational, objective, verbal perception, or an imaginative, fluid, musical one" (32). This first conversation with Angel follows upon Ellie's having received a telephone call from her brother asking her to come to Scotland and care for their invalid mother while he and his family go on a much needed vacation. Ellie is estranged from her mother, whom she refers to as an "old witch" (28), and despises her brother. Although she had desperately longed to give a resounding "No" to her brother's pleas, she had been unable to say anything, and he had interpreted that as a "maybe." Now she has been anguishing over what to do. She has just made up her mind that she will not go to Ayrshire when Angel manifests.[6] Angel is argumentative, maddeningly logical, a bit of a scold, and a wit. Her first remark to Ellie, who is out for a walk on a cold day, is "'You should have brought a wooly'" (32). When Ellie pleads for "'sensible consolations' or mystical vision or *something*," Angel adopts the tone of a scolding schoolmistress: "'Oh grow up, Ellie,'" said Angel unsympathetically, "'you are most unlikely at present to get a mystical vision because you think you know what kind you want, which is precisely what a mystical vision isn't. And you don't need sensible consolations because as a matter of fact you get more than most people, you just don't recognise them'" (33).

Angel counters Ellie's insistence that Angel is not a mystical vision with an argument worthy of the medieval scholastics. "You have to be clear about this. You hear my voice—you frequently complain that I'm intrusive or bossy and make you do things you don't want to—so, diagnostically, you've only got two choices: I'm either a physical manifestation of the divine glory—that is to say a mystical experience—or you have a serious psychiatric illness. Henry would probably tell you it was treatable"

(33). Not only does this angel speak, but she eschews a spiritualized or pious language in favor of one that is colloquial and highly empirical. At times she sounds more like a hardheaded social scientist than a denizen of the heavenly court. When Ellie wonders why she had never been aware of Angel's presence until recently, Angel replies, "'Menopause. . . . Lots of physical changes take place in women at the climacterium, gaining consciousness of your angel may very well be one of them. We're not sure, there is a shortage of data'" (41).

When one of Ellie's dinner guests, an American psychiatrist, proclaims that "'Angels do not, in any meaningful sense, exist; therefore anyone who communicates with them is delusional'" (79), Ellie feels hatred, which she realizes is a sign that she is frightened. She is too intimidated to offer her genuine response, but only thinks it: "'Well, speaking personally, I have an angel, a rather tiresome one as a matter of fact, who jabbers at me constantly, and I don't murder small children'" (80). Later another guest, a priest, asks Ellie privately if she believes in angels. Her positive reply elicits from him the comment, "'Lucky you,' . . . and she knew he meant it" (86). This exchange reflects Maitland's felt need for more remythologizing. The natural explanations offered for much of what passes for extraordinary, paranormal, or mystical experiences, especially by Henry and his friends in the psychiatric field, fall short. When Ellie asks Henry what he intends to do for his patient who hears voices, he replies, "'I hate voice hearers. . . I really do. They push the whole issue too far. I don't know. Drug her, I suppose. That's what we do'" (87). Ellie knows that "she could never tell him about Angel. Never" (88).

Yet Angel has a stubborn reality in the novel, refusing to be reduced to a matter of Ellie's *corpus callosum*. Angel's earthy language, wit, and penetrating insights give her palpability. Although she can be comforting and companionable, she is also adversarial, forcing Ellie to confront things she would prefer to ignore.

Ellie's earthy angel is one of the ways—but certainly not the only one—in which Maitland subverts the traditional matter-spirit dichotomy, which has always plagued Christianity. In *A Big-Enough God* Maitland insists that humans should not try to find God by fleeing from the material, but rather by looking more deeply into it. "This conviction that human ingenuity will reduce the influence of God seems to me to grow, once again, out of that fundamental dualism which supposes that matter is somehow less God's than 'spirit' is."[7] She argues that moving beyond this dualism, together with humility in the face of new scientific understanding of the nature of matter, makes it possible for us to retrieve an almost forgotten article of the faith: the resurrection of the body—not as some sort of metaphor for spiritual perpetuity, but as a physical reality.

We have restored to us the resurrection of the body, which, if you can bring yourself to like bodies as much as God clearly does, is nothing but good news. If there is no way of being a self, if there is no personhood without material reality (i.e., a body)—with all the elements and parameters and constructions I have suggested and more—then there is no resurrection without the body, because there is nothing to resurrect. The resurrection of the body, as Paul makes clear, is the ground of our hope and love and joy.[8]

In Maitland's work the body matters. Matter matters.

Perhaps the most conspicuous example of Maitland's determination to celebrate the goodness of the material and heal the divorce between matter and spirit is her treatment of homosexuality. In *A-Big Enough God* Maitland praises the flamboyant diversity of creation:

The goodness of God may be hard to argue from the creation—the flamboyance, the abundance, the sheer ebullience of God however is not. The generosity of a God who can create a universe so highly complex, so intricate, so random that there can be reverse time in the atom, and *diversity of sexuality* [emphasis added] in the human, and death among the far-flung stars is a generosity that should encourage not only gratitude but awe. All these things are essential to what it is to know God.[9]

Thus Maitland sees homosexuality not only as a *given*, a part of the way things are—but as something to inspire awe and gratitude. She makes no explicit or even implicit judgment about the morality or immorality of homosexual acts.[10] Even in our day, when homosexuals are regularly portrayed sympathetically in books and films and when homophobia is one of the few "sins" acknowledged by the secular world, Maitland's treatment of homosexuality in *Brittle Joys* is remarkable. Her portrayal of gays both underscores their goodness as human beings and partakes of that ebullient joy in diversity referred to in the passage above, at the same time that she generates tremendous sympathy for their suffering from HIV/AIDS. Her two best friends are a lesbian and a gay man; her protégé in her glass studio is also a lesbian. Although Ellie herself is heterosexual, she does not enjoy a robust, healthy sexuality. Her libido seems to be very low. She and her husband have "not had sex for over ten years" (112).

Ellie and Judith, her closest woman friend, form a group of two. "'One of the things it is to be a feminist, is to be in a Group,' Judith said, 'and this is our Group Meeting. It's not our fault it's so small.'" (46). Judith, a consultant and fundraiser, has an Italian lover, whom she calls La Carissima and sees periodically. Ellie and Judith greatly enjoy their "delectable and highly alcoholic lunches" (46), and one source of their merriment is their enjoyment of their role as fag-hags. Judith purports to be working on a research project called *The Natural History of the Fag-Hag*. Simply put, a fag-hag is a woman who enjoys the company of gay men. In a short piece entitled "Fag Hags: A Field Guide," which is included in her collection of stories *Angel Maker*, Maitland offers an extensive definition of a genuine fag-hag. In addition to enjoying the company of gay men, her other characteristics are that she is over forty, verbally witty, extremely good at her job, sensitive, though bossy at times, not a good mother (although she thinks she is), and fond of having lunch with women friends.[11] Ellie perfectly embodies this definition.

Judith is a flamboyant and likeable character. Her scintillating displays of wit are an overlay for a deep and abiding affection for Ellie. "They loved each other. The showing-off which they both found enormous fun was also a cover for an enormous tenderness" (15). When Judith arrives for one of her lunches with Ellie having "the transparent look of someone with cancer" (162) and reveals that she has just learned that La Carissima is getting married, her grief is palpable.

> "*I'm* a lesbian, Ellie, I'm a goddamn dyke, and she is my lover, my sweetheart, my girl friend, my *numero uno*, and so on and so forth *ad nauseam*. *Mia Carissima*. I'm forty-two years old and I thought this would hang about fairly effortlessly until I was too old to care. I thought I had it made. I feel like a complete idiot quite apart from . . . well . . . quite apart from the fact that I'm soft on her, and I never bloody knew it until now. So I feel like an idiot in spades." (163)

When Ellie tries to comfort her by suggesting that maybe the marriage won't make any difference, Judith reminds her that when Ellie had told her about Henry's new love, she had not suggested that it would not make any difference, thus placing Ellie's heterosexual marriage and Judith's homosexual love affair on a plane of equivalence.

Late in the novel Ellie attends the "wedding" of two gay male friends. The ceremony is described with a sense of high-spirited fun. Noting the wedding cake with two grooms on top, Ellie wonders if they had had "to buy two sets and throw away the brides, were there somewhere two tiny dollies all in white plastic lace seeking partners and finding each other?" (199). The ceremony itself is "mocking, gay, exhibitionist and joyful." Jim and Stuart vow "to share the onerous duties of maintaining the cat litter tray in a hygienic state" (200). Later Ellie discovers that one of the guests is Neil, a good friend from art college. He and Ellie had briefly been lovers, but Neil had gone on to be "a wildly active gay man in the USA" (205). Although they haven't seen each other for twenty-five years, they talk of their present lives and not just their shared past "so they knew that it was still a friendship, not merely a nostalgic delight" (205). At the same time that Neil's homosexuality is very much to the fore, especially in the presence of his current lover, his tenderness and affection for Ellie, his delight at seeing her, his outrage that Henry has left her, and his candid self-revelation of his own life continually push his humanity into the foreground, but without lessening our awareness of his homosexuality.[12]

Ellie's protégé in her studio is Mary, an extremely talented young lesbian who Ellie feels will probably surpass her someday in the art of glass-making. Mary is completely comfortable in her sexuality, probably because of her happy and secure childhood. "Her parents had been joyful middle-class hippies, never worn to sordidness but high-spirited and peace loving and vagrant" (93). Because she had died in childbirth, Mary's mother "remained always for her the lovely flower child of devoted photographs" (94). Her father is described as

> the ideal man, born at the ideal moment in time, to be a single father. He had received a tiny baby in the dark from a dying woman and found in that gift a sort of magical trust . . . but he remained, perhaps because of the extraordinarily delightful experience of bringing up a child, somehow carefree in every respect except in his devotion to his daughter. Mary had had what many people would call a ramshackle childhood, but it was also a blessed and golden one. (94)

Here Maitland contravenes the stereotype of the homosexual as the victim of an unhappy childhood, having suffered from—at best, insufficient love and nurturing, at worst, hostility and domination. One could argue that Mary's lack of a mother had an adverse effect on her sexual development, but such an interpretation seems discordant with Maitland's clear determination to portray her as a happy, secure, well-adjusted person. Maitland suggests that although Mary was deprived of her biological mother, her father's girlfriends supplied her with a "selection of kindly women to be, never stepmothers, but fairy godmothers." (95). Furthermore, her life was enriched because "her infant years were brightened by a father who fathered, a father who—by force of circumstance and his good will—mothered" (95). When Mary tells her father that she is a lesbian, he feels "rewarded in complicated ways. . . . Subliminal jealousy was dealt with forever. And he loved her. He really loved her" (95).

Another aspect of Maitland's determination to attenuate the matter/ spirit dichotomy is her attempt to retrieve belief in the miraculous. Until recently a belief in miracles was a staple of the Christian faith. Classic Christian arts portrays countless scenes of angels, saints, or Christ Himself appearing to humans. Old and New Testament miracles, as well as those ascribed to saints, are favorite subjects. This aspect of Christian belief has been greatly attenuated, especially among more educated believers. Some Biblical scholars have demythologized the miracles to the point that they are acceptable even to the most skeptical, rational mind: the healings were a psychosomatic response to the charismatic Jesus; the multiplication of the loaves and fishes was really the generosity of Christ's listeners who, inspired by His words, shared their lunch. Maitland argues that Christians need to develop what she calls a "second naïvety" and that demythologizers "have a rather arid understanding of what it is to be a human being and of what it is to tell the truth."[13] Maitland wishes us to see that much of what we regard as natural is really nothing short of miraculous.

> It never seems to occur to the demythologizers that turning water into wine by the ordinary method (fermentation) is every bit as extraordinarily startling, bizarre, even "miraculous," as what happened at the wedding feast in Cana. The demythologizers absolutely fail to recognize that a little more awe and wonder, a little more immaturity and magic, an honest delight in lucky (and of course virtuous) Daniel surviving the night while the lions prowl and roar and do not hurt him, would do none of us any harm.[14]

A miracle, after all, is matter infused with spirit. The spirit world refuses to leave matter to the ways of nature and pulls it in a new direction, giving it a new form. Maitland stretches the parameters of what can be believed. While medieval painters struggled to convey the reality of angels by depicting them as human beings with enormous wings, Maitland does it by giving Angel a voice—a palpable, insistent voice, oozing with personality.

Maitland tries to retrieve the mythical and transcendent by subverting our ordinary experience of time and sense of self. Suddenly Ellie seems to become someone else in another period of time. Out for a walk on a cold morning, without warning she is a child in the hold of a Phoenician merchant ship caught in a storm. The ship carries ingots of glass among its cargo, and when one of them reflects the flame of a cooking fire, she "sees deep inside the ingot an answering flash of blue flame, dazzling" (38). Tucking the treasure into her tunic, the child has it with her when a huge wave sweeps her from the ship. Another time Ellie is riding a London bus when she is suddenly a fourteen-year-old Venetian apprentice glassmaker, who is running away, not because she is ill-treated or unhappy, but because she wants to make another kind of glass. *Cristallo*, the glass her father has taught her to make, is "highly-wrought, elaborate, magical. It will take colour like sugar icing, and still be so fine that the light comes through the colour like the reflections in the water of the canals of the Republic in the sea" (52). But she has seen drawings of glass made in England. "Heavy. Solid. Cut like jewels are cut. Not playful, exuberant, airy, coloured, but serious, and so clear" (52). She is running away because she wants to make glass like that.

At a time when Ellie is feeling particularly vulnerable and scared, after Henry has left her, another of her friends has died from AIDS, and she longs for someone to take care of her, she is suddenly present at a Mass where a priest with trembling hands is using a glass chalice. It is "a magical chalice, the treasure of this cold fenlands church, the *diatreta*, which is the green of fresh peas, in reflected light and glows violet pink in transmitted light" (120). The time period seems to be the early medieval period, for the dragon ships of the Danes have been spotted and the terrified congregation knows there will be "blood and rape and death before dawn" (121). The use of glass chalices has been forbidden by the Church, but this is an old magic chalice, and the people in desperation have turned to their old gods. The priest himself is torn between the old and the new faith. "The gods have fought here, Christ and Thor have fought along the bones of these fingers and the priest is not certain who has won" (121). In his terror the priest drops the chalice, which shatters, spilling the consecrated wine, "the sacred blood of the Saviour" (121) on the floor. So shaken is Ellie by this vision, that she immediately runs to her history of glass and turns to the section on chalices, which confirms her certainty that glass chalices had been prohibited by the Church in the ninth century. This vision correlates strongly with Ellie's inner state at the time. Just as a "long moan of fear and loss shakes the congregation," (121) Ellie is overwhelmed by loss: the loss of her marriage, the rivalry of her protégé, the death of another of her friends from AIDS. Also like the congregation, she clings to her faith for succor but is beginning to feel desperate. "'Angel,' she cried, 'do something. Get God to do something.'" (122).

In another fantasy Ellie is at an art show, admiring a beautiful green glass vessel made by a colleague and rival. As she reaches out to touch it, suddenly the hand touching the vessel is not hers, but "chocolate coloured, more elegant, ringed heavily" (172). Immediately Ellie knows that she is now the Queen of Sheba, admiring the vessel she has requisitioned as a gift for Solomon. According to legend, this vessel eventually wound up at the Last Supper, thus becoming the Holy Grail, and is now in the Cathedral Church of San Lorenzo in Genoa. As Queen of Sheba, Ellie laughs, perhaps because she knows the curious history of this piece of glass, or perhaps "just because the bowl is beautiful and in her wisdom all beauty fills her with joy and the joy spills over into laughter like a mountain stream" (173). This linking of the sacred (the Holy Grail) and joy is an emblem of Maitland's ideas about the need for an artful theology: "The production of art is quite simply a particular participation in the divine; it is a specific and vital form of theology."[15] Furthermore, such an art should be a wellspring of joy, for in Maitland's view, God's work of art is a comedy rather than a tragedy.[16]

The title *Brittle Joys* directs us to Maitland's overriding concern with joy in this novel. In *A Big Enough God* she argues that joy is not just a by-product of a lucky break or fortunate circumstance, but a necessary response to an amazing universe. "An immediate and necessary response is a humbled and shaken ejaculation of 'Oh wow.' . . . This wowed posture, it seems to me, is what is meant by that odd word 'joy.'"[17] Even more important, joy is an important part of any response to God. It "is in fact an ethical imperative in response to God's creative power as revealed in the whole created universe."[18] Maitland clarifies that she is not talking about the kind of blithe, carefree attitude recommended by some latter-day hippies and self-help gurus, compounded of equal parts of self-esteem, nonjudgmentalism, and rejection of guilt feelings. Rather, Maitland means "something about the area called 'hope, faith and love'—a product, as it were, of the struggle to engage with and live with these harsh and demanding virtues."[19]

On the other hand, Maitland insists that this joy is not something heavy and relentlessly serious. In the last section of *A Big Enough God*, "Notes on the Practise of Joy," she lists among other aids to joy, like prayer and anti-individualism, the startling recommendation "Have more fun."[20] The use of the word *fun* is somewhat surprising, suggesting the most trivial kinds of pleasure, associated mostly with boisterous children and rebellious adolescents. Yet while fun is certainly not the same thing as joy, it is not entirely unrelated either: "Fun is not joy, but it is not happiness either: fun is something we can choose, as we cannot choose happiness, and it is a better form of joy training than the traditional gloomy self-denial and mortification enjoined on us by too many spiritual manuals."[21]

Ellie is trying to cultivate the practice of joy, and having fun is certainly part of her regimen. Her bantering with Judith is an example. She invites Judith to a private art showing, saying, "'Listen, hon, in your baggy school knickers you'd be chic. This one will be fun and we'll look divine and everyone will say, "Dear God who is that stunning woman with Ellie Macauley? How does the old bag find such gorgeous friends?"'" (171).

"They won't," said Judith darkly, "they'll say, 'Why hasn't she brought someone pretty for little me to play with?'"

"No they won't," said Ellie, bold in her affection, "all the brighter people, those who know enough even to think that, will say instead, 'Ellie Macauley? I never knew she was *that* way inclined. That explains a lot.' And my stock will rise and I will be able to buy you presents as wonderful as the ones you buy me."

"Flattery, Héloïse Macauley, as you very well know, will get you just about anywhere. OK. You're on. Where and when?" (171)

In order to see this playful repartee for the courageous act that it is, it is necessary to recall that at this time Ellie is struggling with the loss of her marriage and Judith with the impending marriage of her lover. The two go to the show, "looking indeed wonderful and depending on each other, grateful and affectionate in their need. It was fun" (172). Another striking example of Ellie's propensity for fun is that on the day she accompanies her gay male friend, Hugo, when he has a blood test for HIV, they pass the anxious hours waiting for the test results walking about Hampstead Heath. After a particularly tense moment, Ellie challenges him to a race. "They were children, running and laughing, innocent and loving. They were adults who carried bitterness and fear and complexity as close as their skins and now tossed that all away for the delight of chasing each other down a steep hill on a spring day" (242).

Ellie's penchant for fun could be seen simply as a version of the "I have to laugh in order to keep from crying" syndrome, especially when she is trying to cope with an impending calamity like the end of her marriage or the possibility that her dear friend has AIDS. Yet for Maitland, fun is more than just a coping mechanism. As she says in *A Big Enough God*, fun is preparatory work for the practice of joy and, thus like joy, an ethical imperative. Maitland drives this point home in an amusing way by recounting the act of defiance that had led Ellie to break with her family and leave home. Her dour Presbyterian mother had volunteered Ellie to plant crocus bulbs on the minister's lawn. Ellie had planted the colored bulbs so that when they came up they spelled, *"Ave Maria," "Viva il Papa,"* and *"Orate pro nobis"* (35). Ellie's moment of fun is transformative.

Not only is this prank an indication of Ellie's incipient interest in Catholicism, but it facilitates her escape from a life of stifling and rigid conformity, the freeing of her creative and artistic abilities, and the beginning of her rewarding relationships with women. The first of these women is her new quasi-mother Megan, a teacher at the school who invites Ellie to live with her and eventually becomes Ellie's trusted and much loved business manager. As Ellie says, "'With Megan, and the Blessed Virgin Mary . . . who needs psychological maturity?'" (36).

Yet breaking free is not enough. The joy that Maitland sees as an ethical imperative is not simply a matter of breaking through barriers and throwing off whatever pains you. Fun is not the only preparation work for joy. Equally important is the infinitely more arduous task of facing the darkness within. Ellie needs to confront some painful challenges to her stubbornness, self-righteousness, and need to control. These challenges pertain to her family: her mother, her brother, and her daughter, Stephanie.

Since leaving home Ellie has had only minimal contact with her family. She looks down on their provincial world of puritan piety. From her affluent, fashionable London life of art shows and good restaurants, she thinks condescendingly about her brother Alan's home. "I bet they keep the phone in the hallway, in a draughty corner. I bet they have a telephone table, with a Dralon-covered seat, and a little drawer with a fake brass knob to keep the directories in. I bet Betty wipes the phone with a damp cloth, a cloth damp with disinfectant, every morning, in case of germs" (29). When Alan calls to ask if she would be willing to care for their elderly mother while he and his family take a much needed vacation, Ellie is horrified at the prospect of spending time with her mother, who at their last meeting had told her that she was "'no daughter of hers'" and that "'she never wanted to see [her] again'" (28). Ellie's failure to clearly say no is taken by Alan as a qualified yes, but although wracked with guilt, Ellie is determined not to go. Her determination is shaken, however, when "infuriatingly" and "with complete clarity" (30) she suddenly remembers when her daughter Stephanie had been so ill she almost died, and she asks herself "who had been constant, loving, supportive, quiet, present, prayerful? The old witch herself. Down the path that Ellie had walked when Henry could not, or would not, follow, but her mother had. Dour, upright as ever, . . . she had kept vigil with her granddaughter" (30). Before she can clarify to her brother that she is not going to come, her mother dies. Ellie does go to Ayrshire, not to care for her mother, but to attend her funeral. There she is forced to confront the genuine love Alan and his wife Betty had for her mother. At the funeral she is at first put off by their stoicism, comparing it unfavorably with the emotional outpouring of grief there had been at the funeral of one of her gay friends:

> Then, just when she was feeling securely superior to their small-minded lives, she glanced at Betty and saw in her face an agony of loss that was as real as Robbie's keening at Tim's funeral. Had Betty loved her mother? Had she lost something, some claim to identity? Ellie knew suddenly that it was not Robbie's sort of loss that she saw in Betty's face, it was her own—it was how she felt about Henry. Caring for her mother had given shape and meaning and therefore joy to Betty's life—it was the thing that she did, that made a framework, and out of that doing something, that might as well be called love, had indeed been formed, and now it was gone. She found that she had no words of comfort for her sister-in-law; that she, warm-hearted, tender, kind, understanding Ellie, to whom her friends turned in their distresses knowing they would find comfort, was just a minor snob who gained gratification by being the woman who understood queers. (185)

A further recognition of Alan and Betty's moral stature is forced upon Ellie, when it is discovered that her mother has left all her money—not to Alan and Betty, her faithful caregivers—but to Ellie's estranged daughter, Stephanie. They are "extremely noble about it," insisting that they "'didn't look after her to get anything out of it.'" (186).

While walking from the funeral to the reception, Ellie has a vision of her own life as a little girl, which gives her a new perspective on her mother:

> A little girl in a place that, even if it was not much fun, was perfectly safe, a child fed, organised, educated, cared for. She saw a woman, not laughing or joyous, but solid and brave and honourable according to her own rules, a woman of rigour and not unuseful. Ellie neither loved nor liked that woman; that was sad, but it was not the whole story. Betty had loved her; Alan had loved her. . . . She was even, briefly, glad that she had come" (185–86).

It is as if for a few moments Ellie has stepped outside her own skin and seen her mother through other, more objective eyes. Although the sympathetic feeling of the moment is ephemeral, this epiphany is important in enlarging Ellie's sense of moral clarity and extending the boundaries of her sympathy to those she does not like or find attractive. This moral expansion is given concrete expression when Angel tells her she should make a glass tear for her mother, as she has done for all her gay friends who have died. At first she refuses, but Angel convinces her that there "could be loss without love" (188). Ellie is too honest to lay claim to a love she does not feel. Genuine love is too precious to be dishonored by a cheap imitation. Ellie is not mourning the loss of something she once had; rather she is mourning the fact that she never had a warm, nurturing mother. But she does see her mother through a wider, more honest lens, and she will honor her by making her a tear.

A second indication of Ellie's moral growth is her decision to be gracious about the divorce. It is not that she has changed her mind. She does not want to lose her marriage, but she tells Henry, "'It's all right Henry. I consent. I don't like it, but you should feel free. I've been silly'" (221). She also tells him that she hopes that they can be friends even as she knows that she wants him as a husband, not a friend. He thanks her, and she feels herself "fall free" (222).

The third major sign of Ellie's moral growth is the letter she writes to her daughter Stephanie. Throughout the novel Ellie has been mentally composing letters to Stephanie but never actually writes them. They vary wildly in tone: plaintive, outraged, whining, curt, sarcastic. In the end, however, she writes this short and simple note:

> Dear Stephanie,
> I'm sorry I behaved so badly.
> much love, Mummy. (228)

Why does Ellie actually mail this one while all the others never make it outside of her own head? It may have something to do with her last conversation with Angel and her final mystical experience.

Angel has confessed to being responsible for the glass pieces that have been disappearing from the studio. "'I loved it too much. Then I wanted it too'" (226). Angel is being recalled for "assessment" because she has been seduced by all the delight in the material world—especially glass. Ellie feels she cannot bear the loss of Angel. Yet after Angel departs, she "knows a moment of perfect emptiness. Because she has given everything away she experiences both loss and freedom" (226). As Ellie begins to blow a piece of glass, she has her final vision, but not like the others where she assumed a different identity. This time she simply sees "improbably and certainly" a young dark Palestinian girl. As Ellie blows the glass bubble, seeing simultaneously the Palestinian countryside, she does something she has not done before: she transfers the bubble to another rod, removes the blowing tube, and taps it free. She then hears an angel-voice say, "'Do not be afraid, Mary, for you have found favour with God.'"(227). The narrator says, "This is the annunciation." The Biblical event merges with Ellie's life:

> There is a silence at this conception, as intense as the sun, as deep as the blue lake, as translucent as glass, and deep within the blue there is a flash of lightning. . .
>   . . . Ah, sobbed Ellie, and she was open, open and unafraid of her own openness. She wanted, almost to her own surprise, to have sex, to make love, to open, open herself up for . . . for . . . it was not for anyone and she would not do it, but she who never wanted to have sex wanted it now. She learned how to receive so that receiving was a gift, a gift of fearlessness, of power and love. (227)

In the very next scene Ellie mails to Stephanie her simple, honest, and straightforward letter. This act, which represents for Ellie a giving over of her own will and submission to a higher good, is linked to Mary's surrender to God. What Ellie has conceived is fearlessness, power, and love. Her longing for sex suggests that she recognizes that her vulnerability had resulted in a brittleness that kept real emotional intimacy at bay. Now she has the power to be open to love and is willing to risk the pain that it may entail.

Angel's confession of her love affair with glass brings to a culmination the central symbol of glass, which is indicated by the first word of the title, *brittle*. Angel shamefully confesses to Ellie that she has stolen a bowl, a cube, a bauble, a paperweight, and a teardrop—all beautiful glass objects made in Ellie's studio. "'I really love glass . . . its transparency, its brittleness, you know. . . . But I got carried away; I started getting confused'" (224). At her dinner party early in the novel, Ellie had argued that a love of material beauty is not only *not* bad, but it might actually get you into heaven if you "'found in it an image of the beauty and brilliance of its creator'" (81). But the seductive lure of physical beauty can be overwhelming and requires a delicate balancing act to keep it in the correct perspective. In discussing glass with her assistant, Ellie expresses her dislike for "pretty" glass. "'Glass inclines to be pretty—it can't be ironic; prettiness is the great temptation of glass, like natural is the great temptation of clay. . . . Glass has to be beautiful, transcendent, technical or . . . not pretty'" (98). At one point when Ellie is thinking about the earliest glassmakers, who she believes worked "in northern Palestine, around the time when BC and AD met" (147), her reverie is saturated with the language of mysticism and divinity.

> "They must have worked in faith, those Semitic glassworkers, for they made nothing that had not been made before and more easily by moulding and slumping and working, but this was a new thing that they did. And did the desert stars roar overhead? And were they struck with awe by night and sunstroke by day? Did they see angels and watch the bushes burn and burn and burn and yet be not consumed?" (147–48)

Since Maitland has argued in *A Big Enough God* that human creativity is not only a reflection of God's creativity, but one of the most fitting ways to honor Him and enter into intimate communion with Him, it is not surprising that she invests the art of glassblowing with such transcendent qualities. Furthermore, glass is particularly apt for expressing the transcendent: "Something else about glass that she loved—her contact with it, while she was working on it was infinitely tender, intimate, maternal, but never sensual: it was fierce inside, this thing that looked so cool and smooth. It had to be kept at a distance, the distance of glove or pontil; not like clay which snuggled up to you puppylike, inserting itself into the gaps between the cells of your skin" (149).

Glass keeps working its way into metaphors. When Henry first tells Ellie that he wants a divorce, "a glass bubble . . . anneals, hardens and holds her" (114), and after venting her anger at him and just before she begins to cry, "the glass bubble which had seemed so tough around her began to crack" (116). After she and Hugo are told that his HIV test was negative, they feel as though they are "walking on thin glass, thin transparent glass which was none the less strong enough to carry their weight" (246). The symbol of glass gathers to itself the paradoxical quality of human emotions—strength coupled with fragility.

Like most human artifacts, glass is made of the most ordinary materials ("a measured mixture of roast crushed flints, bright red lead-oxide, tartar, borax, saltpetre—nothing fancy, nothing hard to come by"), and by an amazing process of transformations becomes something "so soft, so flowing, so gently malleable" and then hardens "into something so strong and wonderfully clear with an innate sparkle," which will "quite unexpectedly, ring like a bell when . . . tapped" (149). In its evolution into this thing of astonishing beauty, however, it becomes extremely vulnerable. It becomes brittle.

The glass that Ellie makes and that Angel steals exemplifies those acts of human imagination that are a reflection of God's creativity and transcendent beauty and are thus "artful theology." The title *Brittle Joys* and the metaphors used to describe peak emotional moments also suggest that the properties of glass—its source in ordinary *stuff*, its amazing transformative process, its vulnerability—make it a metaphor for the joy that, as Maitland reminds us, is one of the fruits of the Holy Spirit.

Maitland's epigraph for the novel tells us that the title phrase comes from a sermon of St. Augustine. "For in life we must struggle to hold on to brittle joys" (Augustine, Sermon III).[22] The subject of this sermon is the Beatitudes, and throughout it Augustine is contrasting the ephemeral nature of earthly joys with the everlasting joys of heaven. Earthly goods decay and can be lost or stolen, and what is worse, they can lead one astray from the path of virtue. "Riches indeed can be lost; and I only hope they get lost without getting you lost too."[23] Earthly delights are insignificant in comparison with the joy of being with God in heaven. "Whatever we do, whatever we do well, whatever we strive for, whatever praiseworthy objects we are crazy about—well, when we attain to the vision of God, we won't seek such things anymore. What after all is there to seek, if you have got God?"[24] Thus Augustine's purpose seems to be to devalue earthly joys and encourage his hearers to set their sights on heaven.

Maitland, on the other hand, seems to have quite a different purpose in mind in her depiction of earthly joys. She would certainly agree with Augustine that these delights are ephemeral. Yet rather than exhorting us to "Reckon earthly things as worthless"[25] and prefer heavenly joys, Maitland wants to make us appreciate them all the more, not least because they are a reflection, a hint—no matter how imperfect—of the transcendent beauty and joy of the Creator. The use of the word *brittle* to describe them clearly links them with her central symbol, glass, thus stressing that they are "fiercely beautiful" (146), with "an innate sparkle" (149), "Fragile and tough. Hard and soft" (226), "transcendent" (98). But like all brittle things, they are very vulnerable and have a tendency to shatter.

The most precious of these "brittle joys" are those that draw us close to human love. As Maitland says in *A Big Enough God*: "When we feel in need of more explanation we need think only of that moment when we see another human being and find in them the delineations of beauty, the possibility of love and delight. For at that moment we act as God acts to the whole of creation: it is not for anything—it is beauty, delight, joy, fun, creativity. It is love."[26] As if to illustrate this point, Maitland ends the novel with a scene between Ellie and Hugo. They have just received the news that his HIV test was negative. Not only does this mean he is not presently under sentence of death, but also that he will be able to be a surrogate father for the baby that Mary wishes to have. Despite the morally questionable nature of Hugo's sexual activity and Mary's decision to become pregnant by a sperm donor, Maitland concentrates on the human good that is present even in these circumstances. "Joy. Pure, unalloyed joy. She could hardly identify the feeling, it was so rare: not relief, not happiness, just this bubble, this inspiration of disinterested, pure joy, transparent as glass and as lovely. She rejoiced and was glad because her friend was well" (246).

Brittle joys are precious. They are also not for the faint of heart, for they are fraught with risk. Risk is a strong theme both in *A Big Enough God* and *Brittle Joys*. Risk is not the same as recklessness; but it does comprise a certain boldness, together with a willingness to let go of the comfortable, the familiar, the secure. Maitland sees our amazing, diverse, unpredictable universe as a sign that God Himself is not averse to taking risks. "God does throw dice, God is a gambler. There is risk at the heart; and God, bolder than we are, consents to the risk." Furthermore, joy, the cultivation of which Maitland sees as an ethical imperative, is "born out of contingency and risk and uncertainty."

The most obvious example of risk in the novel is the sexual behavior of Ellie's gay friends, which has resulted in many of them becoming ill with a deadly disease. Ellie cautions Hugo, "'You can take responsibility and take risks—you just have to take responsibility for those risks. No whining'" (218). At the same time that Ellie cautions Hugo, she cannot help but admire the boldness with which he takes risks. She sees him "winding himself up to run wild risks because without them he was not himself, which was of course why, cautious, almost cowardly by nature, she loved him so much" (221). She also clarifies that *risky* does not just mean unconventional behavior. On the contrary, "'Commitment can be risky too'" she argues (195). Ellie refuses to pass moral judgment on anyone else's behavior, as long as the only potential harm is the person's own and he is willing to take the risks involved, yet it is important to see this as Ellie's perspective, but not necessarily that of the novel, which is quite clear about the fact that the suffering and pain resulting from this sexual activity extends far beyond those who choose to engage in it.

Maitland's fondness for her homosexual characters is given comic emphasis when Angel admits to Ellie that angels not only love sex, but have a soft spot for gays. "'I'll tell you an embarrassing secret: Almost all angels like gay men better too. We have a soft spot—I mean for those sexually active liberated ones. Queers. Angels like queers'" (89). Angel elaborates:

> "We identify I suppose; they're more like us than most of you are. . . .
>
> "Well, you know; no begetting, no permanence, lots of highly enjoyable experiences which aren't forced into a social framework, which aren't built on for something else, built into anything. Oh it's hard to explain. Something to do with camp, of course, but more . . . look, angels adore sex. We aren't fixed by gender, even Milton knew that, we're free, we're what you would call promiscuous, though we think of it as generous; we don't trade delight for anything else, and we can't make it permanent even if we wanted to. We love sex, and when it comes to bodies we are inevitably a bit voyeuristic." (89)

Another major example of risk in the novel is glassmaking. Ellie has been burned. She has "scars, whiter whorls and dashes against the whiteness of her arm" and a "long scar, down the outside of her thigh" (2). Furthermore, even if the glass survives all the critical steps—the heating, blowing, kneading, cutting—even if it attains the perfect shape, there is always the danger that it can shatter. The novel includes other more subtle examples of risk-taking, as when Ellie decides to answer honestly when the priest at her dinner party asks her if she believes in angels, and she replies, "'Yes, I do'" (86). Although the priest seems sincere when he replies, "Lucky you," he laughingly tells Henry that he should ask his patient who insists she talks to an angel to bring him a feather. Ellie thinks that he has "no right to envy what he was not prepared to run any risk for" (86).

Although *Brittle Joys* is the first novel Maitland wrote after her conversion to Catholicism, there is no account of Ellie's conversion, no intimation of what led her, once she had thrown off her parents' Protestantism, to embrace Roman Catholicism. Her youthful prank of planting bulbs that would spell out *Viva il Papa* and *Orate pro nobis* can be seen as simply the rebellious act of an angry adolescent, who knows that Catholicism is her parents' *bete noir*. In the depiction of her life as a successful glassmaker, wife of an older psychiatrist who wants a divorce, and friend of lesbians and gays, Ellie's Catholic life weaves in and out in little unobtrusive ways. At one point she decides to make gratitude for her women co-workers her next Mass intention. While she is at Mass, the only point in the novel where we actually see Ellie actively practicing her Catholicism, a distinction is made between her public and private faith. Whereas some of the critics claimed to find a religious meaning in her work because of the "way that she buried colour deep inside her glass, so that it would flash unexpectedly," the truth is that "really what she most liked about institutional religion was that it was pretty tedious" (50). As a celebrity, Ellie presents to the public a solidly intellectual faith, lit by a certain high camp flamboyance which was both self-protective and loyal to her Church. Outside of the rites, her faith was flashy, public; she made sure it was mentioned in any interviews; . . . and she was, in as much as it mattered, a well-known and articulate supporter of advanced post-conciliar Catholicism. But that was not the point: the point was this mild boredom, a blessed and almost certain reward for forgoing her bath to be here. (50)

In her private life, Ellie's Catholicism takes on a more inward, serene, mellow, almost zen-like quality. As she attends Mass and "the canon [drones] on from the altar," she realizes that she does not "really even want glimpses of heaven and meaningful eucharistic experiences. She truly desired this slight absence of mind, this quiet drift, this essentially known place" (50). Here Maitland captures something essential about Catholic life that is as puzzling to outsiders as it is comforting to insiders. Traditionally, Catholics' attachment to their faith has not depended on a charismatic minister, inspiring sermons, or a stimulating variety in the services.[27] Whereas non-Catholics often wonder why Catholics, especially before Vatican II, did not get bored listening week after week to a Latin Mass they could not understand or praying the monotonous, repetitive rosary, Catholics themselves usually experienced these rites as a bracketed space of sacred time. The ritual itself connects the believer with a continuum that is outside earthly time and space.[28] Although it may appear monotonous and repetitive to an observer, the rite is often experienced as both mesmerizing and soothing. Ritual's repetitiveness and monotony is also akin to the chants and rhymes that accompany children's games, and to nursery rhymes and stories that children never tire of hearing again. Their function is not so much to convey information as to induce a state of feeling and to transport the hearer to another world.[29]

Ellie's connection to other Catholics is evident in the fact that she is offered a commission to make a glass panel for a convent because, as her German architect friend tells her, the sisters "are wanting very much to have women, and to have Catholics also" (108). Hugo's reference to Ellie's "dour Presbyterian soul, regardless of her fancy Catholic pretensions" (168) reminds us of the ongoing tension between her childhood religion, which she threw off, and the one she adopted as an adult. Ellie's Catholicism is present in brief allusions to Catholic practices, such as her confession after she slashes Henry's face with a fish knife when he asks for a divorce ("she heard a sharp intake of breath. She had never managed to provoke a personal reaction through the grille before" (117) and lighting a candle when her friend Robbie dies of AIDS (129).

These allusions and outward behaviors mark Ellie as a Catholic, but even more significant identity markers are her fierce love of beauty and the material world. According to Catholic theologian Lawrence Cunningham, "a sacramental attitude demands (indeed it presupposes) a healthy and robust love for the world in all of its beauty and delight. It is an attitude which sees real value in good art, in friendship, in the world of nature, in culture, in play."[30] Catholicism's oldest and most persistent enemy is gnosticism, which sees matter as inherently evil, and Ellie's fierce love of beauty and the world mark her as a daughter of the Church.

In addition to valuing the material world and the beauty that expresses its inherent goodness, Catholicism is also a religion that takes the supernatural seriously, that is wary of demythologizing, and that refuses to see Christianity as simply a program for ethical behavior and humanitarianism. Ellie is clearly open to the transcendent and the mystical. Although her apparent approval of a homosexual lifestyle is in tension with Catholic moral theology, Ellie, with her love of flamboyant beauty, her serious attention to her art, her love and compassion for her friends, her exuberant affirmation of the world, and her intimacy with an angel, is an exemplar of much that is distinctive and good in the Catholic tradition.

NOTES

1. Maitland, *Big-Enough God*, 74.

2. Maitland, *Big-Enough God*, 185–86.

3. Sara Maitland, *Brittle Joys* (London: Virago Press, 1999), 32. Hereafter cited in the text by page number. There are several versions of the protagonist's name. Her given name seems to be Héloïse, but her friends call her Ellie, and her family calls her Nelly. When her sister-in-law addresses her this way, Ellie corrects her: "'Héloïse,' she said firmly" (25). She is also addressed at one point as Helen (36).

4. Maitland, *Big-Enough God*, 189.

5. In a lecture at the University of Notre Dame given in 1998, Maitland told of difficulties she was having with her British editor, who objected that her angel character did not have enough human personality. Maitland's reply that the character was an angel, not a human being, apparently did not satisfy her editor. Her American publisher who had published her other novels in the United States refused to publish *Brittle Joys* because of the angel, insisting that the enthusiasm for angels in popular culture would not allow her novel to be taken seriously. According to the *Catechism of the Catholic Church*, "The existence of the spiritual, noncorporeal beings that Sacred Scripture usually calls 'angels' is a truth of faith." *Catechism*, 328.

6. *Manifest* is the verb Maitland uses to indicate that Angel is making her presence felt and getting ready to speak to Ellie.

7. Maitland, *Big-Enough God*, 44.

8. Maitland, *Big-Enough God*, 105.

9. Maitland, *Big-Enough God*, 43.

10. This is an important point since official Catholic teaching, as set forth in the new *Catechism of the Catholic Church*, distinguishes between the homosexual condition ("they do not choose their homosexual condition; for most of them it is a trial") and deliberately chosen homosexual acts ("Homosexual persons are called to chastity"). *Catechism*, 2358, 2359.

11. Sara Maitland, "Fag Hags: A Field Guide," in *Ângel Maker: The Short Stories of Sara Maitland* (New York: Henry Holt & Co., 1996) 111–118.

12. Maitland is yoking together two realities which, at least for many traditional Christians, are in tension, if not in outright contradiction: that this person is a sexually active homosexual *and* a likeable, generous, loving person. Maitland's technique here is reminiscent of G. K. Chesterton's analysis of orthodoxy: "By defining its main doctrine, the Church not only kept seemingly inconsistent things side by side, but, what was more, allowed them to break out in a sort of artistic violence otherwise possible only to anarchists. . . . It has kept them side by side like two strong colours, red and white, like the red and white upon the shield of St. George. It has always had a healthy hatred of pink." Chesterton, *Orthodoxy*, 103–4.

13. Maitland, *Big-Enough God*, 185.

14. Maitland, *Big-Enough God*, 185.

15. Maitland, *Big-Enough God*, 121.

16. Maitland, *Big-Enough God*, 112.

17. Maitland, *Big-Enough God*, 156.

18. Maitland, *Big-Enough God*, 163.

19. Maitland, *Big-Enough God*, 162.

20. Maitland, *Big-Enough God*, 180.

21. Maitland, *Big-Enough God*, 181.

22. I am unable to locate a translation of this sermon that matches Maitland's version.

23. Saint Augustine, Bishop of Hippo, *The Works of Saint Augustine*, ed. John E. Rotelle, O.S.A., Sermons III, translated by Edmund Hill, O.P. (Brooklyn: New City Press, 1991), 53A.4.

24. Saint Augustine, Sermons III, 53.6.

25. Saint Augustine, Sermons III, 53.15.

26. Maitland, *Big-Enough God*, 64.

27. This is not as true in the post-Vatican II Church as it was before the Council. As the Catholic Mass came to incorporate elements characteristic of Protestant services—congregational singing, more emphasis on preaching, a service that showcased the priest/minister (as opposed to the way the priest was "hidden" in the Latin rite, even having his back was to the people)—Catholics also look for more stimulating services, better music, and more inspiring preaching, often judging the "quality" of the Mass by the charisma of the priest. In this sense, Ellie is acting more like a pre-Vatican II Catholic.

28. C. S. Lewis makes a similar point in *Letters to Malcolm: Chiefly on Prayer*: "Novelty, simply as such, can have only an entertainment value. And [churchgoers] don't go to church to be entertained. They go to *use* the service, or, if you prefer, to *enact* it. . . . It works best—when, through long familiarity, we don't have to think about it. As long as you notice, and have to count, the steps, you are not yet

dancing but only learning to dance." C. S. Lewis, *Letters to Malcolm: Chiefly on Prayer* (New York: Harcourt, Brace & World, 1964), 4.

29. In writing about Norman MacLean's *A River Runs Through It,* Theodore Weinberger quotes Johan Huizinga: "the ritual act has all the formal and essential characteristics of play . . . particularly in so far as it transports the participants to another world." Johan Huizinga, *Homo Ludens: A Study of the Play-Element in Culture,* (New York: Roy Publishers, 1950), 18, quoted in Thomas Weinberger, "Religion and Fly Fishing: Taking Norman Maclean Seriously," *Renascence* 49, no. 4 (summer 1997): 282.

30. Lawrence S. Cunningham, *The Catholic Experience* (New York: Crossroad, 1987), 134.

IV

PIERS PAUL READ

13

A Rebel with a Cause:
Monk Dawson

*Imaginary evil is romantic and varied, full of charm, while imaginary good is
tiresome and flat. Real evil, however, is dreary, monotonous, barren. But real
good is always new, marvelous, intoxicating.*

—Simone Weil

*If the Divine call does not make us better, it will make us very much worse. Of
all bad men, religious bad men are the worst.*

—C. S. Lewis, *Reflections on the Psalms*

Monk Dawson, Piers Paul Read's third novel (1969), is a serious examination of the perilous position of religious faith in the second half
of the twentieth century. The novel examines the trajectory of a naïve, unexamined faith that is suddenly confronted with a virulent and aggressive
secularism, exposing the vulnerability of a religion that barricades itself
and fails to truly engage with the larger world. *Monk Dawson* also shows
how "engage with" can quickly modulate into "conform to" when not
firmly anchored in its theological tradition and fortified by a healthy respect for and recognition of the forces of evil that course through what
Saint Augustine called "the city of man."[1]

Set in the 1950s and 1960s, *Monk Dawson* delineates the flaws and
weaknesses in both the pre-Vatican II Catholic Church and the winds of
change that blew through the post-Vatican II Church in the name of reform. It also explores the perennial question of the interrelationship of
faith and morality. Do a person's beliefs really matter, or only what he
does? After all, Christ said, "None of those who cry out, 'Lord, Lord,' will

enter the kingdom of God, but only the one who does the will of my father in heaven" (Matt. 7:21) and states forthrightly that only those who
feed the hungry, clothe the naked, and perform the other corporal works
of mercy will enter heaven (Matt. 25:31–46). Yet there is also abundant
scriptural support for the idea that good deeds cannot earn salvation and
that a right relationship with Christ is imperative. The novel suggests
that trying to sever the link between right belief and right action is
fraught with danger. These themes are explored through the experience
of a likeable and genuinely good man, Edward Dawson, caught up in the
turmoil that was unleashed when the Catholic Church tried to reform itself during the permissive and rebellious 1960s. Religious faith is the
overarching theme of the novel. Even when Dawson has lost his own
faith and surrounds himself with other nonbelievers, its absence is a
defining element. Characters talk about why they no longer have faith,
or how they lost it, or how life is better or worse without it.

The novel begins when Dawson as a young boy is brought to Kirkham,
a boy's boarding school run by Benedictine monks. He arrives at the same
time as another student, Bobby Winterman; and the two remain close
friends throughout their school days. The two young boys exhibit the
kind of unreflective and trusting belief manifested by children who have
been well catechized and who live in a tightly-knit, religiously homogeneous community. Nevertheless, even at this early age, there are signs of
tension with religious faith and its authority figures. A paragraph in the
first chapter sets up a dichotomy between nature and faith:

> The school and monastery were built in different styles and stones, all ugly,
> but the valley before it was always beautiful—especially in the autumn when
> a shallow mist clung to the ground beneath the brown trees and the sun
> shone above it. Gradually, as we grew older, we became aware that there
> were other elements in the valley, as in the world at large, that had been there
> for more than the hundred years since the monastery was founded: which
> had been there before Saint Benedict, before Christ, perhaps before Adam,
> when the melting glacier, the last remnant of the ice age, had burst through
> the soft clay to the sea. . . . There was wheat where the farmers had planted
> it for countless generations, and there were cows and sheep and insects with
> no religion at all. And in ourselves we felt pleasure in the sun or exhilaration
> at a ground-frost and the emotions of hatred, affection and indifference
> which were found among us and all men before popes and bishops, synods
> and councils: and these, like the dandelion which grew in the paving stones
> between monastery and abbey church, these infiltrated the community of
> boys and men.[2]

One can almost hear Shakespeare's line about finding "sermons in stones"
or Wordsworth proclaiming that "One impulse from a vernal wood/May

teach you more of man,/Of moral evil and of good,/Than all the sages can."[3] The contrast between nature—monumental, imposing, powerful, peaceful, dignified—and institutional Christianity—ugly, a latecomer, and relatively ineffective in the face of the irresistible forces of nature—is striking. Like the persistent dandelions that inevitably push their way through paving stones, the flaws, frailties, and vices of human beings seem stubbornly resistant to the attempts of the Church to reform or even curb them.

This remarkable passage is filtered through the consciousness of Winterman, who is narrating this chapter.[4] Since Winterman loses his faith when he grows up, this description may be simply forecasting Winterman's own eventual loss of faith. The passage has wider implications, however. This evocative paragraph images the faith/world dichotomy that is developed in the novel. The Christian, and specifically Catholic, faith is often *not* attractive, especially when compared with powerful natural forces, which seem to be much more compelling. The Church may not be as old, powerful, or seductive as nature; but it does have its own kind of dogged persistence. Like the ugly stone building and the paving stones, it does make it a little harder for nature to have its own way.

The novel also problematizes religious faith by suggesting that it sometimes seems to be artificially *imposing* meaning on the random flux of life, claiming that it is only seeing the meaning that is there—whereas to the eye of the nonbeliever, the so-called meaning is nothing more than wishful thinking. When Dawson is trying to make up his mind about whether or not he should become a priest, Father Timothy tells him about a priest who wondered the same thing.

> "Well, he couldn't make up his mind about his vocation, so he said to God— if I see a spider in the next twenty-four hours, without looking for one in particular, I shall take it as a sign that you are calling me to the priesthood. He said this at six in the evening, and by four the next afternoon he had not seen the spider. Then, at five past five, he took a book from a shelf and one of those very, very small spiders was hanging from it." (25)

Needless to say, the young man in the story became a priest. Father Timothy follows this story with the remark that "'God has ordained that his priests be equal to the angels'" (25), thus implying that this exalted view of the priesthood is perhaps on the same plane as using spiders to discern God's will. In fact, a high regard for empirical truth—especially historical facts—does not seem to be a high priority for people of faith, as evidenced by the fact that the Church has honored as saints many people about whom little or nothing is known. Dawson ponders the fact that the "special place in the Church of the Curé of Ars is "unaffected by the discovery that his patron, Saint Philomena, had never existed" (40).

The early part of the novel contains an interesting observation on how faith is passed on. The argument is often made that the poor catechesis that was common in the decades following Vatican II is responsible for the loss of many of today's young Catholics, who stop practicing the faith as soon as they are out of the family home.[5] Yet the catechesis Dawson receives in the 1950s (*before* the Council) does not appear to be particularly good.

> Religion was never forced on us at Kirkham: religious instruction was the least important subject on the curriculum, and we all left the school particularly ignorant of the substance of our supposed beliefs. But this was not the product of negligence. The monks of this order of Saint Benedict were only following the tactics of another order, the Society of Jesus. Ten years in a monastic institution could be assumed to have left its mark at a far deeper level than that of mere consciousness. No one could decide to forsake what they had inexorably become. No one could deny his own identity. For years, now, for fourteen years we had been to mass every day of the term, and twice on Sundays. On Thursdays there had been Benediction. On Sunday evenings, Vespers. Every morning there were prayers before classes with the headmaster: every evening, prayers before bed with the housemaster. God entered into everything we did. No aspect of our lives was without its good or bad, its right or wrong. Faith became as automatic as the habits of hygiene . . . and we thought as little of being Catholics as of brushing our teeth. (21)

This passage is remarkable in a number of ways. In no way can it be read as a vindication of pre-Vatican II catechetical methods. Quite the contrary. Particularly the last sentence would seem to make it a stinging criticism of an approach that made religion perfunctory and routine. After all, both the narrator and Dawson lose their faith as adults. The fact that the boys leave school "particularly ignorant of the substance of [their] supposed beliefs" suggests that, although the religious instruction of this era may have had more substance than that of the post-Vatican II period, it was still inadequate. Yet the narrator articulates a way of transmitting the faith that is more subtle, but perhaps in the long run more powerful and effective, than classroom instruction: immersion in a Christian community where regular prayer and liturgical worship are part of the ordinary routine of daily life. As Winterman puts it, this routine "left its mark at a far deeper level than that of mere consciousness. No one could decide to forsake what they had inexorably become." This observation suggests that in spiritual matters, one first works on external behavior—deeds and words—and then the internal disposition will follow—whether trying to develop one's own faith or that of others. Such a belief was behind the practice of having children memorize catechism answers, attend school masses, say the rosary and other prayers—even though these practices were "forced" on them and in no way were expressions of genuine piety. As the devil in C. S.Lewis's *The Screwtape Letters* says, "All mortals tend to turn into the thing they are pretending to be."[6]

Yet despite the tenacious power of early training, faith is easily lost. Winterman's loss of faith seems to begin with his realization that "'everyone else seemed to get on quite well without it,'" reinforced by his decision that "'chastity's absurd'" (85). The fact that Winterman and Dawson both move out of the sheltered, homogeneous religious environment at a time when secular society is questioning faith more aggressively than ever before suggests that, although their faith might have survived if they had stayed in a sheltered supportive environment, the modern world's antagonism to religion exposes the vulnerability in the kind of faith formation they experienced.[7] Modern secular society presents challenges to religious belief and practice that were simply unimagined in a time when, despite sectarian differences, people lived their whole lives among other believers in a society that fostered and protected Christian values.

As if to further emphasize the precariousness of faith in the modern world, Read provides another example of a loss of faith in Jenny, the woman Dawson lives with after he leaves the priesthood. Unlike Dawson and Winterman, Jenny was not brought up Catholic, but is a convert. In fact, she was instructed by Dawson himself after he becomes a priest. She became interested in Catholicism because one of her lovers during her marriage came from a Recusant Catholic family.[8] "This Recusant made a strong impression on Jenny, if only for hurrying his sperm-smeared body to church that Sunday morning. She took to going to mass, under his influence, first to this church, then to the cathedral" (128). When Dawson visits Jenny shortly after leaving the priesthood, she tells him that her Catholic days are over. Just as there doesn't seem to be any substantial reason for her converting, so there is no substantial reason given for her leaving. But her (apparently) whimsical conversion, quickly followed by de-conversion, represents a phenomenon that has raised questions about conversions based on an attraction for a particular Catholic or community of Catholics, rather than on careful examination of Catholic doctrine and an informed decision to embrace it.[9]

Monk Dawson is primarily the story of one man's spiritual journey, yet its setting in a period that inaugurated some of the greatest change in the history of the Catholic Church constitutes a critique of both the situation that engendered the call for reform and the forces of upheaval that followed the Second Vatican Council. Dawson's own growing awareness of deficiencies in the pre-Vatican II Church typifies a common experience for many Catholics during those years. His new perspective begins with his questioning the apostolate of the community of monks he has joined. In what sense could educating the sons of the rich and powerful be seen as a faithful following of Jesus? His confessor cites the traditional principle, "*cujus regio, ejus religio.* Secure the prince, and you have his subjects'" (42). Even though the priest admits that things have changed a bit since the days of princes, he still thinks the principle is valid. Dawson, however, is not so sure. When Pope John XXIII issues the encyclical *Mater et Magistra*, he realizes that the pope himself is calling for "a total reversal of the Catholic Church's traditional attitude on social questions. No longer were the pious permitted to believe that the material plight of their fellow men was irrelevant to the quest for eternal salvation" (43).

Dawson enthusiastically welcomes the pope's call for more sustained attention to social justice. From the very beginning of the novel, his strongest characteristic is his compassion. Only a month after arriving at school, he and Winterman go for a walk and see the bullocks that are owned by the monastery. Noting their "gentle and affectionate gaze," (3) Dawson is horrified to learn that they are raised only for meat. The realization brings tears to his eyes. For the next three nights, he refuses to eat the meat that is served in the refectory, even though he is beaten as a result. Although he eventually gives in and eats meat, Dawson's empathy and compassion remain his defining attribute. When he and Winterman discuss what they want to be when they are grown up, Dawson tells him, "'I'm going to help people'" (4). As a young priest, Dawson gets in trouble with his superior for taking it upon himself to install an impoverished deserted wife and her six children in a room behind the stage of the school theater. Defending himself to the abbot for having acted without getting permission from the proper authority, he asserts, "'The Church . . . I mean, a certain sort of establishment within the Church has always been against . . . against the more positive acts of charity. Saints have usually done good in spite of the Church'" (51). Dawson's action may have been impetuous and imprudent, but his conviction that the Church's record on charity and social justice has at times been less than impressive is an attitude that was shared not only by some theologians, but also by many laypeople who were invigorated by and enthusiastic about this new challenge to live the gospel more fully.

Another insalubrious aspect of the pre-Vatican II Church is an unwholesome, suspicious, and problematic attitude toward sex. The innuendoes about homosexual priests and a reference to a monk with very little beard, "though he was said to shave and the monastery was known to reject vocations where a vow of chastity would be superfluous" (7) lend credence to the familiar view that those who elect a life of celibacy are either homosexual or lack any kind of robust sexuality. The monks are "acutely aware of the dangers of pederasty" (9), surely not an unreasonable concern at any single-sex school. Yet their efforts to prevent it are extreme.

So obsessed were the authorities with the possibility of sentimental and sensual relationships between boys—a custom that was rampant in most other schools of this kind—that they invented a complex of extra taboos. It was not difficult for them to do this in such a small, enclosed society as the school and monastery of Kirkham and so an atmosphere was created in which a boy could not be seen in normal, friendly conversation with another of a different age. (9–10)

If any boy were discovered doing "something or other" with another, he would be isolated until his parents would come and get him. "The monks had no clear idea of what it was—a grave sin or a mental aberration—but they knew it was contagious and thought it was incurable" (10). When Dawson is sixteen, he rescues one of the younger boys who on a school holiday gets stuck in a cave in a limestone quarry. With his arm around the boy's shoulder, Dawson is "inflated with a stronger emotion than he had ever felt in his life before" (14). With his other hand he begins touching the skin of the boy's flank, stopping only when the hear they voices of other boys from the school.

This experience is troubling to Dawson, and he talks it over with his mentor, Father Timothy. He has admitted that he was fond of this boy, and Father Timothy's chilling rejoinder is, "'When an older boy becomes fond of a younger one, his wish, even if he doesn't know it, is to misuse the other boy's body. . . . What starts as a gesture of affection, Eddie, can quickly become the groping of lust'" (17–18). Although the pre-Vatican II Church excoriated Freud's theories, which saw sex lurking everywhere, even in apparently innocent acts and wishes, ironically, this priest's advice sounds curiously Freudian. Yet Freud saw these actions and desires as evidence of a perfectly natural and healthy instinct (although one that had to be kept under control for the good of society),[10] whereas Father Timothy's advice inculcates a fear of sexuality as something dangerous and perverse. Father Timothy suggests that Dawson submit to a "mild beating" to discipline the flesh, and he complies (18).

Another factor in Dawson's failure to develop healthy sexual attitudes is simply his lack of exposure to females. Except for his mother and sister, whom he sees only during school vacations, he has almost no contact with females. Consequently, when he becomes a priest and women come to him in confession, he realizes that "to him the female of our species was a category of creature as new and as strange as the giraffes at the Regent's Park zoo" (69). His segregated upbringing, education, and seminary formation have not prepared him to deal with half the souls to whom he would be ministering. But Dawson's inadequacy in this respect is not due simply to lack of exposure to females. Even more detrimental is the philosophy of chastity he has been taught and the hyperbolic rhetoric in which it was enshrined. Dawson discovers a enormous gulf between the traditional presentation of chastity and the lived reality of women's lives:

> The Church, after all, had always had such a special place in its heart for the purity of its daughters: virginity was not just a state of experience, but a precious, jewel-studded, gold-encrusted ivory citadel given by God to every female child.
>
> ... Certainly, the armies of chastity were demoralized by the indifference or hostility of those who lived around them. The gold, the ivory and the jewels were somehow out of fashion and, as Dawson himself said to his penitents, there was little use in crying over sacked cities: but even his exhortations to further resistance and counter-attack were reluctantly listened to. If morale seemed high for further encounters, it was often just enthusiasm for a second defeat. (69–70)

This passage manages to be both gently mocking and savagely critical. It exposes Dawson's gullibility in having uncritically accepted this line of thinking, and the overblown regal and military metaphors render the Church's valuation of chastity ridiculous, suggesting at least a partial explanation of why it is so ineffective in regulating the sexual experience of young women.

This critique is not unusual in the post-Vatican II period. Indeed, after *Humanae Vitae*, the chorus of voices raised in protest against the Church's teaching went far beyond its condemnation of contraception to encompass every aspect of its teaching on sexuality. What makes Read's treatment of this subject noteworthy is his inclusion of some counter voices as well. For example, neither Dawson's all-male education, his lack of good sex education, nor his being trained to associate sexuality with fear and danger seem to have done him serious harm when he takes up his own sexual life with a sexually experienced woman. He feels awkward at first but learns quickly, and soon they enter into "months of pleasant life for both of them" (134). When Dawson is commissioned by an editor to write some newspaper articles, the editor encourages him to include something personal, the "'unnatural demands of celibacy—something like that'" (142). Dawson's unexpected reply is, "'That really wasn't a problem'" (143). The editor clarifies that celibacy being a nonproblem is not what his readers want to read. "'I don't want to hear about what went on with the choir boys behind the altar, but we've got to have something that'll cover the sex angle because our readers think about it and sweat about it and they don't want to read about someone who says he can do without it'" (143).

Thus Read succeeds in presenting a more nuanced description of the conflicted and incendiary issue of sex and the Catholic Church than many contemporary writers who seem to see only one side of the problem: either all health and normalcy is on the side of the secular culture, and the Church's sexual teaching is simply twisted and neurotic; or the Church proffers wholesomeness and spiritual health while the secular culture is mired in pernicious, soul destroying vice. Read is fully cognizant of the way in which the Church throughout its long history became infiltrated with unhealthy attitudes and practices with regard to sex—especially in the training of the young.[11] Read makes no attempt to whitewash it. No excuses about how those strains are not *truly* Catholic, but aberrations of the Gnostics, Jansenists, or some other heretical group can really alleviate the embarrassment and resentment that many contemporary Catholics feel about this aspect of Catholicism. On the other hand, Read is also aware of the way the secular culture loves to sensationalize Catholic problems with sex, both for their entertainment value as well as opportunities to undermine the moral authority of one of the last critical voices challenging contemporary sexual mores.

If the novel is clear-sighted about the failures and inadequacies of the pre-Vatican II Catholic Church, it is no less discerning in depicting the turmoil and distortion that infected the Church once John XXIII opened the windows to the modern world. It would be too much to claim that Edward Dawson is a kind of Catholic Everyman figure navigating the tumultuous waters of upheaval that coursed through the Church during and after the Council. His education by monks in a secluded boys' boarding school is certainly not normative; and his seminary training and his career as a priest—although a short one—also sets him apart from the average Catholic. Nevertheless, many of Dawson's emotions and reactions as he tries to take what he thought was a settled and incontestable faith and correlate it with a world exploding with the sexual revolution, the feminist movement, and rebellion against all forms of authority resonate with Catholics who lived through those years. Change took on a life of its own, and like the sorcerer's apprentice, created havoc. "Nuns who had been encouraged to make themselves pertinent by changing their robes and cowls for contemporary and conventional skirts, in some cases decided that their vocations were as out of place as their veils. Indeed many individual monks and nuns decided that if the life they had led until then was somehow irrelevant, then no reform could help it. And so they left" (44).

Dawson's initial confusion eventually gives way to "a frenzy of reformist zeal" (45). Although he had apparently lived happily with the Latin Mass all his life, he now joins other young priests in asking the abbot for permission to say the Mass in English.[12] His reformist zeal soon goes beyond matters of liturgy. He agitates for the abolition of the Officers' Training Corps at the school, lectures his confessor about the new ideas of the Council, and again questions how teaching the sons of the rich can be a legitimate apostolate. In fact, he is so hard on his confessor that the old priest requests a transfer and is given a post as chaplain to an unreformed community of nuns.

As Dawson's confusion and agitation grows, he does what many others did in those tumultuous times: he latches on to the one thing he can be sure of: humanitarianism. It was Pope John XXIII himself who had taught in *Pacem in Terris* and *Mater et Magistra* that Christians must realize that improving the lives of the poor—their material conditions, not just the state of their souls—was imperative. Dawson begins to channel his confusion into efforts to help the poor and disadvantaged, housing an abandoned wife and her children in the room behind the school theater. Eventually his conflicts with the monastic community lead him to have a breakdown, and the abbot decides to transfer him to the secular clergy.

Serving in London's Westminster Cathedral, Dawson's horizons are considerably broadened. One young penitent confesses to having premarital sex; but as Dawson gently questions her about the frequency and circumstances, he learns to his horror that her sexual partner is her father, who is forcing himself on her. Realizing that this situation requires the help of social workers, he convinces the girl to go with him to seek help from the Children's Officer, the result being that the girl and her younger brothers are provided with separate living quarters. From a material standpoint, Dawson's intervention certainly does improve the girl's situation. However, it also raises a difficult issue that began to surface as more and more Catholics enthusiastically threw themselves into works of social justice. As the demarcation between religious practice and social work became blurred, it became evident to some that although Catholicism and secular humanitarian efforts might *look* similar on the outside, they answer some important questions differently. Helen Sweet, the girl Dawson has helped, who obviously was enough of a practicing Catholic to have gone to confession, is confused by some of the things the social worker has said:

> "Mr Simmonds told me that Dad ought to have got married again. He says it's hard on a working man, not having a wife."
>
> "Yes, I think he's right."
>
> "And he says I mustn't think of m'Dad as plain wicked, you see, because there's lots of men who'd act like that if they lived all cramped up, like we were."
>
> "Did he say that?"
>
> "Yes, Father. And I don't quite understand, you see, because what he did was a sin, wasn't it?"
>
> Father Dawson looked down at his hands and twisted them together. "It was a sin so far as we know, Helen, but only God can see right into your father's heart and judge just how bad he was to do it.". . .

"But it's true, isn't it, that there ought to be more Council flats, and bigger ones?"

"Yes."

"And will there be less sins when there are?"

"I don't know, Helen. Only God can tell us that." (65–66)

This passage dramatizes one of the problems that ensued when after Vatican II Catholicism decided to be more open to the modern world. Advances in psychology and the other social sciences were making morality, which had once seemed a simple matter of right and wrong, appear infinitely more complex than they did in an earlier era. The powerful influences of environment, education, heredity, addiction, and family dynamics—together with huge discrepancies among the advantages with which people begin life—rendered the issue of moral guilt much more complicated. Although the social sciences provided helpful insights into moral questions, the underside of this development was that simple people like Helen, the young and uneducated, were deprived of a relatively simple moral code that had provided clear guidelines. Although Catholic moral theology had always insisted that circumstances can mitigate one's degree of culpability and that God alone could know the extent of a person's guilt, some of the conclusions of social science seemed to be doing away with guilt altogether.

While Dawson is doing parish work, Winterman, now a journalist, enlists him to write some columns on religious subjects for his newspaper. It is ironic that, these articles, at least as Winterman paraphrases them, seem to make a clear distinction between religion and humanitarianism:

Do not confuse faith with humanitarianism. Sympathy for your fellow man is not a religious sentiment but an animal emotion. Like other forms of human love—sensual, parental or brotherly love—it is of no theological significance. Thus Christians are not notably more humanitarian than non-Christians. We help others in obedience to an instinct that preserves the unity of society: Faith in God is quite another question. (87–88)

What seems to be getting short shrift here is that other question. Glib affirmations of the dignity and unique status of faith were easily made in the years following the Council, but seldom was that status explained or defended in any meaningful way. On the other hand, humanitarian efforts were much more likely to engender enthusiasm than a reasoned defense of the Virgin Birth or the Real Presence. Humanitarian efforts need no defense. Their goodness is self-evident. *Every* religion advocates them. The very physicality of preparing dinner at a homeless shelter or refurbishing a house for a poor family can be energizing—even exhilarating—and the feeling of righteousness that usually follows is also welcome. For these reasons, emphasis on social justice came to be the centerpiece for many catechetical programs, and Confirmation preparation for the young often included a substantial service requirement; whereas the knowledge of doctrine, Church history, apologetics, and Scripture were greatly de-emphasized. An unintended result was that many young people realized that they did not need to subscribe to the Christian creed and its rigorous sexual ethic in order to engage in humanitarian good works. So they set about being good secular humanists.

Eventually, Dawson himself becomes a secular humanist. As he writes his articles, often late at night, he begins "to examine and question his be-haviour in relation to his beliefs," concluding that often his priestly min-istry does not really help people (his childhood ambition) but makes their lives more difficult (88). Ironically, the final stage of the unraveling of his faith occurs at a Trappist monastery, where his superiors have urged him to make a retreat. He finds the monks' life senseless and their sacrifices, such as giving up meat, pointless. In the quiet of the monastery, he must face the questions that have been tormenting him. He asks the prior if he can "'think of any way in which a Catholic is better or better off than a non-Catholic'" (94). The prior's answer of the Eucharist is unconvincing. Dawson is unable to pray and ends up concluding that he has lost his faith. As he explains to Winterman, "'I don't believe in it any more, in any of it. Not even in God. I've reached my maturity at long last. I've out-grown all the nonsense that we were taught at Kirkham and now I want to live as deeply as I can before I die'" (96).

Dawson's experience here again exemplifies a common dynamic in the post-Vatican II years. The enthusiasm for more attention to social justice led some Catholics to put greater emphasis on one part of the gospel—"You will know them by their deeds" (Matt. 7:16)—and less on another equally important part of the gospel, the necessity for a right relationship with Christ—"No more than a branch can bear fruit of itself apart from the vine, can you bear fruit apart from me" (John 15:4). It is no surprise that Dawson's inability to pray is the prelude to his loss of faith. The arid-ity of his spiritual life, as well as his inability to come up with cogent an-swers to hard questions about the efficacy of prayer and the reasons for being a Catholic, suggest that the pre-Vatican II Church may have insuffi-ciently prepared Catholics with the spiritual and intellectual resources they would need in a world after the Council, a world no one could have imagined.

In retrospect, the post-Vatican II Church's embrace of the modern world seemed to some people to have been too eager, naïve, and indiscrimi-nate.[13] Catholics took to heart Pope John XXIII's metaphor about opening the windows to let in the fresh air of the world. Some commentators have wryly suggested that the timing was unfortunate in that this openness came just as the air outside was beginning to turn noxious.[14] The rush to social justice opened an engagement with the larger secular world, which eventually came to embrace other aspects of that world that had nothing whatsoever to do with social justice, but a great deal to do with sex.

Dawson's entry into the secular world marks the beginning of his sexual education. His introduction into sexual knowledge first comes by way of the confessional as he encounters tales of sexual passion spinning out of control, including the girl being sexually abused by her father. One penitent asks Dawson to visit her home and counsel her promiscuous daughter. Dawson does so, and one visit culminates in an embrace and kiss. After he leaves the priesthood, it is not so much the desire for sex, which in the London of the 1960s is promoted and advertised in "the tableaux of titillation and innuendo . . . all around him" (111), as it is loneliness and the desire for love that causes him to seek out a woman. He finds her in the person of Jenny, the woman he had instructed in the faith. When he meets her again, he learns that her husband had been killed in an auto accident and the attractive young widow is available. Having lost her newly acquired faith, she has no scruples about taking up with a former priest, and they are soon happily living together, enjoying a robust sex life and luxuriating in the pleasures made possible by Jenny's large income. His lack of information about sex and limited exposure to women has not impeded his ability to perform sexually. For a while their life seems perfect, and Dawson is the envy of the other men in Jenny's circle of friends. In addition to their sexual delights and other pleasures, they also enjoy conversations about their higher awareness and their having outgrown the need for religion.

"Why is it," she once asked, "that people live in so much confusion, not knowing what to do with their lives?"

"I think the only explanation is an ethological one: that at an early state of evolution, the human being needed this anguish, a sort of guilt about living, to foster feelings of social obligation which kept the tribe together and at peace with itself."

"Yes, I see. And now?"

"And now we no longer need the taboos because we understand, rationally, the nature of society. Intuition is redundant."

"It is an exciting time to live in, isn't it?" Jenny said.

"As you say—the maturity of man."

"But what's to be done about people who don't see all this?"

"Inevitably, there are individuals who lag behind the communal level of understanding. Religion has some function for them, I suppose." (138–39)

Dawson and Jenny's bliss does not last. Not only is his feeling for Jennie diminished by her arrogant and rude behavior to tradesmen and waitresses, but he dislikes her rich friends, whose lifestyles seem decadent and pointless. Also, his delight in his newfound sexual freedom is compromised by his growing sense of the costs of irresponsible sex. He learns that Jenny's daughter is not really the daughter of her late husband and that, in fact, Jenny is not sure which of her two lovers is the father. Working as an investigative reporter, Dawson visits an orphanage, where he is confronted with the problem of all the unwanted children. The matron explains that half of the children are colored and hard to place. Many of the others are born to Irish mothers who have the baby in England but stipulate that it must be placed with a Catholic family, which is not easy to do in England. Sexuality, which at first had seemed simply a wholesome adult behavior, nature's way of assuaging loneliness, has a dark underside.

The scene that dramatically shows the nadir to which Dawson's embrace of the secular world has led is his participation in a black mass. He, Jenny, and some friends attend a charity ball, and during the dinner his friends urge him to say a black mass.

> There were candles and flowers already on the table but Benji and Henry Poll now arranged them as decoration for an altar. Hands cleared it of plates and glasses. Jenny was then naked. "Pray, Father, on my back or my front?" she asked, looking at Dawson in the face for the first time since she had returned to the room.
>
> "On your back," said Sylvia, "it's always on your back, at least I think so." And this was what Jenny did. She lifted herself on to the table and lay down on her back. Benji and Henry Poll, like two sub-deacons, brought the goblet and one of the two rolls in front of Dawson. And Dawson began: "He, on the day before he suffered death, took bread into. . . " But here he stopped. He felt suddenly sick and involuntarily he vomited, a trickle of half-digested brandy, coffee, strawberries, sucking-pig and consommé-en-gelée dripping from his mouth on to the table-cloth and on to the stomach of his naked mistress, collecting in part in her navel. (161–62)

Dawson's embrace of the secular world, which began with his benevolent desire to be a humanitarian, has led him to engage in an act that his earlier self would have found abhorrent and sacrilegious.

Has Read carried the "slippery slope" argument too far? As the novel suggesting that if one tries to disengage the "fruit" of good works from the "vine" of orthodox Christian belief and practice (including the contested rules for sexual morality), one will inevitably wind up in a morass of depravity? Obviously, some people do lose their faith but continue to engage in humanitarian acts of service without becoming sexually profligate, dishonest, or abusers of alcohol. Yet *Monk Dawson*, like many of Read's other novels, suggests that an indiscriminate embrace of the contemporary secular world and its values does pose significant risks—not only to faith—but to common decency and integrity.

Another critique of the post-Vatican II church is actually embedded in the early pre-Vatican II portion of the novel. In the section of the novel where Winterman is describing how the schoolboys imbibed their religion—not through excellent religious instruction—but through the routine of religious practices, he goes on to describe being in church during a Sunday service:

> As the monks filed into the church before a ceremony, or as the procession moved out afterwards with the great silver crucifix bright beside the candles, the fourth-formers all in white, the tall monks all in black, the novices, the prior, the abbot and finally the celebrant in his bright robes—as all this happened before our eyes, it was inevitable that some of our minds would be touched by its theatre. Thoughts would surely turn to the highest form of heroism that we had been taught to recognize—the heroism of sanctity. (22)

The point of this passage is that these splendid ceremonies caused some of the boys to think about a possible vocation to the priesthood. Since *Monk Dawson* was published in 1970, it would have been written when the revised vernacular liturgy was still very new. For many Catholics, it was not until the new liturgy and all the experimentation that accompanied it had been in place for several years, that they began to cast an eye backward to the more formal, ornate, and ritualistic liturgy of the pre-Vatican II Church and conclude that something valuable had been lost. The use of the word *theatre* in the above passage may seem to be pejorative, but it is not necessarily.[15] There is no explicit comparison of pre-conciliar and post-conciliar liturgy in the novel, for Dawson leaves not only the priesthood but Catholicism itself before the liturgical changes really take hold. Nevertheless, for readers with thirty or more years of the new liturgy behind them, this passage can be a reminder of the power and compelling beauty of ritual, ceremony, and tradition, which some believe was too carelessly tossed aside.

Having discarded his Catholic faith, and even his belief in God, Dawson has shifted his spiritual energies to secular humanism, but he finds he must shift them once again when he realizes that the secular press, which he had seen as an instrument for helping to solve social problems, has its own vested interests and is not really committed to the welfare of ordinary working men. He finds himself attracted to the communist ideals of a strike organizer.

> Was he, then, to become a Communist? There came from his memory images of Communism—Russia, Stalin, torture and totalitarianism—things his mother had told him, things he had been taught at school. But McKeon [the

strike organizer] had not had the face of a torturer. . . . A kind of weariness came over Dawson. The enthusiasm passed, leaving a backwash of depression. Could he change again? Could he say, to Jenny and others, that he had found the answer for a third time? (180)

Dawson had thought he had found a moral center in the humanitarian impulse. The goodness of humanitarian acts seemed self-evident, not requiring any foundation of philosophical principles. But without a strong theoretical basis, the persistent encroaching presence of human greed, jealousy, and self-interest renders it increasingly difficult to anchor these acts of benevolence within any kind of stable framework. They become more and more privatized. Dawson finds these shifting perspectives make his writing difficult.

> There were other people's points of view—the readers' prejudices and the editors' concept of their responsibility. Moreover, there were the rights of the human beings he might write about—the tramp's idea of himself, the drunk's idea of himself. These imagined pressures and opinions came down on each thought as it began to take shape. He felt himself a pig-in-the-middle with no point of view of his own. (198)

After his loss of faith, Dawson's belief in the self-evident goodness of humanitarian work and his love for Jenny had been the two props that held him up and filled the void left by the departure of faith. His disillusionment with journalism, which he has seen as the voice of benevolent secular humanism, is still fresh when Jenny leaves Dawson to go off with another man. He is now left with nothing but the vague sense of wanting to help others, the sympathy that had revolted at eating the flesh of trusting animals. He makes an unfortunate marriage with a woman he does not love, and the result is tragic. His motivation is never made very clear. His explanation to Winterman is simply, "'Oh, I don't know. . . . We both just rather wanted to get married'" (197).

The marriage quickly deteriorates. Winterman suspects sexual difficulties, commenting that "any erotic sentiment can turn sour" and revealing that "they made love infrequently and when they did it was, as often as not, when they were drunk" (197–98). As his marriage disintegrates, Dawson and his wife, whom he first met as a priest, counseling a skeptical adolescent rebelling against her mother's Catholicism, reverse their original roles, she defending Catholicism, he dismissing it out of hand.

> "Don't you think," she once asked, "that the Church is right, really, to make marriage a binding institution?"
> "No. Why?"
> "Well, it is a practical business, isn't it, and not so romantic?"

"That's true to the extent that priests can't conceive of love, so they can't write it into Canon Law." (199)

Depressed and neglected by Dawson, his wife dies in what appears to have been a suicide attempt.

The end of the novel finds Dawson, not only back in the Catholic Church, but ensconced in one of its strictest religious orders—the Trappists. The intervening period of time during which Dawson rethinks Christianity and makes the decision to become a monk is passed over. We see him through the eyes of Winterman, who is driving near the monastery and stops and asks permission to see Dawson. He claims that he needs to see him for spiritual advice, a falsehood that clashes with the "rage" he is feeling at monks who are "obsessed only with perverting nature in the name of supernatural law" (213). "What could they have done to Dawson now, when they had already destroyed his life? What kind of broken man was I to see? What species of lunacy? What variety of despair? I was not surprised that they were going to let me see him. I knew the arrogance of these clerics" (213).

Winterman does not find a broken man, and their meeting suggests that Winterman's claim to be seeking spiritual advice may turn out not to be so disingenuous after all. Much of their conversation is rendered in summary form. "He explained how he had regained his faith . . . and spoke of the soul and of God as though the soul was the only facet of his identity and God the only person of any account. . . . He said he thought that there was great confusion in our generation between social and religious morality—between the exigencies of human life and the deference that was due to God" (215). When Winterman asks him how he can be so sure that his beliefs are true, Dawson gives an answer appropriate for a contemplative monk, but one that would certainly not convince a skeptic. "He then described the state of absolute concentration that he had reached through meditation and self-denial, where the truth of a proposition may be measured by the physical sensation of ecstasy and release that it provokes in the brain and spine" (215). Goading him on, Winterman asks him if he considers the kind of life he (Winterman) leads evil. Although refusing to judge his friend's life, Dawson insists that whether or not Winterman calls evil by that name, certain kinds of behavior are undignified, "contradicting the tight logic of [his] being with negative and destructive patterns of thought and behaviour. One did not attain a state of grace through a continuous succession of right actions, but by the understanding of the contradictions within oneself, a containment of them and hence the preservation of moral integrity" (216).

This exchange might have been more convincingly rendered in dialogue, yet one can also see why Read might have wished to present it at a remove. Filtered through Winterman's memory, it is cushioned by his skepticism and resistance, saved from being as didactic as it would be in Dawson's own words. What comes across most strongly is not so much what Dawson says as the sense of peace. "There was no sign of the passing of time. The curve of the lake shore below us, the squares of the buildings and the lines of the stone walls that ran up the side of the green hills, all became a placid, abstract pattern whose repose permitted a stillness of mind. We talked further, and then for moments there was silence and the silence took on a value equal to the speech" (216–17). To Jenny, who insists that Dawson must be either mad, broken, or sick, Winterman asserts that he seemed "so much at ease with himself" (219).

If Read's portrayal of Jenny and her self-indulgent, decadent friends are taken as a representation of the secular world over against the sacred, this dichotomy seems too stark, too histrionic. What helps to provide some balance is the brief but touching depiction of Dawson's sister, Sally, and her husband Arnie, whom Dawson visits when he first leaves the priesthood. According to Sally, Arnie "'hates religion'" and she herself admits that she hasn't really given it up, saying, "'Never had it really'" (103). They lived together before marrying and now have a baby son. She seems to have no great emotional investment in her home. "'I mean you're just there to watch telly and eat and sleep, aren't you? We got this place on a mortgage'" (105). To Dawson it seems that their lives are filled with distractions that keep them from talking to one another: "the newspapers in the morning, television in the evening and . . . reading at night" (106). Such conversation as they do have is practical: "let's take Jamie for a walk before it rains: peas or carrots; there's a Humphrey Bogart on Channel two" (107). Hearing from Sally about Arnie's work as a research chemist, he asks her if he lives for his work. Sally's incisive answer is, "'You must stop thinking of people as living for something. Most people live because that's the way they find themselves'" (106).

Dawson at this point still sees the secular as an inverted religion, with its own set of first principles and ultimate ends. Yet, as Sally perceptively notes, as lived reality (as opposed to what is preached by idealistic secular philosophers), secular life is more often characterized by routine, boredom, distraction, than by grand visions or goals. Later when the couple visits Dawson and Jenny in London and Arnie speculates about the cost of their expensive house, he gives vent to his cynical views about money:

"A fat chance I'd ever have of making that kind of money."
"Some people do."
"Not at anything honest. It's all either inherited or made in some swindle. It's this sort of thing that's sickened me with England." (165)

Sally and Arnie, solidly middle class—neither the miserably oppressed poor nor the extravagant and decadent rich—represent one kind of secular life in which the most predominant experience is boredom. Although their actions and conversation are not as repellent as those of Jenny and her friends, they engender a sense of emptiness and despondency that is not far from despair.[16]

What is the significance of having Dawson lose his faith at the same place where he chooses to live his re-found faith: a Trappist monastery? Trappists are not only one of the strictest orders in the Church; they are also contemplative. Unlike most religious orders, they undertake no "good works." They do not serve the poor or tend the sick. They run no educational institutions. They do not even give retreats, except insofar as they welcome laypeople to come and spend some time in prayer and meditation at the monastery. Even secular people can admire those religious orders who engage in social service. They can even approve of those who minister to the laity by conducting religious services, administering sacraments, providing religious instruction and preaching— even though these functions do little in the secular view to make a better world. But contemplatives seem to do no good for anyone else, their whole life being devoted to their own search for spiritual peace and union with God. At best, such a life is seen as neutral—not harmful, but not admirable since it contributes nothing to society—and at worst, self-indulgent and perverse.

Thus Read's choice of a Trappist monastery for Dawson's final spiritual home is both a comment on Dawson's own earlier efforts to justify his religious vocation in terms of humanitarian work and the larger tendency of the Church to conflate the two in the years after Vatican II. It suggests that although much about religion is comprehensible to a nonbeliever, even to one who does not see the "cumulation of probabilities"[17] that lead one to take the leap of faith, the essence of that faith is really comprehensible only from the inside. Jenny's response to Winterman's account of Dawson—that he is mad, broken, or sick expresses—the inability of the secular to understand the religious. In an open letter to Dean Inge, an Anglican clergyman hostile to the Catholic Church, Hilaire Belloc used the following analogy:

> You are like one examining the windows of Chartres from within by candlelight, and marvelling how any man can find glory in them; but we have the sun shining through. . . . For what is the Catholic Church? It is that which replies, co-ordinates, establishes. It is that within which is right order; outside the puerilities and the despairs. . . . Within that household the human spirit has root and hearth. Outside it is the night.[18]

In Belloc's analogy the people looking at the stained glass windows at night are those who have never been inside during daylight. Dawson, however, *has* been inside during the day, but once he is in the dark, the windows look just as dark to him as to one who has never experienced their glory from within—perhaps even darker. He admits that the "stained glass windows" of faith can make you feel happier, but considers them "'a childish illusion all the same'" (199). He equates lack of faith with having grown up and dislikes being around Christians, finding "'something soft and unpleasant about them'" (199). The novel dramatizes how easily the memory of the sun streaming through the stained glass windows can be lost and forgotten once one decides to move into secular "darkness."

Read has been accused of being too doctrinaire and didactic and writing thinly disguised theological tracts. Although there is never any doubt about which side Read is on, such a view fails to account for areas in his fiction that are more open and polyphonic, where he clearly resists comfortable, tidy moral judgment. One example is the issue of homosexuality and pederasty in *Monk Dawson*. Obviously, the monks' tendency to be suspicious of any closeness or tender feelings between boys is distorted and neurotic. Similarly, Father Tim's insistence that Dawson should submit to a beating to discipline his body because of his fondness for a younger student seems to be the expression of an impaired and distorted sexuality. Yet on the other hand, the monks' fears are not entirely misplaced. It is clear that Dawson's feeling for the boy did go beyond simple fondness; there was a physical, sexual attraction. Later in the same year, that same young boy, "was abducted and debauched by three sixth-formers from another house" (18). There *was* a real danger. The Church may have used dehumanizing, injurious methods of trying to ward off evil, but the evil was and is real. When a reformed, more humane Church tried to throw off its sexually repressive measures, the evil still remained, as menacing and predatory as ever. The old approach was clearly inadequate, but the new approach is either nonexistent or naive and quixotic. The menace of evil remains.

Monk Dawson, published only five years after the close of the Second Vatican Council, seems amazingly prescient in delineating the shadow side of reform and the dangers for faith once the windows were opened too wide.

NOTES

1. Saint Augustine writes:

And thus it has come to pass, that though there are very many and great nations all over the earth, whose rites and customs, speech, arms, and dress, are distinguished by marked differences, yet there are no more than two kinds of human society, which we may justly call two cities, according to the language of our Scriptures. The one consists of those who wish to live after the flesh, the other of those who wish to live after the spirit. *The City of God*, Book XIV, chapter 1, trans. Marcus Dods, D.D. (New York: Modern Library, 1950), 441.

2. Piers Paul Read, *Monk Dawson* (Philadelphia: Lippincott, 1970), 8–9. Hereafter cited in the text by page number.

3. *As You Like It*, II. i. 17; "The Tables Turned," lines 21–24.

4. The narrative point of view of the novel is a little problematic. Winterman explicitly narrates the first and last chapter and some other ones in which he plays a direct part. Most of the other chapters, however, seem to revert to a straight third person narration and concern events and thoughts of which Winterman could have no knowledge unless Dawson had filled him in on all the most intimate details of his life, which seems highly unlikely.

5. Of course, other factors such as the sexual revolution, fewer Catholic schools, a drastic reduction in the number of religious sisters, brothers, and priests as teachers, and an antireligion bias in both higher education and the media are also important factors in the large scale rejection of Catholicism by young people. To what extent each of these factors is responsible is a problem for sociologists of religion. Nevertheless, it is widely believed that the eviscerated catechesis that followed Vatican II has taken a terrible toll.

6. C. S. Lewis, *The Screwtape Letters* (New York: Macmillan, 1953), 54.

7. Such a sheltered environment might be a tightly knit enclave of people of the same religion, such as were much more common in an earlier age.

8. Rucasants were Catholics who resisted the attempt of Henry VIII to bring the Reformation to England and held fast to their Catholic faith through all the persecutions and penalties imposed on Catholics by Henry and subsequent English monarchs.

9. Although Jenny receives instruction from a priest, in the 1980s the Rite of Christian Initiation for Adults replaced private instruction by a priest. This rite was really a return to the practice of the early Church whereby converts underwent a period of catechetical, liturgical, and spiritual formation within the community. In 2003 an article in *Our Sunday Visitor* listed as concerns about the current RCIA process:

- Seemingly high dropout rates within a few years of RCIA.
- A perceived lack of knowledge about Church teaching, not only among many participants, but often among the Catholics giving instruction.
- An emphasis on the "experience" of community, rather than on the substance of our common Catholic life, which sets participants up for a fall when the program is over. "Why the RCIA Needs Improvement," *Our Sunday Visitor*, 2 March 2003, 2.

10. See the fifth lecture of Freud's *Five Lectures on Psychoanalysis*.

11. In an essay originally published in 1982, Read writes, "It is certainly undeniable that the Church mistrusts the sexual drive in men and women." Acknowledging that erotic liaisons are the staple of the novelist's art, he adds, "It is therefore with some sorrow that I have come to accept that the Church is right and that novelists are wrong." "Upon This Rock," in *Hell and Other Destinations*, 59, 60.

12. Once the new rite for the Mass was translated and approved, it became the norm; but there was a period of transition, which is being described here.

13. Richard John Neuhaus, writing in *First Things* says, "I once asked a bishop who had played a major part in drafting the constitution [*Gaudium et Spes*] whether the document was not marked by a certain naïveté about the modern world. After a moment's thought, he said, Perhaps. He then quickly added, But, if so, it was an evangelical naïveté. Richard John Neuhaus, "The Public Square," *First Things*, Aug./Sept. 2004, 99.

14. Michael Novak puts it this way:

At the very moment during which some of us were urging an "open church" and "opening the windows of the Church to the world," we neglected to notice that the vehicle in which we were riding was just entering a long tunnel filled with noxious fumes. We opened those windows at an inopportune moment. Thus the "popular" culture in which the young find themselves has at its disposal the most powerful instruments ever—television, cinema, rock music, etc.—and is at the same time perhaps the most toxic in history. Michael Novak, "Abandoned in a Toxic Culture," *Crisis*, December 1992, 15–16.

15. Thomas Merton's friend, Edward Rice says that Merton once explained the Mass to his friend Seymour Freedgood as "a kind of ballet, with similar precise, prescribed movements and gestures." Edward Rice, *The Man in the Sycamore Tree: The Good Times and Hard Life of Thomas Merton* (New York: Image Books, 1972), 97.

16. What is seldom depicted in Read's fiction is the fulfilled and happy secularist, who does not lead a decadent life, but one which conforms to traditional standards of decency and integrity. Occasionally, his characters will begin their secular life this way but usually fall into either degeneracy or numbing despair. Secular readers (and even some Christian ones) are apt to find such a portrayal unbalanced and unfair to the potential for good within the natural order.

17. According to Newman scholar, Ian Ker,

It is in fact, Newman argues, the cumulation of probabilities, which cannot be reduced to a syllogism, that leads to certainty in the concrete. Many certitudes depend on informal proofs, whose reasoning is more or less implicit. . . . Such implicit reasoning is too personal for logic. The rays of truth stream through the medium of our moral as well as our intellectual being. Ian Ker, *The Achievement of John Henry Newman* (Notre Dame: Univ. of Notre Dame Press, 1990), 64.

18. Hilaire Belloc, "A Letter to Dean Inge," in *Essays of a Catholic* (New York: Macmillan, 1931), 304–5.

14

✛

The Absurdity of
Being Polish: *Polonaise*

One must have experienced the grim humorlessness of contemporary revolutionary ideologies to appreciate fully the humanizing power of the religious perspective.

—Peter Berger, *A Rumor of Angels*

Suppose that Christendom—the deep unity of Western culture through the years—survives best not when it is trying to respond to the relentless thud with which secular history marches, but when it dances a little.

—Joseph Bottum, "God & Bertie Wooster"

*P*olonaise (1976) is Piers Paul Read's sixth novel. It follows the lives of Stefan and Krystyna Kornowski, the children of a Polish aristocrat, who loses the family fortune, forcing his children into genteel poverty. Since the novel begins in the late 1920s, Stefan and Krystyna live their new lives against the background of the Great Depression, the spread of Communism, the rise of fascism, the Spanish Civil War, and the expansion of the Third Reich. *Polonaise* dramatizes the way in which these violent and catastrophic events militate against religious faith. The brother and sister soon discard the Catholicism in which they were raised and look for new systems of meaning in the competing ideologies of the day. They are attracted to Communism, but eventually become disillusioned with it as well. In the final section of the three part novel, Read leaps ahead to the peaceful 1950s and explores the tenuous situation of moral innocence in the relatively stable world that has emerged from the horrific events of World War II. Throughout the novel the traditional antagonists of faith—basic human concupiscence and undisciplined sexuality—play a large role as well.

We first meet Krystyna and Stefan as sheltered, privileged, and naive adolescents. When Krystyna is twelve, her mother dies of emphysema, in spite of the children's prayers that she be spared. A few years later, their father is on the point of bankruptcy, and Krystyna learns that the family might lose Jezow, their country estate. When the repulsive Mr. Stets, the representative of the bank that holds the mortgage, suggests that there could be "bonds" between the two of them that might make it possible to write off the debt or postpone its repayment, Krystyna impulsively offers to marry him. When Mr. Stets explains that he is already married, Krystyna is naive enough to believe that letting him have sex with her will save the estate. She is wrong, and the family still loses the estate.

This appalling incident is the first of many in which Read depicts a vicious, unbridled lust. Even when the participants are young and attractive, he manages to make the physicality of sexual intercourse repulsive. In the case of Mr. Stets, however, the disgust begins with the description of the man. "His appearance, even on a fine day, was not healthy. He was a man of indeterminate middle age, with a huge belly, a sagging face and grey skin which grew yellowish around the eyes and mouth. He was partly bald and what hair he had was greasy. He was not tall and waddled like a toad."[1] The encounter is described from the point of view of Stefan, who follows Krystyna and Mr. Stets to the summerhouse. From up in a hayloft he hears "a slight whimpering in a higher pitched voice . . . a grunt, then a cry (in a higher pitched voice), then a grunt, then another grunt, a curse, a grunt—all quickly together—and finally a long-drawn-out curse which ended in a sort of sigh" (22). He then hears Mr. Stets berating Krystyna. "'Why aren't you a woman? I'm not a hammer and chisel, am I? No, I'm a man, that's all. Not a *battering ram*'" (23). When Stefan gets the nerve to look down, he sees "a moving grey shape which he suddenly recognize[s] as a white pair of buttocks belonging to Mr. Stets who, dressed only in a shirt, was looking for his trousers" (23). This fragmented description of disembodied voices and isolated body parts is a strong image of the kind of uncontrolled sexuality that is such a disruptive and destructive force in the novel.

Stefan is obsessed with sex. "Hormones flowed in his blood to his brain, infecting it with their narrow obsession. He could not stop thinking about women" (37). Although preoccupation with sex is not unusual in adolescent boys, Stefan's frustrated desires manifest themselves in bizarre fantasies and fragments of fiction—the inauguration of his vocation as a writer. In his first written fantasy, a student has sex with an old family servant. The sexual encounter is crudely described: "He plunges—he reaches under her skirts, and shoves his hands deep into the mass of wool, flesh and bulbous veins. . . . He removes one hand, inserts another, rummages around to find an orifice. Hooks it with a finger and leads the old peasant to his room. She lies on his bed. He covers her face with her skirts. The stink" (38). This fragment is soon followed by another, in which the characters are a voluptuous princess and her jester. Although the tone is decorous, the brashness of the princess, who commands him to give her his "cock," is startling (39). These two idiosyncrasies of Stefan's youthful sexuality—his propensity for fantasies marked by violence, and revulsion at disgusting sights and smells associated with the flesh—continue to be a central part of his writing and fantasies, as well as of his actual sexual life. For Stefan, the boundary between fantasy and reality becomes blurred and stays blurred for the rest of his life.

It is significant that when Stefan is first attracted to Rachel, the woman he eventually marries, he is drawn to her not as a whole person, but as individual body parts. "The colour of the skin was light brown: the wisps of hair were black, and the lobe of her right ear was pink" (76). Even as Rachel's attraction to him becomes evident and she invites a sexual relationship, Stefan's attitude is conflicted between desire and dread. In fact, the day before he first goes to her house, he writes his fantasy of what their rendezvous will be like. It starts with an erotic embrace but ends with his biting her Achilles tendon and her sobbing and running to her room. In fact, when the meeting actually does occur, they end up becoming lovers. Although Stefan does not bite her Achilles tendon, his first sexual experience is disappointing. "With disbelief he felt her hands on his buttons, then on his flesh; then he resigned himself to the necessary experience, as if he was at the dentist, and after some twisting, puffing and the final, unmistakable ejaculation, he realized with inexpressible disappointment that the whole thing had happened as it should have done—that he and Rachel were lovers" (108).

In addition to its association with violence and the disgust he often feels at the sight and smell of the flesh, Stefan's sexuality is marked by another odd quality—detachment. Even at the beginning of his love affair with Rachel, he is as much observer as actor. "He watched himself copulate with equal horror and fascination. Years of sexual speculation had estranged his mind from his genitals. He observed his own sensations with the same detachment as he watched her body quiver, her mouth loll open, her eyes grow glazed" (117). Apparently immune to passion himself, he enjoys arousing it in another, but not out of a desire to give pleasure, but from a desire to humiliate. "She was driven into ecstasy while he never lost control. He then was a man (consciousness) and she a beast (instinct). She was totally humiliated and Stefan, as a result, was triumphant" (117).

Stefan is a voyeur—not only with regard to other people's sexuality— but with regard to his own. In fact, Stefan's unbridled intellectual curiosity destroys his capacity to experience true sexual pleasure, intimacy, or joy. In his notebook he writes, "My passion is curiosity, but unlike all other passions it can have no moment of rapture. The saint, the sensualist or the huntsman—they all have their moment of total concentration—the orgasm of the kill: but for me the moment never comes. It is destroyed by the thought: 'Is this oblivion?'" (208).

Stefan's sexuality is characterized by detachment, disgust, violence, and a desire to hurt. The more tender, affectionate acts of eros become displaced, even on his honeymoon, by delight in power. "He took less pleasure in the ever-present and compliant body of his young wife than in shouting a command and having breakfast brought to his bedside by a polite young maid in a starched apron" (123–24).

After his marriage, Stefan's sexuality continues to be strongly intertwined with his fantasy life and expressed in bizarre and violent ways. Through his writing, Stefan comes to the attention of the Princess Czarniecka, who invites him to elegant parties and offers him the use of a room in the palace as his private writing studio. One day the Princess's fifteen-year-old daughter Tilly comes to his studio and questions him about his writing, about the possibility of a war, and about how she is practicing keeping her finger in a flame so as not to be afraid of pain. Soon she asks him to teach her about pleasure, specifically "*Les plaisirs d'amour*" (204). Stefan is happy to oblige, and leads her through holding hands, kissing, stroking, and using his toe to give her a little orgasm. The final lesson is to be full-fledged intercourse. His plans for this event, however, go beyond the simple seduction of a gullible adolescent. Having achieved renown as an avant-garde writer, he has been invited to be an honorary guest on the maiden voyage of a new steamship, the *Jagiello*. His plan is to have Tilly meet him in the hotel where he will be staying the night before he leaves on the voyage. There he plans—not only to have sex with her—but to kill her!

Stefan's linking of sex and violence has become increasingly evident in his writing, both in his published works and his private fragments. In his notebook he had writtten that for him ecstasy is being able "to provide immortality by fusing perfect pleasure (orgasm) with perfect pain (death)" (208). At one point he had written a sketch about two children, brother and sister, whom he was tutoring. He was curious about them and wished—not to do things to them—but to see things done to them. In his sketch, he directs them first to undress and then to do sexual acts; finally, he has the boy stab his sister and jump out the window. In one sense Stefan's fixation on sex makes him a recognizable twentieth-century man.[2] Yet his failure to integrate his sexuality with any kind of tenderness or affection, his proclivity to see human beings, especially potential sexual partners, as fragmented body parts, his frequent sense of disgust and revulsion, and repeated instances of violence—at least in his fantasies—are strong indications of a pathological dimension in his personality.

Krystyna and Rachel also discard traditional sexual mores, although neither of them has her sexual desires and fantasies laid open in such detail as is the case with Stefan. When Rachel takes up with Stefan, she has already had at least one other sexual liaison with another member of their Communist cell. Having lost her virginity at an early age with the repulsive Mr. Stets, Krystyna does not hesitate to become sexually involved with Bruno, a fellow student and friend of Stefan. Their sexual appetites, once roused, are not easily suppressed. After Rachel marries Stefan and becomes pregnant, she admits to Krystyna that she is glad she is pregnant while her husband has gone off with Bruno to volunteer in the Spanish Civil War because it has diminished her libido. She admits to Krystyna, "'I mean before I did it I never thought about it—at least not much—but once you get used to it, you really need it, don't you?'" (154).

Krystyna obviously agrees, for with Bruno, now her husband, also gone to fight in the Spanish Civil War, she begins an affair with Michael, the leader of their Communist cell. He is not at all physically attractive. In fact, he is in some ways reminiscent of the repulsive Mr. Stets. But there is a strong, unmistakable sexual aura about him:

> He was an ordinary man in appearance—small, plump and balding, with smooth skin on his cheeks and an aroma of pomade: but he had, all the same, some sort of physical presence. His suit was a little tight and he seemed in the fading light to bulge in many different places; and from these bulges there seemed to come some strange, hypnotic energy which Krystyna had never felt when she had studied him in the cell. He did nothing . . . yet he gave a signal of some sort which was both invisible and obscene. (155)

The language here has a strong association with animal sexuality—a mating instinct communicated by smell or some other emanation. No human language or specifically human characteristic is involved. Krystyna begins fantasizing about Michael, and those fantasies soon become real. So dependent does she become on satisfying her sexual needs with him that when Bruno returns from Spain unexpectedly, rather than being overjoyed at his return, she sees him as an inconvenient interruption of her affair with Michael. Perhaps if Bruno had returned with a hearty and zestful lust, she might have easily shed her craving for Michael; but in fact, Bruno has been traumatized by his experience in Spain and seems interested only in his baby son, Teofil. Krystyna manages to carry on her affair clandestinely. The horrifying culmination of Krystyna's conflicted feelings is that she and Michael agree that he will use his influence to have Bruno arrested so that she and Michael will have their freedom to carry on their affair as before.

As for Rachel, after her twins are born, she slides into a kind of contented domesticity, in which her sexual desires are dormant. Not only does she no longer desire sexual satisfaction for herself, she tells Krystyna that she wouldn't mind if Stefan had an affair. Since there is no longer any "sexual current at all" (190), between them, and he really is not a provider (her wealthy father basically supports them), she realizes that Stefan was not a good choice as a husband. She is not much upset by her realization, however, for she is now focused entirely on her children.

Of all of them, Bruno seems to be the least concerned with sex. Although he had been passionately attracted to Krystyna, after they marry, his concerns about social injustice, his devotion to the party, and most of all, his love for his baby son displace sexual passion. Krystyna suspects infidelity when he returns from one of his trips on Party business and she finds a bottle of French scent in his bag. His explanation, however, that it was meant to be a surprise for her seems sincere and convincing. Bruno's demeanor is simply not that of an adulterer.

Besides their disordered sex lives, another defining characteristic of these four young people is their atheism. Stefan, Krystyna, Bruno, and Rachel have all discarded the trappings of religious faith. Stefan boldly tells Krystyna in the second chapter that God does not exist. Krystyna, who is seventeen at the time, insists that she will pray that they don't lose their estate; but Stefan's sarcastic rejoinder is "'Pray, then. . . . Just as you prayed for Mama.'" (9). Similarly, Krystyna prays that Mr. Stets will not come to foreclose on the estate. Yet Mr. Stets does come, and Krystyna loses—not only her home—but her virginity. Failure to have prayers answered precipitates the loss of faith for both brother and sister. Whereas Krystyna never seems to give God another thought once she is initiated into the ways of the world, Stefan's atheism is much more ongoing and deliberate conscious choice, and it gives purpose to his existence. He writes in his notebook, "Since there is no God and no after-life, no good, no evil, no Heaven, no Hell—then ecstasy is everything. It is what we should purse—ecstasy prolonged—indefinite ecstasy" (208).

Stefan's early dismissal of a God who will not answer prayers to preserve the life of a dying mother leads him into an intellectual conundrum as he finds that the values he adopts lack a firm ontological grounding. He sometimes has conversations with himself (or, more precisely, with his imaginary *alter ego*, Raymond de Tarterre) about this problem, and the word that surfaces most often is *absurd*.

"But perhaps, *mon cher Stefan*, you are not a Marxist at all, but have merely persuaded yourself that you are."
"Why should I do that?"
"Fear of the void."

"Nonsense. I accept absolutely that my purpose and fulfilment lie with history, with socialism, with revolution."

"But that, my dear fellow, is the *absurdity* [emphasis added]. For you know as well as I do that without God, there is no obligation. Each man is sovereign. Even if he sees a pattern in history, why should he follow it?" (128)

Stefan goes on to argue with Raymond that some values are compelling because there must be a bond between humans, only to be told that it might be to one's advantage to bond with others, but that is all it is: enlightened self-interest. Any rationale devised to support that bond is nothing more than a human invention. Ideologies should never be taken seriously, for they are simply matters of taste. "'What you must not do,'" says Raymond, "'is confuse your aesthetic preference for an ethical value: or talk in terms of right and wrong'" (129).

Even as an adolescent, Stefan had spent much time in "Cartesian speculation" (9). Like Descartes, who doubted everything but his own consciousness, Stefan lives in an entirely self-referential world. This aspect of Stefan's atheism is accentuated when he decides to distill the essence of his thought, and begins with Descartes's famous maxim, "I think therefore I am," adding, "my thought is my being" (228). He makes a list of his major principles. The first is that there is no God since there is neither sensory nor rational evidence of His existence. The second is that the only reality that is real to him is what is inside his head. The third is that the only purpose of power and freedom is to achieve pleasure and happiness. The fourth acknowledges that his pleasure might entail the suffering of others. Similarly—point five—his happiness might consist in being protected from another. In both instances, however, the ultimate purpose is the pursuit of one's own pleasure, contentment, and self-interest. No other considerations are relevant. A morality may be invented to justify one's course of action, employing lofty intellectual constructs, such as human dignity, personal responsibility, and so forth. One may even sincerely believe that these principles are grounded in some kind of reality. Yet according to Stefan, they are nothing more than inventions, as much figments of the imagination as the stories and fantasies he concocts. His sixth point is that it is possible to hate what is usually regarded as health, nature, and wholesomeness, and perversely take pleasure only in pain and degradation, usually inflicting it on others, but in some cases, even enjoying one's own pain. This convoluted linking of pleasure and pain Stefan readily acknowledges is his own. His final point is that his "pleasure" requires a foolish, gullible victim, like the young Tilly; and that is her misfortune. He forcefully resists any feelings of responsibility or sympathy for her. All of these points flow from Stefan's initial foundational principle, "There is no God" (228).

As Stefan plots his seduction and murder of Tilly, his infatuation with his power takes the form of self-divinization. "'When I come back I shall be a God. I shall have eaten of the Fruit of the Tree of Knowledge. Good and Evil will have been made subject to my will" (239). Stefan's framing of his reverie in terms of the Fall evokes the understanding of Original Sin as—not a decisive historical act that explains human depravity—but as a mythic account of the moral drama that is replayed in every human life. In his version, however, Satan is not a liar. Eating the forbidden fruit really *will* make Stefan a god.

Unlike Stefan's self-conscious atheism, Krystyna's rejection of God is simply a given. She does not ponder its philosophical implications or its ramifications for morality. She is too busy seeing to practical matters after the loss of the family fortune: getting the family moved into a flat in Warsaw, getting a job, buying and cooking food, and taking care of her child. Her love affair with Bruno, though genuine and tender, is a short interval that briefly illuminates her grim round of work and responsibility. When she reappears as a middle-aged matron in the last part of the book, she is in more comfortable circumstances, but her personality and approach to life are basically unaltered: she is realistic, practical, and tough. Krystyna's no-nonsense approach to life can easily be explained by the traumatic events of her life, yet her admirable ability to cope and survive has a kind of barrenness that speaks of the loss of something that might have provided a more stable framework of meaning and a source of hope.

There is no comparable sense with Rachel. Her atheism seems the easiest of all. She is the privileged child of well-to-do Jewish parents who have a sentimental attachment to their cultural heritage but do not seem to be religious. Rachel's only real religion is Communism, but once her twin children are born, she settles easily into comfortable domesticity, and all concern with social justice or workers' rights evaporates. "There was now no trace of the racy, radical independence. Conservative instincts and values had risen in her mind as surely as the milk in her bosom" (189). Her opinions are "expressed in her own voice but with meaning and intonation indistinguishable from her mother's" (189–90). Rachel's contentment makes her almost as solipsistic as Stefan. "Like a cow sensing a storm, she had settled down on her dry patch of grass and chewed cud with her calves. She was protected from anxiety by the kind of complacency which maternity engenders: nothing outside her family circle could threaten her because nothing outside her family circle was real" (226–27).

Stefan, Krystyna, and Rachel exemplify different ways of being an atheist. Stefan's disbelief is a Sartrean existentialist choice forced upon him by the absurdity of life. It is for him the defining principle of his identity. Krystyna's is also a deliberate choice, resulting from the inadequacy of her childhood belief in a father-God who would answer all her prayers.

Such a faith sufficed in her sheltered and privileged childhood, but disintegrated when faced with the harsh realities of life. Unlike Stefan, however, once she discards belief in God, she never gives it a second thought, but is completely absorbed with practical details of living. Rachel seems to have always lived blissfully without God. Her youthful attraction to Communism is not so much a substitute religion as a way of asserting her independence from her parents and enjoying the company of bright and stimulating young people. Her dedication to socialist principles dissolves into contented domesticity once her children are born, and her worldview then extends no further than the walls of her own home. Rachel is an example of the happy secular humanist, who finds joy and meaning in family and simple domestic joys and is simply uninterested in a transcendental dimension. She is the type of atheist that frustrates evangelizing Christians who are convinced that all atheists must be desperately searching for some transcendent meaning and living unhappy, unfulfilled lives. In fact, some of them are quite happy, as Rachel would have been had Hitler not come along.

Like the other young people, Bruno does not believe in God; but it does not seem to be such a conscious decision to discard religion, as with Stefan, and to a lesser extent, with Krystyna. He does, however, have purer ideals than the others. Stefan, however, is not content to let Bruno rest comfortably in his idealism. In discussions with him, Stefan argues that Communism is really living on Christian capital.[3] He pursues this line of argument, asserting that Bruno's idealism has really nothing to do with justice or morality. He admits that socialism may be the wave of the future, but asks him "what moral imperative obliges [him] to swim with the tide rather than swim against it" (135). Bruno thinks the answer should be self evident, that once you have seen the misery of others, it is clear you must work to improve their lives. For Stefan, however, this conclusion is not axiomatic as it is for Bruno.

> "Why? Why must I? What does their condition matter to me?"
> "But men are brothers. . . ."
> "They are not. And even if they are, am I my brother's keeper? Only Christ says that I should be; only He insists that men must love one another; and if Christ was God, then I might pay some heed to what He said—if only to protect my own interests in the next world. But there is no next world; Christ was not God; there is no God. And because there is no God, there is no obligation. There is only force, and a calculation of interest. . . ." (135–36)

Stefan is convinced that all so-called moral choices are really nothing more than a matter of taste and an attempt to veil the frightening void. He continues to press the notion that moral positions are really nothing more than preferences, more akin to aesthetic taste than to principled decisions.

"'I am not convinced that your distaste for suffering is any different from mine for Stravinsky'" (136). He contends that it is foolish for any form of idealism to claim to know what will benefit humanity, for the whole notion of human happiness is "'elusive and paradoxical. Men strive for security, yet danger exhilarates them. They have soldiers and police to protect them, then climb mountains, or travel to the North Pole to escape from their suffocating safety.'" He subjects Bruno's belief that men are brothers to a grueling scrutiny, pointing out that "'whenever they can they compete, just as animals compete, in games and races and tests of endurance and skill'." (136)

Stefan's argument is provocative because, although ostensibly addressed to an idealistic 1930s communist, a breed that has almost vanished from the face of the earth, it is equally applicable to a type of contemporary ecumenical pluralism that sees all religions as equally valid and valuable precisely because of certain broad humanistic values, such as the golden rule, which they hold in common. The very fact that the injunction to do good to others is found in all major religions seems to provide its authoritative basis. Yet, as Stefan perceptively points out, these comforting, ennobling sentiments are not the whole truth about humanity. Along with the desire to bind ourselves to others is the desire to separate ourselves from others, to compete, struggle, and prevail. If ubiquity determines what is valid in religion, why do we see the humanistic values as true and good and the competitive and aggressive ones as perverted and evil? Is it, as Stefan suggests, merely a matter of taste?

In fact, as G. K. Chesterton pointed out a century ago, it is simply untrue that the religions of the world differ only in their rites and forms and not in what they teach. "It is false; it is the opposite of the fact. The religions of the earth do *not* greatly differ in rites and forms; they do greatly differ in what they teach."[4] Chesterton discounts the common humanistic values found in all religions because he thinks they are grounded in nature, not in a divinely revealed religion.

> That Buddhism approved of mercy or of self-restraint is not to say that it is specially like Christianity; it is only to say that it is not utterly unlike all human existence. Buddhists disapprove in theory of cruelty or excess because all sane human beings disapprove in theory of cruelty or excess. But to say that Buddhism and Christianity give the same philosophy of these things is simply false.[5]

Chesterton would agree with Stefan that looking to nature or universal human experience alone as a grounding for one's morality is inadequate.

As Stefan continues to dissect Bruno's idealism, he attacks the only apparent source of their validity, their apparent universality, by pointing out the prevalence of opposing tendencies. When Bruno insists on the genuineness and purity of his desire to improve the lives of others and thus elevate human nature, Stefan counters with the charge that Bruno fails to recognize the roots of his own idealism. "'Do you know why you and all other Communists want to civilize man, and change nature? Because you still believe in God, in original sin, and in the perfectibility of the soul. Your mind is moulded by twenty centuries of Christian belief, and though you say you are atheists, your whole philosophy is shaped by Christian beliefs and has no justification without them (137).'" Stefan's argument suggests that atheists may fail to think through their atheism to its logical conclusion. They like being idealistic and enjoy the self-satisfaction of being righteous without God, yet they might be severely discomfited by confronting the philosophical underpinnings of their value system.

The reader is told that this argument goes on for hours, but there is no indication of what else is said. Although the two shake hands and part as friends, "nothing had been resolved" (137). Shortly afterward, Bruno goes to Spain to fight for the Republicans in the Civil War, where his idealism is severely tested. Stefan hears rumors of torture and assassination in Barcelona, where Bruno is working for the Party. When Bruno comes home, his appearance bespeaks the trauma he has suffered. "His cheekbones protruded so that his eyes seemed sunken in their sockets, and their expression was unlike any she had seen before—a mixture of callousness, despair and exhaustion" (191). Bruno refuses to talk to Krystyna about his experience in Spain, but his behavior—waking at night with a cry and clinging to her like a frightened child—attests to his inner torment. Krystyna learns from her lover and fellow party member that in Barcelona Bruno had been involved in "'the unpleasant but necessary Party work'" of liquidating Anarchists and Trotskyists, had lost his nerve, and deserted (196). If Bruno's ideals have not been destroyed, the apparatus he had adopted for fulfilling them has been. On Christmas Eve, Bruno astonishes everyone by going to Midnight Mass with Aunt Cecylia and the family servant. From this point on, Bruno plays little part in the story. He is sent away to prison, and not long after he is released, he leaves to fight against Hitler. At the time it is not clear whether Bruno's Christmas Midnight Mass signals a genuine turning to God or is simply an impulsive gesture, expressing his frustration and disappointment at discovering the dark underside of his ideal. Late in the novel, however, Teofil sees a letter to Krystyna from a soldier who served with Bruno, informing her of Bruno's death at the hand of the Nazi's while trying to help Rachel and her family escape. The letter mentions that Bruno prayed every night that God would keep Krystyna and Teofil safe (288).

Parts One and Two of the book are set against the horrific cataclysms of
the rise of fascism, the Spanish Civil war and the looming shadow of the
Third Reich. Part Three, however, takes place during the peaceful 1950s.
Here the villains are not Stalin, Franco, Hitler, or the Communists party
bosses, but the arrogance, venality, and depravity of the British upper
class. Far from trivializing the evil that is desired and pursued in decorous
drawing rooms in comparison with that precipitated by societal upheavals of war and dictatorship, Read discloses the kinship between them.

In Part Three, Bruno and Rachel have both perished in World War II,
but Krystyna (now married to a Frenchman) and Stefan have survived by
getting out of Poland in time and are living in Paris. As if to replace Bruno
and Rachel, another young couple fills out the quartet. They are
Krystyna's grown son, Teofil, and Annabel Colte, a young Englishwoman,
who is studying at the Sorbonne and boarding with Krystyna and her
husband. Teofil and Annabel are strong contrasts to Krystyna, Stefan,
Bruno, and Rachel, for they have come of age in a relatively peaceful
world and enjoyed a stable environment that has protected their innocence. Annabel has been brought up in an aristocratic family, and Teofil
has been educated at Downside, an English Catholic boys' boarding
school, and at Oxford.[6] Their innocence with regard to sex is conveyed,
not by any explicit account of their lack of experience, but by the way they
discover and express their growing love for each other. When Sarah, another English girl boarding with Krystyna, questions her about their relationship with Teofil, Annabel says, "I don't think of him in *that* way. It's
funny, isn't it? Because he's awfully handsome and attractive. But I can't
imagine ever . . . touching him" (292). Sarah had previously told Annabel
that her boyfriend was asking for more than a kiss and asked what she
would do in such a situation. "'I wouldn't let him,' said Annabel severely" (278). Annabel's sexual restraint is not based on religious scruples,
for she does not believe in God. It is when Annabel goes home to England
for Easter that she and Teofil realize how much they care for each other,
yet their first meeting after her return is hardly marked by an abandonment to passion.

> Teofil had kissed girls before and had not taken much pleasure in it, which
> was why he had never gone further. For the same reason he dreaded the mo-
> ment when he would have to kiss Annabel but knew that it had to be done;
> and rather than have it hanging over him, he decided to get it over with. . . .
>   It was a definite kiss but quite unpractised. Both pairs of lips barely
> opened, but were pressed together in imitation of the older kind of film; but
> Teofil's arms went around her shoulders and Annabel's came up to clutch the
> coat on his back with the clenched grip of a baby.
>   "I love you," he said awkwardly, like a boy playing a part he had not
> rehearsed.

"So do I," she said. "I love you." And she spoke with just as little conviction; but they were both so delighted to have got it over and done with that
for the rest of the evening they hardly let go of one another's hand or looked
anywhere but into each other's eyes. (303–4)

The tone of this passage seems to mock the two young lovers as naive,
awkward, and silly. Their innocence is hardly portrayed as wholesome.
The fact that Teofil had never enjoyed kissing a girl is troubling, and this
lack of pleasure has probably kept him sexually pure as much as his
moral principles. Similarly, Annabel's awkwardness is due to her overprotective upbringing and domineering mother more than to principled
virginity. Furthermore, it is later revealed that her father had tried to
sexually molest her.

These disturbing facts suggest that Read is not drawing up some simplistic dichotomy between the sexual promiscuity of the secular radicals in
the Poland of the 1930s and wholesome sexual innocence in the England
and France of the 1950s. Nevertheless, the fact that Teofil's and Annabel's
innocence has been preserved—even if not for the best of reasons—is an
important difference. Even after they become engaged, Stefan is puzzled
by "the persistent absence of any sign of lust in either of the two young
lovers" (310). As clumsy as their initiation into sexual love is, there is a
sense that it is opening out into something larger, stronger, and filled with
more possibilities than that of the older couples. Once Teofil and Annabel
know that they love each other, they plan to marry as soon as possible. Although Annabel, an only child, is the sole heir to her parents' fortune, they
decide that they will give away most of her money. Teofil also decides that
he will not continue in banking but will become a lawyer and defend poor
people. "'After all, if God has given one an intellect, one shouldn't use it
just to get rich. . . . I'd much rather live modestly off what I earn, doing
what I think right, than be enslaved by someone else's money'" (331–32).
They also plan to have lots of children. These decisions are based partly on
self-interest: "'I'm all for a big family,' said Teofil. 'We were both only children, you see, and not particularly happy'" (332). Yet Teofil and Annabel's
choices are not the result of self-interest alone, but of generosity, honesty,
and care for others. Virtue may be more important than passion in their
keeping love alive.

Teofil and Annabel's love may be innocent and virtuous, but it is also
clearly vulnerable. When Teofil and his family come for a visit to
Annabel's home, Mulford Park, her parents, who have only pretended to
overcome their objections to the marriage, devise a diabolical plan to have
a friend, a notorious philanderer, seduce Annabel before the marriage can
take place. This "friend," one of the other house guests, is a charming
older man named Jack Marryat, who ingratiates himself with the other

men when the ladies withdraw after dinner. Even Stefan is captivated by the "perfect manners and flawless charm" of Jack Marryat (326). Marryat has "an extraordinary effect on everyone in the house." Although he is not "obviously handsome, witty or charming," he exerts a power over people because of "his most engaging quality," his modesty. (327)

Only the crafty, dissolute Stefan is perceptive enough to realize that Marryat is deliberately rousing Annabel's latent passions. Noticing that Marryat is always with her, Stefan becomes convinced that "Marryat needs only time. Nothing can be done against him" (329). When he sees Annabel playing tennis with Marryat, he is struck by the excitement he sees in her eyes:

> There was more, much more, than a game of tennis in her eyes. They were wild and excited. She was hypnotized by Marryat as he hurled himself against the ball. She met each volley with her whole body: each stroke was a response to each stroke of his. Her breasts were abandoned to her movement; her buttocks jumped and twisted; her arms stretched; her legs were open and alert and on her face was a smile—a smile of unmistakable complicity which seemed to confess that the game was not a game but a deadly game of courtship. (335–36)

This extraordinary passage could almost have been written from a classic Freudian perspective that sees every aspect of life, including the most off-hand remark or slip of the tongue, as either an expression or repression of sexual desire. Such a starkly simplistic account, however, would be reductionistic. Read's language here reflects an awareness of the way that sexual energy is intertwined with other kinds of energy, that the buoyant excitement and stimulation of vigorous exercise, especially when shared with a partner of the opposite sex, can easily become a precursor of erotic desire. Stefan's intuition here may be nothing more than an impulsive guess, born of his own twisted lascivious fantasies, yet subsequent events validate his conjecture. The precariousness of such an attraction, once removed from a supportive and protective community, is underscored.

Teofil and Annabel—young, naive, weak, and inexperienced—seem doomed in the face of the powers arrayed against them—older, cynical, powerful, rich, and shrewd. It is only through the intervention of Stefan— a person as deeply steeped in evil as they, but one who for some reason has now rejected his lifelong impulse to destroy innocence and is determined to preserve it instead—that their love is able to come to fruition. Stefan has resisted his own desire to seduce Annabel, telling himself that Teofil and Annabel belong together. His alter-ego Raymond de Tarterre, however, finds this idea laughable. "'On the contrary, they belong apart. They are both empty and immature—two timid hermaphrodites waiting and longing to be depraved'" (296). He says that Teofil is a dandy who "'shrinks from women and the mushy bog of their sex and affection'" (296). Raymond's censure typifies the kind of criticism that the sexually experienced make of the chaste, yet it has a grain of truth in it. Clearly, both Teofil and Annabel have each been scarred by their childhoods and feel a bit stiff and awkward about entering the world of sexuality. Their naive and anemic sexuality, which puzzles Stefan because of its apparent lack of lust, has a certain sweetness about it; but it is clearly shown to be inadequate—not only in its failure to be a well-developed, robust, adult sexual appetite—but also in its vulnerability to the raw, predatory power of the depraved amorality that surrounds them.

The strongest link between the two sections of the book and the key to the whole novel is Stefan. He is the only character that plays a substantial role in both parts. Also, he is the most peculiar character, the one to whom ordinary readers would find it most difficult to relate. Krystyna is the practical businesswoman and harried wife and mother, Rachel the well-meaning but pampered only child of indulgent parents, Bruno the starry-eyed idealist. Despite their affiliations with political radicalism, they are all firmly enmeshed in the familiar bourgeois everyday world of ordinary and prosaic details. Their thought patterns are recognizably familiar.

Stefan, however, is strange and exotic—an artist—more specifically, an artist solidly and thoroughly in the grasp of the ironic temper. To understand how not only Stefan's art, but also his temperament and his whole approach to life are shaped by irony, it is useful to consider the ideas of literary critic Northrop Frye. In his *Anatomy of Criticism*, in which he associates literary modes with the seasons of the year, Frye links irony with winter.[7] Frye sees the literary modes determined primarily by the situation of the hero. "If inferior in power or intelligence to ourselves, so that we have the sense of looking down on a scene of bondage, frustration, or absurdity, the hero belongs to the *ironic* mode."[8] Stefan "reads" human life in this way. Stefan is like the ironic fiction writer, who, according to Frye, "like Socrates, pretends to know nothing, even that he is ironic. Complete objectivity and suppression of all explicit moral judgements are essential to his method."[9]

Also, according to Frye, irony "begins in realism and dispassionate observation. But as it does so, it moves steadily towards myth, and dim outlines of sacrificial rituals and dying gods begin to reappear in it."[10] Stefan's stories usually begin with a very realistic, recognizable setting and situation but descend into violence, mayhem, and bloodshed. Furthermore, not only Stefan's characters, but Stefan himself conforms to Frye's description of a tragic hero who is isolated and alienated without being noble or tragic.[11]

Stefan's penchant for using the word *absurd*, especially in his dialogues with his alter-ego, Raymond de Tarterre, inevitably suggests literature of the absurd, of which Stefan seems to be a forerunner. This literature, which came into vogue after World War II, is based on the idea that the human condition is essentially absurd, that we live in an alien and unintelligible universe, and there is no metaphysical foundation for our values. Literature of the absurd is characterized by illogic, inconsistency, and bizarre fantasy. Besides the word *absurd*, two other things associated with Stefan serve as a kind of emblem for him: his Polishness and his grimace. His Polishness is often equated with the absurdity of his life and is expressed by his grimace.

Stefan has this to say about the Polish people: "'We seem so foolish, so hopeless, so superstitious, that somehow we don't deserve to be a nation. When a German or a Frenchman looks at me with contempt, I feel contemptible. The Russians despise us—even the Bolsheviks—because we are despicable. We aren't strong or brave. We're poseurs, voyeurs, the lackeys of the French'" (110). To Bruno's rejoinder that he must love his country as one keeps a wife or a new pair of shoes, even if at first they hurt, and wear them until they fit, Stefan replies, "'That's why I shall always be unfaithful, and always unfulfilled'" (111). As he makes this remark, Stefan's face is "twisted into the Kornowski grimace" (111). Polishness, absurdity, and the Kornowski grimace: this triad forms a kind of leit-motif that follows Stefan through the novel.

The fact that his grimace is often identified as the Kornowski grimace suggests that it is a genetic inheritance from his father, a transmitted physical feature no more significant than hair color. Yet the fact that his father was an extravagant profligate, a cruel and unfaithful husband, a neglectful father, and at the end of his life insane suggests that the "Kornowski grimace" is more than a physical characteristic and that—whether it was learned behavior or genetic predisposition—Stefan bears the burden of his forebears' disordered lives.

What is one to make of Stefan's fetish about Polishness, his contempt for his own nationality? Leaving aside the fact that it must be offensive to patriotic Poles, is it not another example of the kind of crass ethnic bigotry that has led to so much suffering, particularly in the twentieth century? Even if slightly less abhorrent because directed at one's *own* nationality, it still is tendentious and disturbing. On the other hand, it could be symbolic of the kind of human nature that Stefan knows best because he lives inside of it. Furthermore, because he is extraordinarily intelligent, reflective, and insightful, he sees it more thoroughly and honestly than most people do. Stefan's concept of Polishness as "the trait in the national character which lives in fantasy and never follows anything through" could be referring to something inherent in the human condition (233). Without discounting significant differences among nationalities, people around the world can recognize their national character in Stefan's description. The Kornowski grimace is like the mark of Cain, the emblem of the sinful, fallen human race.

Stefan's reaction to his "Polishness" is sinister amusement and bitter disgust. G. K. Chesterton's chapter "The Flag of the World" in *Orthodoxy* provides an instructive contrast to Stefan's attitude. Chesterton argues, "Our attitude towards life can be better expressed in terms of a kind of military loyalty than in terms of criticism and approval."[12] He insists that his loyalty is not due to a kind of naive optimism. On the contrary, he sees the world's faults, but he loves it without a reason. He loves it because it is his country. Does this sound suspiciously like the kind of unthinking "Polishness" that Stefan excoriates? It really is not because Chesterton is not recommending a kind of patriotism that is blind to its country's faults and failings. On the contrary, the loyal patriot *must* criticize when he sees danger or fault. "A man who says that no patriot should attack the Boer War until it is over is not worth answering intelligently; he is saying that no good son should warn his mother off a cliff until she has fallen over it."[13] What Chesterton eschews is not a critical spirit, but criticism that does not emanate from love, arguing that the "evil of the pessimist is, then, not that he chastises gods and men, but that he does not love what he chastises—he has not this primary and supernatural loyalty to things."[14]

But how can one develop this loyalty? How can Stefan love Poland? Chesterton offers an intriguing hypothesis about the source of such a loyalty. He denies a common idea about the foundation of the social order:

> But [social theorists] really were wrong in so far as they suggested that men had ever aimed at order or ethics directly by a conscious exchange of interests. . . . They gained their morality by guarding their religion. They did not cultivate courage. They fought for the shrine, and found they had become courageous. They did not cultivate cleanliness. They purified themselves for the altar, and found that they were clean. . . . Anarchy was evil because it endangered the sanctity.[15]

Chesterton further argues that only the person, who has this kind of loyalty, will really help to improve his country. "The more transcendental is your patriotism, the more practical are your politics."[16]

If the "Polishness" that Stefan derides is really the human frailty that he sees up close, Stefan's flaw is his inability to accept his own humanity and that of those around him. His penetrating intelligence and keen sense of irony lead him to see it in terms of ridiculousness and absurdity rather than evil and moral weakness. Because Stefan's critical spirit is not infused with love, it settles into a grim, sullen gloom. Chesterton clarifies that the healthy patriotism he advocates is not one in which love and criticism blend together and neutralize each other. "We do not want joy and anger to neutralize each other and produce a surly contentment; we want a fiercer delight and a fiercer discontent."[17]

Furthermore, seeing the world as part of a story—even a story with tragic elements—can produce, not just stoic endurance, but joy. Chesterton relates his surprise at discovering that when he came to believe that the world was really fallen, he actually felt better about the world and his place in it. "The Christian optimism is based on the fact that we do *not* fit into the world."

> The optimist's pleasure was prosaic, for it dwelt on the naturalness of everything; the Christian pleasure was poetic, for it dwelt on the unnaturalness of everything in the light of the supernatural. The modern philosopher had told me again and again that I was in the right place, and I had still felt depressed even in acquiescence. But I had heard that I was in the *wrong* place, and my soul sang for joy, like a bird in spring.[18]

Chesterton's discovery that acknowledgement of humanity's fallen state can actually bring joy may not seem logical, but for some people, it hits home with a frisson of recognition. It is somewhat akin to the relief that a sick person feels when his disease is finally diagnosed, even though he is still suffering and the cure will be long and difficult. *Absurd* is indeed the correct word to denote Stefan's attitude toward the "Polishness" of humanity, for he fails to place it within a framework of meaning that would invest it with significance and offer hope for its improvement.

Stefan's obsession with Polishness is reflected in the novel's title, *Polonaise*, which refers to the traditional Polish dance and the famous music Chopin composed for it. Yet this expression of Polishness—far from being absurd—is actually salvific, for the dance is instrumental in Stefan's saving Annabel from the sinister machinations of her parents and Jack Marryat. The absurdity of being Polish, like the absurdity of belonging to the fallen human race, has its glorious as well as its ludicrous and shameful aspects.

The conclusion of the novel provides Stefan with an opportunity to break through his commitment to absurdity. When he meets Annabel and Teofil, he has just recently returned to Europe from living in the United States, where he had been trying to write, but with disappointing results. He hopes that a return to Europe will enable him to produce something worthwhile. He tells Annabel that he wants to write a story with a happy ending but that it is impossible because "'art depends upon life and in life there is no happy ending'" (273). As he gets to know Annabel and Teofil and gives up his initial temptation to seduce her, he becomes drawn into fostering their union. This project and his writing become conflated. He records in a notebook every detail about their burgeoning relationship; it will be his "living masterpiece" (310).

When the scene shifts to Mulford Park and Stefan realizes with horror the plot that is being hatched to destroy the innocent love of Annabel and Stefan, he seems for the first time to see human evil for what it is. When enmeshed in fascist dictatorships and the machinations and savage brutality of political factions, he could not really recognize evil as evil. It was "absurdity." Now, however, at Mulford Park he can name it, and he acts to circumvent its deadly power. Perhaps he recognizes evil because it threatens the "masterpiece" he is writing: the relationship of Annabel and Teofil. Throughout his life, the only thing Stefan has really cared about is his writing. Now writing and life are merged.

On his return to Paris from England, Stefan tries to finish writing his masterpiece, which will end with the marriage of Annabel and Teofil. As he works on his story, he finds that "some sort of preamble would be necessary to lift the narrative from a sentimental romance into a novel of ideas" (345). He tries to write some kind of philosophical introduction, but finds himself pondering these questions:

> What is the happiness that my characters unknowingly pursue? What is their innocence? Why is the narrator so sure that there is one way, one truth? That the other is evil and wrong? Is it a random preference with no significance beyond the gratuitous choice? . . .
> . . . It is not instinct which finds joy in the triumph of innocence over corruption: it is conscience. But if conscience can be in conflict with nature— then what directs it? What can be beyond nature? (346)

The questions Stefan is struggling with here are ultimately questions about the existence of a transcendent God—not a God that is simply a name we give to our own subjectivity—but one that has an objective existence beyond the human being and that makes the universe meaningful by giving His creatures an ultimate end and enabling them to reach it through their exercise of free choice. Once again Chesterton's *Orthodoxy* offers a helpful insight by elucidating the difference between a religion that stresses God's immanence and one that stresses God's transcendence:

> By insisting specially on the immanence of God we get introspection, self-isolation, quietism, social indifference—Tibet. By insisting specially on the transcendence of God we get wonder, curiosity, moral and political adventure, righteous indignation—Christendom. Insisting that God is inside man, man is always inside himself. By insisting that God transcends man, man has transcended himself.[19]

This energy that flows from belief in a transcendent God and a meaningful external reality offering both real danger and real rewards leads, according to Chesterton, to better stories, more vibrant and robust religion, and the true reforming spirit. "That external vigilance which has always been the mark of Christianity (the command that we should *watch* and pray) has expressed itself both in typical western orthodoxy and in typical western politics: but both depend on the idea of a divinity transcendent, different from ourselves, a deity that disappears."[20]

Stefan's insistent pondering of conscience, his growing sense that it points to some meaningful context for our moral choices is reminiscent of the argument of John Henry Newman in *An Essay in Aid of a Grammar of Assent*:

> Inanimate things cannot stir our affections; these are correlative with persons. If, as is the case, we feel responsibility, are ashamed, are frightened, at transgressing the voice of conscience, this implies that there is One to whom we are responsible, before whom we are ashamed, whose claims upon us we fear. . . . These feelings in us are such as require for their exciting cause an intelligent being.[21]

A few months after Stefan's return to Paris, Annabel and Teofil are married, and when they stop in Paris on the way back from their honeymoon and confide that they think Annabel may already be pregnant, Stefan knows he has the happy ending for his "masterpiece." It is noteworthy that he now sees in the couple's eyes that "erotic complicity which Stefan had once looked for in vain" (345). Their sexuality which before had seemed so awkward and infantile now appears to have become mature and robust within the bonds of matrimony. Stefan calls Krystyna and asks her to have lunch with him because he needs to tell her something. He asks her if she remembers what he told her in the summerhouse at Jezow when their father went bankrupt. She does not remember but asks why it is so important. Stefan's answer is that he was wrong. He never gets to tell his sister, however, for when she arrives, she finds him dead, "his features in repose" (346). What he had told her that day in the summerhouse was that God did not exist.

NOTES

1. Piers Paul Read, *Polonaise* (London: Orion Books, Phoenix, 1997), 9. Hereafter cited in the text by page number.

2. This is not to suggest that before the twentieth-century no people were obsessed with sex; but once Freud raised our awareness of the strong current of sexuality in all human beings, and as twentieth-century culture became increasingly

open about sexual matters, the permissive culture allowed for much more explicit expression of these desires and also led people to more easily discover them in themselves and others—a bit of a self-fulfilling prophecy, or an instance of seeing what you expect to see.

3. Francis Canavan sees this dynamic writ large in American society. "Liberal democracy has worked as well as it has and as long as it has because it has been able to trade on something that it did not create and which it tends on the whole to undermine. That is the moral tradition that prevailed among the greater part of the people." Francis Canavan, "The Dilemma of Liberal Pluralism," *The Human Life Review* 5, no. 3 (summer 1979), 7, quoted in Stanley Hauerwas, *A Community of Character: Toward a Constructive Christian Social Ethic* (Notre Dame, Ind.: University of Notre Dame Press, 1981), 217.

4. Chesterton, *Orthodoxy*, 135. For example, different religions have different understandings of the origin of the world, the nature of the Creator, the final destiny of human beings and the basis of their claims to have a revelation from God and to authoritatively teach the truth.

5. Chesterton, *Orthodoxy*, 137.

6. Although some might argue that Oxford could in no way be considered a "sheltered environment," one must remember that this is Oxford of the 1950s—not the 1960s; and Teofil's reply to Stefan when he encourages him to make love to Annabel—"It would be a sin" (340) suggests that even at Oxford Teofil had found an environment that allowed him to keep his traditional moral code intact.

7. Northrop Frye, *Anatomy of Criticism: Four Essays* (Princeton: Princeton University Press, 1957), 33–34. Comedy is associated with spring, romance with summer, tragedy with autumn, and satire, as well as irony, with winter.

8. Frye, *Anatomy of Criticism*, 34

9. Frye, *Anatomy of Criticism*, 40.

10. Frye, *Anatomy of Criticism*, 42.

11. Frye, *Anatomy of Criticism*, 41.

12. Chesterton, *Orthodoxy*, 72.

13. Chesterton, *Orthodoxy*, 74.

14. Chesterton, *Orthodoxy*, 74–75.

15. Chesterton, *Orthodoxy*. 73.

16. Chesterton, *Orthodoxy*, 76. Richard Weaver of the University of Chicago evidently agreed with Chesterton when he wrote that "service to others is the best service when the effort of all is subsumed under a transcendental conception." *Ideas Have Consequences* (Chicago: University of Chicago Press, 1948), 77.

17. Chesterton, *Orthodoxy*, 77. Chesterton's idea here anticipates his point about orthodoxy which he makes later in the book. He argues that the truths of orthodox Christianity are best expressed in paradox because it keeps two apparently contrasting beliefs together (for example, that Christ is fully human and fully divine; a man has infinite worth and must be abjectly humble) and refusing to blend them into some moderate golden mean. *Orthodoxy* 103–4. See chapter 12, "Holding on to the Good: *Brittle Joys*," endnote 12.

18. Chesterton, *Orthodoxy*, 85–86.

19. Chesterton, *Orthodoxy*, 141–42.

20. Chesterton, *Orthodoxy*, 141.

21. John Henry Cardinal Newman, *An Essay in Aid of a Grammar of Assent* (Garden City, N.Y.: Doubleday, Image Books, 1955), 101. Newman goes on to argue, "If the cause of these emotions does not belong to this visible world, the Object to which his perception is directed must be Supernatural and Divine; and thus the phenomena of Conscience, as a dictate, avail to impress the imagination with the picture of a Supreme Governor, a Judge, holy, just, powerful, all-seeing, retributive, and is the creative principle of religion, as the Moral Sense is the principle of ethics" (101). Certainly it would be a stretch to suggest that Stefan's insight here goes as far as Newman in explicitly linking the impulses of conscience to the Judeo-Christian God. Nevertheless, his instinctual gropings are definitely tending in the same direction.

15

The Mystery
of the Resurrection:
On the Third Day

For the others,
        of whom I am one,
                miracles (ultimate need, bread
of life) are miracles just because
      people so tuned
              to the humdrum laws:
gravity, mortality—
      can't open
              to symbol's power
unless convinced of its ground,
      its roots
              in bone and blood.

      —Denise Levertov, "On Belief in the
      Physical Resurrection of Jesus"

"On the third day, he rose again from the dead." This statement from the Apostles' Creed is the epigraph for Piers Paul Read's novel *On the Third Day* (1990). Read places at the heart of this book the Christian doctrine that is most incomprehensible, most mysterious—perhaps even repugnant to human reason—and yet absolutely central to the Christian creed: the bodily Resurrection of Jesus Christ. In spite of repeated efforts to spiritualize or allegorize its meaning, this doctrine stubbornly refuses to go away. St. Paul says, "if Christ has not been raised, our preaching is void of content and your faith is empty too" (1 Corinthians 15:14).

Belief in a literal resurrection cannot be separated from belief in a literal crucifixion, and Read conjoins the two in a startling way. The Crucifixion and Resurrection exact from the Christian something akin to the obedience God demanded when he asked Abraham to sacrifice his beloved Son. The Christian must be humble and submissive in the face of this staggering reality. Read's imagination is always drawn to the way that creedal beliefs and the moral life are intertwined, and this novel suggests that trying to "tame" this doctrine shrinks the soul, whereas affirming it liberates the soul and is morally invigorating.[1]

Beginning with the Higher Criticism and the demythologizers of the nineteenth century, and continuing into the present, some theologians and scholars have attempted to preserve the significance of this tenet of Christian faith without requiring belief that an actual physical human body died (by a particularly gruesome means of execution) and then a few days later was in some way reanimated into a life that, although different from its previous mode of existence, was still physical. Some scholars maintain that the Resurrection is not so much about Jesus as it is about his disciples. The story of the empty tomb is seen as a literary device to explain the way in which Christ's followers were inspired by His teachings and empowered by His memory, such as this interpretation by a Jesuit theologian:

> My understanding of the resurrection does not support the necessity of an empty tomb in principle. Resurrection faith today is not belief in an external miracle, an empirical historical event testified to by disciples, which we take on the basis of their word. A reflective faith-hope today will affirm Jesus risen on the basis of a conviction that Jesus' message is true, because God is the way Jesus revealed God to be.[2]

Read's novel, however, compels the reader to consider a very literal, historical, physical understanding of the Resurrection. He does this by opening the novel with a shocking event. Some archaeologists find a skeleton in the Old City of Jerusalem, and persuasive evidence suggests that it is the skeleton of Jesus Christ.

For the characters that hold to a physical resurrection, convincing evidence that the skeleton is indeed that of Jesus threatens their Christian faith. For others who hold to a more spiritual interpretation of the Easter story, the discovery will not destroy what is truly essential in Christianity. Another group of people actively seek to undermine Christian faith and are overjoyed at the prospect that this discovery will deal a deathblow to a religion that they despise. All three groups have a strong personal investment in the outcome of the investigation. The intensity of their passions and the hostility that is generated give the novel its dramatic tension.

As is always the case with Read, his fictional universe does not minimize or gloss over the presence of evil in the world. On the contrary, Read depicts evil in a particularly graphic way, often through grotesque or unsavory images. One of these occurs in the first chapter with the image of a corpse hanging by the neck from a window in a monastery. The body turns out to be that of Father Lambert, an eminent archaeologist, renowned for both his scholarship and his holiness. The body is discovered by Andrew, a young novice who reveres the older monk. With the help of some other monks, the young man manages to pull the corpse inside. "He shrank back, horrified to see a face he had revered already blackened and distorted, with the tongue protruding from between the teeth and the unfocused eyes bulging from their sockets."[3] This grotesque image of a saintly monk is a reminder that the holy are not only *not* safeguarded from evil, but are often its favored target.

This powerful image introduces a novel with many examples of moral evil: timid, mendacious monks who would rather publicly lie than admit to an embarrassing fact, a callous young man who routinely uses young women as sexual partners for three months and then dismisses them, parents who blatantly favor one child and are coldly distant with the other, the betrayal of a sister by her brother, attempted assassination, and international terrorism. The goodness in the world is often crowded out by the more aggressive, obstreperous force of evil.

Through the particularity of his description, Read renders a secular world that has the dense, rich texture that is such a marked characteristic of his fiction The account of the way Henry, Andrew's older brother, concludes his dates is a good example:

> Henry always arranged a three-course dinner, beginning with soup and ending with a sorbet, with smoked salmon, gravadlax or game pie in between. He did not prepare it himself; someone else came in during the day; but he served it methodically by candlelight at the polished antique table in the corner of his living-room.
>
> There was always, too, a half bottle of Meursault or Montrachet and a full bottle of some fancy claret, then a choice of liqueurs to drink with their coffee. (70)

The description of Henry's flat is also done with a richness of suggestive detail.

> He intended, now, to replay the tape of *Newsnight* which had been recorded automatically earlier in the evening; but he did not reach for the controls which, with the press of a couple of buttons, would have brought sound to the speakers and an image to the screen. Instead, he sat in quiet obeisance, before the dead set as if praying before his household god. It was a fine god—a Bang and Olufsen: when it was switched on, its colours outshone the flames of the gas log fire. So, too, the video recorder was the best of its kind,

slim and grey like a revolver, with twinkling numbers and symbols waiting
to obey those invisible rays which emanated from the small box which Henry
held in his hand. (75–76)

The objects in Henry's flat take on an eerie quality suggestive of a futuristic, robotic, dehumanized universe, albeit one in which he is fully in control. This richly textured secular world is the matrix within which Read
explores his central theme: the Resurrection of Jesus Christ. What do
Christians mean when they profess to believe it? How central is it to
Christian faith? What would it mean for Christianity if it were proved that
there was no physical resurrection of Jesus?

Speculation about the cause of Father Lambert's death—whether suicide
or murder—takes on special urgency when it is revealed that he was mysteriously summoned to Jerusalem right before his death because his friend
and colleague, Michal Dagan, a Jewish archaeologist, had unearthed a cistern containing the skeleton of a man crucified in the first century. Several
factors suggest the possibility that it might be the skeleton of Christ. As Dagan's son says to his sister Anna, "'Dad's dug up the body of Jesus'" (92).

Some contemporary Christians who prefer to concentrate on Jesus as an
ethical teacher rather than an incarnate God, dismiss as irrelevant
whether the story of the empty tomb signifies a revivified body, a stolen
body, or simply the renewed faith and courage of the disciples. Even for
those who still hold to belief in a physical resurrection, the event depicted
in Renaissance art and stained glass windows as someone in a toga, holding a banner, while Roman soldiers cower at his feet, seems an other-
worldly phenomenon, incomprehensible, even unimaginable for a modern person. Yet through his use of a dramatic, concrete scene, drenched in
details and earthy particularity, Read thrusts this doctrine into the mate-
riality and familiarity of the twentieth century world.

> It was only when he was standing on shingle which had collected at the low-
> est point, that Dagan noticed a large earthenware jar, cracked and lying on its
> side.
> The jar was not unusual. Like the cistern, it was of a kind common to the
> period, used for storing olives or grain, with a wide neck and a tapered stem.
> It was too heavy to have been used to draw water from the cistern, and per-
> haps for that reason had been left there, submerged under the surface. (3)

It is not revealed at first what the archaeologists find in the jar. Eventually,
however, Dagan's son tells his sister Anna that their father has found the
skeleton of Jesus in a cistern under the Temple Mount.

> "You mean the remains of a crucified man?"
> "As described in the Gospels."

"There are marks?"

"Yes. On the wrists; the ribs, the skull. And a long nail through the ankles."

"What kind of marks on the skull?"

"Scratches."

"The crown of thorns?"

He shrugged. "I guess so." (92–93)

These details seem slim evidence on which to conclude that the skeleton is that of Jesus, especially since many people were crucified in first century Palestine. Additional support comes from the Vilnius Codex, "'a fragment of the Slavonic version of Josephus' *Jewish War*'" (93). According to Anna's brother, "'It contained a passage not found in any of the other editions, to the effect that the Romans might have smuggled the body of Jesus out of the tomb hidden in a storage jar and had built it into a cistern beneath the Temple'" (93). Thus Read takes the doctrine of the Resurrection, traditionally considered the lynchpin of Christianity, extricates it from the domain of ancient history, myth, Biblical scholarship, and Renaissance art, and plunges it right into the world of the 6:00 news. Such a startling juxtaposition is unsettling, to say the least.

Even before it is confirmed whether or not this is the skeleton of Jesus, the mere possibility pushes this most incredible of all religious beliefs into a harsh spotlight, forcing the reader to confront the question of how important a physical resurrection is to his or her own Christian faith and what it would mean if it were definitively proved that Jesus did *not* actually rise from the dead.

Even the saintly Father Lambert is shaken by this discovery. When, shortly after his return from Jerusalem, his body is found hanging from his window, Andrew, his devoted protégé, fears that Father Lambert had lost his faith and committed suicide in despair. This hypothesis is reinforced when he learns that hours before his death Father Lambert had sought out Veronica Dunn, a woman with whom he had been in love, told her he had lost his faith, and made love with her, for their love "'was now the most precious thing in his life and . . . he did not want to die with it unfulfilled'" (42).

Andrew's own faith is also undermined when he actually goes to the site of the discovery. As Father Lambert's graduate student, he is instructed by the head of the order to go to Jerusalem and inspect the evidence. Although he is plagued by faintness, dizziness, and fear in the tunnel on the way to the cistern, after seeing the skeleton, he is surprised at how well he feels: "When at last, he took off his paper cap[4] and stepped out into the hot, bright sunshine, he did not drop this role [of an objective archaeologist] for that of an anguished believer who had just had the rug pulled out from under his feet. Instead, he felt a sudden, irrepressible burst of high spirits which made him want to run across the plaza and jump for joy" (135). Andrew at first interprets his exuberance as relief "at returning unaffected by what he had seen" but then realizes that "unlike Father Lambert, he had discovered the truth before it was too late" (135). He feels liberated.

Some nonbelievers think that Christians hold on to their belief because it is comforting, a kind of spiritual security blanket, and that they lack the fortitude to face the world and human life on their own terms.[5] Conversely, Christians often think that nonbelievers are opting for the easier, more comfortable route, unwilling to accept the demands and challenges of a Christian life. Each thinks he has chosen the harder way. Read's depiction of Andrew's reaction to this purported discovery of Christ's skeleton would support the Christian view. Andrew's apparent willingness to throw over his years of prayer, discipline, sacrifice, and study in preparation for living as a celibate monk—all on the basis of his first view of the skeleton without even waiting for subsequent study—suggests that the magnetic appeal of a life free from the obligations and sacrifices demanded of the Christian (and even more so of a monk) is so strong that even a momentary crack in the structure of faith is enough to send one charging into the delights of the secular life.

Read portrays with considerable subtlety the complex dynamic involved in both coming to faith and losing faith. Perhaps more than any other Catholic novelist since Graham Greene, he dwells on *belief*—in the sense of believing a certain set of propositions, accepting as true that certain events really occurred in history—and not just *moral* conversion as central in coming to faith. Yet faith is not as simple as a neat set of free-floating intellectual propositions. Those beliefs are inextricably and mysteriously entangled with the moral life. Once Andrew has decided "that if Christ did not rise from the dead, then all the struggle to be unselfish was futile" (136), he wastes no time in leaving the monastery, checks into a hotel, persuades Anna to move in with him, unburdens himself of chastity, and tries to make up for lost time.

At first everything is wonderful, but soon Andrew is behaving in ways that disturb him. Only a few days after beginning this new life with Anna, Andrew tells her about Father Lambert's sexual encounter with Veronica Dunn. Telling her "how Father Lambert had apologized not for what he had done but for what he had done badly, . . . a cruel grin crossed his face, and a callous laugh accompanied his conjecture as to whether Father Lambert had been unable to finish what he had started, or whether it was all over before it had properly begun" (198). No sooner does Andrew repent of his arrogant attitude and ridicule of the man he had so loved than he catches himself again in behavior that his former self would have considered shameful. He is walking along the streets of Jerusalem when he notices two tall scantily dressed European girls. "One of them was not only pretty, but gave Andrew a fleeting glance of interest, which, involuntarily, he returned, wondering, before he was aware of what he was doing, what it would be like to sleep with her—wondering, and then wanting to try her for size, to give her the benefit of that skill and vigour which had left Anna with such a fresh complexion and happy smile" (198–99). Although Andrew repents of these desires, as he had repented of his unkind thoughts about Father Lambert, the thought of going to confession or even praying a decade of the rosary now seems foreign to his nature. He rationalizes that such acts are really those of a monk, and he is no longer a monk. Andrew is astute enough to recognize that his sudden loss of faith has fragmented his personality:

> It was as if the change he had made in leaving the Simonite order, and living with Anna, had not resulted in a straightforward metamorphosis from celibate monk to devoted lover, but had rather fragmented his personality so that two or even three different characters now lived within the same mind— the kind and humble Christian; the loyal and devoted husband of Anna;[6] and this new, strutting embodiment of brute nature that gloried in what was healthy, strong and triumphant and despised what was feeble, needy and poor. (200)

Andrew's experience also dramatizes the way a change in belief affects the way one sees everything else. Just the prospect of a major challenge to his faith causes Andrew to view everything through a new lens, and things look quite different. Shortly after arriving in Jerusalem, Andrew goes to the Church of the Holy Sepulchre, which he had always seen as evidence of the universality of Christianity. Although he had always found it a "gloomy church" and had never liked the "hotch-potch of its architectural styles," he now observes the artifacts from a more distanced and critical point of view. "Here, again, where once he had knelt to pray, he merely studied the intricate silverwork which surrounded the painted faces of the Greek icons; looked up at the twinkling vulgarity of the candelabra; and noted the naïve depiction of Christ on the Cross." (117) This scene provides a perceptive commentary on the role of art and artifacts in religious experience, especially within the Catholic tradition. Catholicism's reliance on statues, paintings, and other kinds of religious artifacts to stimulate religious devotion has been as derided by its critics as it has been loved by its adherents. Most of the Reformers objected to this art because they considered it idolatry, whereas in more recent times Catholics themselves have criticized it because much of it was not good art and thus not worthy of its subject.[7] Andrew's experience in the Church of the Holy Sepulchre suggests that the effect of religious art is not so much a function of its artistic merit as it is of the interior disposition of the viewer. Bereft of religious faith, the observer can relate to it only in terms of its aesthetic value.

Read's depiction of the loss of faith also delineates the way in which a person who has been formed in the faith rarely makes a clean break. It is difficult—if not impossible—to completely disentangle the threads of Christianity from the fabric of one's personality and values. When Anna tells Andrew about her previous lovers, he is shocked and angered enough to lash out at her, but "the lingering monk, whom he had tried so hard to shake off during the days which had gone before, stepped forward with the reflex gentleness and humility which came from the years of religious life" (201). Andrew, like Bruno in *Polonaise*, is living on his Christian capital.

As Andrew is losing his faith, his skeptical brother, Henry, is moving toward faith. Henry first appears as a confirmed atheist, who is convinced that he completely sees through the religious illusions of his brother and other misguided believers. He believes a religious vocation like Andrew's is "'the symptom of a psychosis'" (66) and considers it "'demented to lead a life in which you suppress all your natural desires'" (67). Henry is convinced that he understands the psychological dynamic underlying Andrew's faith: "'It's so patently obvious to me that after being deserted at a vulnerable age by our weak father, and then bullied in adolescence by our emasculating mother, Andrew found a psychological haven in the Catholic Church with its strong but kindly God the Father and passive, patient and ever-loving mother of Mary'" (67).[8]

Read's portrayal of Henry is another example of the way he includes both familiar and not-so-familiar arguments against Christianity and the Church and states them in a particularly forceful way—forceful because of the passion and intensity which draws them forth, the anger and sarcasm with which they are enunciated, and even their persuasiveness—the way they seem to fit the facts and explain the phenomenon of religion. For example, when Anna tells Henry that Andrew is kinder and gentler than anyone else she knows, Henry responds that Andrew's kindness is due to his "'fear of life. He's like a monkey, threatened by a stronger monkey, who lies down and proffers his genitals to deflect the other's aggression'" (71). He considers Andrew a victim "'of all those repressed pederasts and menopausal spinsters who run the Roman Catholic Church'" (72). Henry delivers a caustic attack on Catholicism's relationship with sexuality:

> "Sooner or later [Andrew] was bound to discover that you can neither change human nature nor deny it; you can simply pervert it. Most dangerous of all is the celibacy of priests, because all that energy which should be dissipated in sex is obliged to find other outlets like pride, ambition and the sin-

ister pleasure which priests take in exploiting, and manipulating the weakness and uncertainty of others." (72–73)

Yet at the same time that Henry is making these arguments that have a certain plausibility, he undermines his credibility by revealing his own cynicism and bitterness. Arguing with Anna that liking and loving are incompatible, he maintains, "'love is just a gloss on the crude instincts which ensure the survival of the species'" (72). He further insists that human beings are "'isolated individuals in relentless pursuit of gratification and power'" (72). The religious may be deceived in their motives for their choices as to how to manage their erotic energy, but Henry's callow, calculated, and self-serving use of women hardly seems more admirable or enlightened.

Henry's life epitomizes many of the best things that the secular world has to offer: money, women, an elegant car, expensive clothes, and a fashionable, beautifully furnished flat. Eventually, however, a certain tedium sets in. "He felt he was watching life from the auditorium when he should have been on stage. He was sure that there must be more to achieve than what he had achieved already" (82). Yet even as he yearns for some more glorious destiny, he reminds himself that man is "no more than an evolved baboon" (82).

When Henry is distressed and frightened by some minor ailments which turn out to have simple explanations—blood in his basin due to a nosebleed, weight loss caused by his cutting back on alcohol—he is forced to encounter his own mortality, or rather *his reaction* to the thought of his mortality. Even after he realizes he is not in danger of death, he still feels anxiety, which he finds difficult to explain. "It was not that he feared death, which he supposed was simply oblivion; he was, rather, annoyed in advance by the business of dying, just as he was exasperated when any of his machines broke down" (167). Henry likes to feel that he is in control and can make everything in his life run efficiently. Just the thought of any lessening of control is unsettling.

In a chance meeting with Veronica Dunn, whom he had once met, Henry tells her about the skeleton. She maintains that Henry's belief that the skeleton is that of Jesus is just as much a "faith" as the faith of religious people who are certain that it is not. She asks him to look into the possibility that the find is a hoax and makes a bet with him that it is fraudulent. Asked what she is proposing as a wager, she answers that they are playing for their souls.

The first crack in Henry's nonbelief appears when he finds himself unable to concentrate on his work because he is distracted by the discovery of the skeleton and the ramifications it will have—not only religious ones, but political ones as well. Having lived mostly with other agnostics,

Henry is shocked to realize how many people in the world believe in the Resurrection of Jesus Christ. He begins to have "the uneasy feeling that there might, after all, be more to life than he had supposed" (182). Henry is in an in-between state, no longer comfortable in his agnosticism, yet still repelled by religion. "He still felt a repugnance for religion, and thought it absurd to suggest that a God powerful enough to bring the whole universe into existence should choose to become a sweating, defecating, human being" (183). This passage conveys the powerful literal meaning of the Incarnation, which is almost lost among idealized art, pious stories, and overly familiar Biblical language. The central tenet of the Christian religion is indeed a preposterous proposition! Henry is allowing the possibility of the existence of a divine savior to enter his conscience, but as something to be dreaded, rather than embraced. In fact, when his reverie is interrupted by a phone call from a researcher with information about the Vilnius Codex that seems to support the opinion that the discovered skeleton is that of Jesus, like Andrew emerging from the tunnel, he actually feels relief. "As Henry stepped back from the abyss of Christian belief he felt a sudden surge of physical well-being, like a man who wakes up to find himself cured of a debilitating disease. Life—life on the earth and in the air—appeared once again as something of extraordinary beauty. Why had he faltered?" (185).

The solidity of his atheism has been undermined, however. It is further weakened during a conversation he has with his friend Edward Meredith, a Moscow news correspondent, who is helping him investigate the possibility that the discovery might be a fraud. When Henry insists that Christ's skeleton must be somewhere because he can't have risen from the dead, Meredith, whom Henry respects as intelligent, replies, "'Nothing is impossible for God.'"

> "Do you believe that?"
> "If there is a God, it's only common sense."
> "And is there a God?"
> "That's a very deep question, Henry. We must talk about it some other time." (188)

Meredith's remarks, while hardly a robust confession of faith, leave the door open for the possibility that an intelligent, sophisticated person could consider faith in God as something other than an absurdity. Later the reader is told that Henry is seen in a Catholic church, kneeling in front of a crucifix, but the scene is strictly third person reportage, with no access to Henry's thoughts.

After learning that the skeleton is a hoax and that Anna has had an affair with Henry, Andrew, confused and angry, returns to the monastery in

London. Henry visits him there and admits that he is no longer so sure that God does not exist. After he leaves Andrew, he again goes into a Catholic church; but this time the reader *is* privy to Henry's introspection. Looking at the tabernacle, he thinks that the Holy of Holies in the Temple of Jerusalem "for all its magnificence," could hardly be compared with this one, "a little cupboard covered with embroidered cloth, . . . if it did indeed house the living God" (273). Henry, who is convinced that Andrew ought to leave the monastery and marry Anna, then addresses that possible presence in the tabernacle:

> "Let him go," he said in the silence of his mind. "Let him go, and I will believe in you, in what you taught, yes, even in your Resurrection. Let her be happy with Andrew, and let Andrew be happy with her, and, if you need a life to atone for the wretched Father Lambert, then take mine. Show him the way out, as you show me the way in. Cut through his guilt and neurosis as you cut through my egoism and doubt." (274)[9]

Aside from the gaining and losing of faith, and the centrality of belief in the physical Resurrection in Christianity, Read's other important theme in this novel is the polarization within Catholicism since the Second Vatican Council. Father Lambert fears that in the era of openness ushered in by Pope John XXIII's call to "open the windows" and reinvigorate the Church, the opinions of liberal theologians have been harmful—not only to the laity—but to the clergy as well. According to Veronica Dunn, Father Lambert thought "'that so many of the younger priests had been corrupted in the seminaries by the liberal theologians. They were no longer taught to believe in Hell, but without Hell the whole idea of salvation loses its meaning and there is no point to the suffering of Christ'" (43). The lack of cohesive belief in the Resurrection—at least as traditionally understood—is symptomatic of the harm that Father Lambert feels has been done by liberal theologians.

Father Lambert, however, is not simply a watchdog for orthodoxy. He also has a reputation for holiness. Although he is the "most distinguished" (7) of the Simonite monks, being a world-famous archaeologist, "neither his fame, nor his dedication to uncovering the past, had ever distracted him from his obedience to his calling as a Catholic priest. He said mass every day, at an altar in a church or at a table in a tent; and when in London he would sit in the confessional for an hour every Saturday morning, waiting for penitents who rarely came" (8).

Read emphasizes those qualities of Father Lambert that are at odds with the more popular image of the good priest which evolved in the years after Vatican II. In reaction against a clerical culture in which priests had been seen primarily as distant and austere authority figures and treated with deference often disproportionate to their deserts, there was great enthusiasm for humanizing the priesthood. Many priests asked to be called by their first names, or "Father" plus their first names. Priests were encouraged to be friendlier, wear secular clothes, and to chat with parishioners after mass. As more ministries in the Church were delegated to laypeople (with the good intention of helping them realize the fullness of the priesthood of the laity), and they began to read the Scripture from the pulpit, distribute Holy Communion, act as hospital chaplains, and in some cases, even preach, the identity markers between ordained priest and laity became less distinct.

Father Lambert, however, not only "mortified his flesh in a way that was quite out of fashion," but his "expression was stern, and his manner remote, even forbidding. Few people called him John or even Father John: it was always Father Lambert" (8). His resistance to the more egalitarian and genial style of priesthood suggests that he may see it as eroding the special nature of the ordained ministry. Although Father Lambert's "remote, even forbidding" manner might not seem a desirable trait in an ideal priest, Read seems to be at pains here to differentiate the priest from the man. He stresses the fact that in his priestly work Father Lambert is diligent, kind, and faith-filled. "People crossed London when it was known that he was preaching" (8).

The celibacy of the Roman priesthood is another contentious point in the novel. Clerical celibacy had always been encouraged and often mandated, and clerical marriage in the Western Church was forbidden in the eleventh century.[10] After the Reformation, Catholics generally regarded their celibate clergy as a point of pride, but after Vatican II there was increasing agitation for married priests.[11] Clerical celibacy would no doubt have been challenged during the cultural revolution of the 1960s—Council or no Council. Yet the swiftness and intensity with which Catholics changed their minds—from seeing celibacy as honorable and noble to seeing it as inhuman and pointless—suggest that there had not been a clearly realized and well-communicated theology of the celibate priesthood. Many Catholics simply could not see any good reason why celibacy was intrinsic to priesthood and why it should be mandatory rather than voluntary.[12]

For Andrew, as for many young men who consider becoming a priest, the prospect of celibacy is problematic. Andrew has "instincts common to a man of his age" (44). He is neither undersexed or homosexual, common explanations often given for the willingness of many priests to give up marriage and family. According to Father Lambert the reason for a celibate priesthood is not, as is commonly supposed, the argument from practicality, "the avoidance of the encumbrance of a wife and family so as to dedicate oneself entirely to the Lord," nor the idea of simply giving up something pleasant and good in itself as a sacrifice to God (44). Father Lambert's argument for priestly celibacy is this: "In a priest, he had said, the man must transcend the male: holiness was incompatible with the qualities which women sought in their lovers. That was why Jesus had been celibate, and had asked those who would follow him *à outrance* to make themselves eunuchs for the sake of the Kingdom of God" (44). It is difficult to know which traits Father Lambert thinks women seek in their lovers (virility? dependability? sensitivity?) that would be incompatible with holiness. Perhaps Father Lambert has in mind more negative masculine traits: competitiveness, aggression, lust. At any rate, different women value different traits. What is important about Father Lambert's theory, however, is that it is based on an understanding of gender as an important and real (not simply culturally conditioned) category and one, which has theological significance.[13]

Andrew is convinced and is glad to undertake this sacrifice for the good of the priesthood. His confidence in Father Lambert's argument is shaken, however, when he learns that in the last hours of his life, his role model had broken his vow of celibacy and slept with a woman he had been in love with for years. Andrew feels "misled, if not actually deceived. He felt like a boy who had caught his teacher reading a pornographic book" (45). Andrew here embodies the dilemma of the many Catholics with regard to the celibate priesthood. The theology and ideals of consecrated celibacy are noble in theory, but so often contradicted and dishonored in practice.[14] Would it be better to have a less noble theory but one which is more consistently observed?

Read articulates not only the common arguments *for* celibacy (freedom for a more total devotion to ministry, sacrifice for love of God) as well as Father Lambert's more theological one but also the arguments *against* it. Henry speaks for the typical secular view of this countercultural life choice when he asks Anna if it isn't "'demented to lead a life in which you suppress all your natural desires'" (67). Anna, whose opinions are not as ossified as Henry's, is irritated by his doctrinaire attitude and retorts, "'Perhaps you just don't have the imagination to envisage a life that is different from your own'" (67). Henry's response is that he *can* imagine it, but he explains it as a way of coping with psychological, emotional, or sexual immaturity.

Although Henry's opinion is delivered with a self-righteous, arrogant tone, it does have plausibility. Undoubtedly some priests have been drawn to a life of celibacy for the wrong reasons. Yet Henry's argument goes further, for he believes that if his understanding of this psychological dynamic is correct, it inevitably precludes the presence of other factors: grace, the Holy Spirit, love of God. Read himself subscribes to the idea that psychological factors, especially those based on one's early family life, can be formative in the growth and shape of a person's faith. That does not mean that it is any the less a genuine faith.[15]

Once Andrew is convinced that the skeleton that was found is truly that of Jesus, he loses his commitment to celibacy along with his belief in a divine, resurrected savior. In his mind the two are intimately linked. As he explains to Anna,

> "It must be difficult for you to understand, but my concept of celibacy was tied up with my belief in the Resurrection. It was as if the sexual act somehow initiated the decay of the flesh, as a fig must split open to release its seed. The Resurrection of Jesus, like the Assumption of Mary, was linked in my mind to their virginity. Then, suddenly, this afternoon, when I realized that Jesus, and Mary too, had a body like yours or mine, which flourished when they were living, but eventually putrefied like the corpse in the cistern, then virginity seemed absurd—in fact not just absurd, but wrong, sterile, a denial of life. And that's what suddenly made the monastery seem intolerable—the thought that behind those doors were fifteen or twenty wretched men struggling to suppress their God-given desires." (163)

Andrew's reflections on celibacy amplify the novel's case for the centrality of the Resurrection in Catholic belief—belief not just in the sense of the Creed, but in the whole fabric of Catholic life: piety, liturgy, morality, and consecrated, celibate religious life. If Andrew's statement were that his belief in Christ's *divinity* was tied to his belief in the Resurrection, it would be more understandable. All Christians, married or unmarried, would acknowledge that link and presumably face the same crisis of faith as Andrew if they were to learn that Christ's skeleton had been found. But linking celibacy and the Resurrection is curious. Many Christians believe in the divinity of Christ, validated by His Resurrection, but do not believe that such a belief calls for celibacy. Furthermore, Andrew's belief that "the sexual act somehow initiated the decay of the flesh" is reminiscent of medieval or Jansenistic theologies that stressed the spirit-flesh dichotomy, saw most sin as rooted in the flesh, and often encouraged what amounted to a hatred of the material world. Although such attitudes are out of favor in the contemporary Church, their legacy is reflected in Andrew's attitude. The novel reflects the distortion in Andrew's opinion by the impulsive way in which he goes from one extreme to the other, in a matter of twenty-four hours discarding his commitment to celibacy and undertaking a vigorous sex life.

The issue of celibacy is never resolved in the novel. In the end it seems as if Andrew is headed for a healthy sexual life, leaving the reader with the idea that his understanding of celibacy in religious life had been immature and distorted. This sense is reinforced by his skewed theory about his ability to somehow "save" Father Lambert from eternal punishment by giving up Anna, returning to the monastery, and living the rest of his life as a monk. When Henry asks him if he really believes he can save Father Lambert's soul as well as his own, Andrew's confident reply is, "'Yes. By seeing it through, right to the end, my life for his life—a return, no more, for what he did for me'" (268). Andrew says he has returned to the monastery—not to save his own soul—but that of Father Lambert. Henry is understandably horrified by this theology of substitute salvation—as any reputable Catholic theologian would be.[16] Andrew is clearly confused. Yet his impetuous changes of mind about celibacy and his torturous agonizing about it do cast a light on this ancient practice of the Church. Although his reasoning may be flawed, these discussions suggest that the tradition is more than a pious sacrifice or a pragmatic strategy to allow the priest to concentrate more fully on his ministry. Andrew's intuitive sense that it is somehow connected to Christ's Resurrection may not be entirely off the mark.

The arguments for married priesthood that have been common since Vatican II and been given new force by the sexual scandals in the Church have engendered much analysis of this ancient discipline. Some views— that it was primarily based on the Church's desire to keep ecclesiastical property from being bequeathed to priests' legitimate offspring, or that it was a holdover from the ancient view, common in the ancient world, that sexual activity was incompatible with the sacred—are not without substance. Likewise, the pragmatic factor of greater availability for service and the witness of celibacy as a sacrificial offering for the sake of the gospel are also relevant. Yet one of the most powerful arguments for a celibate priesthood is that the priest is an icon, a sign of another dimension that does not contradict natural human good (which includes marriage and family) but which goes beyond them. If there is no life beyond the grave, then indeed it makes no sense to give up the great goods of marriage and family. Our faith in that transcendent dimension is, as St. Paul says, grounded in the Resurrection. So Andrew's intuitive sense that there is a link between celibacy and the Resurrection is not without substance.

Yet the tension and polarization in the post-Vatican II Church go far beyond priests' demeanor and preferred form of address or arguments about celibacy. They touch on the core beliefs of Catholicism. Even secular Henry knows that liberal theologians "don't believe in the empty tomb" (104). The finding of the skeleton under the Temple Mount serves as a fulcrum around which whirl the conflicting opinions in contemporary Catholicism. The clerics and theologians which come together to discuss this discovery and its implications are like a microcosm of the Church. As they discuss the situation, a kind of Bakhtinian dialogic play of voices ensues.[17]

Liberal theologians are represented in the novel by Father van der Velde, "the distinguished Dutch Dominican from the Ecole Biblique" (137), who is called to Jerusalem, along with Andrew and Cardinal Memel, the head of the Simonite order, to give his opinion on the archaeological find. Van der Velde speaks the idiom of contemporary liberal theology: "'We may look at the question of whether Jesus rose from the dead or not in a literal sense—and whether, in consequence, the skeleton discovered by Professor Dagan could be his—without doubting any article of the Nicene Creed'" (142).

> "The question we must consider, Your Eminence, is not 'Did Christ rise from the dead?' because it is an article of our faith that he did, but 'What do we mean when we say that Christ rose from the dead?,' or 'In what way did Christ rise from the dead?' Is it possible, we must ask ourselves, that Christ rose from the dead in a way that left his body itself on earth?" . . .
> "So the answer must be yes, because the Jesus of before the crucifixion did not disappear into thin air, whereas the risen Jesus did, and so, we must suppose, was physically real only in a spiritual sense and not in an actual, scientific sense that would exclude the existence of his mortal remains." (144)

Father van der Velde points out various facts about the gospels that weaken the case for a bodily resurrection. He believes that the disciples did find the tomb empty but offers the hypothesis that the Romans stole the body because they actually wanted to foster the new religion, thinking that it would be easier to govern the Jews if they followed a messiah who insisted that his kingdom was not of this world. Father van der Velde goes on to offer an alternate version of the New Testament account of the time after the finding of the empty tomb. Perhaps Peter was released from prison—not by an angel—but by the Roman authorities.

> "Is it not even possible that the sudden change which came over the apostles at Pentecost, when they no longer cowered afraid in an upper room, but came to speak openly of Christ in the market place, came about not just because of the descent of the Holy Spirit but because of assurances by the Roman authorities that Christian preachers would be protected? Is it not even conceivable that the hearing of the apostles by many men of different nationalities—each in his own tongue—came not as a result of a miracle, but because the Romans themselves provided interpreters to spread the message of Our Lord Jesus Christ?" (147)

This is the gospel according to van der Velde. He insists, though, that this reconstruction of the traditional story is not simply his own creation, "'but the conclusion reached by several theologians and exegetes, and it was evolved some time before the discovery of the Vilnius

Codex'" (149). Although he appears to believe that such an understanding of the New Testament events is perfectly compatible with Christianity, he points out that he and his colleagues have not dared to make their theory known in public since it would cost them their jobs in Catholic universities. He employs one of the favored poses of liberal theologians: the victim of the Inquisition.

Cardinal Memel, the head of the Simonite order, is a career churchman—prudent, cautious, and intent on preserving the good name of the Church. According to the Cardinal's secretary, Father Pierre, he is "'quite convinced that the Holy Spirit has already chosen him as the next Pope, and he seems to think that the best way to ensure this destiny is to run for the post as one would for the Presidency of the United States'" (125).

Father Pierre is cautious in a different way. He is skeptical about the claim that the discovered skeleton is that of Jesus and is wary of getting caught up in the enthusiasm of the moment and making an impulsive judgment. He repeatedly points out how the hypothesis being put forth fails to take account of other facts or more plausible explanations. He has a no-nonsense, cynical attitude and is not afraid to make impolitic statements, such as "'I mistrust the Jews. . . . They have always been the enemy of Christianity'" (140). The others are horrified by Father Pierre's statement and defend the Jews by pointing out the sensitivity they have shown about the Christian holy places. "'Of course,' said Father Pierre. 'Pilgrimages are a source of foreign currency. But even here they try to denigrate our faith by turning the Holy Land into a Disneyland'" (140). Father Pierre is the only member of the group who is not prepared to give credence to the claim that the skeleton is the bones of Jesus.

Prior Manfred, the German prior of the Simonite monastery in Jerusalem, where these churchmen have gathered to ponder the implications of the discovery, is motivated primarily by piety and, to a certain extent, by fear. He speculates that perhaps this discovery is sent to test their faith, suggesting that "'perhaps, if these are the bones of Christ, then they are uncovered to test us further, to see if our faith in Christ can survive despite the evidence that there was no bodily resurrection'" (141). When he points out that many Scripture scholars doubt the bodily resurrection and yet have not lost their faith, there is "an almost crazed look in his eyes as he spoke. It was quite evident to Andrew that . . . he was closer to a crisis than any of the others" (142).

Andrew takes a minor role in this discussion, serving as the lens through which the reader observes the proceedings. As the character that is best known to the reader, his feelings, concerns, and fears are present as a backdrop. At this point Andrew's own religious beliefs are in turmoil, and he doesn't quite know what he believes. In this respect, he may represent the state of mind of the reader after hearing all of these arguments.

Read's sympathies clearly lie with the more traditional and orthodox view represented by Father Lambert and Father Pierre. Yet his incorporation of stimulating and provocative new versions of the foundational story in the Christian gospel keeps this section of the novel lively and prevents the narrative bias from becoming too heavy-handed. Here again Read shows his ability to articulate arguments against the grain of the authorial perspective. Unfortunately, however, the characters that give voice to these ideas are often so unattractive that one feels that the secular or liberal viewpoint is not given a fair hearing. The bitter, cynical, and selfish Henry is hardly representative of a humane and enlightened secularity. Still, the breadth of viewpoints that Read articulates is stimulating and engaging.

Read's ability to encompass and engage a variety of perspectives contributes to his success in creating interesting minor characters, such as Michal Dagan and his wife, Rachel. In terms of the plot, Michal Dagan is essential in that he is the archaeologist who oversees the excavation of the skeleton and is responsible for involving Father Lambert. Yet he is present in a relatively small portion of the novel. In Michal Dagan Read portrays a Jew of deep religious sensibility, struggling to maintain his fidelity to the teachings of the patriarchs and prophets at the same time that he recognizes that the security of the state of Israel may require compromises with that tradition. Rachel, a woman who has suffered much, is presented with sympathy and understanding.

Another merit of Read's fiction—though probably one of interest only to the Catholic reader—is his remarkable ability to capture subtle nuances of Catholic life that are frequently experienced but rarely articulated or even consciously recognized. Yet once they are pointed out, the Catholic reader thinks, "Yes, of course, that's just how it is!" An example is Read's description of Andrew's ambivalent attitudes about sexuality at the time he decides to leave the Simonite order. "His only knowledge came on the one hand vicariously from his brother's cynical adventures, and on the other from the blend of romanticism and sentimentality which so often affects the attitude of the clergy towards the love they have sacrificed to pursue their vocation" (196). Here Read articulates that curious kind of moral schizophrenia that has plagued so many Catholic youth, for whom their only models of lived sexuality are either the irresponsible, hedonistic embrace of sex in the secular world or the chastity of those who view sex either with hostility and fear or with a hopelessly romantic idealism. What they too rarely see modeled is faithful, responsible married sexuality that is positive, passionate, and joyous.

Piers Paul Read's *On the Third Day* is a multifaceted examination of the centrality within Christianity of the Resurrection of Jesus Christ—understood in a literal, physical sense—and not simply as metaphorical, symbolic, or spiritual. In giving voice to the various strands within Catholicism, and allowing them to confront and interact with another major religion and a very powerful and vigorous secular world, Read has produced an engaging and exciting tale. The novel provokes serious thought about what is at stake in a physical understanding of the Resurrection. Sometimes in making arguments for a nonliteral understanding of this doctrine, people will say, "Nobody is really interested in corpses." *On the Third Day* proposes that, on the contrary, people are *very* interested in whether one particular corpse—the dead body of Jesus—was raised to a new and glorious life, a life that was physical enough to include eating breakfast and whose wounded flesh could be felt by Thomas. This is not to deny that the meaning of the Resurrection includes many different forms of dying and rising to new life. Yet as Denise Levertov says in her poem "On Belief in the Physical Resurrection of Jesus," the power, the ground, and the roots of the symbol are in "bone and blood."[18]

NOTES

1. Read is perhaps trying to make the same point for orthodoxy—the fullness of Christian doctrine—that Simone Weil is making for moral goodness when she says, "Imaginary evil is romantic and varied, full of charm, while imaginary good is tiresome and flat. Real evil, however, is dreary, monotonous, barren. But real good is always new, marvelous, intoxicating." (Quoted in Edward T. Oakes, "Stanley Fish's Milton," *First Things*, Nov. 2001, 23). Correct belief and moral behavior may both seem in the popular imagination to be restrictive and stifling, whereas, in fact, they are expansive and liberating, though not easy. In fact, they require great courage. Thus he also echoes G. K. Chesterton's contention that "There never was anything so perilous or so exciting as orthodoxy" (*Orthodoxy*, 107).

2. Roger Haight, S.J., *Jesus, Symbol of God*, n.p. (Maryknoll, N.Y.: Orbis, 1999), quoted in Edward T. Oakes, S.J., "Reconciling Judas: Evangelizing the Theologians," *Crisis*, Oct. 2004, 33.

3. Piers Paul Read, *On the Third Day* (London: Secker & Warburg, 1979), 14–15. Hereafter cited in the text by page number.

4. As Professor Dagan says, they are entering "holy ground" (127). The Jews therefore are wearing yarmulkes, and they provide paper skull caps for the gentiles.

5. The nonbeliever may not see what Bonhoffer called "the cost of discipleship," or he may be observing Christians who have adopted a very comfortable kind of Christianity that takes no account of the rigorous demands of the gospel.

6. After their first night together, Andrew tells Anna that he considers themselves married (191).

7. Before Vatican II, Catholic churches were easily distinguished from Protestant ones by the abundance of religious art. Ironically, since the revovation of Catholic churches to make them plainer (see chapter 1, "The Theory of the Catholic Novel," endnote 88), some Protestant churches, especially Anglican and

Lutheran, are now using more religious art. Hence, this traditional difference between the two traditions is now more muted than formerly.

8. An interesting corollary to this scene is provided in an autobiographical article by Read himself, who indicates that he finds psychological explanations perfectly valid in explaining why a person has the kind of faith he does. Speaking of his own faith, he says "just as my mother's tyrannical nature has always made it difficult for me to form a mental image of the Virgin Mary, so the presence of a just and loving father made it easy for me to believe in God." He adds, however, "to explain my faith in this way is not, I suggest, to explain it away." Piers Paul Read, "A Confession," *Crisis*, Sept. 1995, 15.

9. Read here employs the motif of sacrificial substitution, where a person makes a bargain with God, offering his suffering or even his life in return for the good of another person. One of the best known is Sarah in Graham Greene's *The End of the Affair*, who offers to give up her lover Bendrix if God will let him live. Thomas Woodman says, "The way that individual human suffering can be caught up into Christ's and thus both be redeemed and—in a sense—itself be made redemptive has been a very distinctive doctrinal and devotional bias of Roman Catholicism as opposed to Protestantism." Woodman, *Faithful Fictions*, 133.

10. The earliest document regarding clerical celibacy is from the Council of Elvira (300–310). It reminded married clergy that they were bound by a vow of perpetual continence.

11. The argument for a married priesthood refers primarily—if not exclusively—to diocesan (also known as secular) priests, who serve in parishes. For members of religious orders, who live in community, a married priesthood would obviously be impracticable.

12. The argument that a priest could not be totally devoted to his ministry if he had a wife and family seemed obviously contradicted by the many examples of fine Protestant married clergy who seemed able to combine a vibrant pastoral ministry with marriage and family life.

13. In this respect, Father Lambert's thinking is in harmony with much of the recent argument for the all-male priesthood, i.e., that a priest is an icon of Jesus Christ, who was a male, that his bride is the Church, and that a female priest would violate this important imagery.

14. This fact became painfully obvious during the sexual scandals in the American Catholic Church in 2002. A careful reading of Church history, however, reveals that a failure to live up to the vow of chastity is not peculiar to the late twentieth century. Indeed, during the medieval and Renaissance periods it was not unusual for priests to have concubines and bastard children. The great Catholic humanist Erasmus was the son of a priest.

15. See endnote 8. Psychologist Paul Vitz turns Henry's thesis on its head in his book *Faith of the Fatherless*. He challenges the widespread assumption "throughout much of our intellectual community, that belief in God is based on all kinds of irrational, immature needs and wishes, whereas atheism or skepticism flows from a rational, grown-up, no-nonsense view of things as they really are." He proposes, "atheism of the strong or intense type is to a substantial degree generated by the peculiar psychological needs of its advocates." Vitz also claims "there is no systematic empirical evidence to support the thesis of childhood projection being the

basis of belief in God. Indeed, the assumption that religious belief is neurotic and psychologically counterproductive has been substantially rejected. Instead, there is now much research showing that a religious life is associated with greater physical health and psychological well-being." Paul Vitz, *Faith of the Fatherless* (Dallas: Spence, 1999), xiv, 3, 9.

16. Andrew's theory of substitutive salvation is substantively different than the motif of sacrificial substitution which has been a frequent motif in Catholic novels and which is exemplified by Henry's offer to adopt the faith if Andrew can be freed to marry Anna. The sacrifice is to benefit one who is living. Although Catholics do believe that prayers for the dead can help those who are in Purgatory, Andrew seems to believe that he can overturn the condemnation of one who may be damned—a highly unorthodox idea.

17. See chapter 3 "The English Catholic Novel Today," endnote 78.

18. Denise Levertov, "On Belief in the Physical Resurrection of Jesus," in *The Sands of the Well* (New York: New Directions, 1996), 115–16.

16

Conclusion: A Future for the English Catholic Novel?

The difference between a believer and a non-believer is not that the believer has one more item in his mind, in his universe. It is that the believer is convinced that reality is to be trusted, that in spite of appearances the world is very good.

—Eamon Duffy, *Faith of Our Fathers*

The Christian, together with everyone who has genuine hope, fights his way through the meaninglessness of the world. He establishes cells and islands of conspiracy, networks of hope in the kingdom of the dark lord of the world.

—Hans Urs von Balthasar, *You Crown the Year with Your Goodness*

Is there a future for the English Catholic novel? We have seen that several critics have argued that the Catholic novel reached its zenith in the golden age of the 1930s, 1940s and 1950s and after Vatican II went into a long decline. Since these analyses were made more than two decades ago, perhaps by now these critics would pronounce the Catholic novel—not dying or in decline—but dead.[1]

Should there be a future for the Catholic novel? Some people might say "Good riddance," seeing the classic Catholic novels as too parochial and provincial, reminiscent of a Church they would rather forget.[2] Even readers who are open to fiction with religious themes may prefer that the emphasis be on Christianity rather than on Catholicism. The denominational mentality is embarrassing now, even to many Catholics.[3] Gregory Wolfe, the founder and publisher of *Image*, a journal of the arts and religion, says that earlier Catholic writers made what he calls a "grand gesture" in response to "drastic secularization," whereas now it seems more suitable

351

for writers who wish to incorporate their faith into their writing to make a "quiet gesture."[4] Others have spoken of the "shouts" of earlier writers (with reference on Flannery O'Connor's assertion that "for the hard of hearing you shout") compared to the "whispers" of the current ones.[5]

Despite the predictions of the death of the Catholic novel and of the distinctively Catholic culture, which gave it birth, many people hope it will survive. Noting that Catholicism places more importance on free will than does Lutheranism or Calvinism, Thomas Woodman argues that "Catholic novelists have not only been found to write with great moral subtlety but have sometimes quite clearly privileged character as the centre of the novel in the most traditional fashion."[6] That fact may explain the popularity of Catholic novels with non-Catholic and even secular readers: they provide an experience somewhat akin to reading those weighty Victorian novels, fraught with moral seriousness and ethical concern, in which human acts had momentous import in a meaningful universe. Bernanos, Mauriac, Greene, Waugh, and Spark were not catapulted into literary prominence *only* by Catholic readers.

For Catholics, however, the survival and flourishing of Catholic novels is even more consequential than for secular readers, who see them simply as a species of enjoyable fiction. Like everyone, Catholics enjoy reading about their own experience. When Sara Maitland published *Brittle Joys*, one reviewer commented "'this is not a novel for atheists.'"[7] The implication is that people do not like to read novels about anything that is not part of their own experience—which raises questions about why white people like *Beloved,* or gentiles like *My Name is Asher Lev.* Maitland says that she wanted to ask the reviewer, "And what do you think we theists have been reading for the last 200 years? We have had to consume an unmitigated diet of post-Enlightenment bourgeois humanism, if we wish to read novels at all."[8] It is only natural for Catholic readers to enjoy spending time in a fictional space with Catholic furniture.

Yet, Catholic fiction *is* more problematic than *Beloved* or *My Name is Asher Lev* because people do not mind stepping beyond the bounds of their own experience to read about slavery or Hasidic Jewish life. On the contrary, most readers delight in stretching their awareness to include other lives in other milieus, finding them colorful, quaint, intriguing, charming, stimulating, or provocative. The Catholic novel, however, makes other demands, invoking a supernatural dimension that, for the secular reader, simply does *not* exist; or conveying a sense of urgency and an imperative tone that is perceived as making a moral claim on the reader, thus eliciting charges of evangelism or sugar coated apologetics. One might argue that the popularity of magical realism shows that secular readers are not averse to the presence of the supernatural in fiction; but these forays into the metaphysical realm are more acceptable because there is a sense that magical realism is a "game," that the author does not *really* believe that these things happened, and that he or she certainly does not invoke them as credible, authoritative signs of a transcendent order which claims one's allegiance and makes moral demands. Furthermore, a Catholic author who has a public presence as a Catholic, who writes and speaks on Catholic matters—as Sara Maitland, Alice Thomas Ellis, and Piers Paul Read have done—is more likely to be suspect by secular reviewers and readers.

Catholics hope for a future for the Catholic novel, not only because it reflects their own experience, but because it helps them understand their faith better. Bernard Bergonzi in his essay "The Decline and Fall of the Catholic Novel" says that in *How Far Can You Go?* Lodge "moved down from those dangerous peaks and rarefied air [the world picture of the old Catholic novels] to the flat, populous plain where most of us live our daily lives. If we are Catholics we shall discover in this excellent novel what we were and what we have become, and non-Catholics should find the discovery interesting too."[9] Although the Catholic life that Lodge depicts in *How Far Can You Go?* is certainly more familiar to the average Catholic than the Catholicism of the aristocratic Lady Marchmain of *Brideshead Revisited* or the whiskey priest in *The Power and the Glory,* one could argue that those novels, as well as those about Mauriac's Jansenists and Bernanos's humble curé who converses with the devil, have enabled Catholics to stretch their Catholicism beyond their own parochial or catechetical boundaries. It gives them more a of a sense of the universalism at the heart of Catholicism. The loss of such novels would impoverish Catholic life.

It is somewhat disconcerting to suggest a utilitarian reason for the production of future Catholic novels. Yet the fact remains that they nourish Catholics in a way nothing else does. American Catholic novelist Ron Hansen puts it this way:

> In the finest of our fictions, whether it be Willa Cather's *Death Comes for the Archbishop*[10] or Walker Percy's *the Moviegoer,* we have a sense of humanity functioning as it generally does, but at a higher and inspired level where harmonies are revealed, order is discovered, the questions that lie hidden in our hearts are given their just due. We think, if we are Christians, that this is what it is to live fully in the presence of grace. We glimpse, if only through a glass darkly, the present and still-to-come kingdom of God.[11]

The fact that some of the strongest statements about the decline of the Catholic novel come from nonbelievers who are also highly critical of its flaws (criticism that is as valuable as it is perceptive) raises again the question of whether the Catholic novel is a literary genre that can be fully appreciated only by another Catholic, ideally one who embraces and practices the faith in its fullness. Sonnenfeld admits, "My elegiac preface is not a song of lamentation, for I am neither a reactionary and romantic would-be aristocrat nor a believer."[12] Richard Gilman, writing in the *New York Times Book Review* in 1984, does not so much say that Catholic novels are in decline as say that the world has moved on and they are no longer meaningful. They now appear to him to be marred by "contrivances, flaws, arbitrary endings, rhetorical interventions, and the attempts by the author to play God." Gilman admits that his "own drift to unbelief" is a factor in his judgment, but argues that there has been a "seismatic shift" in society, and it is no longer part of our culture "to believe that the drama of sin, damnation, and salvation lies at the heart of the human condition."[13]

The seismic shift that Gilman noted in 1984 is even more pronounced twenty years later. In 1968 more than 75 percent of Britons said they believed in God. In 2004, only 44 percent said they did. Church attendance fell from 12 percent in 1979 to 7.5% in 2000.[14] Cardinal Cormac Murphy O'Connor of London is quoted as saying that Christianity has been "almost vanquished" in Britain.[15] Piers Paul Read in an interview given in 1999 said, "To judge from my children and some of their friends, the problem today is not atheism but people not being interested in religious questions at all, a lack of curiosity about whether there is any religious truth. This is partly because of a kind of consensus of humane values which seem to them an entirely sufficient moral system, without the need to bring God into the equation."[16] What Catholics have been facing in recent decades is not so much the kind of anti-Catholicism faced by Bernanos, Mauriac, Waugh, and Greene, but rather *indifference* to religion in general and Christianity in particular.[17]

The four contemporary novelists we have been considering exemplify how the current state of affairs has impacted the Catholic novel. Their fiction is directed at a very different readership than that of Mauriac, Bernanos, Waugh, and Greene. In his book on the Catholic novel, Donat O'Donnell speaks of the "still and gnawing despair" in France after World War I.[18] To the Europeans who were traumatized by the war, the depression, and the rise of the fascist dictatorships, the Catholic novels of this period, even with their emphasis on sin and shades of Jansenism, offered a vision of a rich interior spiritual life, which readers found a compelling alternative to the death, destruction, and despair around them. For many Europeans, however, World War II did not spawn the same kind of despair. The existentialism of John-Paul Sartre and the theater of the absurd did have a certain vogue among intellectuals in the 1950s; but as the century wore on, ordinary people were more interested in the benefits offered by the post-war welfare states, and growing prosperity even kept fears of Communism at bay.

The sense of ultimacy and of impending doom in earlier Catholic novels is missing from the recent ones. Although the fiction of Ellis, Lodge, Maitland, and Read treats serious themes and is clear about the reality of evil, there is an awareness that it is addressing readers for whom, on the whole, life is quite good and who, rather than being passionately for or against religion, are largely indifferent to it. Considering how the earlier Catholic novelists defined themselves in opposition—to secularism, to industrialism, to modernity itself—these writers seem quite comfortable within their larger social unit and relatively uninterested in political systems. They do not hate modernity as such, nor do they seem to have the contempt for the middle class that some of the earlier writers evinced.

Similarly, these Catholic novelists are not so hard on their own Catholic community. Whereas Bernanos, Mauriac, and Greene castigated middle class, "pious" Catholics for their materialism and smug self-righteousness, these novelists have empathy with ordinary Catholics and appreciate their struggles. Their scorn is much more likely to be directed at the clergy and hierarchy for unrealistic and inhumane sexual teaching (Lodge), ridiculous "reforms" in the liturgy and Church discipline (Ellis), patriarchy and inadequate appreciation of the feminine (Maitland), and the failure to promote a vigorous and coherent orthodoxy (Read).

To some extent, these attitudes reflect the fact that there has been a seismic shift in Catholicism as well as in the larger society. Reflecting the ecumenism and the greater openness to the secular world of the post-Vatican II Church, recent Catholic fiction does not depict such a sharp demarcation between the supernatural world and the secular world. The novels are not as strongly focused on sin and salvation as the earlier ones, reflecting the tendency of post-Vatican II catechesis and homiletics to concentrate more on social justice and human flourishing and less on sin and the possibility of damnation.[19] Nor do these novels put as much stress on conversion in the traditional sense. Many of the classic Catholic novels depicted the move from nonbelief to faith (*The Viper's Tangle, Brideshead Revisited, The End of the Affair*).[20] Although David Lodge's first novel, *The Picturegoers*, was about a skeptic who converts to Catholicism, his subsequent fiction does not evince much interest in conversion. In fact, he seems more interested in the loss of faith or in the permutations of faith as it moves through periods of skepticism to a more tentative or ambivalent form of faith. Neither, I suggest, are Maitland and Ellis much interested in a clear-cut movement from nonbelief to faith. Like Lodge, they are more inclined to describe the ongoing conversion and re-conversion that is necessary for living the Christian life and in the tensions, problems, doubts, consolation that are part of being Catholic at the end of the twentieth century. Read shows more interest in conversion than the others, but in none of these writers does conversion to Catholicism have the prominence that it had in the classic Catholic novels.

The question of the future of the Catholic novel is inextricably entwined with the condition of the Catholic Church. In an essay published in 1980 David Lodge acknowledged this connection between the state of the Church and artistic production:

> The fact is that contemporary Catholicism no longer constitutes the kind of unified, sharply defined challenge to secular or Protestant values that it once did, and thus no longer provides an organizing principle or rallying-point for intellectual and artistic programmes. It is, I believe, a much more decent, humane, open-minded Christian community than it once was, but it is also rather blander, duller, and more amorphous.[21]

Bernard Bergonzi agrees. "The collapse of the Catholic world-picture lifted a great load of anxiety, but it seems to have left behind a shrunken world, where Catholics share most of the assumptions of a secular, hedonistic society, and religion seldom appears as a mode of transcendence or transformation."[22] Dull it may be, but Lodge finds a more pluralistic secular world a more comfortable place to live and work. "I would rather work in a pluralist secular state than in one in which the Church played a dominant or militant cultural role."[23] In this view what we have is a Catholicism that is easier to live with but that may not be conducive to great Catholic novels.

In a 1995 interview, Lodge addressed the additional problem that whereas the older Catholic novels could reach a readership around the world because, despite regional differences, the Church had a strong core of universal identity, now the situation is quite different:

> Now [the Church is] very pluralistic, very split and divided within itself, culturally very diverse. Catholicism in one country or on one continent is very different from Catholicism somewhere else. I think those differences and divisions were concealed before by the very powerful and centralized control of the Vatican. . . . So I would expect that there wouldn't be any identifiable Catholic novel that would be saying the same things in different countries, but rather that the fragmentation of the Church would be reflected in a wide variety of novels.[24]

Church historians have suggested that the transformations that have altered and, to some extent, traumatized the Catholic Church in the post-Vatican II period have been the most profound since the Reformation. The sociological data that points to lower levels of belief and practice among contemporary Catholics raises questions about what English Catholicism will look like in the future. Will it be, as Lodge suggests, so distinct as to seem foreign to Catholics from other countries or continents? Will the universality that it claims be all but invisible? These questions are important because Catholic novelists, more than most other Christian writers, bring a denominational mentality to their work.[25]

In a recent essay "The Catholic Novelist in a Secular Society," Piers Paul Read says, "The question for the future is therefore this. Will the Catholic novelist in the next millennium increasingly dissociate his faith from his work?"[26] To some extent that will depend on the extent to which the novelist is willing to alienate some critics and limit his audience. Read reports that an American critic said of him, "The Catholicism that provides Read's fiction with its moral center could prove to be the artist's liability, narrowing the subjects or circle of readers he can touch."[27] Even more important, however, will be the state of the Church.

Most social indicators point to a smaller Church in the future, yet one in which the members are more committed to their faith than in the past when so many people were Catholic simply because of ethnic or family heritage or because of social pressure. As David Lodge said to me when I asked him what he thought about Catholicism in Europe, "Well, it seems to be dying, doesn't it? But on the other hand, those that are there really want to be there."[28] Commenting on recent developments in the English Church, sociologist Michael Hornsby-Smith, writes, "From being an ascribed collective cultural identity, Catholicism became much more an achieved and voluntary individual identity and it had to compete with all the other leisure time pursuits on offer in the booming consumer-oriented culture at the end of the century."[29] Even Pope Benedict XVI subscribes to the view that this trend represents the direction of the Church in the coming decades. In *Salt of the Earth* he writes, "The Church . . . will assume different forms. She will be less identified with the great societies, more a minority Church; she will live in small vital circles of really convinced believers who live their faith. But precisely in this way she will, biblically speaking, become the salt of the earth again."[30]

What will be the nature of this Church? The post-Vatican II Church (at least in western Europe and America) is quite polarized, although perhaps more so in the United States than in Europe. There are conservatives, whom liberals refer to as reactionary restorationists who want to undo the reforms of Vatican II, and there are liberals, whom conservatives deride as "cafeteria Catholics" who are unfaithful to the Magisterium and want to turn Catholicism into another branch of liberal Protestantism.[31] Will the future Church continue to be so polarized, or will it evolve intermediate position that combines the best of both positions? Two recent books by American Catholics argue that the Church must go strongly in one direction if it is to flourish, be faithful, and reverse some of the losses of the post-Vatican II years. In 2003 Peter Steinfels, a former senior religion correspondent for *The New York Times* published *A People Adrift: The Crisis of the Roman Catholic Church in America.*[32] In the same year, sociologist David Carlin published *The Decline and Fall of the Catholic Church in America.*[33] Although these two books specifically focus on the American Church, their analyses and predictions apply to England as well as to the United States.[34]

Steinfels claims that American Catholicism "is on the verge of either an irreversible decline or a thoroughgoing transformation."[35] Carlin predicts that unless the Church "reverses its process of liberalization, it will . . . decline even more, finally falling into irrelevancy."[36] Steinfels, however, believes that the demoralization, dissent, confusion, low level of practice, diminishing number of priests and religious, and loss of so many of the young are due to the retention of a hierarchical model of authoritarian leadership and the failure of the Church to fully implement the reforms envisaged by Vatican II. In particular, he points to the failure to fully empower the laity, the refusal to ordain married men and women, and the stubborn adherence to outmoded and unpersuasive teachings on contraception, homosexuality, and divorce. Steinfels believes that such positions are untenable and liberalization almost inevitable. "Maintaining these defenses always consumes tremendous amounts of spiritual energy, intellectual credibility, and institutional authority, inevitably diverted from engaging rather than staving off new ideas and historical shifts. And yet these defenses prove to be brittle and inflexible bulwarks that eventually collapse before the pressures of change or are outflanked by them."[37] Steinfels argues that if these changes do not come to pass, Catholic life will decline, Catholics' worship and reception of the sacraments will become even more irregular, and their faith will be superficial and increasingly marginalized. He does not rule out the possibility that the American Church could implode, as has happened in Ireland and French Canada.

If Steinfels's hopes are born out and the liberal agenda is enacted, Catholic novels would most likely be more Christian than recognizably Catholic, thus making them less "different," as Peter Hebblethwaite hoped in 1967. We would probably see more "whispers" than "shouts," and the Catholic novel would become subsumed under the Christian novel, one that conveys the "centre of coherence" that Hebblethwaite preferred to a denominational mentality.[38] Liberal Catholicism wishes to move the Church into closer conformity with secular ideals and contemporary standards and, in line with the Common Ground project of the late Cardinal Bernardin, to stress the beliefs we have in common with non-Catholic Christians. The election of Joseph Ratzinger as Pope Benedict XVI has disappointed liberals who hoped for a more progressive pope to succeed John Paul II (although given his age, his reign is not likely to be a long one). This situation may result in Catholic fiction critical of the Vatican and the hierarchy, detailing the suffering caused by what liberals perceive as outmoded and untenable policies.

David Carlin, however, contends that the current crisis in the Church is caused by a failure of fidelity, the influence of dissenting theologians, irresponsible liturgical experimentation, a disastrous "dumbing down" of catechetics, and a naive accommodation with certain aspects of the secular culture, such as the sexual revolution, New Age spirituality, and the therapeutic mentality. Like Pope Benedict XVI, he thinks the future Church will be smaller, a "saving remnant."[39]

Carlin also believes that traditionalists will outnumber liberals in the future because they are far more likely than liberals to believe that the Catholic Church is the true church of Christ and to persevere even when disappointed in the current state of the Church. Liberals, on the other hand, are more inclined to see Catholicism as only one expression of Christianity are therefore more likely to leave it if things don't improve. He also argues that liberals are less likely than conservatives to successfully pass on the faith to the younger generation. Although liberals who grew up before Vatican II may retain their adherence to Catholicism,

> their children and grandchildren have received a very different kind of education in Catholicism, a more liberal education. For them, the Church is an instrument, a means to an end. The Church can help the individual to live in hope and charity, and it can help bring justice to the world. . . . But if the Church . . . proves to be ineffective at promoting these many good things, then it is a defective instrument, and it can be discarded.[40]

Carlin believes that the future Church, as well as being primarily committed to traditional Catholic orthodoxy, could take either of two forms. It might return to "a new Catholic quasi-ghetto. But unlike the old Catholic ghetto—which was optimistic, building up its strength, . . . this new ghetto will be pessimistic, carrying a memory of failure."[41] This scenario sounds almost as grim as the situation faced by Bernanos and Mauriac, who did not see much genuine or vigorous Catholicism in "Catholic" France. On the other hand, the saving remnant might not be weak and pessimistic, but vigorous, energetic, and hopeful. In order for this to happen, the Church will need to strongly resist the idea that Catholicism is simply one sect among many, that all religions are simply different paths to the same truth.[42] Carlin argues that the Church must emphasize that which is distinctive in the Catholic tradition, such as the doctrine of the Real Presence, Marian devotion, the communion of saints, and the practice of private confession.

Carlin also contends that the Church must recognize that it is confronting a serious enemy. The Church has always had enemies: polytheists,

Docetists, Gnostics, Pelagians, Albigensians, Muslims, Protestants, and Communists. It is a psychological truism that having a common enemy crystallizes a sense of identity and galvanizes loyalty. In this ecumenical age and since the fall of Communism, the Church is less focused on a particular enemy, and instead concentrates on the enemies we share with all people of good will—poverty, hunger, ignorance, and discrimination. While this solidarity with others is welcome, the Church may be failing to fully recognize the danger and power of its current enemy, secularism.[43] By *secularism* Carlin does not mean simply a significant number of non-Christians, but rather an aggressive anti-Christianity that is vigorously promoting "a moral and political agenda that is flatly incompatible with Christianity."[44] Although liberals also denounce the pernicious elements of our secular society, Carlin argues that only a vigorous orthodoxy can withstand such an enemy. "By increasingly incorporating secularist beliefs and values while retaining the music and poetry of religion, liberal Christianity progressively empties itself of all genuine Christian content, until finally it becomes nothing but an empty shell and collapses upon itself."[45]

If the Church's future is that described by Carlin and Pope Benedict the XVI, we are likely to see more distinctively Catholic novels. Thomas Woodman hopes that specifically Catholic insights will not be "dissolved in a bland ecumenical consensus that offers no real Christian challenge to the status quo."[46] A smaller remnant Church that nourishes a vibrant orthodoxy and gives loving attention to those aspects of the faith that are distinctly Catholic would forestall the development of that "bland ecumenical consensus" that Woodman fears. It would also retrieve some of the factors that lent drama and power to earlier Catholic novels but are attenuated in today's Catholicism. If part of the vitality of the Catholic novel resulted from Catholics' sense of apartness, as Lodge and Bergonzi argue, or their being "in opposition" to the surrounding culture, as Kellogg maintains, and from the sense of the Church as unchanging (at least in essentials), something approaching that situation may exist in the future. The sense of salvation and damnation as truly momentous questions may once again exist in a small group of people with a strong Catholic faith. The situation will hearken back to the time when Catholics were an even smaller minority in England than they are now, evoking that aura of the exotic that has always been part of the appeal of Catholicism in England. Perhaps their minority status and the fact that being a serious Catholic in England has always been more rare in England than in the United States accounts for the flourishing of the Catholic novel in that country. In addition to the major figures mentioned in this study, the past eighty years have seen high-quality Catholic novels by Maurice Baring, A. J. Cronin, Compton Mackenzie, Antonia White, J. R. R. Tolkien, John Braine, Rumer Godden, and Anne Redmon.

Another reason that the prospect of a smaller but resolutely orthodox Church seems to hold out more promise for distinctively Catholic novels with the kind of power and drama that characterized earlier Catholic fiction is that conservatives seem more attentive to the supernatural mysteries of the creed, whereas liberals are more concerned with social justice and with Church governance and oppressive authority.[47] Conservatives are more likely to give robust assent to the ongoing occurrence of miracles, the intercession of the saints, and the power of intercessory prayer. They have also retained a stronger sense of personal sin, the need for repentance, confession to a priest, and a vivid belief in an afterlife—including hell. Also, conservatives' attachment to traditional devotions like the rosary, the Stations of the Cross, novenas, and exposition of the Blessed Sacrament increases the likelihood of fiction informed and enriched by the imagery and symbolism of these traditional devotional practices.[48] All of these factors point to the prospect of novels with a richer Catholic texture.[49] Such novels may not convince nonbelievers of supernatural realities, anymore than did those of Mauriac, Bernanos, Waugh, and Greene, but they may tap into some of the power that animated those earlier books.

Yet no matter what the shape of the future Church—large or small, conservative or liberal—the most crucial factor for the future of Catholic fiction is belief. I agree with Scott Appleby, noted scholar of American Catholicism, who says that the ideological issues of the past fifty years will not be the defining feature of the Church in the near future. "Rather, the Church will be engaged by a far more profound and disturbing crisis of belief and meaning. In light of the extent and depth of this crisis, the attention given to 'Catholic culture wars' will come to be seen as an unaffordable luxury."[50] The pervasive atheism and nihilism that dominates so much of academic and intellectual life, which is disseminated through the media and popular culture, together with the growing confrontation with Islam and other religions in our increasingly multicultural world, will deepen this crisis and bring it to a point. If the ecumenism of the last fifty years has caused Catholics to see the good in other religions, the next fifty will require them to see and reaffirm the good in their own. The great Catholic novels emerged from an intense and profound belief in the truth of the Faith, not just as an antidote to despair and meaninglessness, but also as initiation into a sacramental community and nourishment from a tradition of wisdom. The great Catholic novels emerged from an intense and profound belief in the truth of the Faith.

Andrew Greeley argues that the "enchanted world" of the Catholic imagination is nurtured by liturgy and ritual, religious art, and the stories of the saints—what he calls "the richest repertory of images and metaphors of any of the world religions."[51] I suspect, however, that this imagination is also sustained by a belief in the supernatural doctrines of the creed, the efficacy of the sacraments (understood as powerful in and of themselves, and not simply because of a charismatic minister or because of the aesthetics of the rite), and a system of clear and consistent moral teaching.[52] It is this intellectual dimension that keeps the liturgy, ritual, art, and stories from becoming merely superstition or quaint custom. Both the "enchanted world" of liturgy, ritual, sacred art, stories, and devotional practices, *and* a clearly defined and robustly promulgated moral theology and a strong belief in the supernatural elements of Christianity are necessary to nourish the Catholic imagination.

In any event, the novels of Ellis, Lodge, Maitland, and Read can help us to speculate on the characteristics of future Catholic fiction. The four Catholic novelists whose work we have been considering are clearly the inheritors of a tradition. We see in their work some of the techniques of their predecessors: the skeptical narrator (Winterman in *Monk Dawson*), the obnoxious Catholic (Bede Harrington in *Therapy*), sacrificial substitution (Henry in *Monk Dawson*), and the inclusion of the miraculous and mystical in the work of Ellis and Maitland. These hallmarks of the Catholic novel will almost certainly continue to reappear. Read has written the novel of ideas, a genre popular with earlier Catholic novelists. Also, just as Mauriac, Bernanos, and Greene wrote basically realistic fiction against the grain of stream of consciousness and other modernist techniques (and found a grateful audience for their works), so also do Ellis, Lodge, Maitland, and Read evince a preference for realism. David Lodge asserts, "I like realistic novels, and I tend to write realistic fiction myself."[53] Although that remark is from an early essay (1969), all of Lodge's novels have been basically realistic, although he does not entirely eschew experimentation. He explains in a later interview why most of his novels also include some sort of experimental technique, such as stepping into metafiction (fiction that proclaims its own fictionality, often becoming playful about the nature and methods of fiction) for a few pages to remind the reader that all this is a story and comment on his own fictional technique, or writing sections as part of a television script or series of postcards:

> I still "believe" that it is worthwhile creating that effect of recognition which the classic realist text can produce, that sense of fidelity to history and to social texture. I like to give that to my readers, but I don't any longer think that it is enough to do just that; it no longer satisfies me to do it throughout a book, so the metafictional apparatus of *How Far Can You Go?* questions the realist convention at the same time as the book is using that convention.[54]

These playful interpolations, however, do not detract from the basically realistic mode of the narrative.

Similarly, Sara Maitland and Alice Thomas Ellis work primarily in a realistic mode, but do not hesitate occasionally to tear open the illusion of realism to allow for visits from an angel or a nun levitating on the streets of London. Again, the word that seems apt here is *playful*, but the play is serious in a way that the play of magical realism is not, for it is the writers' way of speaking of subjects in which they profoundly believe. Some people have suggested using the term "spiritual realism" to refer to the work of religious writers who stretch the parameters of naturalistic realism to allow for the inclusion of what they see as the profoundly real operations of the Spirit. One might say that for typical writers of magical realism, the emphasis is on magic (in the sense of trick); whereas for christian writers, the emphasis is on *realism*.[55] This combination of a basically realistic style enriched by a playful or even somber stretching of the borders of observed reality in order to convey the spiritual or supernatural seems very congenial to the Catholic novel.

Of the four novelists we have been examining, Piers Paul Read hews most closely to realism. In fact, most of his novels convey an extremely strong sense of connection to the objective world. Read's ability to capture the ambience and details of ordinary life, to produce realistic dialogue for characters from hugely disparate backgrounds, together with his talent for embedding his fictions in milieus that are rich in historical and factual detail, give his novels a realistic texture that at times seems close to that blending of fact and fiction known as the nonfiction novel.

I suspect that future Catholic novelists will gravitate toward a greater use of realism than their contemporaries. Possibly the very fact that they are including a religious dimension in their fiction will suffice to mark their work as different or original without their having to resort to experimentalist techniques. Much experimental writing is called forth from the postmodern temper, which seems inhospitable to writing undergirded by Christian faith. Roger Lundin explains, "the postmodern self no longer harbors hopes of discovering truth or secure principles. Instead, driven by the ideals of therapy and consumption, it seeks, by whatever means will work, to provide satisfactions for the unencumbered self; it strives to reduce all individual moral actions to matters of choice for which there are no authoritative guidelines or binding principles."[56]

As with the preference for realism, future Catholic novels will probably be more likely than others to suggest closure. As Maitland acknowledges, the novel form leans toward closure, and the truly open ending may be impossible to achieve in the genre, especially when written by someone who believes there really are meaningful answers to ultimate questions. Read is the one of the four novelists who is most likely to favor closure in his endings. With Monk Dawson's becoming a Trappist monk, Stefan's realization that he does believe in God, and the discovery that the alleged disproof of Christ's Resurrection was actually a hoax, Read's fiction resembles the conclusions of earlier Catholic novels, where Lord Marchmain returns to the faith on his deathbed and a new priest comes to replace the martyred whiskey priest. Yet the more open endings of Lodge, Maitland, and Ellis are probably more typical of what we can expect in the future.

I suspect that Maitland's conviction that an open ending is more compatible with transcendence, mystery and "a big enough God," is not only more congruent with contemporary literary tastes, but also reflects the fact that, even for traditional Catholics, the struggles, upheavals, and scandals in Catholicism in the second half of the twentieth century have left them uncomfortable with endings that suggest definitive answers or the inevitable triumph of Catholic truth. There is a widespread distrust of easy answers or formulaic apologetics. In spite of their effectiveness as a teaching tool for children, the catechism questions and answers that instructed earlier generations of Catholics fail to convey the complexity, ambiguity, and mystery that are tangled together at the heart of Catholicism. Furthermore, they suggest a kind of glib certainty. All the questions *did* have answers. The assurance that there were easy answers ready at hand, may, in fact, have helped to form a readership more amenable to closed endings and the inevitable triumph of the faith.[57] Catholic readers of today and tomorrow, however, no matter how conservative their theology, are unlikely to favor closure that suggests a facile triumphalism.

They will certainly not have anything approaching the comfortable assurance that characterized a significant portion of earlier Catholic readers. As if the secular media's relentless reminders of anti-Semitism, the Crusades, the Inquisition, and the condemnation of Galileo were not enough, triumphalism will seem arrogant and silly in the wake of the chaos, liturgical mayhem, dissent, and sexual abuse scandals that marked the post-Vatican II Church. All readers—Catholic and non-Catholic—are likely to reject any Catholic fiction that does not carry within it a sense of humility.

Another characteristic of contemporary Catholic novels that will probably become even more prominent is the *rapprochement* with secularity. In his 1970 book *Christ and Prometheus* Jesuit William Lynch called for a new image of the secular in literature. "There is a long tradition of the religious writer who allocated all that was good to the sacred and nothing but the flat, the neutral and the nonhuman to the secular."[58] Criticism of the secular world is the birthright of the Catholic novel. The fiction of Barbey d'Aurevilly and (the later) Huysmans in France and Belloc and Benson in England saw little of value in the secular world without the redeeming grace of Catholic Christianity. Even Chesterton, whose jovial nature would not allow him to disparage the natural joys of eating and drinking, fellowship and family, was clear that these natural joys tended to become sour and perverse if not rightly ordered within an acknowledgement of God's sovereignty. Mauriac, Bernanos, Waugh, and Greene—and even some of the earlier writers—did not reserve *all* goodness to the sacred, yet a certain suspicion of and hostility to the secular *was* insinuated in their novels. The grimness, venality, and materialism in the France of Mauriac and Bernanos, the decay and death that pervade "Greeneland," and the brittle sterility of Waugh's satires may be as much a reflection of their authors' belief in original sin and a critique of the lifeless faith of nominal Catholics as it is censure of the secular world.[59] Nevertheless, the goodness of the secular world in those novels remains muted, sequestered, and understated.

This perspective annoys secular readers even when they are drawn to Catholic novels for other reasons. Some nonbelievers feel that the Catholic writer cannot see the secular fully or fairly. Is it possible for a person of faith, who believes that only through grace and faith in Christ can human life be lived in all its fullness, to see the secular without diminishing its goodness or minimizing its potential? Future Catholics will have to face the challenge of the secular. Even if the Church does become a much smaller Church of committed believers, Catholics certainly will not live in insular, enclosed communities like the Catholic ghettoes of the past. They will have to band together in a world in which such faith is increasingly countercultural, but the boundaries of their communities will be extremely porous. Contemporary life simply will not allow for the kind of sheltered existence provided by the old Catholic ghettoes. Nor would that kind of protected faith be desirable, even if it *were* possible. As Sara Maitland says, "The healthy Catholic self may well be the one who lets in the most from outside, who takes into themselves the influences, the presences of the Other and who feeds them back to the community."[60]

Such Catholics may be ideally situated for the kind of rapprochement with secularity that Lynch desires. He calls for "a new image of secularity whose first stage will be the acceptance of secularity . . . 'taking the secular risk.'"[61] Allowing the secular to be itself will actually invigorate the Christian imagination.

> But as further exploration leads to deeper knowledge of the complete identity of this world, its magnitude, dignity and horror (and the true dimensions of the task of redemption), the religious imagination will have to rediscover its own complete identity in order to deal with it. That will not be in order to impose itself and its forms as master, even as master of meaning, but to serve the world as servant in the tortuous search of the world for identity and salvation.[62]

Yet since the publication of Lynch's book in 1970, subsequent developments have led some people to see secularity through a less benign lens.

Archbishop John J. Myers apparently agrees with David Carlin when he says, "the particular form that secularism takes in America is in an undeclared war with our faith."[63] It should be noted that what Carlin and Archbishop Myers see as inimical to Catholicism is *secularism*, which refers to specifically anti-Christian elements in the secular world, whereas Lynch's term is *secularity*, a more neutral term indicating the natural order devoid of revelation and grace. *Secularism* would seem to call for a more combative attitude, but in the end it comes down to a matter of discrimination: the ability to sort out and repudiate the increasingly toxic elements in secular culture while at the same time fully recognizing and appreciating the natural goods the secular order.

As with the challenge of the open ending, achieving this kind of attitude toward the secular will always be difficult for a person who really *does* believe that the secular order simply does not have within itself satisfactory answers to the meaning of life and adequate resources for dealing with evil. Yet Lynch encourages religious writers to portray the secular *"without the perpetual concern that something is missing from the picture"* (emphasis in the original).[64] Sara Maitland and David Lodge demonstrate a remarkable ability to allow the goodness of the natural order to remain fully itself, at the same time that they have no illusion about its fallen nature, thus avoiding the myopic vision of the nineteenth century Transcendentalists. Alice Thomas Ellis and Piers Paul Read are more wary of the secular order. Yet even in their fiction there is a sense that grace builds on nature, that the natural goods of friendship, marriage, and children are the necessary foundation for recognizing the greater good of the order of grace.

I have suggested that a core of orthodox committed Catholics and a more positive attitude toward secularity may contribute to a more vibrant Catholic fiction. Is this combination really an oxymoron? Can a committed orthodox Catholic be truly open to the secular? Although disparaging the world has a long history in traditional Christian piety and rhetoric, Catholics need to realize that the compelling power and truth of the faith is not dependent on denigrating the secular. On the other hand, if rapprochement becomes conflation, if the attempt is made to merge the sacred and the secular, and the boundaries are not preserved, the sacred will be diminished and in danger of being engulfed by secularity. Only a vibrant and resolute faith, committed to its moral precepts, nourished with prayer and liturgy, confidently rooted in the fullness of its tradition, while fully aware of the failings of the human institution of the Church—only such a faith has the resources to allow the secular to be itself, to embrace its goodness while seeing it clearly. As Lynch says, "To live and breathe in the modern world is no task for a disarmed imagination."[65]

This more positive attitude toward secularity will most likely continue to characterize Catholic novels and will probably also be reflected in subject matter and themes, especially with regard to sex. Earlier Catholic novels almost always presented sex primarily as sin and an obstacle to holiness. In Greene and Waugh there was still a strong emphasis on sexual sin but with an acknowledgement that even sinful sex (Sarah's love for Bendrix in *The End of the Affair*, Charles's homosexual love of Sebastian in *Brideshead Revisited*) is a reflection of a divine love and can be an entrée into a relationship with God, although that sinful love must be given up in the new life of faith. What is new with these contemporary Catholic novelists is that they are more likely to imply that this love, although sinful in its inception, will be incorporated into the character's new life (Bernard's love for Yolande in *Paradise News* and Andrew's love for Anna in *On the Third Day*). These novelists are simply much more comfortable with sexuality, sensuality, and the whole physical realm, not seeing the physical in such stark contrast to the spiritual, but rather as a reflection of God's immanence in His creation. They can describe sex in terms of tenderness and joy, something almost unheard of in earlier Catholic novels.[66] Future Catholic novelists will almost certainly continue this trend to broaden the scope and increase the perspectives from which sexuality is described, including sympathetic portrayals of homosexuals and appreciative depictions of women's bodily experience. For some readers, the muting of a sense of sexual sin in Catholic novels is problematic. To some extent the formidable challenge of the Christian novelist is akin to that of all Christians: to love the sinner and hate the sin. The best Catholic novels have managed to do this. Of course, some readers still found them moralistic, but that is inevitable. As for the future, much will depend on whether the Church will recover a strong sense of sexual sin, cogently and robustly promulgated in homiletics and catechetics.

Steinfels points out that "the church has come to recognize marriage and sexuality as paths to holiness no less authentic, demanding, and rewarding than that of the ordained or vowed celibate—not just as a principle tucked away in theology texts, but in the religious instruction and culture of ordinary Catholics."[67] A novelist familiar with Pope John Paul II's theology of the body might take up the challenge of portraying a married sexuality that is—or at least trying to be—total, fruitful, faithful, and free, the characteristics John Paul II ascribes to sex lived according to God's plan. Such a sexual life might be good, but would it make a good novel? John Paul II is clear about the difficulty of trying to live this ideal. A novel could conceivably portray it as demanding and exciting—and more dramatic—than any adultery. Whether or not a portrayal of married love as an adventure would appeal to readers—even pious Catholics—is debatable. It is worth noting, however, that the novels of Henry James and Virginia Woolf contain little outward dramatic action but focus almost entirely on thoughts and conversations. Their novels are outstanding exemplars of the possibility of great fiction concerned with the inner life and the intricate nuances of human relationships with little exterior dramatic action. The adventure of Christian marriage—even without adultery—suggests intriguing possibilities for future Catholic novels.

Sara Maitland has demonstrated how women's bodily experience and religious experience (often intertwined) can function as the center of a rich fictional matrix with important religious themes. In addition to the obvious technique of describing women's lives with care and attention, she has effectively incorporated the hitherto marginalized stories of Biblical women. For Catholics, of course, Mary is the preeminent Biblical woman, and Maitland's epilogues featuring Mary in *Daughter of Jerusalem* not only serve to humanize Mary, but invest the fictional account of a contemporary woman's experience with greater depth and a connection to the transcendent. Some Catholics are uncomfortable with the long tradition in the Church of focusing almost exclusively on Mary's submissiveness and humility, feeling that it has acculturated Catholic women to an oppressive, patriarchal social order. Nor have the saccharine, sentimental portrayals of Mary in much religious art (especially bad devotional art, such as holy cards) endeared her to contemporary people who prize strength, initiative, and courage in a woman. Yet younger Catholics who have not been negatively affected by early presentations of Mary and some older Catholics who are open to a reevaluation of her are discovering in Mary that strength, initiative, and courage that they value. They may welcome her presence in future Catholic novels.

In any event, future Catholic fiction will undoubtedly draw more on women's religious experience—not simply to "even the score" because male characters dominate most of the classic Catholic novels—but because women's religious experience is often significantly different from men's. For Catholic women, the long tradition of an all-male priesthood and the privileging of celibacy as the spiritual ideal, together with the tendency to associate women with lust, the flesh, and the downward pull of matter, means that they often lived their faith in a distinctively different matrix than did Catholic men.

Another feature that is likely to be prominent in future Catholic fiction is the comic mode. There is still a lingering sense that the comic mode is not suitable for writing with a serious religious theme, yet any reader of Flannery O'Connor knows that is not true. The satires of Evelyn Waugh are often incorporated into his Catholic *oeuvre* as portrayals of the emptiness of a world without God. Yet the uses of the comic surely go beyond simply "clearing space" for the sacred. It was mentioned in the chapter on the theory of the Catholic novel how scholars and critics have pointed out the philosophical fit between Christianity and the comic. The shape of Christianity is descent followed by ascent. Original sin is referred to as a the *felix culpa* (happy fall) because it earned such a blessed Redeemer. Jesus was crucified but rose victorious. The last book of the Bible, Revelation, depicts the final victory over the forces of darkness. The greatest poem of the Middle Ages, Dante's account of a journey through hell, purgatory, and heaven, is called *Commedia*—not because of its ability to produce laughter, but because it ends in heaven and the protagonist's reassurance that he will ultimately be among the saved.[68]

Muriel Spark, David Lodge, and Alice Thomas Ellis have opened up exciting new possibilities for Catholic fiction that takes seriously the affinities between Catholicism and the comic mode. In an essay published in 1966 David Lodge remarked on the fact that in Graham Greene's later fiction, marked by irony and the comic mode, "the possibility of religious faith has all but retreated out of sight in the anarchic confusion of human behaviour."[69] Yet this essay was written before Greene's late *Monsignor Quixote*, which uses the comic mode and gentle irony to make a searching and thoughtful probing of the nature of faith. Lodge himself and Alice Thomas Ellis have demonstrated that the comic vision is not antithetical to religious concerns.[70]

One way in which the comic is appropriate to writing within a faith dimension is its ability to be subversive, especially in the form of satire. Because religion has often been aligned with the forces of economic and political power, it tends to be seen as inherently conservative and inimical to transformation or innovation. But such a view ignores the Jesus who challenged the conservative religious leaders of his day, upset the establishment, and talked about the folly of putting new wine in old wine skins. Comedy can be cleansing and reinvigorating for religion—especially institutional religion.

Many writers, including David Lodge, have been influenced by the ideas of the Russian theorist Mikhail Bakhtin, who sees the comic mode as always antiauthoritarian, satirizing hierarchies of power. Lodge says that comedy is "not just entertaining but performs a very valuable hygienic cultural function: it makes sure that institutions are always subject to a kind of ridiculing criticism."[71] To see the Church as always in need of reform (*semper reformanda*) is not disloyalty. Both liberals (Steinfels) and conservatives (Carlin) agree that the Church must transform itself if it is to survive. Satire will keep that reforming/transforming imperative sharp, distinct, and vigorous.

Comic novels can be especially appealing for those who feel that Greeley's "enchanted world" is not the whole story of Catholicism. The Catholic world does not seem so enchanted to someone whose adolescence was burdened by Jansenistic guilt over normal sexual desires, or who was berated in the confessional for having doubts about the faith, or who couldn't be a bridesmaid for her dear Methodist friend because Catholics were not allowed to take part in any Protestant services. The fact that these situations are not characteristic of today's Church matters little to those who bear emotional scars and seriously question whether an institution which once endorsed such policies can really claim to have divine authority. Good Catholic novels in the comic mode can help to expunge some of the hurt that still lingers for those who experienced the Church as harsh, punitive, misogynistic, or overly scrupulous and open the door to a more life-giving and joyful faith.

Although the comic spirit does sometimes endorse subversion, it also celebrates community and social cohesiveness, and has a natural affinity for forms of order that facilitate a healthy and flourishing society. Unlike tragedy, which focuses on the individual, comedy is more directed at the good of the whole society.[72] David Lodge says, "Comedy reasserts the body, and the collectiveness of the body is what really unites us rather than ideologies."[73] Its thrust is to affirm the good of the social order and to implement a healthier social group by expelling some undesirable element. Hence the tradition of comic dramas ending with a marriage, which contains the promise of renewing and strengthening the social fabric. The comic mode then is ideal for expressing the communal aspects of the Catholic tradition. When asked in an interview if he had so many characters in *How Far Can You Go?* in order to emphasize that the historical dilemmas of Catholicism are communal, Lodge affirmed that he did.[74]

Another reason why future Catholic novels may look to the comic mode is the aforementioned need for humility after the chaos and upheavals of the last forty years. As David Lodge reminds us, the older image of the Church as an impregnable, monolithic entity is untenable, if not ludicrous today. One can love and honor the Church and still see aspects of it that are laughable. Chesterton says, "A characteristic of the great saints is their power of levity. Angels can fly because they can take themselves lightly."[75] Catholics also need to take themselves lightly. We need to have a sense of humor about the contortions caused by the flawed human side of the Church. Comic irony may be the most appropriate lens for seeing our naiveté in underestimating the effects of our open embrace of contemporary secularity, the bad taste of some of our liturgical reforms and church renovation, and the implausibility of thinking we could eviscerate catechetics of everything but drawing pictures and expressing feelings and not produce a religiously illiterate generation.

One of the functions of comedy is to promote emotional health by allowing us to laugh at our follies, but in that laughter there is also hope and promise, as with the elderly Sarah in the Old Testament, who laughed when the angel said that in the next year she would bear a son. Chesterton believes that although sorrow is inherent in the Christian view of the world, joy is by far the larger component:

> Christianity satisfies suddenly and perfectly man's ancestral instinct for being the right way up; satisfies it supremely in this; that by its creed joy becomes something gigantic and sadness something special and small. The vault above us is not deaf because the universe is an idiot; the silence is not the heartless silence of an endless and aimless world. Rather the silence around us is a small and pitiful stillness like the prompt stillness in a sickroom. . . .
> Joy, which was the small publicity of the pagan, is the gigantic secret of the Christian.[76]

If Christians truly believe that the answers to the big questions are affirmative—that there is meaning, that there is a point to the universe, that we are created and loved and are not simply a cosmic accident, that death is not the final answer, but life is—we will be energized to face the truth about our failures. We need to be able to laugh at the all too human side of the Church, even as we mourn for the suffering and loss of faith caused by its transgressions. We need to laugh in order to have hope. And good comic Catholic novels can help us to do that.

It pleases me that the four novelists I have discussed are comprised of two men and two women, two converts and two cradle Catholics, two conservatives, one liberal, and one (Maitland) whose theology is quite conservative but whose strong identification with feminist concerns is more typically associated with liberals. Two (Lodge and Ellis) are hilariously funny; two (Read and Maitland) are more solemn and serious in tone—although Maitland certainly has her whimsical and playful side. (It seems to me that most of Maitland's humor is concentrated in *Brittle Joys*, the first novel she wrote after becoming a Catholic.) Yet as different as their work is, they all live in Greeley's "enchanted world"—but with one eye on the dirt and muck in the corners. These novelists do not hesitate to delineate with trenchant irony, biting satire, or simply devastatingly realistic description the ways in which the Church fails. Their angles of vision diverge and their critiques are distinctly different, focused on sexual teachings (Lodge), patriarchy (Maitland), or post-Vatican II developments (Read and Ellis). Yet they still see their world through the categories, the symbols, the stories, and the rituals of Catholicism—not just because they are literarily useful, but also because they undergird the story with a meaning that transcends the secular.

Taken together, their fiction leaves one with a sense of the capaciousness of Catholicism. Although to outsiders Catholicism often appears as a constriction of the imagination and the obstruction of free thought, Chesterton says that anyone who wants to become a Catholic must broaden his mind. "He must grow more used than he is at present to the long avenues and the large spaces."[77] He illustrates his point with this analogy:

> St. Mark's Cathedral at Venice is in some ways a very curious building, and to some northern eyes does not look like a cathedral at all; but it does look like a thing coloured with the sunrise and the sunset, in touch with the very ends of the earth; open like a harbour and full of popular poetry like a fairy-palace. That is, it does express the first essential fact that Catholicism is not a narrow thing; that it knows more than the world knows about the potentialities and creative possibilities of the world, and that it will outlast all the worldly and temporary expressions of the same culture.[78]

The Catholic novel partakes of the capaciousness of Catholicism. There is a place for the realistic novel describing the day to day life of ordinary Catholics; the novel that foregrounds the inherent drama of the faith by using exotic settings, odd or eccentric characters, and highly exceptional situations; and the novel that makes little explicit use of Catholicism but through symbolism, imagery, or simply invoking the paradigmatic Christian stories to shape its narrative expresses Catholic beliefs. The most problematic part of the phrase "the Catholic novel" is the article *the.*

When earlier Catholic novelists directed their critique at the Catholic community, they often focused on a lack of charity in smug, self-righteous Catholics and in spiritually dead parishes. Yet Ellis, Lodge, Maitland, and Read seem more concerned with the power of charity than with the lack of it. They tend to see the transformative power of charity in the life of an ordinary Catholic—Bernard's kindness to his aunt, Anna's generous help to a family with a handicapped child—rather than to critique "bad" Catholics. They seem more interested in the "little way" of Saint Thérèse of Lisieux, the small little moral struggles in everyday life that lead to incremental change and growth in the spiritual life.

Yet as important as charity is in this fiction, I suggest that the overarching virtue in these contemporary Catholic novels is hope. Sally Cunneen says that Sara Maitland makes the reader "aware of the sacred potential within and outside of each of her characters' consciousness."[79] To some extent, this sense of potential is born of clarity, an ability to see secularity, as Lynch recommends, with a greater openness and honesty about both its strengths and weaknesses. As Maitland says,

> We know perfectly well that honest atheists, agnostics, and adiaphorists live virtuous lives of civic service, psychological health, and ethical integrity. Faith is not about goodness, but about holiness. It is about creating and maintaining the tiny holes and narrow rips in the membrane between time and eternity, between immanence and transcendence, between the divine and the mortal, between God and humanity.[80]

Maitland also says in *A Map of the New Country: Women and Christianity*, "You have to set out before you know what you are setting out for."[81] This statement captures well the dynamic sense of forward movement that I see, not only in Maitland's work, but in that of Ellis, Lodge, and Read. Yet the phrase "before you know what you are setting out for" conveys the lived experience of faith—its tentativeness, its ambiguities, its doubts, its character as both overwhelming gift and willed decision—that these novelists convey so well.

In *The Portal of the Mystery of Hope*, Charles Péguy says:

> The faith that I love the best, says God, is hope.
>
> Faith doesn't surprise me.
> It's not surprising.
> I am so resplendent in my creation
> . . . .
> Charity, says God, that doesn't surprise me.
> It's not surprising.
> These poor creatures are so miserable that unless they had a heart of stone,
> 　how could they not have love for each other.
> . . . .
> But hope, says God, that is something that surprises.
> Even me.
> That is surprising.
> That these poor children see how things are going and believe that tomorrow
> 　things will go better.[82]

Péguy's idea that even God is surprised by human hope suggests why it is such a natural and fruitful theme for Catholic novelists. It is the locus of the drama, passion, and energy at the heart of the life of faith.

Yet a note of caution is in order. What I detect in the fiction of Ellis, Lodge, Maitland, and Read is not some kind of easy optimism or cheap grace. Some Catholics have been put off by the avalanche of post-Vatican II rhetoric about community and the love of God with nary a word about evil, sin, or damnation. They miss a certain toughness and hard-edged realism that—for all its severity—seemed more in touch with reality. These novelists have toughness. They all see in the world and in the Church much that is twisted, wrong, and badly in need of healing. The hope I see in them is not a palliative born of illusion. It is a determination to hold to what they see as good. As Ellis says at the end of *Serpent on the Rock*:

> The gates of Hell shall not prevail. That promise was the only hope I could see until I remembered the moment in the Creed at which we kneel, at the words *et homo factus est* and realise that God so loved us that he lived on earth and died for us. This reminder of the absolute reality of self-sacrificial love, of total goodness, is all we can hold on to in a climate dedicated to the

pretence of fellowship and loving-kindness, to schmaltz, self-conceit and heresy [emphasis in the original].[83]

Ellis clings to hope born of the incarnational faith embodied in the Church, Read sees in Catholicism a source of clarity and moral order, Maitland detects "rips in the membrane between time and eternity," and Lodge describes some fairly good grounds for believing that the human story, like all good comedies, will have a happy ending, including—if not an earthly marriage—some kind of celebration of God's gifts of gender and sexuality.

Liz hopes.
Mary says "Robin . . . ?"
Christ's tomb is still empty.
The answer to the question is "Very good news."

NOTES

1. Kellogg's *The Vital Tradition: The Catholic Novel in a Period of Convergence* was published in 1970; Sonnenfeld's *Crossroads: Essays on the Catholic Novelists* was published in 1982.

2. One English professor at a Catholic university, when presented with the idea of offering a course in the Catholic novel, spoke disparagingly of such literature as "ghetto literature."

3. An example is "A Note to the Reader" in the 50th anniversary edition of Thomas Merton's *The Seven Storey Mountain* by William H. Shannon, the president of the International Thomas Merton Society:

> At the time Merton wrote his book, Roman Catholic theology had become a set of prepackaged responses to any and all questions. Polemical and apologetic in tone, its aim is to prove Catholics were right and all others were wrong. . . .
> . . . Today, as we hover on the verge of a new millennium, we can identify with his searching, if not always with the specific direction it took. Merton's personal magnetism, the enthusiasm of his convictions, the vivid narratives of this born writer, transcend the narrowness of his theology. His story contains perennial elements of our common human experience. This is what makes it profoundly universal.

William H. Shannon, "A Note to the Reader," *The Seven Storey Mountain*, by Thomas Merton, 50th anniversary edition (San Diego: Harcourt Brace & Co. 1998)., xx–xxi.

4. *Ethics and Culture: The Newsletter of the Notre Dame Center for Ethics & Culture,* Spring 2005, 4.

5. O'Connor, "Fiction Writer," 34.

6. Woodman, *Faithful Fictions*, 163.

7. Maitland, *Novel Thoughts*, 2.

8. Maitland, *Novel Thoughts*, 2.

9. Bergonzi, "Decline and Fall," 187.

10. *Death Comes for the Archbishop,* like the earlier novels of Sara Maitland, is not strictly speaking as a Catholic novel since Cather was an Episcopalian; but even more than Maitland's *Daughter of Jerusalem* and *Virgin Territory,* it is completely immersed in Catholic life, ecclesiology, and Church history—so much so that after it was published, Cather received letters from readers asking her when she had converted to Catholicism.

11. Hansen, *A Stay Against Confusion*, 24–25.

12. Sonnenfeld, foreward to *Crossroads*, viii.

13. Richard Gilman, "Salvation, Damnation, and the Religious Novel," *New York Times Book Review,* 2 December 1984, 58. Quoted in prologue to Fraser, *Modern Catholic Novel*, xi.

14. Dwight Longenecker, "Indifference to Religion on the Rise in Great Britain," *Our Sunday Visitor*, 30 January 2003, 4.

15. Greg Watts, "Gandalf in London,"*Our Sunday Visitor*, 7 March 2004, 19.

16. Read, "Piers Paul Read on the Future of the Church."

17. In the case of Bernanos and Mauriac, it was both. Because almost all Christianity in France was Roman Catholic, hostility to religion meant hostility to Catholicism. There simply was not much of a Protestant presence—a very different situation from that in England.

18. Donat O'Donnell, *Maria Cross*, 235.

19. Even in earlier Catholic novels, sin was almost never exclusively, or even primarily sexual sin. Like Dante, who placed sins of lust in the "highest" (least bad) circle of hell, the great Catholic novelists seem always to have known that pride, despair, and a cold heart were much worse. Nevertheless, the reality of sexual sin was a much stronger presence in the earlier novels and was often entangled with these other sins of pride, despair and so forth.

20. It will be recalled that Sara Maitland, while not focused on movement into the Roman Catholic communion, *does* make conversion in the larger sense the centerpiece of her novels.

21. David Lodge, "The Catholic Church and Cultural Life," in Lodge, *Write On*, 36–37.

22. Bergonzi, "Decline and Fall, 186.

23. Lodge, "Catholic Church," 37.

24. David Lodge, Interview, *Contemporary Authors* (Detroit: Gale Research Inc., 1995).

25. In the summer of 1999 I took part in a seminar on literature and religion sponsored by the Erasmus Institute. When I presented some work I was doing on Catholicism in the fiction of David Lodge, some non-Catholic members were puzzled about why I insisted on focusing on Catholicism instead of simply Christianity. My sense is that it is very difficult for non-Catholic Christians to understand why the Catholic tradition is so seminal to the way Catholics conceptualize and live their Christianity.

26. Read, "Catholic Novelist," 212.

27. Read, "Catholic Novelist," 209.

28. Lodge, Interview with the author.

29. Michael P. Hornsby-Smith, "English Catholics at the New Millennium," in *Catholics in England 1950–2000: Historical and Sociological Perspectives*, ed. Michael P. Hornsby-Smith (London: Cassell, 1999), 293.

30. Ratzinger, Joseph Cardinal, *Salt of the Earth: Christianity and the Catholic Church at the End of the Millennium* (San Francisco: Ignatius Press, 1997), 222.

31. I have yet to meet a liberal or a conservative who is willing to be identified by those names. Part of the problem is that they see their own constellation of convictions as too complex and nuanced to be subsumed under the words *liberal* or *conservative*. Furthermore, they prefer words like *moderate, centrist, orthodox* or *traditional*, thus implying that they really represent the mainstream and that their opponents are at the extremes. Nevertheless, the words *liberal* and *conservative* are continually used in common parlance, and I use them for the sake of simplicity. Although most people insist that they do not like those labels, they all know very well what beliefs and opinions characterize believers designated by the terms.

32. Peter Steinfels, *A People Adrift: The Crisis of the Roman Catholic Church in America* (New York: Simon & Schuster, 2003).

33. David Carlin, *The Decline and Fall of the Catholic Church in America* (Manchester, N.H.: Sophia Institute Press, 2003).

34. Certainly there are notable differences between English and American Catholicism. The Church in England (at least after the Reformation) never enjoyed the kind of ascendancy that pre-Vatican II Catholicism enjoyed in the United States with its far-flung system of thriving Catholic schools and colleges, its seminaries and novitiates filled to capacity, and its high rate of Sunday Mass attendance and intermarriage. Even in the mid-twentieth century, Catholicism in England seemed somewhat exotic. Yet as large numbers of Irish immigrants swelled the ranks of Catholics in both countries, the two Churches have become more similar. Steinfels's and Carlin's analyses would not, of course, apply so well to the Church in Africa or Latin America.

35. Steinfels, *A People Adrift*, 1.

36. Carlin, *Decline and Fall*, 7. Carlin quotes Charles Morris's argument in *American Catholic* (New York: Vintage, 1998) that "large numbers of very active core Catholics, whose commitment is *chosen* rather than merely inherited or imposed, have created an extraordinarily vibrant and participatory grassroots parish life" (320). Carlin agrees that "there are many signs of vitality in the Church in the United States" but asks "Is it truly *Catholic* vitality? Or is it a vitality more proper to generic Christianity? Religions undergoing a process of dissolution due to the abandonment of traditional doctrine often experience, in the short term, a great burst of energy, especially ethical energy" (382).

37. Steinfels, *A People Adrift*, 306.

38. Hebblethwaite, "How Catholic Is the Catholic Novel?" 678.

39. Carlin, *Decline and Fall*, 277.

40. Carlin, *Decline and Fall*, 276–77. One that suggests that Carlin's prediction is coming true is a small but significant trend among young adults to embrace traditional religion (not only among Catholics, but among Protestants and Jews). This phenomenon is described in the book mentioned in the Preface, Colleen Carroll's *The New Faithful*. Also, conservatives tend to be more interested than liberals in making converts, as exemplified in the organization Catholic Answers, which

has revived Catholic apologetics, and which espouses conservative, orthodox Catholicism. Similarly, the vast majority of the Catholic bloggers on the internet are conservative (Jonathan V. Last, "God on the Internet," *First Things*, December 2005, 34–40). Also noteworthy is the fact that religious orders that live in community, wear a habit, and perform traditional ministries seem to attract both more attention from the secular world as well as more applicants to join their orders than do those who dress like the laity and live what looks like a secular lifestyle. Peter Steinfels, however, finds this claim "oversimplified and misleading" (*A People Adrift*, 9).

41. Carlin, *Decline and Fall*, 277–78.

42. This attitude, of course, has never been officially sanctioned by the Church, which teaches that the fullness of Christian faith subsists in Catholicism, yet this mentality has infiltrated Catholic preaching, catechetics and journalism, thus influencing the way the average Catholic thinks about Catholicism.

43. It is necessary to clarify what I mean by *Church* in this context. Both Pope John Paul II and Pope Benedict XVI have spoken out strongly about the danger of secularism, particularly in terms of the "culture of death" and relativism. The popes' warnings, however, seem not to have much influence on the tone or content of homiletics, catechetics, or popular Catholic literature. In the parish milieu—except in the area of abortion—one still has a sense of a quite comfortable accommodation with contemporary secular values.

44. Carlin, *Decline and Fall*, 351.

45. Carlin, *Decline and Fall*, 352. Carlin mentions as examples of the agenda of secular liberalism making morally acceptable nonmarital cohabitation, nonmarital teenage sex, out-of-wedlock childbearing, divorce, and homosexuality; and the legalization of abortion (already achieved), pornography, gay marriage, physician assisted suicide, and euthanasia (353–55).

46. Woodman, *Faithful Fictions* 164.

47. This is not to imply that conservatives are not concerned with social justice. They are. They do, however, tend to pay more attention to the supernatural aspects of Catholicism than do most liberals; and humanitarian ideals, while important, are not *distinctively* Catholic but are held by all people of good will.

48. Of course, these are all generalizations that allow for many exceptions. Nevertheless, based on the books and articles written by conservatives, many of whom are converts, it does not seem unreasonable to see them as more focused on the supernatural, the miraculous and traditional Catholic devotions and practices. Liberals' attention is much more focused on what they want to change in the Church.

49. Another reason why a more orthodox Church may be better for fiction is that in times of great change, confusion and doctrinal uncertainty, Catholic fiction is seen as a forum for competing models of what the Church should be. Bishop Rembert Weakland said, "We are living in a time in which we must re-imagine the Catholic Church" (Eugene Kennedy, *Re-imagining American Catholicism* [New York: Vintage, 1985], 19.) Anita Gandolfo, with reference to American Catholic fiction, writes, "Contemporary fiction of Catholic experience is expressive of the unique situation of the Church in the United States at this particular historical moment and . . . forms an important vision of cultural change." She also asserts, "This

fiction . . . offers a model of spiritual development that should be the preamble to any new model of church" (Anita Gandolfo, *Testing the Faith: The New Catholic Fiction in America* [New York: Greenwood Press, 1992], 206, 209). Fiction that is a reflection of a more settled Church is more likely to concentrate on the great interior drama in the soul of a believer, which is what the great Catholic novels have always been.

50. R. Scott Appleby, "Surviving the Shaking of the Foundations: United States Catholicism in the Twenty-First Century," Contextual Introduction to *Seminaries, Theologates, and the Future of Ministry: An Analysis of Trends and Transitions,* by Katarina Schuth, (Collegeville, Minn.: Liturgical Press, 1999), 11.

51. Greeley, *Catholic Revolution,* 115.

52. It may be objected that Catholic theologians have been arguing with each other since New Testament times and that moral teaching has gone through many permutations—even what appear to be downright contradictions, such as the teachings on usury and religious freedom. Nevertheless, until the present, most lay people were not aware of these disputes and experienced their Church as a source of clear, consistent teaching. Although they did not always like what was taught or obey it, the teaching was perceived as a clear, cogent, and consistent set of moral principles, impervious to social change. That is why the widespread dissent to *Humanae Vitae* was so alarming. It threatened to overturn this perception, and for many Catholics, it did.

53. Lodge, "Novelist at the Crossroads," 32.

54. Haffenden, "David Lodge," 157.

55. This is not to deny that non-Catholic religious writers employ spiritual realism, an outstanding example being Toni Morrison. My remark, however, is meant to be understood within the context of a discussion of the probable direction of Catholic fiction in the future.

56. Roger Lundin, *The Culture of Interpretation: Christian Faith and the Postmodern World* (Grand Rapids: Eerdmans, 1993), 75.

57. Anita Gandolfo evidently believes this to be the case in American Catholic fiction. "Another vestige of the preconciliar paradigm is the tendency toward closure. . . . The preference for didacticism in art characteristic of preconciliar Catholicism is susceptible to the lure of the theses-ridden fiction of passionate intensity." Gandolfo, *Testing the Faith,* 207.

58. William F. Lynch, S.J., *Christ and Prometheus: A New Image of the Secular.* (Notre Dame, Ind.: University of Notre Dame Press, 1960), 33.

59. According to Ian Ker, "Above all what Greene needed and wanted was a religion that had hard and certain things to say about evil." *Catholic Revival,* 119.

60. Maitland, *Novel Thoughts,* 5.

61. Lynch, *Christ and Prometheus,* 15–16.

62. Lynch, *Christ and Prometheus,* 126.

63. John J. Myers, "The Church vs. the Culture: The Score Thus Far," *Crisis,* May 2004, 20.

64. Lynch, *Christ and Prometheus,* 135.

65. Lynch, *Christ and Prometheus,* 142.

66. I insert the word *almost* because I am reluctant to generalize, but in my reading of earlier Catholic novels, I have never read anything to compare with Lodge's

description of his first feel of Maureen's breast or Maitland's description of Liz and Ian's first act of intercourse. These passages celebrate the beauty, tenderness and joy of erotic love. I remember that when I first read Greene's *The End of the Affair*, I thought that if I knew nothing about sex other than what I read in that novel, I would certainly not think it an activity that I would care to engage in.

67. Steinfels, *A People Adrift*, 329.

68. Dante called his poem merely *Commedia*. Later admirers prefixed the modifier *Divina*.

69. Lodge, "Graham Greene," 117.

70. Lodge is widely recognized for seeing the comic aspects of Catholic life in the post-Vatican II period and rendering them with humor that is pungent without becoming caustic or bitter. It is not, however, as widely recognized that, as I hope I have demonstrated, there is also attention to more serious underlying religious concerns.

71. Haffenden, "David Lodge," 166.

72. In an article entitled "Comedy and Christianity: Surveying the Ground," Peggy Thompson makes this interesting point:

> Medieval Catholics were able to enjoy what seems to many of us a disconcerting injection of comedy in their religious dramas in part because their religion shared with comedy an insistence that the individual was to be understood only in terms of the larger community, in this instance, of the one true church. Religious literature drew much less frequently on comic conventions after the Reformation because, in practice, the church community was fragmented and, in Protestant theory, individuals defined themselves more immediately in relation to their God, seeking a place in the only city that mattered, the heavenly city. *Christianity and Literature* 44, no. 1 (autumn 1994): 60–61.

73. Haffenden, "David Lodge," 167.

74. Haffenden, "David Lodge," 154.

75. Chesterton, *Orthodoxy*, 127.

76. Chesterton, *Orthodoxy*, 167.

77. G. K. Chesterton, *The Well and the Shallows* in vol. 3 of *The Collected Works of G. K. Chesterton* (San Francisco: Ignatius Press, 1986), 452.

78. Chesterton, *Well and Shallows*, 453. Chesterton's point here echoes the view of the nineteenth century French novelist Barbey d'Aurevilly: "Surely Catholic wisdom is larger, fuller, more straightforward and more robust than the moralists of free thought imagine." Barbey d'Aurevilly, preface, 13.

79. Cunneen, "Big Enough for God," 135.

80. Sara Maitland, "The Future of Faith," *Cross Currents*, 50, no, 2 (spring/summer 2000): 155.

81. Maitland, *Map of the New Country*, 191.

82. Charles Péguy, *The Portal of the Mystery of Hope*, trans. David Louis Schindler, Jr. (Grand Rapids: Eerdmans, 1996), 3–6.

83. Ellis, *Serpent on the Rock*, 223.

Bibliography

Ableman, Paul. "Booted About." Review of *A Married Man*, by Piers Paul Read. *The Spectator*, November 24, 1979, 21.

Ackroyd, Peter. "Out of Sight." Review of *The Sin Eater*, by Alice Thomas Ellis. *The Spectator*, December 24, 1977, 29–30.

Amis, Kingsley, "How I Lived in a Very Big House and Found God." *Times Literary Supplement*, November 20, 1952, 1352.

Appleby, R. Scott. "Surviving the Shaking of the Foundations: United States Catholicism in the Twenty-First Century." Contextual Introduction. Pp. 1–23 in *Seminaries, Theologates, and the Future of Ministry: An Analysis of Trends and Transitions*, by Katarina Schuth. Collegeville, Minn.: Liturgical Press, 1999.

Augustine, Saint. *The City of God*. *The City of God*, Book XIV, chapter 1, translated by Marcus Dods, D.D. New York: Modern Library, 1950.

———. The Works of Saint Augustine, edited by John E. Rotelle, O.S.A. Sermons III, translated by Edmund Hill, O.P. Brooklyn: New City Press, 1991.

Bakhtin, Mikhail. *The Dialogic Imagination: Four Essays*. Austin: University of Texas Press, 1981.

Barbey d'Aurevilly, Jules Amédée. *Oeuvres de J. Barbey d'Aurevilly*. Preface to *Une Vieille Maitresse*. Nouvelle Edition. Tome Premier. Paris: Librairie Alphonse Lemerre, n.d.

Bellah, Robert. *The Good Society*. New York: Random House, Vintage Books, 1991.

Belloc, Hilaire. *Europe and the Faith*. New York: Paulist Press, 1920.

———. "A Letter to Dean Inge." In *Essays of a Catholic*. New York: Macmillan, 1931.

———. *Survivals and New Arrivals*. New York: Macmillan, 1929.

Benson, Robert Hugh. *The Dawn of All*. London: Hutchinson, 1911.

———. *Lord of the World*. London: Sir Isaac Pitman & Sons, 1907.

Berger, Peter. *A Rumor of Angels: Modern Society and the Rediscovery of the Supernatural*. Garden City, N.Y.: Doubleday Anchor, 1970.

Bergonzi, Bernard. "The Decline and Fall of the Catholic Novel." In *The Myth of Modernism and Twentieth Century Literature*. New York: St. Martin's Press, 1986.

———. "A Conversation with David Lodge." In *War Poets and Other Subjects*. Aldershot, U.K.: Ashgate, 1999.

Bernanos, Georges. *The Diary of a Country Priest*. Trans. Pamela Norris. New York: Carroll & Graf, 1983.

———. *Under the Sun of Satan*. Trans. Harry L. Binsse. New York: Pantheon, 1949.

Boffetti, Jason. "Tolkien's Catholic Imagination," *Crisis*, November 2001, 34–40.

Bradbury, Malcolm. "A Case of Ilychitis." Review of *A Married* Man, by Piers Paul Read. New *York Times Book Review*, December 30, 1979, 3.

Bretall, Robert, ed. *A Kierkegaard Anthology*. Princeton University Press, 1946.

Brockway, James. "Going Down Bravely." Review of *Polonaise*, by Piers Paul Read. *Books and Bookmen*, Feb. 1977, 22–23.

Buckley, F. J. "The Satirist of the Fall." *Crisis*, January 2003, 27–31.

Caldecott, Stratford. "The Lord & Lady of the Rings: The Hidden Presence of Tolkien's Catholicism in *The Lord of the Rings*." *Touchstone*, January 2002, 51–57.

Canavan, Francis, "The Dilemma of Liberal Pluralism," *The Human Life Review* 5, no. 3 (summer 1979), 7. Quoted in Stanley Hauerwas, *A Community of Character: Toward a Constructive Christian Social Ethic* (Notre Dame, Ind.: University of Notre Dame Press, 1981), 217.

Carlin, David. *The Decline and Fall of the Catholic Church in America*. Manchester, N.H.: Sophia Institute Press, 2003.

Carroll, Colleen. *The New Faithful: Why Young Adults are Embracing Christian Orthodoxy*. Chicago: Loyola Press, 2002.

Catechism of the Catholic Church. New York: Doubleday, Image Books, 1995.

Chesterton, G. K. "On the Novel with a Purpose." Pp. 225–29 in *The Thing: Why I Am a Catholic*. Pp. 133–335 in *The Collected Works of G. K. Chesterton*. Vol. 3. San Francisco: Ignatius Press, 1990.

———. *Orthodoxy*. San Francisco: Ignatius Press, 1908, 1995.

———. *St. Thomas Aquinas*. Pp. 419–551 in *The Collected Works of G. K. Chesterton*. Vol. 2. San Francisco: Ignatius Press, 1986.

———. *The Well and the Shallows*. In Vol. 3 of *The Collected Works of G. K. Chesterton*. San Francisco: Ignatius Press, 1990.

Christ, Carol P. *Diving Deep and Surfacing: Women Writers on Spiritual Quest*. Boston: Beacon Press, 1980.

Collins, James. *Pilgrim in Love: An Introduction to Dante and His Spirituality*. Chicago: Loyola University Press, 1984.

Collins, James Daniel. *The Mind of Kierkegaard*. Chicago: Henry Regnery, 1953.

Conrad, Joseph. *The Secret Agent: A Simple Tale*. Cambridge and New York: Cambridge University Press, 1990.

Copleston, Frederick, S.J. *Modern Philosophy: Schopenhauer to Nietzsche*. Vol. 7, Part 2 of *A History of Philosophy*. Garden City, N.Y.: Doubleday, Image Books, 1965.

Couto, Maria. *Graham Greene: On the Frontier*. New York: St. Martin's Press, 1988.

Cunneen, Sally. "Big Enough for God: The Fiction of Sara Maitland." *Logos* 6, no. 4 (fall 2003): 122–35.

Cunningham, Lawrence S. *The Catholic Experience*. New York: Crossroad, 1987.

Daiches, David, ed. *The Avenel Companion to English & American Literature*. Vol. 1. New York: Avenel Books, 1981.

Delbanco, Andrew. *The Death of Satan: How Americans Have Lost the Sense of Evil*. New York: Farrar, Straus & Giroux, 1995.

Demers, James. *The Last Roman Catholic*. Carp, Ontario: Creative Bound Inc., 1991.

Desmond, John. "The Heart of the Matter: The Mystery of the Real in *Monsignor Quixote*." *Religion and Literature* 22, no. 1 (Spring 1990): 59–78.

Duffy, Eamon. *Faith of Our Fathers: Reflections on Catholic Tradition*. London: Continuum, 2004.

Duran, Leopoldo. *Graham Greene*. Trans. Euan Cameron. San Francisco: Harper-Collins, 1994.

Eliot, T. S. "Religion and Literature." Pp. 343–54 in *Selected Essays*. New ed. New York: Harcourt, Brace & Co., 1950.

Ellis, Alice Thomas. *The Birds of the Air*. Harmondsworth, Eng.: Penguin, 1983.

———. Interview by author. London. February 7, 2001.

———. *Serpent on the Rock*. London: Hodder and Stoughton, 1994.

———. *The Sin Eater*. Harmondsworth, Eng.: Penguin, 1986.

———. *The 27th Kingdom*. Pleasantville, N.Y.: Akadine Press, 1999.

———. *Unexplained Laughter*. Pleasantville, N.Y.: Akadine Press, 1998.

Ethics and Culture: The Newsletter of the Notre Dame Center for Ethics & Culture, Spring 2005.

Foucauld, Michel. *An Introduction*. Vol. 1 of *The History of Sexuality*, 19–23. Trans. Robert Hirley. London: Allen Lane, 1979. Quoted in Woodman, *Faithful Fictions*, 147.

Fraser, Theodore P. *The Modern Catholic Novel in Europe*. New York: Twayne, 1994.

Friedman, Melvin J., ed. *The Vision Obscured: Perceptions of Some Twentieth-Century Catholic Novelists*. New York: Fordham University Press, 1970.

Frye, Northrop. *Anatomy of Criticism: Four Essays*. Princeton: Princeton University Press, 1957.

Gandolfo, Anita. *Testing the Faith: The New Catholic Fiction in America*. New York: Greenwood Press, 1992.

Gide, André. *Dostoyevsky*, 15. New York: New Directions, 1923, 1961. Quoted in Fraser, *Modern Catholic Novel*, 5.

Gilley, Sheridan. "A Tradition and Culture Lost, To Be Regained?" Pp. 29–45 in *Catholics in England*, edited by Michael P. Hornsby-Smith.

Gilman, Richard. "Salvation, Damnation, and the Religious Novel." *New York Times Book Review*, December 2, 1984, 7, 58–60. Quoted in Fraser, prologue to *Modern Catholic Novel*, xi.

Glendon, Mary Ann. "The Hour of the Laity." *First Things*, November 2002, 23–25.

Godawa, Brian. "Redemption in the Movies." Pp. 433–51 in Ryken, *The Christian Imagination*.

Greeley, Andrew. *The Catholic Imagination*. Berkeley: University of California Press. 2000.

———. *The Catholic Revolution: New Wine, Old Wineskins, and the Second Vatican Council*. Berkeley: University of California Press, 2004.

Green, Julian. *Diary 1928–1957*, 159. Sel. by Kurt Wolff. Trans. Anne Green. New York: Harcourt, Brace & World, 1964, 159.

Green, Martin. *Essays on Literature and Religion: Yeats's Blessinsg on von Hügel*, 116, 74. London, Longman, 1967. Quoted in Woodman, *Faithful Fictions*, 140.

Greene, Graham. *The End of the Affair*. New York: Viking, 1961.

——. "François Mauriac." Pp. 69–73 in *The Lost Childhood and Other Essays*. New York: Viking Press, 1951.

——. *Monsignor Quixote*. London: Vintage, 2000.

——. *The Power and the Glory*. New York: Penguin, 1977.

——. *Ways of Escape*. New York: Simon and Schuster, 1980.

Haffenden, John. "David Lodge." Pp. 145–67 in *Novelists in Interview*. London: Methuen, 1985.

Haight, Roger, S.J. *Jesus: Symbol of God*. Maryknoll, N.Y.: Orbis, 1999. Quoted in Edward T. Oakes, S.J., "Reconciling Judas: Evangelizing the Theologians," *Crisis*, Oct. 2004, 31–35.

Hansen, Ron. Preface to *A Stay Against Confusion: Essays on Faith and Fiction*. New York: HarperCollins, 2001.

The HarperCollins Encyclopedia of Catholicism. Ed. Richard P. McBrien et al. San Francisco: HarperSanFrancisco, 1995.

The Harper Handbook to Literature. 2d ed. Ed. Northrop Frye et al. New York: Longman, 1997.

Hart, David B. "The Laughter of the Philosophers." *First Things*, Jan. 2005, 31–37.

Hebblethwaite, Peter. "How Catholic Is the Catholic Novel?" *Times Literary Supplement*, 27 July 1967, 678–79.

Heppenstall, Rayner. *Léon Bloy*. Studies in Modern European Literature and Thought. Cambridge: Bowes & Bowes, 1953.

Hoge, Dean et al. *Young Adult Catholics: Religion in the Culture of Choice*. Notre Dame, Ind.: University of Notre Dame Press, 2001.

Hornsby-Smith, Michael P., ed. *Catholics in England 1950–2000: Historical and Sociological Perspectives*. London: Cassell, 1999.

——. "English Catholics at the New Millennium." Pp. 291–306 in Hornsby-Smith, *Catholics in England*.

——. *Roman Catholic Beliefs in England: Customary Catholicism and Transformations of Religious Authority*. Cambridge: Cambridge University Press, 1991.

——. "A Transformed Church." Pp. 3–25 in Hornsby-Smith, *Catholics in England*.

Hornsby-Smith, Michael P. and R. M. Lee. *Roman Catholic Opinion: A Study of Roman Catholics in England and Wales in the 1970's* (Guildford: University of Surrey, 1979), 117. Quoted in Hornsby-Smith, *Roman Catholic Beliefs in England*, 183.

Howard, Thomas. "*Brideshead Revisited* Revisited." *Touchstone*, summer 1996, 27–32.

Huizinga, Johan. *Homo Ludens: A Study of the Play-Element in Culture*, 18. New York: Roy Publishers, 1950. Quoted in Weinberger, "Religion and Fly Fishing," 282.

Huysmans, Joris-Karl. *En route*. 3rd. ed. Trans. C. Kegan Paul. London: Kegan Paul, Trench, Trubner & Co., 1908.

Jaspers, Karl. *Way to Wisdom*. Trans. Ralph Manheim. New Haven: Yale University Press, 1954.

Jenkins, Philip. *Hidden Gospels: How the Search for Jesus Lost Its Way*. Oxford: Oxford University Press, 2001.

Johnson, Anne Janette. "Read, Piers Paul." Pp. 353–55 in Vol. 36 of *Contemporary Authors*. New Revision Series. Detroit: Gale Research Inc., 1993.

Karl, Frederick R. *A Reader's Guide to the Contemporary English Novel*. Rev. ed. New York: Octagon Books, 1986.

Kellogg, Gene. *The Vital Tradition: The Catholic Novel in a Period of Convergence*. Chicago: Loyola University Press, 1970.

Kennedy, Eugene. *Re-imagining American Catholicism*. New York: Vintage Books, 1985.

Ker, Ian. *The Achievement of John Henry Newman*. Notre Dame, Ind.: University of Notre Dame Press, 1990.

———. *The Catholic Revival in English Literature, 1845–1961*. Notre Dame, Ind.: University of Notre Dame Press, 2003.

Kermode, Frank. *The Sense of an Ending*. New York: Oxford University Press, 1967.

Kierkegaard, Søren. *The Concept of Dread*. Trans. Walter Lowrie. Princeton: Princeton University Press, 1957.

———. *Fear and Trembling & Repetition*. Eds. and Trans. Howard V. Hong and Edna H. Hong. Princeton: Princeton University Press, 1983.

Kilpatrick, William. *The Emperor's New Clothes*. Westchester, Ill.: Crossway, 1985.

Knox, Ronald and Arthur Lunn. *Difficulties*. London: Eyre & Spottiswoode, 1932.

Kort, Wesley. *Narrative Elements and Religious Meanings*. Philadelphia: Fortress Press, 1975.

Kroll, Jack. "Map of Greeneland," *Newsweek*, April 15, 1991, 75.

Lacey, Paul A. "'To Meditate a Saving Strategy': Denise Levertov's Religious Poetry." *Renascence* 50, Nos. 1–2 (fall 1997/winter 1998): 17–32.

"The Languages of Love." Review of *Daughter of Jerusalem*, by Sara Maitland. *Publishers Weekly*, January 30, 1981, 62.

Last, Jonathan V. "God on the Internet." *First Things*, December 2005, 34–40.

Lawson, Mark. "How Far Did He Go?" *The Tablet*, September 4, 2004, 12–14.

Lee, Hermione. "Marriage à la Mode." Review of *Daughter of Jerusalem*, by Sara Maitland. *The Observer*, October 22, 1978, 35.

Leech, Kenneth. *Experiencing God: Theology as Spirituality*. San Francisco: Harper & Row, 1985.

Levertov, Denise. "On Belief in the Physical Resurrection of Jesus." Pp. 115–16 in *The Sands of the Well*. New York: New Directions, 1996.

Lewis, C. S. *Letters to Malcolm: Chiefly on Prayer*. New York: Harcourt, Brace & World, 1964.

———. *Mere Christianity*. Rev. ed. New York: Macmillan, 1960.

———. *Miracles*. New York: Macmillan, 1960

———. *The Problem of Pain*. New York: Macmaillan, 1962.

———. *Reflections on the Psalms*. New York: Harcourt Brace Jovanovich, 1958.

———. "Religion Without Dogma?" Pp. 129–46 in *God in the Dock*, edited by Walter Hooper. Grand Rapids: Eerdmans, 1970.

———. *The Screwtape Letters*. New York: Macmillan, 1953.

Lodge, David. *The Art of Fiction*. New York: Penguin, 1992.

———. "The Catholic Church and Cultural Life." Pp. 32–37 in Lodge, *Write On*.

———. "Graham Greene." Pp. 87–118 in Lodge, *Novelist at the Crossroads.*

———. Interview. *Contemporary Authors.* Detroit: Gale Research Inc., 1995.

———. Interview by author. London. March 13, 2001.

———. "Memories of a Catholic Childhood." Pp. 28–31 in Lodge, *Write On.*

———. "My Joyce." Pp. 57–69 in Lodge, *Write On.*

———. "The Novelist at the Crossroads." Pp. 3–34 in Lodge, *Novelist at the Crossroads.*

———. *The Novelist at the Crossroads and Other Essays on Fiction and Criticism.* Ithaca: Cornell University Press, 1971.

———. *Paradise News.* New York: Penguin, 1991.

———. *The Picturegoers.* 1960. New York: Penguin, 1993.

———. *Souls and Bodies.* [American edition of *How Far Can You Go?*] New York: Penguin, 1980.

———. *Therapy.* New York: Penguin, 1995.

———. "The Uses and Abuses of Omniscience: Method and Meaning in Muriel Spark's *The Prime of Miss Jean Brodie.*" Pp. 119–44 in *Novelist at the Crossroads.*

———. *Write On: Occasional Essays '65–'85.* London: Secker & Warburg, 1986.

Longenecker, Dwight. "Indifference to Religion on the Rise in Great Britain." *Our Sunday Visitor,* January 30, 2005, 4.

Low, Anthony. "Jon Hassler: Catholic Realist." *Renascence* 47, no. 1 (fall 1994): 59–70.

Lundin, Roger. *The Culture of Interperation: Christian Faith and the Postmodern World.* Grand Rapids: Eerdmans, 1993.

Lynch, William F., S.J. *Christ and Apollo: The Dimensions of the Literary Imagination.* 1960. Notre Dame, Ind.: University of Notre Dame Press, 1975.

———. *Christ and Prometheus: A New Image of the Secular.* Notre Dame, Ind.: University of Notre Dame Press, 1970.

Maison, Margaret M. *The Victorian Vision: Studies in the Religious Novel.* New York. Sheed & Ward, 1961.

Maitland, Sara. *A Big-Enough God: A Feminist's Search for a Joyful Theology.* New York: Riverhead Books, 1995.

———. *Brittle Joys.* London: Virago Press, 1999.

———. *Daughter of Jerusalem.* New York: Henry Holt & Co., 1978.

———. "Fag Hags: A Field Guide." Pp. 111–118 in *Angel Maker: The Short Stories of Sara Maitland.* New York: Henry Holt & Co., 1996.

———. "The Future of Faith" *Cross Currents.* (spring/summer 2000): 154–56.

———. Interview by author. Austin, Tex. June 18, 1999.

———. *A Map of the New Country: Women and Christianity.* London: Routledge & Kegan Paul, 1983.

———. *Novel Thoughts.* Notre Dame, Ind.: Erasmus Institute, 1999.

———. *Virgin Territory.* New York: Beaufort Books, 1984.

Malin, Irving. "The Deceptions of Muriel Spark." Pp. 95–107 in Friedman, *Vision Obscured.*

Maritain, Jacques. "Christian Art." Pp. 53–57 in *Art and Scholasticism: With Other Essays,* translated by J. F. Scanlan. New York: Charles Scribner's Sons, 1924.

Marshall, John. "Catholic Family Life." Pp. 67–77 in *Catholics in England,* edited by Michael P. Hornsby-Smith.

Mauriac, François. *The Desert of Love*. Trans. Gerard Hopkins. London: Eyre & Spottiswoode, 1949.

———. "On Writing Today." In *Second Thoughts: Reflections on Literature and Life*, 16. New York: World, 1961. Quoted in Fraser, *Modern Catholic Novel*, 37.

———. *The Viper's Tangle*. Trans. Gerard Hopkins. New York: Carroll & Graf, 1987.

McDannell, Colleen and Bernhard Lang. *Heaven: A History*. New York: Random House, Vintage Books, 1990.

McFague, Sallie. *Speaking in Parables: A Study in Metaphor and Theology*. Philadelphia: Fortress Press, 1975.

Miller, J. Hillis. "Literature and Religion." Pp. 31–45 in *Religion and Modern Literature: Essays in Theory and Criticism*, edited by G. B. Tennyson and Edward E. Ericson, Jr. Grand Rapids: Eerdmans, 1975.

Milton, Edith. Review of *The Birds of the Air*, by Alice Thomas Ellis. *New York Magazine*, 7 Sept. 1981, 64–65.

Moeller, Charles. *Man and Salvation in Literature*. Trans. Charles Underhill Quinn. Notre Dame, Ind.: University of Notre Dame Press, 1970.

Mooneyham, Laura. "The Triple Conversions of *Brideshead Revisited*." *Renascence* 45, no. 4 (summer 1993): 225–35.

Mustich, James, Jr. Afterward to *Unexplained Laughter*, by Alice Thomas Ellis. New York: Akadine Press, 1998.

Myers, John J. "The Church vs. the Culture: The Score Thus Far." *Crisis*, May 2004, 18–22.

Naughton, John. "Leavisites in Yorkshire." Review of *Daughter of Jerusalem*, by Sara Maitland. *The Listener* 100, no. 2586, (16 November 1978): 658–59.

Neary, John. *Like and Unlike God: Religious Imaginations in Modern and Contemporary Fiction*. Atlanta: Scholars Press, 1999.

Neuhaus, Richard John. "Kierkegaard for Grownups." *First Things*, October 2004, 27–33.

———. "The Public Square." *First Things*, August/September 2004, 86–104.

Newman, John Henry Cardinal. *An Essay in Aid of a Grammar of Assent*. Garden City, NY: Doubleday, Image Books, 1955.

———. *The Idea of a University*. Ed. Martin J. Svaglic. New York: Holt, Rinehart & Winston, 1960.

Nichols, Aidan. *The Art of God Incarnate*. New York: Paulist, 1980.

Nicholson, John. Review of *The Other Side of the Fire*, by Alice Thomas Ellis. *Times* (London) 1 December 1983, 13.

Norris, Kathleen. *The Cloister Walk*. New York: Riverhead, 1996.

Novak, Michael. "Abandoned in a Toxic Culture." *Crisis*, December 1992, 15–19.

———. *The Experience of Nothingness*, 15. New York: Harper & Row, 1970. Quoted in Christ, *Diving Deep*, 14–15.

O'Connor, Flannery. "Catholic Novelists and their Readers." Pp. 169–90 in *Mystery and Manners*.

———. *The Complete Stories*. New York: Farrar, Straus & Giroux, 1971.

———. "The Fiction Writer and His Country." Pp. 25–35 in *Mystery and Manners*.

———. *Mystery and Manners*. Ed. Sally and Robert Fitzgerald. New York: Farrar, Straus & Giroux, 1969.

———. "The Nature and Aim of Fiction." Pp. 63–86 in *Mystery and Manners*.

———. "Novelist and Believer." Pp. 154–168 in *Mystery and Manners*.

O'Donnell, Donat [Conor Cruise O'Brien]. *Maria Cross: Imaginative Patterns in a Group of Modern Catholic Writers*. New York: Oxford University Press, 1952.

O'Faolain, Julia. Review of *Unexplained Laughter*, by Alice Thomas Ellis. *Times Literary Supplement*, September 6, 1985, 972.

Oakes, Edward T. "Reconciling Judas: Evangelizing the Theologians." *Crisis*, October 2004, 31–35.

———. "Stanley Fish's Milton." *First Things*, November 2001, 23–34.

Oertling, Margaret. "A Response to Critics of *Brideshead Revisited*." The Epositor (Trinity University) 2 (1990): 65–75. Quoted in Mooneyham, "Triple Conversions," 232.

Orwell, George. "Inside the Whale." Pp. 215–56 in *A Collection of Esays*. New York: Doubleday, 1954.

Otto, Rudolf. *The Idea of the Holy*. Trans. John W. Harvey. New York: Oxford University Press, 1958.

Péguy, Charles. *The Portal of the Mystery of Hope*. Trans. David Louis Schindler, Jr. Grand Rapids: Eerdmans, 1996.

———. "Un Nouveau théologien: M. Fernand Laudet." *"Oeuvres de prose, 1909–1914*. (Paris: Gallimard/Bibliothèque de la Pléiade, 1961), 1074–76. Quoted in Fraser, *Modern Catholic Novel*, 21.

Percy, Walker. "On Being a Catholic Novelist." Excerpted from *Conversations with Walker Percy*. Eds. Lewis A. Lawson and Victor A. Kramer. Jackson: University Press of Mississippi, 1985. Pp. 193–94 in Ryken, *The Christian Imagination*.

Pieper, Josef. *In Tune With the World: A Theory of Festivity*. Chicago: Franciscan Herald Press, 1973.

Podhoretz, John. Review of *How Far Can You Go?*, by David Lodge. *The New Republic*, 7 April 1982, 37–38.

Radcliffe, Liat. "Log On for Salvation." *Newsweek*, May 31, 2004, 10.

Randisi, Jennifer Lynn. *On Her Way Rejoicing: The Fiction of Muriel Spark*. Washington, D.C.: The Catholic University of America Press, 1991.

Ranke-Heinemann, Uta. *Eunuchs for the Kingdom of Heaven: Women, Sexuality and the Catholic Church*. New York: Doubleday, 1990.

Ratzinger, Joseph Cardinal. *Salt of the Earth: Christianity and the Catholic Church at the End of the Millennium*. San Francisco: Ignatius Press, 1997.

Read, Piers Paul. "The Catholic Novelist in a Secular Society." Pp. 199–212 in *Hell and Other Destinations*.

———. "A Confession." *Crisis*, September 1995, 14–15.

———. *Hell and Other Destinations: A Novelist's Reflections on This World and the Next*. San Francisco: Ignatius Press, 2006.

———. Interview by author. London. April 11, 2001.

———. *A Married Man*. London: Secker & Warburg, 1979.

———. *Monk Dawson*. Philadelphia: Lippincott, 1970.

———. *On the Third Day*. London: Secker & Warburg, 1990.

———. "Piers Paul Read on the Future of the Church." AD2000 November 1999. <http://www.ad2000.com.au/articles/1999/nov1999p8_286.html> (April 6, 2006).

———. *Polonaise*. London: Orion Books, Phoenix, 1997.

———. "Screwtape Returns." Pp. 76–79 in *Hell and Other Destinations*.

———. "Upon This Rock." Pp. 49–61 in *Hell and Other Destinations*

Reinhardt, Kurt F. *The Theological Novel of Modern Europe: An Analysis of Masterpieces by Eight Authors*. New York: Frederick Ungar, 1969.

Rice, Edward. *The Man in the Sycamore Tree: The Good Times and Hard Life of Thomas Merton*. New York: Doubleday, Image Books, 1972.

Ryken, Leland, ed. *The Christian Imagination*. Rev. ed. Colorado Springs: Waterbrook Press, 2002.

———. "Thinking Christianly About Literature." Pp. 23–34. in Ryken, *The Christian Imagination*.

Sayers, Valerie. "Being a Writer, Being Catholic." *Commonweal*, May 4, 2001, 12–16.

Scott, Nathan, *The Wild Prayer of Longing: Poetry and the Sacred*, 49. New Haven: Yale University Press, 1971. Quoted in Neary, *Like and Unlike God*, 114.

Shannon, William H. "A Note to the Reader." Pp. xix–xxiii in *The Seven Storey Mountain*, by Thomas Merton. 50th Anniversary Edition. San Diego: Harcourt Brace & Co., 1998.

Sidney, Sir Philip. *An Apology for Poetry*. Ed. Forrest G. Robinson. Indianapolis: Bobbs-Merrill, 1970.

Sonnenfeld, Albert. *Crossroads: Essays on the Catholic Novelists*. York, S.C.: French Literature Publications Co., 1982.

Spark, Muriel. *The Comforters*. London: Macmillan, 1957.

———. "My Conversion." *Twentieth Century* 170 (autumn 1961): 58–63.

Speaight, Robert. *The Life of Hilaire Belloc*. London, Hollis & Carter, 1957.

Steinfels, Peter. *A People Adrift: The Crisis of the Roman Catholic Church in America*. New York: Simon & Schuster, 2003.

Stumpf, Samuel Enoch. *Socrates to Sartre: A History of Philosophy*. 3rd ed. New York: McGraw-Hill, 1982.

Tarsitano, Louis. "Passing On True Religion." *Touchstone*, December 2001, 15–17.

Thompson, Peggy. "Comedy and Christianity: Surveying the Ground." *Christianity and Literature* 44, no. 1 (autumn 1994): 59–72.

Tracy, David. *The Analogical Imagination: Christian Theology and the Culture of Pluralism*. New York: Crossroad, 1981.

Ulanov, Barry. "The Ordeal of Evelyn Waugh." Pp. 79–93 in Friedman, *The Vision Obscured*.

Unamuno, Miguel de. *The Tragic Sense of Life*, 131. Vol. 7 of *Selected Works of Miguel de Unamuno*. Trans. Anthony Kerrigan. Princeton: Princeton University Press, 1972. Quoted in Lodge, *Paradise News*, 293.

Varone, François. *Ce Dieu absent qui fait problème*. Paris: Cerf, 1981. Quoted in Michael Paul Gallagher, S.J., *What Are They Saying About Unbelief?* New York: Paulist Press, 1995.

Vitz, Paul C. *Faith of the Fatherless*. Dallas: Spence, 1999.

The Wakefield Second Shepherds' Play. Pp. 44–72 in *An Anthology of English Drama Before Shakespeare*, edited by Robert B. Heilman. New York: Rinehart & Co., 1959.

Walsh, Chad. "A Hope for Literature." Pp. 206–33 in *The Climate of Faith in Modern Literature*, edited by Nathan A. Scott, Jr. New York: Seabury Press, 1964.

Watts, Greg. "Gandalf in London." *Our Sunday Visitor*, March 7, 2004, 18–19.

Waugh, Evelyn, *Brideshead Revisited: The Sacred and Profance Memories of Captain Charles Ryder*. Boston: Little, Brown & Co., 1945.

———. "Come Inside." Pp. 3–9 in *The Road to Damascus: The Spiritual Pilgrimage of Fifteen Converts to Catholicism*, edited by John A. O'Brien. Garden City: N.Y.: Doubleday, Image Books, 1955.

———. *The Essays, Articles and Reviews of Evelyn Waugh*, edited by Donat Gallagher. Boston: Little, Brown & Company, 1983.

———. "Fan-Fare." Pp. 300–4 in Evelyn Waugh, *Essays, Articles and Reviews*.

———. *The Letters of Evelyn Waugh*, edited by Mark Amory. London: Weidenfield & Nicholson, 1980.

Waugh, Harriet, "A Modern Emma Woodhouse." Review of *Unexplained Laughter*, by Alice Thomas Ellis. *The Spectator*, August 31, 1985, 24–25.

Weaver, Richard M. *Ideas Have Consequences*. Chicago: University of Chicago Press, 1948.

Weinberger, Theodore. "Religion and Fly Fishing: Taking Norman Maclean Seriously." *Renascence* 49, no. 4 (summer 1997): 281–89.

West, Christopher. *A Crash Course in the Theology of the Body*. Carpentersville, Il.: The Gift Foundation, 2002. Sound cassette, tape 3.

Whitehouse, J. C. *Vertical Man: The Human Being in the Catholic Novels of Graham Greene, Sigrid Undset, and Georges Bernanos*. London: Saint Austin Press, 1999.

Whittaker, Ruth. *The Faith and Fiction of Muriel Spark*. New York: St. Martin's Press, 1982.

"Why the RCIA Needs Improvement." *Our Sunday Visitor*, March 2, 2003, 2.

Wilson, A. N. Review of *The Other Side of the Fire*, by Alice Thomas Ellis. *The Spectator*, December 31, 1983, 22.

Wojtyla, Karol (Pope John Paul II). "Letter to Artists." 1999. <http://www.ewtn .com/library/papaldoc/jp2artis.htm> (10 April 2006).

Wood, Ralph C. *The Comedy of Redemption: Christian Faith and Comic Vision in Four American Novelists*. Notre Dame, Ind.: University of Notre Dame Press, 1988.

Woodman, Thomas. *Faithful Fictions: The Catholic Novel in British Literature*. Milton Keynes: Open University Press, 1991.

Woodward, Kenneth L. *Making Saints: How the Catholic Church Determines Who Becomes a Saint, Who Doesn't, and Why*. New York: Simon and Schuster, 1990.

Wright, Walter F. "Tone in Fiction." Pp. 297–304 in *The Theory of the Novel: New Essays*, edited by John Halperin. New York: Oxford University Press, 1974. Quoted in Kort, *Narrative Elements*, 100.

Other Books of Interest to Readers of Catholic Novels

The Sin Eater by Alice Thomas Ellis

The Picturegoers by David Lodge

Out of the Shelter by David Lodge

The British Museum Is Falling Down by David Lodge

Ancestral Truths (also published as *Home Truths*) by Sara Maitland

Angel Makers (stories) by Sara Maitland

The Married Man by Piers Paul Read

The Free Frenchman by Piers Paul Read

The Upstart by Piers Paul Read

Knights of the Cross by Piers Paul Read

Index

abrasiveness: in Catholic novelists, 67;
in French community, 37
absurd, literature of the, 322, 354
Ackroyd, Peter, 73, 75
afterlife, 165–66n9, 167n17, 169–71,
182–83, 185n14
allegory, 82
Amis, Kingsley, 61n45
Anderson, Sherwood, 15
angels, 262–64, 280n5
Anglicanism, 40, 60n25
Appleby, Scott, 361
Arnold, Matthew, 163
art, religious, 21, 58, 78, 89n45, 164,
335–36, 347–48n7, 361, 362
assimilative writing, 68
atheism, 177, 361, 372
atmosphere, 7
Augustine, Saint, 276, 285, 304–5n1

Bakhtin, Mikhail, 91n78, 343, 369
Balzac, Honoré de, 38
Barbey d'Aurevilly, Jules, 33, 34, 364,
379
Baring, Maurice, 360
belief. *See* faith

Bellah, Robert, 240
Belloc, Hilaire, 42–43, 61n32, 66, 67, 79,
303–4, 364
Beloved, 352
Benedict XVI, Pope, 357, 358
Benson, Robert Hugh, 41, 364
Berger, Peter, 105
Bergonzi, Bernard, 72, 79, 170, 353,
356, 360
Bernanos, Georges, xii, 12, 18, 24, 36,
37–39, 49, 52, 59n16, 59n19, 60n21,
69, 71, 72, 79, 87, 352, 353, 359, 361,
365, 375n17; *The Diary of a Country
Priest*, 5, 37, 38; *Under the Sun of
Satan*, 37, 38
Bernardin, Cardinal Joseph, 358
Bible: Biblical criticism, 154–55; and
the comic, 369; in fiction of
Maitland, 83, 223–34 passim; and
literature, 2; quotations, 16, 106,
107, 177, 209, 224, 228, 230, 233, 237,
243, 285–86, 296, 329; references,
124–25n6, 209, 227, 228, 229
Bloy, Léon, 35, 36
Böll, Heinrich, 13, 27n53, 88n14
Bradbury, Malcolm, 84

393

About the Author

Marian E. Crowe received her B.A. in English from Mount St. Mary's College in California, her M.A. from California State University at Long Beach, and her Ph.D. from the University of Notre Dame. She has taught at Lake Michigan College, Heidelberg College in Ohio, Saint Mary's College, and the University of Notre Dame, where she is now a Visiting Scholar. She has published articles in *Christianity and Literature, Renascence, Logos, Commonweal, America, New Oxford Review,* and *Crisis.* She is married and has three sons and two grandsons. The only thing she likes more than reading good Catholic novels is reading to her grandchildren.